Subsidies for the Theater

A Study of the
Central European System
of Financing
Drama, Opera and Ballet,
1968-1970

by Wallace Dace
Professor of Speech and Director of Graduate Studies in Theater
Kansas State University

Motto on a Museum in Vienna:

DER ZEIT, IHRE KUNST

DER KUNST, IHRE FREIHEIT

—— *To the time, its art*

To art, its freedom

An **A**g PRESS Paperback
Manhattan, Kansas
1972

PN
1582
C4
D3

Acknowledgements

For valuable assistance in the preparation of this book I am indebted to the following persons, professional societies and business establishments:

AUSTRIA
Graz, **Amt der Steiermaerkischen Landesregierung:** Wirkl.
   Hofrat Dr. Bruno Binder-Krieglstein
   Vereinigte Buehnen: Reinhold Schubert, Intendant; Dr.
   Gerald Szyszkowitz, Chefdramaturg; Iris Stark, Sekretaerin
   des Chefdramaturgen
Innsbruck, **Tiroler Landestheater:** Josef Hummel, Verwaltungs-
   direktor; Dr. Walter Lehr, Dramaturg; Mario Alch, Tenor
Linz, **Landestheater Linz:** Eberhart Uebe, Chefdramaturg
Salzburg, **Direktion der Salzburger Festspiele**
Vienna, **Bundestheaterverwaltung:** Prof. Dr. Friedrich Langer,
   Chefredakteur, Pressebuero fuer alle Bundestheater;
   Oberbaurat Dipl.-Ing. Dr. techn. Karl Waska, Leiter der
   Gebaeudeverwaltung; Lothar Knessl, Disponent
   Burgtheater: Dr. Konrad Schroegendorfer, Dramaturg
   und Leiter des Burgtheaterarchivs
   Finanz Ministerium: Reg.-Rat Johann Meyer
   Staatsoper: Hofrat Ernst August Schneider, EM, Leiter
   des kuenstlerischen Betriebsbueros
   Theater der Courage: Stella Kadman, Direktor
   Theater in der Josefstadt: Prof. Franz Stoss, Direktor;
   Prof. Dr. Ernst Haeussermann, Spielleiter; Veronika
   Riegel, Sekretaerin
   Waagner-Biró, A.G.: DKFM. Walter Kristof; Dipl.-Ing.
   Herbert Wallner; Dipl.-Ing. R. Kemmetmueller

GERMANY, EAST
Berlin, **Berliner Ensemble:** Joachim Tenschert, Dramaturg

GERMANY, WEST
Bayreuth, **Bayreuther Festspiele:** Herbert Barth, Presse
Berlin, **Akademie der Kuenste:** Dr. Michael Haerdter; Heide
   Bank, Sekretaerin
   Buehnentechnische Rundschau: Prof. Dipl.-Ing. Walther
   Unruh, Herausgeber und Schriftleiter
   Deutsche Oper Berlin: Dr. Thomas-M. Langner,
   Chefdramaturg
   **Deutsche Sektion des Internationalen Theater-Instituts
   e.V.:** Gerda Dietrich
   Reiche und Vogel, Leuchtkunst, K.G.

Bonn, **Sekretariat der Staendigen Konferenz der Kulturminister
   der Laender in der Bundesrepublik Deutschland:** Dr.
   Langberg-Moellenkamp
   Theater der Stadt Bonn: Dr. Manfred Klein,
   Chefdramaturg
Duesseldorf, **Duesseldorfer Schauspielhaus:** Wilhelm Berner,
   Chefdramaturg
Erlangen, **Siemens, Aktiengesellschaft:** Lutz Kahlenborn
Frankfurt am Main, **Staedtische Buehnen Frankfurt am Main:**
   Dr. Heinrich Minden, Direktor, Presse und Werbung
Hannover-Linden, **AEG-Telefunken (GV)**
Kassel, **Staatstheater Kassel:** Dr. Renate Voss, Dramaturgin
Koeln, **Buehnen der Stadt Koeln:** Dr. Karl Richter, Redakteur
   Deutscher Buehnenverein
Mannheim, **Nationaltheater Mannheim:** Arnold Petersen,
   Chefdisponent; Dr. Peter Mertz, Chefdramaturg; Hedda
   Kage, Dramaturgin
Munich, **Bayerisches Staatsschauspiel:** Dr. Herbert Stolzenburg,
   Betriebsdirektor; Iri Seisser, Sekretaerin
   **Bayerische Verwaltung der staatlichen Schloesser,
   Gaerten und Seen:** Dr. Walter Tunk, Museumdirektor;
   Alois Frisch, Reg. Oberinspektor
Nuernberg-Fuerth, **Staedtische Buehnen Nuernberg-Fuerth:**
   Karl Pschigode, Generalintendant; Erika Mayer,
   Sekretaerin des Chefdramaturgen
Rheinhausen, **Fried. Krupp Maschinen- und Stahlbau**
Wiesbaden, **Maschinenfabrik Wiesbaden, G.m.b.H.**
Wuppertal, **Wuppertalor Buehnen:** Horst Laube,
   Chefdramaturg

UNITED STATE OF AMERICA
Lawrence, Kans., **University of Kansas:** Professor James E.
   Seaver; Professor Henry L. Snyder
Madison, Wisc., **University of Wisconsin:** Professor
   Jonathan W. Curvin
Manhattan, Kans., **Kansas State University:** Dr. Norma Bunton,
   Head, Department of Speech; Bureau of General Research;
   College of Arts and Sciences Summer Fellowship
   Program; Fritz Moore; Hartmut Renger; David von Riesen;
   Wolfgang Schneider; Ilse Slishman; Sherry Valentine
New York, N.Y., **Austrian Institute:** Harald Kreid, Deputy
   Director
   German Information Center: Inge Godenschweger
Washington, D.C., **Austrian Embassy:** Kurt Krejci
   National Endowment for the Arts: Madelyn Mailman

Table of Contents

List of Illustrations

Introduction

Prior to the beginning of the New York theatrical season of 1969-70, the Metropolitan Opera Association announced that it would not be able to open in September, as had been its custom since its move into the new house at Lincoln Center for the Performing Arts. The theatrical craft unions with which the Met must bargain (chiefly, the American Guild of Musical Artists, the American Federation of Musicians, and the International Alliance of Theatrical Stage Employees and Motion Picture Machine Operators of the United States and Canada) demanded wage increases which were beyond the financial resources of the association. Both sides compromised and the season finally began on December 29, 1969 but during the period of the acrimonious dispute, there were those who thought that the Met might never open again. In an article in the **New York Times** for November 16, 1969 entitled "Evil Times, Evil Priorities," the paper's music critic, Harold C. Schonberg, ventured the opinion that

> the United States eventually will have to do what all other civilized nations of the world do — put the arts on some sort of sustaining basis. That eventually might come. But it will not come for some time. The temper of the times is against it, and the priorities are elsewhere. Evil times. Evil priorities. America is sick.[1]

Why must art be "sustained"? Why can't art sustain itself? Why can't moderate charges for admission to an art gallery pay all the staff salaries, maintenance costs on the building, the expense of a new building when needed and the costs of acquiring new paintings and sculpture? Why can't box office income cover the costs of ballet, symphonic concerts, plays and operas?

The answer seems to be that art, throughout the course of western civilization, has never sustained itself. From this, the detached observer concludes that it never will. No country in history has ever spawned a citizenry the majority of whom preferred art to entertainment. Art has always been a genuine necessity for only a cultivated minority of the people. And the only value of art to a people appears to be the world-wide prestige which art can confer on that people. Art is both a product of civilized society and a yardstick for measuring it. A cultivated society makes art available to a large public at a reasonable cost. A coarse society tolerates the existence of art within its borders only if the public is willing to pay for it.

As American society becomes more refined in the next decades, some means will have to be found to sustain the performing arts with public monies. At present, there are two broad arguments against such a policy. One is that the government agency which controls the funds will inevitably control the artistic policy of the theater it subsidizes. The following study of the subsidized theater in Austria and Germany indicates that subsidy does not **necessarily** impose censorship. The claim that there is no censorship in the German-language theater, reiterated over and over by theater managers and directors, appears to be borne out in practice.

The second argument against public subsidy of the theater is that it stifles private initiative. Broadway managers feel threatened by the specter of taxes for the theater. The subsidized organization can take a chance on a new play without running the risk of going under if the show proves to be a turkey. And if the show is a hit, the tax-supported organization siphons off all the gravy.

This argument deserves some thought. It is plain that the private theater on Broadway, over the years, has made a solid contribution to dramatic literature. The plays of Eugene O'Neill, Tennessee Williams and Arthur Miller have been brought to public attention by Broadway producers. So have the musicals of Jerome Kern, Sigmund Romberg, Cole Porter, George Gershwin and Leonard Bernstein. Broadway can take credit for the emergence of the opera composer Gian-Carlo Menotti. Further, many a distinguished foreign play such as Samuel Beckett's **Waiting for Godot** and Eugene Ionesco's **Rhinoceros** has appeared on Broadway to the accompaniment of critical praise and box office losses.

On the other hand, Broadway's critics point out that the producers and their backers take all the monetary profit out of the theater and keep it for themselves. A more enlightened policy, it is thought, would be to employ the profits from say, **Hello Dolly** to finance an interesting, experimental work such as the Brecht-Weill **Mahagonny**, or spend some of the net earnings of **Plaza Suite** to enable theatergoers to have a look at such recent items as Armand Gatti's **Rosa Kollectiv** or Peter Weiss's **Hoelderlin**.

Further, it must be admitted that the Broadway producers have notably failed to keep the great works of the past continuously before the theatergoing public so that Americans can partake of the world theatrical heritage as do people in other countries, not merely by reading great plays, but also by seeing them in the theater. Even the plays of O'Neill, who is the only American dramatist to win a Nobel Prize, are rarely performed

---

[1]Harold C. Schonberg, "Evil Times, Evil Priorities," **New York Times** (November 16, 1969), Sect. 2, p. 19.

professionally in America. When this situation is contrasted with the treatment of O'Neill's great contemporary, Bertolt Brecht, whose plays are performed by professional companies everywhere in the country of his birth, it is plain that something is wrong.

It is not only the theatergoing public which needs a place to go where the best of the older plays and the more interesting avant-garde pieces are being performed on a regular, professional basis. Actors, singers, dancers, directors, scene designers and all other laborers in the theatrical vineyards need a theater in which to nurture spiritual and artistic growth in their chosen profession. The ideal of ensemble acting is possible only in a theater with a permanent company performing fifteen to thirty plays in repertory during a given season. An actor must participate in the production of many plays in order to achieve an understanding of the spiritual, emotional and intellectual range of his colleagues. When a large group of actors has learned, through years of experience, to play together as an ensemble the result can be theater of the very highest quality, as has been demonstrated recently by the appearance in New York of such groups as the Royal Shakespeare Company, the Vienna **Burgtheater** and the Polish Laboratory Theater.

Perhaps the solution to this vexing problem lies in a combination of public and private theaters, not only in New York, but in the rest of the country as well. The freedom and felixibility of the private sector usually provides a healthy stimulus for the tax-supported institution competing with it. The co-existence in America of both private and public schools is a case in point. By maintaining the very highest possible standards of academic excellence in an atmosphere of freedom from public hue and cry, such private institutions as Yale University, Smith College and the Choate School exercise an indefinable but significant influence on American universities, colleges and secondary schools.

Several other realms of human activity across the country are partially supported by tax monies. Passenger rail service has had to be subsidized recently. Large segments of the agriculture industry are supported by taxation. The health of citizens sixty-five years of age or over is protected by federal and state health plans. Whenever it has become clear that a particular service in the public interest must be provided by tax revenues administered by government, American governmental agencies at all levels have provided such services.

These days, the idea of tax-supported theater is being widely discussed. Theater is a public need and the private sector seems unable to satisfy this need. It is the purpose of this short study of the German-language theater, during the period 1968-70, to examine the organization, physical structure, repertory and financing of a group of Central European theaters — both large and small — in the belief that such information may be helpful in the effort to establish a more vigorous theater in America.

Alban Berg's *Lulu* at the Staatsoper, Vienna.

Organizational and Physical Structure
of the Central European Theater

The largest, best organized and most prolific professional theater in the west is the theater of the German-speaking area of Central Europe — West Germany, East Germany, Austria and part of Switzerland. The population of this area, about 90 million people, is served by over 300 professional theaters which are substantially supported by tax revenues.[2] There are also many private theaters located chiefly in the larger cities.

In West Germany, a country about the size of the state of Oregon, there are, in addition to the private theaters, 188 subsidized theaters in 77 municipalities.[3] This figure indicates the number of distinct stages with auditoriums adjoining, but not the number of theater companies. Nearly every permanent company plays in either two or three theaters, often, all under the same roof. The large house is used for opera, operetta and ballet, the small house for classical and modern plays and if there is a chamber theater, it is used mainly for avant-garde and experimental plays of various kinds and genres.

Schiller's *Die Raeuber* at the *Duesseldorfer Schauspielhaus.*

During the 1968-69 season, there were employed in these West German subsidized theaters 23,293 persons. Of these 1,892 were engaged as actors and actresses for the production of plays. For the production of operas, operettas and musicals, the subsidized theaters also employed 1,230 principal singers, 1,966 chorus singers, 1,046 dancers and 2,417 orchestral musicians who additionally gave concerts from time to time either in their own theaters or in nearby concert halls. The production schedules called for the assistance of 8,172 stagehands, property men, sound men and electricians. The artistic staffs, including **Intendants**, stage directors, musical directors, choreographers and **Dramaturgen** numbered 1,095. Finally, the administrative and house personnel totalled 4,665.[4]

[2]**Deutsches Buehnen Jahrbuch 1969** (Hamburg: Genossenschaft Deutscher Buehnen-Angehoerigen) pp. 201 ff.

[3]**Theaterstatistik 1968-69** (Koeln: Deutscher Buehnenverein) pp. 5-27.

[4]**Ibid.**, p. 44.

These theaters offered to their publics 6,102 performances of operas, 3,966 performances of operettas and musicals, 18,607 performances of plays, 625 performances of ballet and modern dance and 378 concerts played by the theater orchestras.[5] For these performances, 18,761,716 tickets were issued.[6]

During the calendar year 1968, income from ticket sales, cloak room fees, sale of programs, touring, radio and television broadcast fees and other sources came to DM 155.3 million. By way of auxiliary income, the theaters needed DM 412.3 million in subsidies to meet their expenses.[7] Thus, the total amount spent by the West Germans to attend their subsidized theaters, in tickets and taxes, was DM 567.6 million, of which 72.6 percent consisted of taxes.

The Germans invest lavishly in professional productions of works of dramatic art because they think of the theater as neither luxury nor entertainment but rather as an intellectual and spiritual need. This craving for live theater manifests itself in the form of three fairly distinct kinds of plays, operas and ballets done in their theaters. First, they feel a need to present the masterpieces of past epochs in the history of the theater to the people who buy their tickets, especially to the people of the lower and middle working classes. The theater — they think — should not be a plaything for the idle rich, a gathering place for the display of social ostentation. Strenuous efforts are made in the German theater to bring the working classes into contact with dramatic literature. After all, in every audience for a performance of **Carmen** or **Lohengrin, Hamlet** or **Faust, Giselle** or **Swan Lake** there are those who are seeing the famous old chestnut for the first time. A play is not old to a man who has never seen it. The cultural achievements of the west in the

[5]**Ibid.**, p. 45.
[6]**Ibid.**, p. 46.
[7]**Ibid.**, p. 49. The official rate of exchange between German and American money in 1970 was about 28¢ to the German mark.

Bernarda Albas Haus **by Federico García Lorca as played at the** *Schauspielhaus Bochum.*

realm of drama, opera and ballet are a measure of the greatness of western civilization, and these achievements should be made available in faithful yet vivid representations to each new generation, and to members of older generations whose economic circumstances prevented them from attending the theater when they were young. As in the case of a great university like Oxford or Yale, the University of Paris or the University of Vienna, where the student can study everything from Sanskrit to socialism, the German-speaking theater has become something of a repository for world dramatic art. In the process, German-speaking peoples have become a race of cultural internationalists. There is very little drama east or west, old or new to which German audiences have not been exposed.

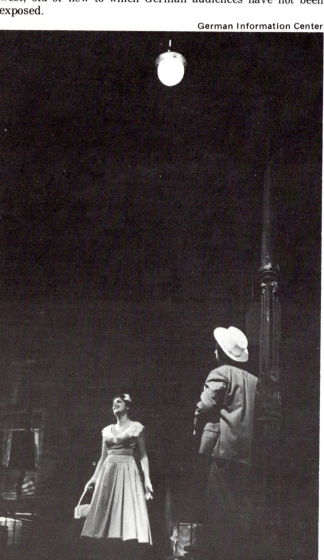

Elmer Rice's *Die Strasse*, with music by Kurt Weill, in Duesseldorf.

The playbills and posters announcing the fortnightly production schedules of the German theaters attest to the international character of their repertories. (See Appendix). Although plays and operas written in German or composed to German texts make up about half the items, the other half consists of an extraordinary variety of fare. On any given night in a given German house one might be able to see a tragedy by Aeschylus, Sophocles, Euripides or Shakespeare, a play by Ibsen, Chekhov or O'Neill, a comedy by Aristophanes, Plautus, Congreve, Molière or Goldoni, a morality piece by Calderon or T.S. Eliot, a venture in absurdism by Ionesco or Pinter, a fantasy by Kalidasa or Karel Čapek, an opera by Janáček, Mon-

teverdi, Ginastera or Benjamin Britten, a ballet by Prokofiev or Leonard Bernstein.

Goethe's *Goetz von Berlichingen* at the Jagsthausen Summer Festival in 1967.

The German theater is thus, in part, a museum. A good museum, that is. The famous works are carefully mounted, artistically performed and available to all at a modest admission price.

The second human need fulfilled by the German theater is the instinctive desire felt by everyone to see what is new in the world. The repertory system of play production, a system followed by all the German and Austrian subsidized theaters, makes it possible for an **Intendant** to schedule a new play for six or eight performances over a six-month period to see how it goes. In a theater mounting a repertory of twenty or thirty plays per season, it is not a matter of life and death whether a new play succeeds or fails. Naturally, along with the author, the **Intendant** hopes that he will develop a hit, in which case he

Schiller's *Don Carlos* at the *Schillertheater* in West Berlin.

SUBSIDIES FOR THE THEATER

Two productions at the *Staedtische Buehne Heidelberg:* **Ernst Toller's** *Hinkemann* **(left) and (top right) Kleist's** *Penthesilea.*

A severe test for any play is whether or not it can cross the language barrier from its own to another country. Since the German-speaking theater provides the greatest number of opportunities for the production of new foreign works and thus the best chance for a work to survive before the public for many generations, it stands to reason that if a work gains acceptance in the German-speaking theater, it has arrived. A work could be produced on Broadway and be hailed as a masterpiece of dramatic art. But if it disappears after a few months and is never performed again on Broadway, how is one to confirm his earlier impression? To paraphrase Oscar Wilde, all the plays of Eugene O'Neill have been done on Broadway — once. It is very seldom that one gets a chance to see O'Neill a second time in a professional New York theater. His reputation as a great playwright probably stems not from the performance record of his plays in America, but from the fact that his works have entered the repertories of the European theaters and stayed there. And this is what probably prompted the Swedish Academy to award him the Nobel Prize in Literature.

The publicly subsidized repertory system of play production enables a new, experimental piece to be tested before a paying public for a very long period of time before history writes its verdict. If a play survives this kind of testing, it has matured from a new play into a work of dramatic literature.

Wagner's *Die Walkuere* **at Bayreuth, 1960.**

schedules it for fifteen or twenty performances the following season at a substantial saving, since he already has the scenery and costumes paid for.

If the play fails, however, he may have the option of cancelling the last few performances and substituting in their place extra performances of some item in the current repertory which possesses a certain amount of reliability at the box office — **Hamlet**, say, or **Faust**. Thus, the failure of a new play does not have the slightest chance of putting a theater out of business, as is the case in the New York commercial theater. Even bad reviews do not determine the issue in a matter of a few days, as the repertory system allows the performances to be scattered out over a lengthy period of time, giving the play every possible opportunity to find its audience, if one is indeed waiting for it.

Because of these factors, the German managers can afford to do a good deal of gambling on new writing talent and they all do. In fact, the German-language theater has become a kind of international proving ground for the assessment of new plays, operas and ballets. The organization is so large that nearly everything new, regardless of the country of origin, can be — and is — tried out.

ORGANIZATION AND PHYSICAL STRUCTURE

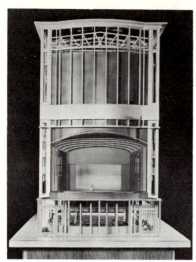

View from the auditorium toward the stage.

View of the work galleries over the main stage and the shop areas over the rear stage.

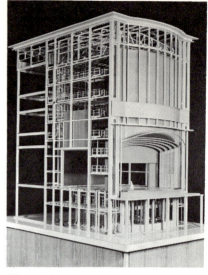

View of the forestage, the areas under the main stage and those to the rear of the main stage. Soundproof doors can be lowered between the main stage and the side and rear stages to permit scene shifts while a performance is in progress.

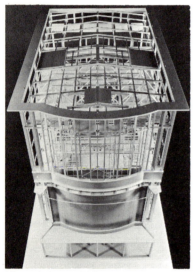

View of the model from the roof area showing the smoke traps and the gridiron. Also, the iron fire curtain is shown in a lowered position.

View of the double decked light bridge and overhead galleries from the left side stage.

View of the trap room and the understage machinery.

View of the trap room and the stage left work galleries.

Model of the *Schauspielhaus Bochum*, constructed for study purposes by the stage machinery contractor Fried. Krupp Maschinen- und Stahlbau, Rheinhausen.

Photos by Fried. Krupp Maschinen- und Stahlbau, Rheinhausen.

Still a third kind of play is regularly performed in the German-language theaters, the play which is not necessarily new nor quite yet a classic, but tends to provoke discussion and controversy where ever it is played. Works by Rolf Hochhuth, Peter Weiss, Armand Gatti and Bertolt Brecht feed everybody's latent penchant for the exchange of political, moral and philosophical viewpoints and the desire to convert others to one's own point of view. Santayana has noted that those who do not remember the past are condemned to live it again, and many Austrians and Germans feel that their theater is a useful instrument to make people think, to enable present generations to achieve **Vergangenheitsbewaeltigung** — an intellectual understanding of past events of history — as distinguished from the visceral understanding possessed by those who lived through it all. By comprehending the past intellectually, it is argued, one can see the shortcomings and failures of the present in proper perspective. Plays which raise questions about the present by showing past events in a certain light are very popular in Central Europe. The theater is considered to be able to mitigate the

Sound Control Room in the *Staatsoper* at Hamburg.

Lighting control apparatus. Left, control room at rear of the auditorium in a typical German theater. Above, the Siemens card system of preset lighting control. The cue is punched into the card, and then reproduced as needed during performance. Each lighting cue is recorded on a card, allowing infinite presetting of the lighting cues for a given production.

ORGANIZATION AND PHYSICAL STRUCTURE

Height indicators for counterweighted pipes driven by traction winches in the *Staedtische Buehnen Dortmund.*

Traction winches in use at the *Staedtische Buehnen Dortmund.*

Maschinenfabrik Wiesbaden, G.m.b.H.

Traction winches used to raise and lower counterweighted pipes over a stage area.

effects of one-sided engagement, to force the viewer to examine his ossified convictions and grapple with a new idea once in a while; in so doing, he may be able to wake himself up to what is going on around him. The theater, in short, becomes a vigorous antidote to intellectual and spiritual apathy.

In addition to the performances of classics, plays of the avant-garde and didactic pieces which arouse discussion and controversy, the German-speaking theater also devotes space in the repertory to children's plays and children's musicals. The belief that the young will profit from exposure at an early age to good music, art and drama has been confirmed everywhere by experience. Today, the education of the young in cultural matters is regarded as a prime obligation of subsidized performing arts institutions.

The Central European theater is essentially a kind of educational institution, intended to preserve knowledge of the past, study the new, provoke discussion of ideas and train the young. As such it is financed in the same way that a public university is financed — the direct user pays a proportion of the cost and by means of taxation, the public pays the rest. In a typical public American university, the student usually pays between 25 percent and 35 percent of the cost to educate him

SUBSIDIES FOR THE THEATER

while the remainder comes from city, state or federal governments, or a combination of these. The financing of the Central European public theaters is similar: ticket sales account for about a fourth of their budgets and government subsidies take care of the rest. Once the theater is envisaged in terms of its educational function for the public good, it is hard to see how it could be adequately financed any other way.

Maschinenfabrik Wiesbaden, G.m.b.H.

Stage lifts at various elevations in the *Stadthalle* at Muelheim/Ruhr. The surface of the orchestra lift is also visible, just below stage level.

Waagner-Biró A.G., Vienna

View from the trap room of the *Theater in der Josefstadt*, Vienna, of the underside of a 12-meter turntable. There is no center pivot, which permits considerable free circulation under the stage. A table elevator is in place beneath a stage trap in the turntable ready to lift an actor from trap room level up through the trap to stage level.

Waagner-Biró A.G., Vienna

Vienna plant of the Waagner-Biró company, one of the largest manufacturers of stage machinery in the world.

Control console for stage machinery. The desk at left contains a control and indicator unit which records position of stage lift and turntable. The panel to the right indicates by means of lights the trim height of the upstage lighting bridge, a batten containing some auxiliary cyclorama lighting units, the main light bridge in the proscenium area, the concert teaser and four curtains in various positions. The exact amount of the opening of the house curtain registers on a horizontal scale. A light on the lower right hand panel indicates whether or not the house curtain is being operated by hand. The lighting bridges used to light the cyclorama can be seen at left.

ORGANIZATION AND PHYSICAL STRUCTURE

Federal Theaters

Tax-supported theaters in the German-language area of Europe may be grouped into three broad categories: federal, state and municipal theaters. A number of private theaters also receive subsidies paid out of tax revenues. Federal theaters are those whose subsidies come principally from the federal government of a country, for example, the Vienna **Burgtheater** and **Staatsoper**, or the **Berliner Ensemble** in East Germany. Large festivals of music and drama are also usually supported chiefly by the federal government of the country in which they take place an example being the Salzburg Festival, held annually in Salzburg, Austria.

State theaters are those whose principal subsidies come from the various **Laender** (states) of Germany and Austria and **Staedtische Buehnen** (municipal theaters) are those whose principal subsidies come from the cities in which they have been erected. Some theaters receive subsidies from two or more government agencies but in every case one agency is designated as the **Rechtstraeger** (official sponsor) which assumes responsibility for the organization. In the following discussion three federal theater organizations will be studied, the **Bundestheaterverwaltung** (Federal Theater Administration) which operates in Vienna the **Staatsoper**, **Volksoper**, **Burgtheater** and **Akademietheater**, the Salzburg Festival and the **Berliner Ensemble**.

Bundestheaterverwaltung, Vienna

The four Viennese theaters operated by the **Bundestheaterverwaltung** are among the finest ensembles of their kind in the western world. The **Staatsoper** maintains an international standard of opera production equalled elsewhere by only three or four houses. The **Volksoper** is one of the few theaters in Europe which specializes in operettas and musicals although a few productions of opera are also mounted there. Finally, the **Burgtheater**, which also performs in the **Akademietheater**, has always been traditionally regarded as the first theater of the German spoken drama.

It is remarkable how a theater building can objectify a deeply felt need in the hearts of the people who regularly attend it, a feeling which is perhaps somewhat religious in character. In the case of the **Wiener Staatsoper**, the building has become both a shrine and a national monument. During its construction, between 1861 and 1869, public concern for the theater became a national pastime. Everybody considered himself qualified to express opinions about the building's architectural style, its seating capacity, its stage machinery, its acoustics, and so forth. Criticism was universal, and it gave rise to a bit of doggerel which haunted the architects for the building, August Siccard von Siccardsburg and Eduard van der Nuell, to their graves:[8]

Der Siccardsburg und van der Nuell
Die haben ihren eignen Stuel.
Ob griechisch, roemisch, Renaissanz,
Das ist den beiden alles ans.[9]

[8]Joseph Wechsberg, ''A Question of Reverberation,'' **The New Yorker Magazine**, XXXI (November 5, 1955), p. 92.
[9]Siccardsburg and Van der Nuell, they have their own style. Greek, Roman or Renaissance, with them it's all the same.

Neither architect lived to see the opening of the theater. Van der Nuell, a somewhat moody man who had already contracted an eye disease working on the project, hanged himself a year before the inauguration and Siccardsburg died a few weeks later. Despite the prognostications of gloom, however, the opera house opened successfully on May 25, 1869, with a performance of Mozart's **Don Giovanni**, sung in German. Over the years, the theater's reputation grew in quality and the Viennese came to take as much pride in it as they took in their great baroque churches and palaces. During the Second World War, many persons stored musical instruments, documents and valuables of all kinds in the large cellars of the building with the mystical conviction that the opera house would be spared. Several American bombs, however, struck the stage house of the theater on the afternoon of March 12, 1945, and the ensuing fire destroyed nearly everything — valuables, documents, instruments, scenery for 120 operas, about 160,000 costumes, stage and auditorium. Only the front of the building and the front lobbies survived. The destruction of the **Staatsoper** was regarded by the Viennese as their greatest collective tragedy of the war.[10]

[10]**Ibid.**, p. 93

The *Staatsoper* in ruins.

Stage and auditorium under construction after the war.

SUBSIDIES FOR THE THEATER

Under the direction of Dipl.-Ing. Dr. techn. Karl Waska the building was restored to its original state, however, and was opened once more in November, 1955 with a production of Beethoven's **Fidelio**. And in 1969, the 100th anniversary of the house was marked by gala festivities among which was a performance of Beethoven's **Missa Solemnis**, conducted by Leonard Bernstein.

The *Staatsoper* as it appears today.

Orpheus motif on the iron safety curtain of the *Staatsoper*

The seating capacity of the **Staatsoper** is 1,642 with 567 places reserved for standees. The proscenium opening is 13 meters wide and 12 meters high. The width of the main stage is 27.50 meters and its depth is 22.50 meters. There are also side and rear stages of comparable size.

Scene shifting apparatus is modern and efficient. The stage area consists of six large stage lifts and a full-stage turntable is available when needed. When not, it can be folded in the center,

FEDERAL THEATERS

picked up and raised into the fly loft. There are 91 pipes for flying scenery and two Linnebach cycloramas which roll up on drums at the sides of the stage when not needed. They measure 57 x 26 meters each; one is dark blue for night scenes, the other light blue for daylight scenes. Seven lighting bridges carry

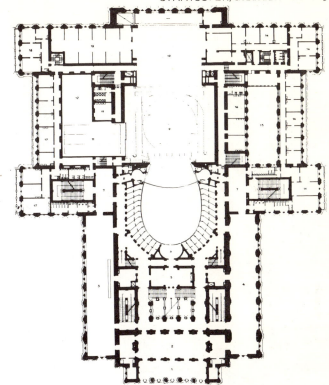

1 Loggia	12 Workshops
2 Foyer	13 Scenery storage
3 Marble Hall	14 Directors' and stage inspectors' offices
4 Tapestry Hall	
5 Teasalon	15 Courtyard
6 Centre Box	16 Chorus dressing rooms (men)
7 Anteroom	17 Chorus dressing rooms (women)
8 Sitting-room	
9 Stage	18 Building administration
10 Rear Stage	19 Juvenile ballet dressing rooms
11 Side Stage	

Floor plan of the *Staatsoper*

Turntable used at the *Staatsoper*. **The unit is 18 meters in diameter and weighs 40 German tons. It can be folded in the middle, picked up by a large hoisting machine and stored in the loft area over the stage when not needed for a production.**

spotlights, striplights, cloud and other projection machines and fluorescent tubes for lighting the acting areas, special effects, and toning the cycloramas. The stage lighting console controls 272 dimmers. The cost of this huge structure with its workshops, dressing and rehearsal rooms, offices, stages, auditorium and many lobbies and foyers was S 260 million.[11]

[11]A. Witeschnik, Hans Felkel, Otto Fritz, Karl Waska, **The Vienna State Opera: Guide** (Wien: Bundestheaterverwaltung, 1955). The official rate of exchange between Austrian and American money in 1970 was about 4¢ to the Austrian schilling.

Maschinenfabrik Wiesbaden, G.m.b.H.

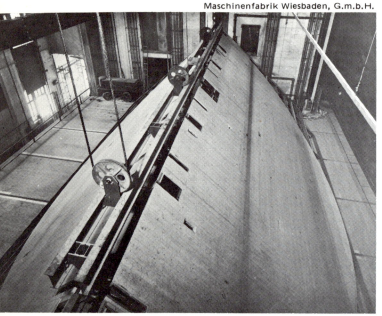

Turntable being flown up to the gridiron.

The repertory of the **Staatsoper** during the season 1968-69 was as follows:

OPERAS		PERFORMANCES
Beethoven	Fidelio	8
Berg	Lulu	8
	Wozzeck	3
Bizet	Carmen	2
Debussy	Pélleas und Mélisande	2
Einem	Dantons Tod	3
Gounod	Margarethe	2
Janaček	Jenufa	3
Leoncavallo	Der Bajazzo	2
Mascagni	Cavalleria rusticana	2
Monteverdi	L'incoronazione di Poppea	5
Mozart	Così fan tutte	8
	Die Entfuehrung aus dem Serail	7
	Die Hochzeit des Figaro	15
	Die Zauberfloete	13
	Don Giovanni	7
Offenbach	Hoffmans Erzaehlungen	9
Orff	Prometheus	2
Pfitzner	Palestrina	2
Puccini	La Bohème	13
	Madame Butterfly	9
	Tosca	9
	Turandot	4
Rossini	Der Barbier von Sevilla	3
Schostakowitsch	Katerina Ismailowa	3
Smetena	Die verkaufte Braut	7
Strauss, J.	Die Fledermaus	3
Strauss, R.	Arabella	4
	Ariadne auf Naxos	8
	Capriccio	4
	Der Rosenkavalier	7
	Die schweigsame Frau	5
	Elektra	3
	Salome	3

OPERAS		PERFORMANCES
Verdi	Aida	4
	Der Troubadour	8
	Die Macht des Schicksals	7
	Don Carlos	6
	Ein Maskenball	6
	Falstaff	5
	La traviata	9
	Othello	3
	Rigoletto	6
	Simone Boccanegra	7
Wagner	Das Rheingold	3
	Der fliegende Hollaender	5
	Die Meistersinger von Nuernberg	3
	Die Walkuere	4
	Goetterdaemmerung	3
	Lohengrin	4
	Parsifal	4
	Siegfried	3
	Tannhaeuser	3
	Tristan und Isolde	2

BALLETS		
Banfield	Le combat	2
Britten	Der Pagodenprinz	2
Chopin	Les Sylphides	1
Czerny	Etueden	2
Einem	Medusa	1
Heuberger/Schoenherr	Hotel Sacher	1
Hindemith	Die vier Temperamente	2
Liszt	Orpheus verliert Euridice	1
Minkus	Don Quixote	2
Ravel	Daphnis und Chloe	7
Strawinsky	Apollo	1
	Le sacre du printemps	7
	Petruschka	3
Tschaikowsky	Der Schwanensee	4
	Dornroeschen	2
	Serenade	1

During the Wiener Festwochen

Gluck	Don Juan	5
Mozart	Divertimento Nr. 15	5
Schoenberg	Verklaerte Nacht	5

The **Staatsoper** thus provided the Austrian public during a ten-month season, from September though June, a total of 181 performances of 54 operas and 54 performances of 19 ballets.[12] Of these works for the theater, a fairly large proportion were composed in the twentieth century. And it is a melancholy fact of our national cultural life that very few of them are known in America. Some have been given scattered performances by the Metropolitan, the City Center, the San Francisco and Chicago opera companies and orchestral excerpts are sometimes heard in the concert hall. It is plain, however, that without large subsidies of public monies the American opera theaters are unable to run the financial risk of partly empty houses to familiarize the public, over a period of time, with what is going on in the world of modern opera.

For example, Alban Berg's enormously influential **Wozzeck** is fairly well known here as the result of some performances conducted by Leopold Stokowski in Philadelphia in 1935, some concert performances by Dmitri Mitropolous and the New York Philharmonic in 1950, a recording of this concert version released shortly afterward, and subsequent performances at the Metropolitan. Berg's second and last opera, **Lulu**, however, is scarcely known in America at all except by recording.

Lulu is based on Frank Wedekind's two late nineteenth-century plays **Erdgeist** and **Die Buechse der Pandora**. Berg devised his own libretto and, prior to his death in 1935, completed the music and the instrumentation for the first two acts and, for the third act, the music in a reduced form but only a portion of the instrumentation. The opera therefore has to be

[12]**Oesterreichisches Theaterjahrbuch** 1968-69 (Wien: Verlag A. F. Koska, 1969), pp. 135-6.

SUBSIDIES FOR THE THEATER

performed as a fragment but it is coming to be recognized, since its first production at Zurich in 1937, as one of the masterpieces of the modern repertory, even as a fragment.

All the dodecaphonic music is derived from a single tone row which appears at the beginning of the **Lied der Lulu** in the second act, starting with measure 491. The various characters are identified by **Leitmotive** and, as in the old morality plays, in addition to being themselves, they appear to stand for certain archetypal traits in human behaviour. For instance, Lulu, who describes herself as a "wild beast," represents the primal "woman-spirit" amorally searching out satisfaction for her insatiable sexual appetites, a Victorian-era Don Giovanni, who brings despair and death to a succession of male and female lovers. Finally, as a London prostitute, she reaches the end of her quest when she makes the mistake of inviting Jack the Ripper up to her bedroom. This final scene of Berg's **Lulu**, played in pantomime against the music of a moving **Adagio**, is one of the most compelling moments on the operatic stage.

Austrian Institute, N.Y.

Berg's *Lulu*, **performed during the Wiener Festwochen, 1963.**

Photo Fayer, Vienna

Janáček's *Jenufa* **at the** *Staatsoper*

Vienna has always been a major port of entry from eastern Europe to the west and it is not surprising that the repertory of the **Staatsoper** includes the music dramas of various Slavic composers. Leoš Janáček's **Jenufa**, a lyrical evocation of Moravian folk life at the turn of the twentieth century has

FEDERAL THEATERS

become firmly established in the repertory since its first performance in Vienna in February of 1918, with Maria Jeritza in the title role. As a critic of the time wrote, "What impresses one about **Jenufa** is its sincerity, the positively austere artistic integrity underlying this dramatic ballad, its avoidance of anything savouring of operatic banality. It is a triumph of spirituality over materialism. As soon as the venerable figure of the white-haired composer was spotted among the artists taking their curtain calls, there was a storm of applause."[13]

A more recent work, **Katerina Ismailova** by the Soviet composer Dmitri Schostakowitsch, has also entered the repertory of the **Staatsoper**. This brutal tale of murder and revenge in a small Russian town is a revision of the composer's early **Lady Macbeth of Mzensk** (1934) which, after some early successes, was roundly denounced in **Pravda** as "a leftist mess instead of human music...fidgety, screaming, neurasthenic."[14] The revised version tones down much of the early shock element of text and music and has become, according to the composer, a means of dramatizing the harsh exploitation of women in nineteenth-century provincial Russia.

Other recent works in the repertory have been Francis Poulenc's **Les Dialogues des Carmélites** and Ildebrando Pizzetti's setting of T. S. Eliot's play **Murder in the Cathedral (Assassinio nella Cattedrale)** which, together with productions of operas by Handel, Monteverdi and Orff, attest to a continuing interest on the part of the **Staatsoper** in operas of a lofty, elevated style with classical overtones, whether in an antique or a modern idiom.

Two other modern operas of interest in the repertory of the **Staatsoper** are Hans Pfitzner's **Palestrina** and Gottfried von Einem's adaptation for the musical theater of Franz Kafka's mordant novel **The Trial (Der Prozess)**. Both these works, although not at all alike, have expanded in a significant way the range of subject matter which appears suitable for adaptation to the lyric theater.

[13]Rudolf Klein, **The Vienna State Opera** (Vienna: Verlag Elisabeth Lafite, 1969), p. 64.

[14]Donald Jay Grout, **A Short History of Opera** (New York: Columbia University Press, 1947), II, p. 519.

Katerina Ismailowa **by Dmitri Schostakowitsch**

Photo Fayer, Vienna

Pfitzner's **Palestrina** is set in the time of the final year of the Council of Trent — 1563 — and the subject matter is unusual for a stage work. The Council is considering a proposal that the traditional polyphonic music be banned from the church and that in its place encouragement should be given to the new Florentine monodic style of music. Cardinal Borromeo, who believes in the spiritual superiority of polyphony over monody, urges his friend Palestrina to compose a new mass in an effort to persuade Pope Pius IV that polyphony can still speak to the peoples of the Catholic church in a time of stress and change brought on by the encroachments of protestantism. But the great musician is dispirited by the recent death of his wife and is unable to compose. A new mass from him seems out of the question and the Cardinal leaves in disappointment. Alone in his study, however, Palestrina is seized again with a desire to create music for the church. Visions of nine past masters of the art of music arouse his creative imagination, heavenly voices are heard and, as an image of his departed wife hovers before his eyes, inspiration touches him once more, for the last time. During the course of a single night he composes the mass which reaffirms the faith of Pius IV in the older, traditional musical means of expressing the word of God to the people.

Pfitzner thought of his opera as a "musical legend" which celebrated the great achievements of the past, a testament to the significance of tradition and the values of the accumulated wisdom of earlier ages of civilization. He once observed, "I cannot entirely disown the hope that at long last the creations of the mind will eventually attain their proper place on earth, and that in the long run, works will not be judged by existing criteria but that existing criteria will be adapted to the creations of the mind. It is the mind that forms of itself a body."[15]

Photo Fayer, Vienna

Hans Pfitzner's spectacle opera *Palestrina* as performed recently at the *Staatsoper*.

Pfitzner's **Palestrina** is a modern opera conceived in the romantic idiom of the past while Gottfried von Einem's **Der Prozess** is just the opposite, an unnerving vision of a future which is void of meaning or purpose, dominated by a faceless bureaucracy which is totally indifferent to the fate of the in-dividual human being. Again, the materials of Kafka's surrealistic novel **The Trial** appear to be just as unpromising a subject for the lyric theater as the learned deliberations of the Council of Trent and again, the skill and originality of the composer demonstrate the contrary.

Josef K, a confidential bank clerk, is arrested one morning on an unspecified charge. He is permitted to continue working at his bank, however. He becomes convinced that he is being watched when a stranger informs him unexpectedly that his trial is about to begin and he must appear before the magistrate. The trial is as curious as the series of events leading up to it. The magistrate refers to Josef K as a carpenter but fails to explain what he is charged with. Josef K tries to defend himself but the magistrate adjourns the proceedings, leaves it up to the defendant whether or not to stay until they are resumed, and disappears. Josef K becomes erotically involved with three women (all played by the same singer), observes the flogging of the two men who arrested him, and tries to interest a lawyer and a painter in helping him with his defense. As length, he finds himself in a cathedral. A priest who identifies himself as the prison chaplain tells Josef K that his trial is over and that he has been found guilty. Two men arrive to conduct the prisoner to his execution.

For this prescient, episodic story Einem has devised a musical framework which he regarded as "soloistic," as distinguished from the "choral" nature of his earlier opera **Dantons Tod**. The music is atonal, but the vocal lines are melodically and rhythmically interesting, reminding one now and then of Montemezzi's **L'amore dei tre re**. Einem has managed to devise a stylistic idiom which consistently conveys to the audience the sinister, dramatic power of the libretto, which was adapted from the novel by Boris Blacher and Heinz von Cramer. The overall effect is that of a nightmare in which the real blends with the unreal, sleep with wakefulness, music with speech and, behind everything, a casual mixture of madness with routine conventionality.

In addition to its operations in the house on the **Ringstrasse**, the **Staatsoper** also performs operas on occasion in the **Theater an der Wien**, site of the first performance of Beethoven's **Fidelio** in 1805, the **Redoutensaal** of the **Hofburg** and in the **Schoenbrunner Schlosstheater**, the small court theater in the Hapsburg's summer residence, **Schoenbrunn**. This theater, which was built in 1767, is one of the best preserved eighteenth-century theaters in Europe. It serves now as the home of the Austrian State Academy of Dramatic Art — the Max Reinhardt-Seminar.

The **Staatsoper** is also noted for the quality of its pit orchestra which regularly gives concerts for the **Musikverein** under its world famous name, the Vienna Philharmonic Orchestra. Its ballet company is also capable of maintaining an international standard when it performs works of the classical and modern periods. Some recent world premières given at the **Staatsoper** were Gottfried von Einem's ballets **Medusa** and **Turandot** and Theodor Berger's **The Seasons**.

By means of the unified administration, the repertory of the **Staatsoper** can be co-ordinated with that of the **Volksoper**, responsibility for the management of which was assumed by the **Bundestheaterverwaltung** in 1945. Whereas the house on the **Opernring** is dedicated to the preservation of the great operatic tradition of the past together with performances of the more challenging modern works, the artists of the **Volksoper** are engaged principally in the production of their speciality, Viennese operetta — works by Johann Strauss, Franz Lehár, Robert Stolz, Oskar Strauss, Karl Milloecker, Emmerich Kálmán, Ralph Benatzky and many others. The theater also produces various operas which are not being done simultaneously by the

[15]Rudolf Klein, **The Vienna State Opera**, p. 65.

SUBSIDIES FOR THE THEATER

Staatsoper and further, has introduced to the public a number of American musicals. As the following list notes, Leonard Bernstein's **West Side Story** received 19 performances during the 1968-69 season, more than was received by any other production in the repertory.

The **Volksoper**, which was built in 1898, seats 1,620 and provides standing room for 136 persons. Its 1968-69 repertory:

WORK		PERFORMANCES
d'Albert	Tiefland	11
Auber	Fra Diavolo	10
Bernstein	West Side Story	19
Donezetti	Der Liebestrank	9
	Don Pasquale	2
	Lucia di Lammermoor	1
Dvořák	Rušalka	4
Einem	Der Zerrisene	4
Fall	Madame Pompadour	2
Flotow	Martha	10
Gershwin	Concerto in F (Ballet)	6
Gluck	Orpheus und Eurydike	10
Kálmán	Die Csárdásfuerstin	11
	Graefin Mariza	7
Kienzl	Der Evangelimann	8
Kodály	Háry János	8
Lehár	Das Land des Laechelns	10
	Der Graf von Luxemburg	7
	Die lustige Witwe	12
Lortzing	Der Wildschuetz	10
	Zar und Zimmermann	2
Milhaud	Minutenopern	3
Milloecker	Der Bettelstudent	3
Mozart	Die Zauberfloete	8
Nicolai	Die lustigen Weiber von Windsor	2
Offenbach	Hoffmanns Erzaehlungen	13
	La Perichole	10
Porter	Kiss Me, Kate	5
Puccini	Der Mantel	6
	Gianni Schicchi	6
	Madame Butterfly	10
	Schwester Angelika	6
Rossini	Der Zauberladen (Ballet)	6
	La Cenerentola	7
Stolz	Fruehjahrsparade	3
Strauss, J.	Der Zigeunerbaron	13
	Die Fledermaus	8
	Eine Nacht in Venedig	10
	Tausend und eine Nacht	11
	Wiener Blut	14
Strauss, R.	Intermezzo	4
Strawinsky	Der Feuervogel (Ballet)	6
Weber	Abu Hassan	3
	Der Freischuetz	14
Wolf-Ferrari	Il Campiello	4
Zeller	Der Vogelhaendler	4 [16]

[16] Oesterreichisches Theaterjahrbuch 1968-69, p. 137.

Photo Hausmann, Vienna

West Side Story by **Leonard Bernstein** at the *Volksoper*.

FEDERAL THEATERS

Three scenes from Gottfried von Einems *Der Prozess*, after Kafka.
Photos by Photo Fayer for the WIENER STAATSOPER

thirteen

Spoken drama is performed in Vienna on the stage of one of Europe's most enduring theatrical organizations — the **Burgtheater** and its associate house, the **Akademietheater**. Founded in 1741 by the Empress Maria Theresia, the original building was called the **Theater an der Burg** and later the **Hofburgtheater**. Under the influence of Lessing's ideas regarding the need for a German national theater, the Emperor Joseph II reorganized the theater in 1776 — the year of American Independence — into a national institution for the public good, a civilizing influence which would spread the Enlightenment throughout the lands of the Holy Roman Empire. The new theater was to perform serious drama of high quality for the propagation of good taste and the refinement of manners. It became the first German national theater organized under an Imperial decree and, after the **Comédie-Française** (founded 1680), is the oldest theater organization in Europe.

The **Burgtheater** has always been somewhat different from its famous French counterpart, however. The **Comédie-Française** was established for a cultivated court elite capable of savouring the subtler nuances of French neo-classic tragedy whereas the **Burgtheater** was intended to educate and refine the audiences, drawn from the general public, which were permitted to attend the performances. In addition, although German dramatists were encouraged, the repertory was not to be concerned first and foremost with German drama. Instead, the Emperor envisaged a world repertory and his first managers inserted this ideal firmly into the daily operations of the company. Thus, unlike the "House of Molière," the **Burgtheater** has always been considered an international theater with catholic tastes in all areas of world dramatic literature. The theater's performing company became famous in the early decades of the nineteenth century not only for its productions of the work of Lessing, Goethe and Schiller but also for mounting the plays of Shakespeare (in the translations of Tieck and Schlegel), its interest in the drama of the Scandinavian and Slavic countries, its productions of the plays of Greece and Rome and, in the twentieth century, a lively concern for the American drama. Recently, the theater has undertaken the production of various cycles of plays, running over a period of years. Among these are a cycle of Shakespeare's history plays, a Grillparzer cycle, and a series of the more significant Greek tragedies. A sampling of American plays performed at the **Burgtheater** since the end of World War II are O'Neill's **Long Day's Journey into Night, A Moon for the Misbegotten, The Straw** and **Strange Interlude;** Thornton Wilder's **A Life in the Sun** and **The Skin of Our Teeth;** Robinson Jeffers' **The Tower Beyond Tragedy;** Tennessee Williams' **Portrait of a Madonna** and **The Glass Menagerie;** William Saroyan's **Lily Dafon** and **The Paris Comedy;** and Arthur Miller's **Death of a Salesman, After the Fall** and **Incident at Vichy.**

Another of the objectives of Joseph II when he established his new national theater was the training of the actors in good manners and good speech so that they could set an appropriate example for the members of the audiences which attended the theater. Eventually, **Burgtheater-Deutsch** became recognized as a national standard of excellence in the speaking of German. The performers who were entrusted with this responsibility were elevated to membership in the Court and in so doing, the Emperor permanently altered the status of professional actors from that of near vagabonds to respected members of civilized society. In return, actors at the **Burgtheater** to this day take very seriously their responsibilities to their audiences. In their performances, they cultivate assiduously the ideal of genuine ensemble acting. No role is too small to be accepted, even by the leading performers, and played as expertly as possible. Even the theatrical convention of the curtain call has been banished from the stage of the **Burgtheater**. The custom can lead to claques and excessive applause for one actor in preference to another, a state of affairs which can turn artist against artist and destroy the spirit of ensemble playing.

Today, the response of the Austrian government to the dedication of the actors at the **Burgtheater** is both generous and humane. After ten years of continuous service with the theater, an actor receives tenure, and at the age of sixty, he may retire with a government pension.

During the nineteenth century, the original building was torn down to make room for various additions to the **Hofburg** and a new **Burgtheater** was erected on the **Ringstrasse** between 1884 and 1888. It was built by the architect Karl Freiherr von Hasenauer after a design by Gottfried Semper. Badly damaged during the Second World War, it was restored to its former state, new stage machinery was added and it opened once more on October 15, 1955 with a new production of Grillparzer's **Koenig Ottokars Glueck und Ende.** The auditorium seats 1,520 and there is room for 200 standees.

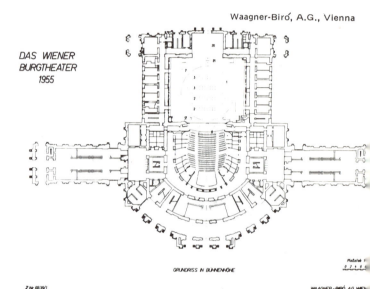

Waagner-Biró, A.G., Vienna

DAS WIENER
BURGTHEATER
1955

Ground plan of the *Burgtheater.*

Waagner-Biró, A.G., Vienna

View from the trap room of the stage lifts installed in the turntable.

SUBSIDIES FOR THE THEATER

The *Wiener Burgtheater* on the Ringstrasse.

Drive machinery for the turntable at the *Burgtheater*.

Model of the turntable with the stage lifts built for study purposes by the stage machinery contractor, Waagner-Biró, A.G. of Vienna.

FEDERAL THEATERS

The proscenium opening of the **Burgtheater** is 12 meters wide and 9 meters high. The stage area is 31 meters in width and 25 meters deep. On it is mounted a turntable 20.8 meters in diameter with four stage lifts forming an integral part of the unit. There are stage wagons for the shifting of full stage settings, 10 lighting bridges and a cyclorama 2,500 square meters in size.

During the season 1968-69, the repertory of the **Burgtheater** was as follows:

PLAY		PERFORMANCES
Aloni	Tante Lisa	2
Beaumarchais	Der tolle Tag	35
Csokor	3 November 1918	3
Goethe	Clavigo	22
	Iphigenie auf Tauris	25
Grillparzer	Die Juedin von Toledo	35
Horváth	Der juengste Tag	29
Madách	Die Tragoedie des Menschen	4
Meged	Hana Szenes	2
Miller	Der Preis	15
Nestroy	Einen Jux will er sich machen	3
Picard/Schiller	Der Parasit	23
Pirandello	Heinrich IV	3
Schneider	Prozess in Nuernberg	17
Scribe	Das Glas Wasser	22
Shakespeare	Coriolanus	19
	Othello	12
Shaw	Die heilige Johanna	37
Wilde	Lady Windemeres Faecher	12 [17]

Koenig Ottokars Glueck und Ende **by Franz Grillparzer at the Burgtheater.**

Although considerable attention is paid to the classics of dramatic literature by the **Burgtheater**, modern plays of distinction are not ignored. During the 1968-69 season the largest number of performances was given to George Bernard Shaw's **Saint Joan**, a play which has always been popular in the German-speaking theater. Another classic of the modern repertory is Friedrich Duerrenmatt's tragicomedy **Der Besuch der alten Dame** which was performed in the 1969-70 season.

[17] Ibid., p. 133.

Grillparzer's *Medea* at the *Burgtheater.*

SUBSIDIES FOR THE THEATER

Duerrenmatt's *Der Besuch der alten Dame* at the *Burgtheater*.

Bertolt Brecht's *Herr Puntila und sein Knecht Matti* in the *Akademietheater*.

Associated with the **Burgtheater** organization is the 542-seat **Akademietheater** which dates from the years 1911-13. In this theater the company performs modern plays and avant-garde experimental pieces. The repertory for 1968-69 was as follows:

PLAY		PERFORMANCES
Albee	Empfindliches Gleichgewicht	22
Ayckbourn	Halbe Wahrheiten	9
Coccioli	Mondhuegel	20
Congreve	Liebe fuer liebe	25
Duras	Ganze Tage in den Bauemen	23
Giraudoux	Die Irre von Chaillot	15
Goldoni	Una delle ultime sere di carnovale	2
Ingrisch	Die Wirklichkeit und was man	
	dagegen tut	14
Kilty	Geliebter Luegner	19
Kohout	August August, August	29
Nestroy	Der Unbedeutende	53
Nestroy/Krejca-		
Kraus	Strick mit einem Ende	2
O'Neill	Alle Reichtuemer der Welt	12
Pinter	Der Liebhaber	23
Raimund	Der Barometermacher auf der	
	Zauberinsel	28
Strindberg	Wetterleuchten	23[18]

The construction and painting of scenery for all productions of the **Bundestheater** take place at the **Werkstaette**, the largest scene shop complex in Europe. Located at some distance from the center of Vienna, these shops include three painting studios 30 meters by 60 meters in size — one each for the **Staatsoper**, the **Volksoper** and the **Burgtheater** — carpentry shops, an ironwork shop as well as other facilities for the building and painting of all types of scenery. In addition, storage areas are provided for the settings for over 300 plays and operas. The shops must prepare scenery for an average of 24 premières a year — of new works and restudied versions of older ones.

[18]**Ibid.**, p. 134.

In order to operate four large repertory theaters with international reputations which offer approximately 1,200 performances to the public in their ten-month seasons, the **Bundestheaterverwaltung** employed during the 1968-69 season 2,705 persons, 100 in general administration and ancillary services, 755 at the **Burgtheater** and **Akademietheater**, 1,187 at the **Staatsoper** and 663 at the **Volksoper**. Of these, there were 110 persons in administration, publicity and directorial categories, 1,003 actors, singers and dancers and 1,592 personnel in the technical departments, making the **Bundestheaterverwaltung** probably the largest single theatrical producing organization in either Europe or America.[19]

The **Bundestheaterverwaltung** receives an annual subsidy from the Ministry of Education. For the period 1965 through 1969, the amounts, in millions of Austrian schillings, were as follows:

Calendar Year	Total Expense	Theater Income from Box Office, Sale of Programs, and Other Sources	Federal Subsidy	Percentage of Subsidy
1965	362.6	107.0	255.6	70.5%
1966	383.0	115.4	267.6	69.9%
1967	448.2	120.0	328.2	73.2%
1968	465.3	124.6	340.7	73.2%
1969	477.3	138.4	338.9	71.0%[20]

A number of American periodicals have noted, with some surprise, that the Austrian government spends more money on subsidies for its four big theaters in Vienna than it does on its foreign service. Although this is not always the case,[21] the comparison is far from inappropriate. In fact, one can feel only admiration and envy for any country which manages to support its performing arts organizations in the manner to which its foreign service is accustomed.

Salzburger Festspiele

A special category of theater organization which is subsidized directly by the federal government of a country is the summer festival of music and drama located, usually, in a small town which does not have a large enough tax base of its own to support such an enterprise. One of the best examples of this practice in Europe is the Salzburg Festival, held every summer in late July and August, which is devoted to performances of plays and operas and concerts of music by Salzburg's most famous son, Wolfgang Amadeus Mozart.

The festival was established in 1920 by Max Reinhardt, Richard Strauss, Franz Schalk and Hugo von Hofmannsthal but the planning had begun considerably earlier. Hofmannsthal thought the tone of the festival should be serious as well as gay, that there should be Greek tragedy as well as modern comedy, opera as well as dance — everything, in short, which makes up the theater. Everything was to be accepted in Salzburg except "darkness without hope or optimism, anything essentially profane, anything lacking sublimity."[22]

The first two seasons were devoted to performances of Hofmannsthal's play **Jedermann**, based on the old English morality play **Everyman**. With Alexander Moissi in the title role, Reinhardt staged the work on the steps of the Salzburg Cathedral, a tradition which has been repeated regularly for half a century. Hofmannsthal later wrote his play **Das Salzburger grosse Welttheater**, after a play by Calderon, for the festival. Productions of Mozart's operas were added as a regular feature in 1922, some of which were conducted by Richard Strauss and others by Franz Schalk. In subsequent seasons the reputation of the festival has grown for its definitive productions of the operas of both Mozart and Strauss as well as those by other composers. New works also have been tried out at Salzburg, notably Gottfried von Einem's **Danton's Tod** in 1947 and his **Der Prozess** in 1953.

While the festival is running one has the impression that the entire city is being used as a production area for music, opera, dance and drama. **Jedermann** is performed in the **Domplatz**, operas in the **Grosses Festspielhaus**, the **Kleines Festspielhaus**, the open air **Felsenreitschule** and occasionally in the **Kollegienkirche**, plays are staged in the **Landestheater** while concerts of Mozart's music are given in the **Mozarteum**, the **Residenz** and the **Erzabteikirche St. Peter**.

Waagner-Biró, A. G., Vienna

The *Grosses Festspielhaus* on the right. Tons of rock had to be excavated to make room for the stage house.

Waagner-Biró, A.G., Vienna

View from the roof of the *Grosses Festspielhaus* of some of Salzburg's churches and the Fortress *Hohensalzburg*, on a hill beyond the city.

[19]**Teilheft zum Bundesvoranschlag: Bundestheater** (Wien: Oesterreichische Staatsdruckerei, 1968, 1969, 1970).

[20]**Ibid.**

[21]Expenditures for the Austrian foreign service for the years 1965-1968 were, respectively, S 248.7 million, 304.6 million, 324.6 million and 375.9 million.

[22]Piero Rismondo, "Theatre Festivals in Austria," Special issue of **World Theatre: Theatre in Austria**, p. 50.

Visitors to the 1970 festival could partake of the following productions:

OPERAS
Beethoven	Fidelio
Cavalieri	Rappresentazione di anima e di corpo
Mozart	Bastien und Bastienne
	Così fan tutte
	Don Giovanni
	Die Entfuehrung aus dem Serail
	Figaros Hochzeit
	Die Zauberfloete
Pergolesi	La serva padrona
Verdi	Othello

PLAYS
Beckett	Warten auf Godot
Hofmannsthal	Jedermann
Horváth	Figaro laesst sich scheiden
Schnitzler	Zum grossen Wurstel
Shakespeare	Hamlet

One of the largest and best equipped theaters in the world, the **Grosses Festspielhaus** was built between 1955 and 1960 for the Salzburg Festival. The architect for the project was Prof. Dr. Clemens Holzmeister and the theater consultant was Prof. Dipl.-Ing. Walther Unruh. Because the theater is used for both plays and operas adjustments can be made in both the seating capacity and the proscenium opening. When the orchestra pit is in use for a production the auditorium seats 2,158 but when large-scale plays are done without an orchestra, the orchestra pit lifts can be raised to auditorium level and 152 extra seats placed on them. In another arrangement, the lifts can be raised to stage level affording an apron stage which extends into the

Waagner-Biró, A.G., Vienna

Interior of the *Grosses Festspielhaus* with the iron safety curtain to the left.

Pressbuero Salzburger Festspiele

Verdi's *Othello* in the *Grosses Festspielhaus*.

Pressbuero Salzburger Festspiele

Emilio de' Cavalieri's opera of **1600** *Rappresentazione di anima e di corpo* performed in the *Kollegienkirche St. Peter.*

FEDERAL THEATERS

Buehnentechnische Rundschau

Ansicht des Proszeniums bei enger Bühnenöffnung (14 m)

Ansicht des Proszeniums bei breiter Bühnenöffnung (30 m)

Drawings showing adjustable proscenium openings in the *Grosses Festspielhaus*. Above, the proscenium width is 14 meters, below, 30 meters.

auditorium for the production of plays requiring close contact between the actors and the audience. The proscenium height is nine meters but the width is adjustable between 30 meters for opera productions and a minimum of 14 meters when plays are performed.

The large stage area is flanked by two side stages from which wagons carrying full-size settings can be shifted on and off. Although there is no **Hinterbuehne**, due to the presence of a mountain immediately in back of the rear wall of the stage, an area for rear-scene projection was cut out of the rock.

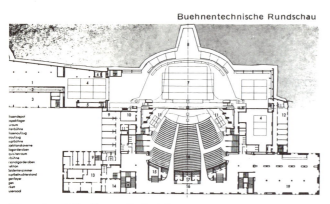

Buehnentechnische Rundschau

Floor plan of the *Grosses Festspielhaus.*

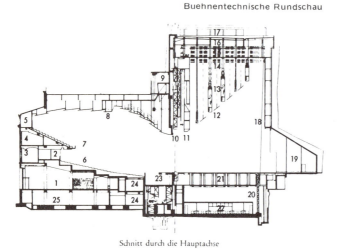

Buehnentechnische Rundschau

Schnitt durch die Hauptachse

1 Eingangshalle; 2 Logen; 3 Logenfoyer; 4 Rangfoyer; 5 Projektionskabine; 6 Parkett; 7 Rang; 8 Beleuchterbrücke; 9 Zuschauerraum-Rauchklappen; 10 Eiserner Vorhang; 11 Portalbrücke; 12 Akustikblenden; 13 Beleuchterbrücken; 14 Prospektzüge; 15 Schnürböden; 16 Rollenboden; 17 Bühnenhaus-Rauchklappen; 18 Arbeitsgalerien; 19 Projektionskaverne; 20 Anlehngitter; 21 Hubpodien; 22 Unterbühnenantrieb; 23 Orchesterhubpodien; 24 Orchestergarderoben; 25 Heizungs- und Lüftungszentrale

Section through the center of the auditorium and the stage house.

The area of the main stage consists of 5 stage lifts each 3 meters deep and 18 meters wide. They are double-decked and can travel from 3 meters below stage level to 3 meters above, either singly or in groups. They can be lowered 25 centimeters so that when the wagons are sitting on them, the level of the wagon can be made level with the rest of the stage. The lifts can also be set in tiers with 25 centimeters representing the height of each riser. Further, for large settings, the four downstage lifts can be extended 3 meters on each side.

Waagner-Biró, A.G., Vienna

Lifts on the main stage of the *Grosses Festspielhaus.* **A stage wagon 9 meters x 18 meters can be seen in the side stage. The iron safety curtain is to the left, and the area for rear-projected scenery is to the right.**

The side stages are separated from the main stage by fireproof, vertically operating iron doors which provide fire protection and a certain amount of soundproofing so that some work can go on in a side stage area even while performers are playing on the main stage. Settings are erected on stage wagons 25 centimeters in height. There are 19 of these wagons, each 3 meters by 6 meters in size which can be fastened together to form units of larger size. Each wagon runs on eight wheels each of which can be turned electrically 90-degrees so that the wagon's direction can be easily changed from parallel to the footlights to perpendicular to them. The wagons are operated by electric winches installed stage left and stage right.

For handling flown scenery such as backdrops, gauzes and some built pieces, 77 hand-operated pipes with counterweight arbors are provided. The pipes are 18 meters long and will accommodate settings for the small stage arrangement. When the large proscenium opening is being used, 10 more pipes on each side from 6 to 7.5 meters in length can be attached to the center group. A pipe thus extended is then handled by three purchase lines controlling the movement of the three counterweight arbors. For concerts, which are sometimes performed in the **Grosses Festspielhaus**, the fly loft can be largely shut off by means of four acoustical diaphragms — large louvers covered with non-absorbing material which pivot on pipes from a vertical to a near horizontal position. When properly adjusted,

SUBSIDIES FOR THE THEATER

they reflect sound out into the auditorium. There are also several spot lines available for handling small units such as trees or lamp posts. To avoid the disadvantages of a double purchase system, the counterweight arbors are mounted on the back wall of the stage house.

Double-decked gridiron over the stage area of the *Grosses Festspielhaus.*

Smoke traps in the roof of the stage house. The traps will open automatically when a certain temperature is reached. The stage house will then act as a huge chimney drawing smoke up from below and out the traps.

Two roll-up Linnebach cycloramas are provided, one which is used for the large stage arrangement and one for the small. The larger cyclorama measures 64 meters by 26.7 meters, the smaller, 52.5 meters by 26.8 meters. They run in tracks which are suspended from the lower of the two gridirons.

The lighting installation is standard for a large German house. Three double-decked lighting bridges, one single-decked unit and two light pipes for strips and cyclorama floods are suspended over the acting area. Two movable lighting towers in the tormentor position provide side lighting mounting positions at several levels. It is from these levels and from the portal bridge that a good deal of follow spotting is carried on during performances in the **Grosses Festspielhaus.** Projection equipment is mounted on all the bridges and a large quantity of fluorescent units is provided for lighting the cyclorama. Acting

One of the Linnebach cycloramas unrolled and surrounding the stage area. Various light bridges support lighting equipment used to light the cyclorama from overhead. The material of the cyclorama is white linen.

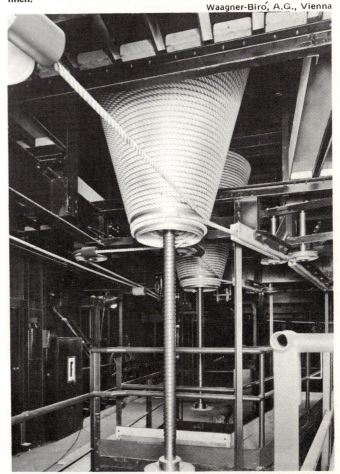

Rope-drum device which stabilizes the speed of the cyclorama as it unrolls from its cone at the side of the stage.

area units as well as high-powered follow spots are mounted in lighting slots in the ceiling and at the sides of the auditorium. The lighting installation is controlled by 290 magnetic-amplifier dimmers in capacities of 2 KW, 5 KW and 10 KW. There are also 18 transistor-device controls for the various parts of the horizon lighting which depend on low-voltage fluorescent units mounted on the portal bridge and on special side bridges mounted perpendicular to the footlights.[23]

Spectators seated in the *Domplatz.*

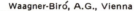

Waagner-Biró, A.G., Vienna

Stage lighting apparatus mounted on the double-decked lighting bridge and on the two tormentors. Scene projectors are mounted on the second deck of the bridge.

The cost of the **Grosses Festspielhaus** was S 210 million. The financial arrangements for the seasons 1968 and 1969 are summarized below. Monetary amounts are in millions of Austrian schillings.

Theatrical Season	1968	1969
Total Expense	65.7840	73.2600
Subsidy, Republic of Austria	10.5592	13.2896
Subsidy, State of Salzburg	5.2796	6.6448
Subsidy, City of Salzburg	5.2796	6.6448
Subsidy, **Fremdenverkehrs-foerderungsfonde**	5.2796	6.6448
Box Office and Other Income	39.3860	40.0360
Ratio of Subsidy to Expense	40.1%	45.3%

The Salzburg Festival has become one of the three or four best known summer festivals of music, drama and opera in the world. Hugo von Hofmannsthal's vision of an idyllic retreat in which one can immerse oneself in poetry, art and nature, untroubled by the strains and annoyances of the outside world has proved to be extraordinarily enticing to visitors from all over the world. The concerts in the churches and palaces, the operas in the **Grosses Festspielhaus** and the **Felsenreitschule**, and the annual playing of Hofmannsthal's own **Jedermann** in the **Domplatz**, with the sound of bells accompanying the lengthening of evening shadows on the facade of the great cathedral — taken altogether, the festival is an entirely fitting monument to the memory of one of Austria's greatest poets and dramatists.

Jedermann gives a banquet for his friends.

Hugo von Hofmannsthal's adaptation of a medieval morality play, *Jedermann,* performed on the steps of the Salzburg Cathedral.

Photos by Pressbuero Salzburger Festspiele

Death comes for *Jedermann*.

[23]Clemens Holzmeister, Wolfgang Teubner and Walther Unruh, "Das Neue Festspielhaus in Salzburg," **Buehnentechnische Rundschau,** LIV (December 1960), pp. 32-42.

Mozart's *Don Giovanni* **in the** *Grosses Festspielhaus.*

Mozart's *Figaros Hochzeit* **in the** *Kleines Festspielhaus.*

FEDERAL THEATERS

Berliner Ensemble

In October of 1948 the dramatic poet Bertolt Brecht returned, after long exile, to Berlin. He had been invited by the East German government to direct a production of his play **Mutter Courage und ihre Kinder** at the **Deutsches Theater**. The production had Helene Weigel in the title role and, after a period of intensive rehearsing, it opened in January of 1949 to a highly favorable response from the critics, the public and — most important — the Communist East German government. They offered to establish a theater ensemble for him with a regular subsidy, give him the use of the **Deutsches Theater** as an operating base and allow him a free hand to mount productions of his own works and the work of other Communist playwrights. The plan included the touring of many of the productions in Communist countries and in the west too, on occasion. After some hesitation, Brecht accepted the offer, although he assigned the exclusive publishing rights to his plays and poetry to a West German firm, the **Suhrkamp Verlag** of Frankfurt am Main. His company was named the **Berliner Ensemble** and, after a number of successful productions, it moved permanently into the **Theater am Schiffbauerdamm** on Bertolt-Brecht-Platz.

This was the same theater which had seen the première of Brecht's biggest pre-Hitler success in 1928, **Die Dreigroschenoper**, the music for which had been composed by Kurt Weill.

The **Ensemble** operates as a regular repertory company. There are over 300 members of the company approximately one-fifth of which are performers. The Ensemble may be said to be the personal creation of Brecht who guided its destinies from 1949 until his death in August of 1956. He was directing a production of his **Galileo** at the time and this work was continued and completed by his associate Erich Engel. His widow, Helene Weigel, is the present director of the **Ensemble** and other associate directors are Manfred Wekwerth and Hans Giersch.

When a new play is undertaken by this elite company rehearsals sometimes last as long as six months. Nothing is opened before the public which is not considered ready by its fastidious directorial staff. As a result, performances maintain a very high standard, indicating that the repertory system is no enemy of quality when it is handled properly. The company performs seven times a week, and their season is eleven months long. The subsidy from the East German government is 50 percent of the budget; the other 50 percent must come in at the box office.

The **Berliner Ensemble** makes a strenuous effort to reach all classes of society, both in Berlin and on the road. The company interests itself in working class citizens, poor people, university students, party functionaries and soldiers of the East German army. The latter, who wear their uniforms when they attend the theater, can sometimes cast something of a pall over the festivities, especially when the satire on soldiery **Mann ist Mann** is being performed, but their education is considered to be part of the responsibility of the theater. As Brecht himself said, the Ensemble had to develop two arts: an art of acting, and an art of teaching.

BERLINER ENSEMBLE—Percy Paukschta

Interior of the *Theater am Schiffbauerdamm* with dove of peace on the fire safety curtain. The theater was built in 1891 and seats 727 persons.

Theater am Schiffbauerdamm, home of the *Berliner Ensemble* in East Germany.

BERLINER ENSEMBLE—Percy Paukschta

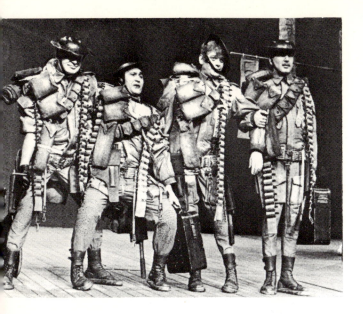

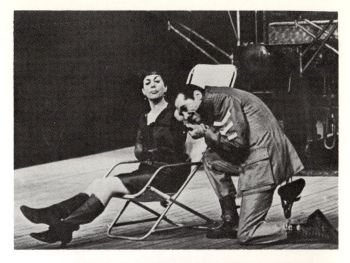

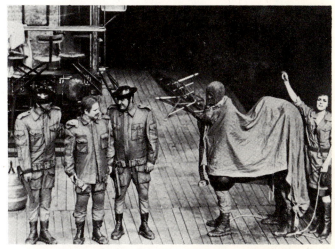

Scenes from Brecht's *Mann ist Mann.*

Photos by Vera Tenschert for the BERLINER ENSEMBLE

The **Ensemble** has toured a good deal more than most repertory houses but part of the reason for its subsidy is the prestige such a theater organization can confer on the **Deutsche Demokratische Republik.** The **Ensemble** has toured both East and West Germany, Austria, Poland, Russia, Czechoslovakia, Hungary, Rumania, Sweden and Finland. It has also played stands in London and in Paris.

The repertory of the **Ensemble,** developed from 1949 through 1968 with the number of performances through July 6, 1968 is as follows:

PREMIÈRE	PRODUCTION	PERFORMANCES
1949	Mutter Courage und ihre Kinder by Bertolt Brecht, music by Paul Dessau	405
1949	Herr Puntila und sein Knecht Matti by Bertolt Brecht, music by Paul Dessau	100
	Wassa Schelesnowa by Maxim Gorki	50
1950	Der Hofmeister by Jacob Michael Reinhold Lenz	72
1951	Die Mutter by Bertolt Brecht, after Gorki. Music by Hanns Eisler	217
	Biberpelz und Roter Hahn by Gerhart Hauptmann	14

PREMIÈRE	PRODUCTION	PERFORMANCES
1952	Der zerbrochene Krug by Heinrich von Kleist	174
	Das Glockenspiel des Kreml by Nikolai Pogodin	51
	Urfaust by Goethe, music by Paul Dessau	19
	Die Gewehre der Frau Carrar by Bertolt Brecht	49
	Der Prozess der Jeanne D'Arc zu Rouen 1431 by Ann Seghers	33
1953	Katzgraben by Erwin Strittmatter, music by Hanns Eisler	62
1954	Hans Pfriem oder Kuhnheit zahlt sich aus by Martinus Hayneccius, music by Kurt Schwaen	5
	Don Juan by Molière, music by Jean-Baptiste Lully	80
	Hirse fuer die Achte by Lo Ding, Tschang Fan and Tschu Dschin-nan	77
	Der Kaukasische Kreidekreis by Bertolt Brecht, music by Paul Dessau	175
1955	Winterschlacht by Johannes R. Becher, music by Hanns Eisler	142
	Pauken und Trompeten by George Farquhar, music by Rudolf Wagner-Régeny	165
	Die Ziehtochter oder Wohltaten tun Weh by Alexander Ostrowski	51
	Der Tag des grossen Gelehrten Wu, a folkpiece from old China	43
1956	Der Held der westlichen Welt by J. M. Synge, music by Hanns Eisler	135
1957	Leben des Galilei by Bertolt Brecht, music by Hanns Eisler	242

Brecht's *Mutter Courage und ihre Kinder.*

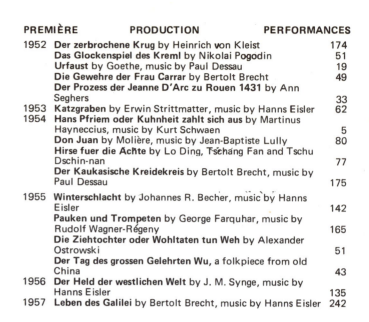

Brecht's *Der Kaukasische Kreidekreis.*

Leben des Galilei **by Bertolt Brecht.**

SUBSIDIES FOR THE THEATER

BERLINER ENSEMBLE—Percy Paukschta

Arturo addresses his followers in *Der aufhaltsame Aufstieg des Arturo Ui* by Brecht.

BERLINER ENSEMBLE—Vera Tenschert

Die Tage der Commune by Bertolt Brecht.

FEDERAL THEATERS

twenty-seven

BERLINER ENSEMBLE—Percy Paukschta

Final scene of *Die Dreigroschenoper* by Bert Brecht and Kurt Weill.

SUBSIDIES FOR THE THEATER

Scenes from *Viet Nam Diskurs*
by Peter Weiss.

Photos by Vera Tenschert for the BERLINER ENSEMBLE

State Theaters

Many of the important theaters of West Germany and Austria are supported mainly by state governments although they may also receive a portion of their subsidy from the city in which they are located. These state theaters are established in the capital cities and some of the smaller cities of the various states. Thus, for example, in the state of Hesse there is a state theater in Wiesbaden, the capital, and another state theater in Kassel. The largest city in Hesse is Frankfurt am Main, however, in which the theater organization is supported entirely by the city. In Bavaria, the largest city — and capital — is Munich, in which the state operates a large and expensive theater complex. The organization in Nuernberg, however, is a municipal theater. Similarly, the theater in Stuttgart, capital city of Baden-Wuerttemberg, is a state theater while the one in Mannheim, another city in the same state, is a municipal theater.

The states of West Germany are Schleswig-Holstein, Hamburg, Lower Saxony, Bremen, North Rhine-Westphalia, Hesse, Rhineland-Palatinate, Baden-Wuerttemberg, Bavaria, Saarland and West Berlin. In Austria, the states are Burgenland, Kaernten, Lower Austria, Upper Austria, Salzburg, Steiermark, Tirol and Vorarlberg.

The financial situations of several West German state theaters during the calendar year 1968 are summarized in the following table. Monetary amounts are expressed in millions of West German marks.

The subsidies for these theaters range from 64 percent to 84 percent of the annual budget, a range of support which appears to be common in West Germany and Austria. We will now examine in some detail three representative state theaters in West Germany, the **Staatstheater Kassel**, the **Deutsche Oper Berlin** and the **Bayerisches Staatsschauspiel**; and three in Austria, the **Landestheater Linz**, the **Vereinigte Buehnen Graz** and the **Tiroler Landestheater**.

Staatstheater Kassel

One is accustomed to seeing good theater in the largest cities of a country. New York, London, Paris, Rome, Vienna and Berlin are the principal theatrical capitals of the west. The real test of a country's artistic vitality is measured in the smaller cities, however, the so-called "provinces" although the medium-sized and smaller cities of Germany and Austria do not seem especially insular or cut off from the artistic and intellectual currents of the outside world. It is possible that this is due, more than to anything else, to the presence in all the medium-sized cities of Central Europe of viable, professional repertory theater companies producing spoken drama, opera, musicals and ballet on a regular basis. Their seasons are ten months long and the theaters offer performances on an average of six nights a week.

It may therefore be of interest to examine in some detail a theater organization in a medium-sized West German city to get an idea of what kind of theater is available outside of Berlin and Vienna. The city of Kassel, in the state of Hesse, provides a useful example. It is located in the central part of the country and its population of some 240,000 (1970) makes it about equal in size to such American cities as Akron, Ohio, Omaha, Nebraska and El Paso, Texas.

THEATER AND LOCATION	SIZE OF COMPANY	TOTAL EXPENSE	BOX OFFICE AND OTHER INCOME	TOTAL SUBSIDY	RATIO OF SUBSIDY TO EXPENSE
BERLIN, BERLIN					
Schiller-Theater, Werkstattbuehne	317	9.107	2.149	6.958	76.4%
Schlossparktheater	130	3.729	0.954	2.775	74.4%
STUTTGART, BADEN-WUERTTEMBERG					
Wuerttembergisches Staatstheater: Grosses Haus, Kleines Haus, Kammertheater	868	23.018	8.182	14.836	64.4%
WIESBADEN, HESSE					
Hessisches Staatstheater: Grosses Haus, Kleines Haus, Studio-Souterrain	534	12.136	2.633	9.503	79.3%
KARLSRUHE, BADEN-WUERTTEMBERG					
Badisches Staatstheater: Grosses Haus, Kleines Haus, Studio, "Die Probebuehne"	469	11.434	2.213	9.221	80.6%
BRAUNSCHWEIG, LOWER SAXONY					
Braunschweig Staatstheater: Grosses Haus, Kleines Haus	364	8.139	1.979	6.160	75.7%
DARMSTADT, HESSE					
Landestheater Darmstadt: Orangerie, Stadthalle, Liebig-Haus, Theater im Schloss	354	7.770	1.176	6.594	84.9%
OLDENBURG, LOWER SAXONY					
Staatstheater Oldenburg: Grosses Haus, Schloss theater, Spielraum	303	5.653	1.146	4.507	79.7% [24]

[24]**Theaterstatistik 1968-69**, pp. 5-27.

SUBSIDIES FOR THE THEATER

View from the *Spohrplatz* toward the *Friedrichsplatz*.

The *Staatstheater Kassel* can be seen at the top right of the picture.

STATE THEATERS

The *Loewenburg* **Castle in the** *Wilhelmshoehe* **park.**

Kassel reflects the influence of post war city planning in Germany. Streets have been closed off to allow pedestrians easy access to stores and shops. One street, in fact, the **Treppenstrasse**, consists of steps which run from one sidewalk to the other permitting leisurely shopping unencumbered by automobile traffic.

The city also boasts a significant cultural tradition. The **Gemaeldegalerie** of the **Hessisches Landesmuseum** includes in its holdings no less than 19 Rembrandts — an important collection. The brothers Grimm composed many of their fairy tales in Kassel and it was here too that there was erected the first festival theater in Germany, **Das Ottoneum**, which still stands. It was built in 1605 to accommodate travelling companies of English comedians but as the Thirty Years' War dragged on it was first converted to an ammunition storage depot and then to a hospital. Today it is used as a museum of natural history.

In the eighteenth century, a **Hoftheater** was constructed in which were performed Italian, French and German opera and ballet, and plays by Lessing, Goethe, Schiller and Shakespeare. During the nineteenth century both Louis Spohr and Gustav Mahler conducted opera in Kassel and during the present century the performing arts continue to flourish with performances of traditional, contemporary and avant-garde works for the theater.

In 1943 the **Hoftheater** on the broad **Friedrichsplatz** was destroyed by bombs and for several years thereafter, plays and operas were performed in temporary structures, a situation much in vogue in Germany at the time. The present **Staatstheater Kassal am Friedrichsplatz** was opened in 1959. The building houses two theaters, one large and one small — the usual custom in the post-war German and Austrian theater buildings. The **Grosses Haus** seats 945 and is used for the performance of operas, operettas, musicals, some plays and a few concerts by the theater orchestra. (Other concerts are given at

SUBSIDIES FOR THE THEATER

the city's **Stadthalle**, seating 1,162). The **Kleines Haus** seats either 534 or, in a different arrangement, 574 and is used mainly for the performance of plays. A feature of this theater is the special performance of plays at 11:30 in the evening, after the regular performance has ended, either on the orchestra lift with the house curtain closed or on one of the side stages — arena-style. These plays tend to be short pieces in the avant-garde mode. Children's plays are given in both the **Grosses Haus** and the **Kleines Haus**.

The architects for this efficient and flexible structure were Paul Bode and Ernest Brundig of Kassel. The theater consultant was Prof. Dipl.-Ing. Walther Unruh of Wiesbaden, editor of **Buehnentechnische Rundschau**, and the acoustical consultant was Dr.-Ing. Werner Gabler of Berlin-Zehlendorf.

The **Staatstheater Kassel**, as do the larger organizations in Vienna and Berlin, produces theatrical works on a repertory basis — that is, a different play or opera is performed each evening on each stage. During the ten-month season some works are performed more often than others enabling the management to depend on the more popular pieces to sustain the financial burden of running new works which need time to attract an audience. The result of this policy is that a good deal of new writing is seen every season in Kassel, in all dramatic forms — spoken drama, opera and ballet. During the season 1967-68, the repertory of the **Staatstheater** included the following works for the stage:

MUSICAL WORKS		PERFOR-MANCES	AVERAGE PERCENT CAPACITY
Antoniou	Klytemnestra	3	44%
Ballet-Abend			
Prokofieff	Symphonie classique		
Egk	La Danza		
Falla	Der Dreispitz	11	49%
Benatzky	Im Weisser Roessl	9	86%
Brecht/Weill	Aufstieg und Fall der Stadt Mahagonny	6	62%
Debussy	Pelléas und Mélisande	3	40%
Kálmán	Die Zirkusprinzessin	26	86%
Kuenneke	Der Vetter aus Dingsda	20	79%
Lehár	Das Land des Laechelns	46	86%
Leoncavallo	Der Bajazzo	16	78%
Lortzing	Zar und Zimmermann	5	95%
Mascagni	Cavalleria rusticana	16	78%
Milloecker	Der Bettelstudent	7	84%
Monteverdi	Die Kroenung der Poppea	8	50%
Puccini	Tosca	5	63%
Rossini	Der Barbier von Sevilla	16	85%
	La Cenerentola	5	65%

Das Ottoneum, near the *Staatstheater Kassel*. The original seating capacity of this early German theater was 625.

Exterior view of the *Staatstheater Kassel* on the *Friedrichsplatz*.

Interior of the *Grosses Haus*.

Interior of the *Kleines Haus*.

STATE THEATERS

Strawinsky	Oedipus Rex	3	
Tschaikowskij	Die Jungfrau von Orléans	8	70%
Verdi	Ein Maskenball	1	70%
	La Traviata	26	72%
Wagner	Lohengrin	5	71%
	Die Meistersinger von Nuernberg	5	92%

PLAYS

Barillet/Grédy	Die Kaktusbluete	42	92%
Bond	Gerettet	10	52%
Bremer	Haende weg von meinem Ferrari	13	79%
Brecht	Der aufhaltsame Aufstieg des Arturo Ui	26	84%
Camoletti	Boeing-Boeing oder Luft und Liebe	13	70%
Capelli	Zweihunderttausend und Einer	15	54%
Diez	Hallo Schatz bist du's?	13	79%
Duerrenmatt	Romulus der Grosse	12	77%
Fos	Hofnarr der kleinen Leute	5	
Gatti	General Francos Leidenswege	12	69%
Gogol	Der Revisor	26	85%
Kesselring	Arsen und Spitzenhaeubchen	1	
Knott	Warte, bis es dunkel ist	16	55%
O'Neill	Fast ein Poet	24	67%
Saint Phalle/Diez	ICH	3	
Schiller	Maria Stuart	19	80%
Shaffer	Schwarze Komoedie	13	60%
Valmain	Mit zwei Fuessen im Grab	10	48%

PODIUM PRODUCTIONS (Only a few seats sold)

Arrabal	Zeremonie fuer einen ermordeten Neger	6	23%
Pinter	Der Liebhaber	5	20%
Saunders	Wirklich schade um Fred	5	20%

CHILDREN'S PLAY

	Peterchens Mondfahrt	47	95%

A typical two-week schedule (the final two weeks of the season — July 1-14, 1968) ran as follows:

	GROSSES HAUS	KLEINES HAUS
July 1	BEATKONZERT: **The Rattles The Rivets The German Bonds**	Zeremonie fuer einen ermordeten Neger
		GASTSPIEL: Open Theater, New York: **The Serpent**
July 2	Die Kroenung der Poppea	General Francos Leidenswege
July 3	La Traviata	Arturo Ui
July 4	Der Barbier von Sevilla	(closed)
July 5	Der Vetter aus Dingsda	ICH
July 6	Die Meistersinger von Nuernberg	Die Kaktusbluete
July 7	Das Land des Laechelns	Die Kaktusbluete
July 9	Die Zirkusprinzessin	General Francos Leidenswege
July 10	Der Barbier von Sevilla	Maria Stuart
July 11	Das Land des Laechelns	Schwarze Komoedie
July 12	Zar und Zimmermann	Maria Stuart
July 13	Der Vetter aus Dingsda	Die Kaktusbluete
July 14	La Traviata	Arsen und Spitzenhaeubchen

Eugene O'Neill's *Fast ein Poet.*

STAATSTHEATER KASSEL—Floris Neusuess

As can be seen, well over 500 performances of operas, operettas, musicals, ballets and plays were mounted in two theaters over a period of ten months. Such a performance schedule requires the services of a sizable permanent company, the extent of which (during the season 1967-68) was as follows:

Intendant, conductors and assistant conductors, stage directors, choreographers, chorus directors, stage managers and their assistants, literary advisers, scene, costume, lighting and sound designers	40
Principal male and female singers	37
Actors and actresses	35
Ballet dancers	20
Chorus singers	42
Orchestra musicians	89
Technical director, painters, carpenters, stagehands, property men and electricians	192
Administrative personnel	39
House personnel	54
Total size of the company of the **Staatstheater Kassel**	548

Attendance at the two theaters and the concert hall during the season of 1967-68 can be summarized as follows:

		Number of performances	Total attendance	Per cent of capacity
Grosses Haus (953)	Operas	116	76,173	68.9%
	Operettas & Musicals	109	85,264	82.8%
	Plays	62	52,864	89.5%
	Ballets	11	5,315	50.7%
	Concerts	5	2,494	52.4%
Kleines Haus (540 or 574)	Plays	267	102,206	69.6%
Stadthalle (1,662)	Concerts	14	17,951	77.1%
	Totals	584	342,267	

As has been noted, the system of publicly subsidized repertory theaters permits a new play to attain the stature of a classic over a period of years. There is hardly a better illustration of this process than the performance history of the plays of Eugene O'Neill in the German and Austrian theaters, not to mention those of other European countries, especially Sweden where there have been several world premières of his work. At Kassel, **A Touch of the Poet**, in a German translation by Ursula Schuh entitled **Fast ein Poet**, opened early in the season and was given 24 performances. In prior seasons the theatergoing public of Kassel had been able to see at their own theater the following plays by O'Neill: **Seltsames Zwischenspiel, Ein Mond fuer die Beladenen, Trauer muss Elektra tragen, Eines langen Tages Reise in die Nacht** and **O Wildniss.**

Fast ein Poet was not done at Kassel, however, simply so the piece could mature gracefully into a classic under people's very noses. It was done because the director, Kai Braak, thought it had something to say to contemporary German audiences. The time of the play, 1828, corresponds to the Biedermaier Period in Germany — a period of sharp political tensions not unlike those of today and marks, further, a time when the modern American nation was being formed. The subject of the play is the role played by illusion in the lives of the people. Is poetry illusion? Does poetry prevent self-understanding? Perhaps the reflections of the poet allow self-reflection in the theater.

These, together with other ideas, prompted the selection of the play for the 1967-68 season. The scene designer, Thomas Richter-Forgách, related the piece to the world of today by adding neon lights to his realistic setting to suggest to the audience the dream world of the characters and the possibility of the seduction of the masses by means of advertising.[25]

[25]Renate Voss, "O'Neill's **Fast ein Poet**, "**Kasseler Theaterzeitung** (September-Oktober 1967) p. 2.

SUBSIDIES FOR THE THEATER

The human desire to study the past in order to recognize in the present the danger signals of tyranny, common in both Germany and America, was satisfied to some extent by the production of Bertolt Brecht's **Gangsterspektakel, Der Aufhaltsame Aufstieg des Arturo Ui**, written in 1941 and first performed in Stuttgart in 1958. A parable on the resistable rise of Adolf Hitler, the piece suggests that gangsters may exist anywhere, at any time, and although Adolf Hitler and Al Capone were contemporaries there is nothing to prevent the reincarnation of either one from again mounting the podium in Germany, America or Sicily.

In order to enhance the allegorical element of the piece the director, Ulrich Brecht, tried to prevent the audience from becoming overly involved in the action, a principle known as **Verfremdungseffekt**, as Bert Brecht called it, and which is applied to a large proportion of idea plays produced in Europe. To achieve this mood, the actors in **Arturo Ui** wore masks which suggested the facial characteristics of their Nazi counterparts — Arturo looked like Hitler, Roma looked like Roehm and so forth. Further, the audience in the theater was never used as a part of the stage audience Arturo was addressing, in contrast to the usual practice in American productions of this play.

Other efforts were made to achieve audience detachment. Tunes used in the Third Reich to herald important announcements over the radio such as Liszt's **Les Préludes** (to proclaim a victory) or Chopin's **Trauermarsch** (to admit a defeat) were reduced to what the composer of the score, Hans-Dieter Hosalla described as **Bumsmusik**. The scene-titles suggested by the author were not used and the costumes were not historically accurate.

The production plan was aimed at making clear the contrast between the ridiculous nature of the means used by Arturo to achieve his rise to power and the terrible nature of the results. In the scene with the actor, Arturo is shown mastering the techniques of mass seduction. In the audience, in a detached way, one observes the fate of both the seducer and the seduced. Further, the director tried to emphasize the fact that Brecht uses many classical devices and allusions in his play to further remove the action from the milieu of Hitler-Capone. For example, much of the dialogue is written in the iambic pentameter of Shakespeare and the classical German drama. There are even rhymed couplets at the ends of various scenes:

"Ja ruf ihn nur! Der Pneu ist leider platt!
Wolln sehn, wer Herr ist in dieser Stadt."[26]

There are many classical references. The Actor, while training Arturo in the art of seducing the masses, quotes from Marc Antony's speech over the dead body of Caesar in Shakespeare's **Julius Caesar**. Also from Shakespeare, the scene in **Richard III** in which Richard expresses a wish to seduce Anna at the coffin of Henry VI is recalled by Arturo's effort, during Dullfeet's funeral, to induce his widow to join the gangsters. Again, the garden scene from Goethe's **Faust** comes to mind during the flower shop sequence in which, while Givola (Mephistopheles) threatens Dullfeet (Marthe), Betty Dullfeet (Gretchen) asks Arturo (Faust) questions about his religion and about socialism.

Even many of the lines are designed to recall lines from the classics of German literature. The audience sometimes finds itself repeating a famous line which is suddenly interrupted by the juxtaposition of something entirely different. Perhaps more than any other element, these classical allusions assist the audience to remain detached from the proceedings at hand and to achieve **Vergangenheitsbewaeltigung**, an intellectualized understanding of the Hitler era.[27]

[26] O.K.! Tell him! The tire is going down!
We'll see who the boss is around this town.

[27] Renate Voss, "Fuer die Freiheit der Fantasie," **Kasseler Theaterzeitung** (Oktober-November 1967) p. 2.

STATE THEATERS

STAATSTHEATER KASSEL—Floris Neusuess

Der aufhaltsame Aufstieg des Arturo Ui **by Brecht. Arturo practices a gesture.**

Of all the functions of the large subsidized repertory house, however, perhaps the most important one is the trying out of new plays, operas and ballets. New works are the life blood of art and the German-speaking theater tries out many new pieces of substance in all theatrical forms each season.

The problem of evaluating the serious new play in the Broadway theater is difficult for several reasons. First, a new play may not last long enough on Broadway for the public to be given an opportunity to come to any conclusions. Second, very few critics offer mature opinion on the merits of a new work whereas thirty or forty critics from papers all over Europe may review a new play opening in a German house. Third, and of even more importance, is the total absence in New York of a permanently established theatrical repertory company maintaining continuously before the public by means of the highest standards of acting and design the masterworks of the theater, an institution which provides a kind of artistic measuring rod against which the new play may be judged in performance. For the art of the opera, the Metropolitan Opera Association well serves this function as does, for ballet, the New

York City Ballet Company. But spoken drama on Broadway is part of the New York entertainment industry, in the same category as movies and television, and is expected by its producer and backers to show a profit. It it doesn't, it is moved out of the theater building it is temporarily occupying to make room for something better suited to the public taste.

It has been observed that if a diamond cutter is continually provided with glass to cut he will soon cease to care whether he cuts diamonds or glass and, in time, will be unable to tell the difference. In the Central European theater glass is regularly studied in the presence of diamonds, not other pieces of glass. When Armand Gatti's new play **General Francos Leidenswege** was given its world première in the **Kleines Haus** of the **Staatstheater Kassel** on November 10, 1967, his work was placed before an audience which had seen, in the same season, plays by O'Neill, Gogol, Brecht, Schiller and Duerrenmatt, among others. In such company, a play has to have something to make its mark.

The French playwright Armand Gatti was born in Monaco in 1924. He fought in the French resistance against the German occupation of France, was captured and condemned to death. He was pardoned because of his youth and interned in Hamburg. He escaped, however, and became a paratrooper until the end of the war. In 1948 he became a journalist and travelled to many countries. He also became an animal trainer in a circus. His professional journey from the animal cage to the theater he considers a natural course of events, saying that a dialogue with a wild beast — even if mute — is, after all, a contact with a living being.

Since the end of the fifties, Gatti has written several plays among which might be mentioned **Der schwarze Fisch, Le Crapaud-Buffle, L'enfant-rat, Le voyage de Grand 'Tschou, Das imaginaere Leben des Strassenkehrers August G, Die zweite Existenz des Lagers Tatenberg** and **Offentlicher Gesang vor zwei elektrischen Stuehlen.** His latest plays are attempts, in the manner of Brecht's **Lehrstuecke,** to assist the various classes of society to understand themselves in an intellectual sense. He is particularly interested in drawing the working classes into the theater where problems and ideas can be expounded in various ways and from many points of view. In fact, the outcome of some of his plays depends on decisions of the audience. Gatti maintains that he does not try to influence the conclusions of his hearers; instead, he lets the problems speak for themselves. He is resigned to the fact that his plays will not change the world. On the other hand, as each person must try to help change mankind, so must the theater — as an expression of mankind's aspirations and idealism — become engaged in the struggle for the betterment of the world.

The title, **General Franco's Lives of Suffering**, refers to the anguish of the people of Spain brought on by the dictatorial regime of the Caudillo. The play attempts to achieve an amalgam of poetry and document. Plot and characterization from the Aristotelian theater are not wholly discarded, and Gatti does not succumb to the temptation — in the style of Hochhuth — to create cardboard figures, often with historical names, who spend their time on stage declaiming platitudes. Ideas are always present in Gatti, and they are made quite clear to the audience, but an effort is made to allow these ideas to mature through the interaction of character and situation rather than by means of verbal statement and counterstatement. The result is the very opposite of propaganda (the simple-minded indoctrination of the audience in the dogma of the author), and by depending on dramatic action to disclose idea, Gatti's work takes a significant place in the theater of politics.

General Francos Leidenswege presents to the audience, in a series of short, clearly etched scenes, the states of mind of a number of refugees from Franco Spain. In one scene, three Spaniards living in Russia are in a plane flying over Moscow from Kiev to Siberia. In another, the daughter of an exiled Spaniard undertakes a holiday trip to Spain and finds, to the discomfiture of her father, that she likes the place in spite of Franco. In a third, a Spaniard whose father was killed fighting for Hitler in Russia comes to Frankfurt as a foreign worker. In still another, a pretty girl flown over from Spain to Cuba is enthusiastically crowned "Miss Tobacco." She becomes disenchanted with Castro, however, and goes to Mexico. Her lover returns to Spain and finds the comrades of his student days, who have been resisting Franco, in jail. Out of these and other lively scenes on a realistic level, there grow dreamlike, hallucinatory sequences in which allegorical elements contribute to the idea content of the play.

The work was in preparation for nearly a year prior to the opening. The distinctions between dream and reality were managed by means of lighting. During portions of the action, a huge rubber doll painted to resemble General Franco hung suspended over the stage like a brooding basilisk. The doll became the target of the emotional outbursts of the immigrants. A large, gray disc, representing the sun looking southward, provided a surface on which were projected scenes from the life of General Franco.

These devices worked very effectively in the performances. The grotesque elements of the play seemed to contain the real kernels of truth; conviction was achieved by means of exaggeration. Often, there were as many as four separate acting areas in use at the same time reflecting the widespread interest on the part of the avant-garde European theater in simultaneous staging.

The artists at Kassel responsible for the production believed in a committed—an engaged—theater. The director, Kai Braak, and the designer, the French painter Michel Raffaelli, had worked with Armand Gatti previously and believed, with him, that the theater ought to take a stand on the issues of the day. Rafaelli, in fact, considered himself the spiritual godfather of the piece since he had suggested the idea to Gatti one night over some spaghetti and wine. He and Gatti are of the opinion that all artists of the theater should work toward some kind of political goal in order to justify dramatic art. A theater organization which exists simply for its own sake, in an artistic vacuum, cannot justify the tremendous expense required to keep it in operation. And the theater can do something. For example, one can see pictures of the results of fighting in Viet Nam on television or in magazines and newspapers, but one is unconcerned and goes his own way. The theater, however, can show us imitations of these same actions which make us suffer, and when we suffer we are willing to act.

By combining in his play segments of the past (the Spanish Civil War) with elements of the present, Gatti projects an image of society's future. This future is revealed through the visions of the people whose fate has enabled them to see. The differences among the characters show the different paths which can be taken toward revolution and restoration of democracy in those places in which it is no longer in evidence, if it ever was.

The première of **General Francos Leidenswege** at the **Staatstheater Kassel** was attended by over 30 critics, representing newspapers and other mass media from the entire German-speaking area of Europe. Among the media which carried reviews of the play were the **General-Anzeiger fuer Bonn und Umgegend**, the **Sueddeutsche Zeitung**, the **Frankfurter Rundschau**, the **Waldeckische Landeszeitung, Handelsblatt**, the **Kasseler Post**, the **Frankfurter Allgemeine**, the **Hessische Allgemeine, Die Welt**, the **Basler Nachrichten**, the **Saarbruecker Zeitung**, the **Rheinische Post**, the **Mannheimer Morgen, Christ und Welt**, the **Nord-Hessische-Zeitung**, and the **West Deutsche Rundfunk**.

SUBSIDIES FOR THE THEATER

Of interest to the free press of Germany was the fact that on the day of the last dress rehearsal before the opening the Spanish government, through its representatives in Bonn and Kassel, made an effort to prevent the première of the play. In spite of this, the **Staatstheater Kassel** opened **General Francos Leidenswege** as scheduled emphasizing the absence of censorship of the theater in West Germany. In fact, the West German constitution guarantees freedom of the theater.

Things turned out differently, however, when Gatti's play was scheduled for production in Paris the following season by the **Théâtre National Populaire**. The first French performance, with a new title and no mention in the text of Franco, was planned for February 11, 1969. As it happened, an important conference on economic matters between Spain and France was scheduled for the same day and the Spanish foreign office protested against the performance of the play. The French foreign minister, Debre, agreed that the play should be forbidden, an opinion which brought him into conflict with the cultural minister, Andre Malraux, who held that the play should be allowed to go on. President Charles de Gaulle settled the matter in favor of his foreign minister. Just before Christmas of 1968, he forbade presentation of the Gatti play in France. There were protests in the French newspapers and a petition condemning the action was signed by many French intellectuals, among whom were Arthur Adamov, Louis Aragon, Roger Blin, Simone de Beauvoir, Marguerite Duras and Jean-Paul Sartre, but the ban remained.[27]

[27]Renate Voss, "Fuer die Freiheit der Fantasie," **Kasseler Theaterzeitung** (Oktober-November 1967) p. 2.

STAATSTHEATER KASSEL—Floris Neusuess

STAATSTHEATER KASSEL—Kaspar Seiffert

Two scenes from Armand Gatti's *Rosa Kollektiv* **(world première).**

Two scenes from Armand Gatti's *General Francos Leidenswege.* **(world première)**

STAATSTHEATER KASSEL—Floris Neusuess

STAATSTHEATER KASSEL—Kaspar Seiffert

The repertory at Kassel the following season (1968-69) included such works as Zimmermann's **Die Soldaten, Martha, Così fan tutte, Der Rosenkavalier** and the Brecht-Dessau **Die Verurteilung des Lukullus** among musical pieces and among spoken dramas, Ibsen's **Gespenster**, Kleist's **Kaethchen von Heilbronn**, Molière's **Der eingebildete Kranke**, the Sophokles-Hoelderlin **Antigonae** together with a new translation of **Antigone** by Claus Bremer, Shakespeare's **Der Widerspenstigen Zaehmung**, Lorca's **Doña Rosita bleibt ledig** and another new play by Armand Gatti, **Die Geburt**. Of these productions, perhaps the most remarkable was that of Bernd Alois Zimmermann's experiment with **Total Theater, Die Soldaten**.

Described by a number of critics after its première at the **Buehnen der Stadt Koeln** on February 15, 1965 as one of the most important modern operas since Alban Berg's **Wozzeck, Die Soldaten** has proved to be an enormously difficult undertaking for every theater company which has staged it. In fact, the Kassel company attracted international attention by being the second theater and the first medium-sized house to mount the opera thus demonstrating that productions of **Die Soldaten** do not have to be limited to the world's largest opera houses.[28]

Zimmermann's opera is based on the play **Die Soldaten** by the playwright and critic Jacob Michael Reinhold Lenz, one of the founders of the German literary movement **Sturm und Drang**. This movement preceded and influenced the early work of Goethe and Schiller although they later repudiated it as excessively subjective and extravagant. Today, as Zimmermann has noted, it is a surprisingly short step from the dramaturgy of the modern theater — with its taste for subjectivity and extravagance — to the ideals of the **Sturm und Drang**. Some slogans from the movement certainly posses a familiar ring: "uebersteigerter Individuallitaetsbegriff" ("do your own thing"); "Autoritaetsfeindlichkeit" ("hostility toward the Establishment"); "Freiheit vom Vorurteil der Gesellschaft" ("freedom from the prejudices of society"); "Freiheit zum persoenlichen Entscheidung" ("freedom of personal choice"); "Leidenschaft anstelle der Moral" ("passion instead of morality"). Are the 1770's trying to say something to the 1970's?

Lenz was born in 1751 in Latvia into upper class Baltic society. He studied theology at Koenigsberg then became a tutor and a free-lance author. He was associated with Goethe at Weimar in 1776 where he met Frau von Stein, Wieland and others. There were scandals involving love affairs and some signs of insanity in his behaviour. He travelled to Riga, then to Russia where he became a teacher. In 1792 he was found dead in a Moscow street.

His chief literary work consists of some translations of plays by Plautus and Shakespeare, a vigorous critical attack on the French idea of the Aristotelian unities, and three plays, **Der Hofmeister** (1774), **Der neue Mendoza** (1775) and **Die Soldaten** (1776). He proclaimed a dramaturgy which was anti-Aristotelian in that the unities of time, place and action were to be replaced by short, disconnected, fragmentary scenes, some of an hallucinatory nature, which would convey to the audience the inner life of the characters. This concept of the theater had a decisive influence on Georg Buechner, and later on Gerhart Hauptmann and Bertolt Brecht. In fact, Brecht wrote an adaptation of **Der Hofmeister**. Of **Die Soldaten**, Lenz said in a letter to Herder that it represented a certain portion of his own being, that it was dramatically truthful, and that this truth would manifest itself despite centuries of indifference to his work. His prediction is interesting in view of the fact that a large number of plays from the seventeenth, eighteenth and nineteenth centuries maintain their essential vigor — if not their original form — as musical adaptations for the opera house.

Die Soldaten is a play, like Buechner's **Woyzeck**, which is charged with social criticism and paints a portrait of a world tinged with insanity. The plot is concerned with the destruction of a middle-class girl by means of elementary force, the kind of force which can suddenly overwhelm a person, and which can destroy civilization. The play was written in 35 scenes. Zimmermann's adaptation for the lyric theater condenses the action to 15 episodes as follows:

The scene is French Flanders, and the composer describes the time of the action as yesterday, today and tomorrow. The heroine, Marie, a middle class girl is in love with Baron Desportes who has secretly left his regiment in Armentières and come to Lille to court her. A young textile worker, Stolzius, is also in love with Marie and wishes to marry her. Marie's father warns her against Desportes but she is attracted by the idea of becoming a **gnaedige Frau** and allows him to seduce her.

In the officers' coffee house at Armentières, the officers tease Stolzius about Marie and her affair with Desportes.[29] Stolzius writes Marie, asking her intentions, but she lets Desportes answer it. The latter breaks the engagement between Marie and Stolzius in a letter which he pretends is from Marie. Stolzius determines to seek revenge.

Some time elapses during which Desportes leaves Marie and the girl sinks into despair. Stolzius takes a position as a soldier-servant to another officer, Major Mary, in the hope of encountering Desportes. Marie tries to see Desportes but the officer tells his batman to prevent her coming. The Jaeger rapes Marie.

Later, Desportes recounts to his friend Major Mary the episode about Marie. Stolzius kills him with a bowl of poisoned soup, then kills himself. On the shore of the river Lys, Marie's father fails to recognize her. A tank with soldiers on it runs over the inert form of the heroine.

The composer, Bernd Alois Zimmermann, who had composed in many forms and was experienced in the modern techniques of twelve-tone and electronic music, chose this play as the basis for his first opera not because of its implicit social criticism but because it illustrates the manner in which brute force, exemplified here by rape, murder and suicide, can engulf us all and destroy us. The degradation of Marie belongs to our time as well as to her own time, and it will belong to all time until the expedient of force is everywhere renounced.

Zimmermann was further attracted to the fragmentary nature of the play because he saw in it an opportunity to experiment with a form of opera he describes as **Total Musiktheater**, an effort to engulf the audience in the action by surrounding it on all sides with music, sound effects, stage action and filmed action. His original plan was to establish twelve small stages clear around the audience with parts of the orchestra in pits in front of each one. Action would go on all around the audience at all times. The scheme suggests that Zimmermann was well acquainted with the **Total Theater** project planned by Walter Gropius for the stage director Erwin Piscator during the 1920's. In the Gropius theater, Zimmermann's ideas could be realized but in its absence, the composer was persuaded by the directors of the **Buehnen der Stadt Koeln**, who commissioned the opera, to rework his material for conventional proscenium theater production. He did so, but he hung on to his original plan in three scenes of the

---

[28]After the first performance of Berg's **Wozzeck** in Berlin in 1925, the second production it received, at Oberhausen in 1929, demonstrated the same thing.

[29]Cf. Berg's **Wozzeck**, Act II scene 2.

opera — the coffee house scene, in which several actions take place simultaneously; the rape scene; and the final scene, in which Marie's past, present and future are all visible to the audience at the same time. Zimmermann thought of the audience as being inside a huge sphere, so that it has no choice but to become totally absorbed in the simultaneous actions surrounding it. Under these conditions, perhaps the faintly academic art of the opera can be dragged into the twentieth century. What is needed, according to Zimmermann, is a pluralistic conception of opera, a concentration of all theatrical media, the exploitation of architecture, sculpture, painting, lyric theater, spoken theater, ballet, film, microphones, television, tape recorders, electronically synthesized music, concrete music, circus music — all the forms of the modern theater combined into a production of theatrical totality. Music must become a collage of the music of all epochs and all forms and, in this way, carry to the audience simultaneously a feeling of the past, the present and the future.

Zimmermann organized his opera around three major lines of development: the fate of Marie, the world of the soldiers, and the three **Total Musiktheater** scenes. All the music of the opera grows from one twelve-tone series of notes.

The scenes detailing the fate of Marie are composed dialogue. The text is easy to understand since the music merely underlines the content of the dialogue. The performers act normally in relation to their own personalities and their positions in life. Details of characterization are carefully underscored in the music. Only during ensembles, does music take some priority over the understandability of the text.

Three scenes depict the lives of the soldiers. Two ideas in the Lenz text suggested a certain kind of treatment of these scenes, both in music and in pantomime. At one point, the soldiers are described as mechanical beings, and at another, as caricatures of humanity, living in a state of wretched singleness. Thus, in the scenes depicting the condition of the soldiery, anonymous figures in the background are silhouetted against a screen, move in marionette-like fashion, and execute stylized, puppet gestures. The effect is to suggest that from the outside they look normal enough, but inside, they are damaged human beings. There are 35 persons required for the coffee house scene, although only a few have lines to sing.

The coffee house scene, the rape scene and the final scene of Marie's degradation constitute the scenes of **Total Musiktheater**. The rape sequence is staged behind a scrim, but it is duplicated on the motion picture screens in many permutations of the theme of a woman dragged slowly into the gutter. Such is the arrangement of the motion-picture screens and the clusters of speakers in the auditorium that the effect is that of the audience, too, being raped.

The coffee house scene is staged on several levels at once and is musically one of the most difficult sections in the opera. The scene begins with a twelve-tone chord whose notes are distributed among twelve solo voices — each singer singing a different note of the chromatic scale. When it is recalled that most ensemble sequences in opera begin on no more than four or six different notes, and these generally in the same key, the difficulties facing the singers, conductor and coaches can be readily imagined.

In the final scene of the opera, mechanical-acoustical-electrical elements dominate the action and the characterization. As Marie's father leaves her, not knowing who she is, a huge tank, the width of the stage, rolls toward the audience and over Marie. Thirty spotlights are aimed directly in the eyes of the audience while a blast of sound from twelve clusters of

speakers surrounding the seating area assails the listeners with screams, shouted military commands in many languages, lines from earlier scenes, war sounds, airplanes, explosions, and — throughout — the heavy tramp of marching boots. On the movie screens are such things as the atomic bomb explosions over Hiroshima and Nagasaki, scenes from concentration camps and other exercises in mass destruction. The effect is the opposite of Brecht's theory of the detached observer in the theater drawing intellectual conclusions about stage actions he coolly witnesses. In Zimmermann's theater, the audience experiences in reality actions which are merely imitated by the performers.

The musical setting of the piece taxes the resources of the very largest opera houses, and the fact that it could be done at Kassel at all is a tribute to the energy and dedication of the theater and a good example of the efficacy of subsidized repertory for enabling the citizenry of a medium-sized city like Kassel to see a new and exciting work of musical theater. The usual opera orchestra must be augmented for **Die Soldaten** with such things as organ (for four hands), cembalo, piano, celesta, guitar, alto flute, and saxophone. Additionally, a huge percussion section is called for: large and small drums, wooden drums, bongos, tomtoms, temple bells, tamtams, gongs, rattle, maracas, triangle, castanets, three hanging railroad rails, tambourine, glockenspiel, xylophone, vibraphone, marimbaphone, high hat, wood block, steel bars, whip crack and cow bells. For some sequences played on the stage, the composer requires a jazz combo of clarinet, trumpet and double bass and several kettle drums.

The orchestra was so big that it couldn't be gotten into the orchestra pit of the **Grosses Haus**, so the percussion section was accommodated during the six performances in the rehearsal room on the eighth floor of the workroom area between the two theaters. An associate conductor followed the conductor's beat by means of a closed-circuit television screen and the noise was relayed by microphones to the speaker clusters in the auditorium.

The music itself posed many problems for singers and orchestra players alike, and required approximately 60 orchestra rehearsals and over 300 solo and ensemble rehearsals. In the coffee house scene there were cases of time changes in every succeeding measure — for example, 3/4, 2/4, 1/4, 3/8, 5/8, 3/8, 1/4, 3/4 and so forth — and the vocal lines often consisted of wide leaps in chromatic intervals, as when the Countess de la Roche is required to sing from b'' to a' to a-flat in quick tempo. It was found that if a singer had to perform a role in the regular repertory on a given night he could not be asked to rehearse the Zimmermann on either the same day or the day preceding.

The music is dodecaphonic and is embellished with liberal use of electronic music, as in the rape scene. Zimmermann employs traditional musical forms such as the chorale and the toccata (as does Berg in his **Wozzeck**) but even more ingenious is his effort to organize length of notes, pitches and dynamics in symmetrical sequences which suggest his idea of the audience in the center of a sphere of reality which contains within itself the present, the past and the future. Musical quotations from the past blend with jazz excerpts from the present to persuade the audience that past and present are one and that there is no escape into the future. That such concepts can be expressed at all in musical terminology is only one of the remarkable features of this significant and revolutionary opera.

Zimmermann has spoken of the influences of both James Joyce and Ezra Pound on his thinking about his opera. Joyce's remark in **Ulysses** "put allspace in a notshall" and Pound's comment "all ages are now" taken together suggest the thematic material — the aesthetical Idea — of **Die Soldaten**.

Opera must say something to the audience, as does the spoken drama, if it is to survive as a viable art form in a world desperately searching for answers to the seemingly insoluble problems of human violence, greed and rapacity. By placing the audience on the rack of genuinely felt experience, Zimmermann hopes to arouse sufficient emotion in his audiences to achieve in them a catharsis of such emotions into an intensely perceived awareness of the agony of a world wracked equally by violence and hate. A historical romance is replaced by historical fatalism — that is, a spoken drama of a past historical epoch achieves new life in a musical setting from today, and tomorrow.[30]

Bernd Alois Zimmermann's opera *Die Soldaten.*

Operas such as **Die Soldaten** and plays such as **General Francos Leidenswege** cannot be effectively staged in primitive theater buildings, and the two theaters which make up the complex of the **Staatstheater Kassel** are as well equipped as modern technology can make them. In fact, the need for a large number of new theaters in Germany and Austria after the last war has stimulated a great deal of experiment and fresh thinking in connection with the age old problems of theater design and construction.

One of the recurring problems of theater architecture is that of the appropriate relationship between the auditorium and the stage. There is a trend nowadays to try and reduce the artificial separation of audience from stage area found in theaters with proscenium arches and attempt a continuous flow from one area to the other. Zimmermann and Gatti are only two among many who envisage a very intimate kind of communion between actor and audience and the two theaters of the **Staatstheater Kassel** complex both provide facilities for the achievement of this relationship.

In the **Grosses Haus,** the area between stage and auditorium, called the portal area, permits either a proscenium situation or a feeling that the stage area flows architecturally into the auditorium area almost without interruption. The proscenium

30F. W. Anders, "Warum **Die Soldaten?,**" **Kasseler Theaterzeitung** (Oktober-November 1968) p. 2.

opening can be varied by the use of movable tormentor towers from a width of 16 meters, to 12 meters, to 8 meters. The proscenium height is controlled by a movable portal bridge, the audience side of which is covered with Swiss pear tree wood. The bottom of the bridge is either broken up into several curved sections for the idea of "flow" from stage to auditorium, or straightened out with the addition of a soffit piece when the proscenium idea of the theater is desired.

Buehnentechnische Rundschau

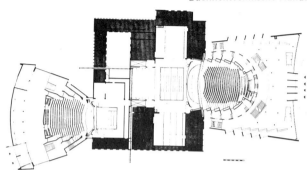

Floor plans of the two theaters in the Kassel complex. The *Kleines Haus* **is left, the** *Grosses Haus* **right.**

Buehnentechnische Rundschau

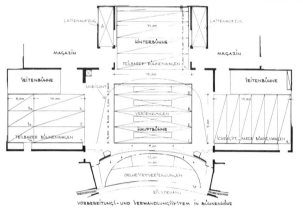

Floor plan of the main stage, side stages and rear stage of the *Grosses Haus* **at Kassel.**

Although the **Grosses Haus,** seating 945, was planned primarily for opera and musicals some plays are performed there too. When the orchestra is not needed the orchestra lift is raised to stage height, a condition which adds an apron four meters deep to the fixed stage area. The lift operates on hydraulic power and is divided into three upstage sections and one downstage section all of which can be operated separately or in groups. The three upstage platforms are double-decked so that if the upper floors are at stage level, the lower ones will be 3.3 meters below. Since the downstage unit can also sink to a level 3.3 meters below stage level an orchestra pit can still be provided even with half the lift being used as a forestage.

Due to the variability of the stage area there are two house curtains in use in the **Grosses Haus** in addition to the **Eisenvorhang** (the iron safety curtain). Downstage of the orchestra pit area is a decorated scenic curtain used when the lift is up at stage level. Directly upstage of this house curtain is the **Eisenvorhang**. Further upstage is the main house curtain used when the orchestra lift is lowered to orchestra pit level. It is made of velour and is suspended from a **Scherenzug**, two pantagraph-like devices which contract and expand like an accordion, carrying the two halves of the curtain with them. Pipes for scrims and sound curtains are hung between the velour house curtain and the portal bridge.

It is of interest that the "proscenium wall" is about five meters thick due to the design of the portal zone of the theater. As a result, dressing rooms can be placed in what, in an American theater, would be the proscenium wall — allowing rapid access from dressing room to stage area.

The main stage is flanked by two wagon side stages and one rear stage wagon. The main area consists of four elevator stages 15 meters wide and a total of 11 meters deep. The elevators will run singly or together in any combination a distance of 3 meters above the stage and 3 meters below. In each elevator is a small table elevator used to bring performers up from the trap room to stage level.

The stage left wagon consists of six sections totalling 9 meters by 15 meters in size. The sections may be used independently or coupled together in groups. The wagon has its own motor drive mechanism. The floor can be sloped toward the audience by raising the back edge of the tops. There are three slopes, steep, medium and mild. Any given slope can be set on the entire wagon in 15 minutes. Many directors in the German theaters like to make use of a raked stage and this wagon makes raking possible on a temporary basis for a given production in the repertory.

The stage right wagon consists of six elements. Three are 3 meters by 10 meters and three are 3 meters by 5 meters; hence, the two wagons are the same overall size. Each small wagon can run on its own power.

The rear stage wagon is 14 meters wide and 11 meters deep. It consists of 4 sections which are coupled together by dovetail joints. The motor drive is installed in a special wagon behind the others which is 14 meters wide and 0.8 meter deep. The motor conveys power to two driveshafts on which are located cog wheels. The wheels move over a cog track in the stage floor only 15 millimeters wide.

The side wagons run on rubber rollers over beachwood tracks which can be replaced when they wear out. The travel of the wagons is very quiet. They are 16.67 centimeters high and when in place on the main stage, the front is masked by a special scenic unit which slopes to the stage floor level.

The stage battens in the **Grosses Haus** were originally hand operated by means of counterweight arbors. Due to the need to move wagons from center stage to either side and to the rear it was not possible to allow the arbors to run along one of the side walls, or the back wall, from stage floor to above the gridiron level. The arbors were rigged to travel part way down from the gridiron and, by means of a double purchase system, the battens travelled all the way up from floor to gridiron. The system is common in American theaters using side stages. It essentially gives a two-to-one mechanical advantage to the batten; the batten travels twice as far as the counterweight arbor. The disadvantage of this system, and it is a serious limitation, is that twice the weight on the batten must be placed in the arbor to overcome the batten's mechanical advantage. Handling the system then calls for twice as many stagehands as are required by the single purchase system installed in theaters without side stages or with only one side stage. Hence, the administration of the **Staatstheater Kassel** soon found it necessary to install winch-controlled battens in the **Grosses Haus** partly to save

manpower and partly to cut down on the noise from the crew as it struggled with the excessively heavy counterweight arbors. Under the direction of Prof. Dipl.-Ing. Walther Unruh, 10 motor winch units were installed 1 meter above the gridiron to clear the existing lines and loft blocks. The hand system was retained so that either hand or motor operation would be possible. The 10 winches can be used, by means of a switching system, to operate a total of 33 battens. Eight of the winches can operate any one of four battens (one operates any of five) while two of the winches are masters into which can be plugged several battens at once. The control console for the system is located on the fourth work gallery which allows the operator to see the rise and fall of the battens more easily than they can be seen from the floor. With the installation of this system, one operator replaced some twenty stagehands at the pin rail.

Maschinenfabrik Wiesbaden, G.m.b.H.

Control console for electric-winch-operated pipe battens in the *Grosses Haus* at Kassel. There are four individual control units, then two master controls, then four more individual controls. The nearest control handle activates the winch which raises and lowers any one of battens no. 3, no. 12, no. 21, no. 30 or no. 38, depending on which button is depressed. The *Aus* (out) button releases the numbered buttons. The master winches can handle several battens each. The handle is pushed forward to raise a batten and pulled back to lower it. The amount of distance the handle is pushed is directly proportional to the speed of the batten's run. Height indicators are next to the control buttons.

In addition to the scenery battens, the overhead equipment consists of the main portal light bridge, two more motor-driven light bridges on which are installed projection apparatus and special units for back and side lighting, a regular light pipe for borderlights and the track for the **Rundhorizont**, or Linnebach cyclorama. This cyclorama has, for acoustical reasons, a 2 percent rearward slope in its 20 meters of height. It is 40 meters wide and, as in most German houses, when not in use it is rolled up on one of two **Wickelkonen** (wrapping cones) at the sides of the stage. The winding operation is motor driven.

Scenery can be changed on the side and rear stage wagons during a performance if necessary as all three areas can be sealed off from the main stage and the auditorium by means of soundproof doors. These doors are made of steel plates backed by layers of sound-absorbent wool. In each sound door there is a small door which gives access to the area closed off without the need to raise the sound door.

Lighting control is executed from a control room at the rear of the auditorium. The console consists of 160 lighting circuits and the dimmer units are magnetic amplifiers. Each spotlight, in addition to being dimmable, is equipped with remote-control color media which allows the operator in the control room complete control over the color from every instrument in the theater. The cyclorama is lighted by 32 large fluorescent tube floodlights with color magazines on each one. Communication between the various lighting stations is achieved by means of two-channel short-wave radio transmitter-receiver units.

Sound equipment is also controlled from a booth at the rear of the auditorium. There are ten speaker clusters in the auditorium fed by various microphone channels and a five-track tape recorder-reproducer unit. Sound effects are generally taped although the theater also has available motor-controlled thunder, wind and rain machines backstage. There are a number of outlets in the house for microphones for radio broadcasts and outlets for TV cameras.

In the **Kleines Haus** the stage machinery is somewhat simpler. The portal zone is 10 meters wide and can be reduced by movable tormentor towers to a width of 7 meters. The portal bridge is dead hung at 5.5 meters above stage level, establishing thereby the height of the proscenium. The theater is designed, however, to give the feeling of an uninterrupted flow of sight and sound between stage and auditorium. For instance, during a production of Kleist's **Penthisilea**, actors who were not participating in a scene on stage were often sitting just downstage of the portal zone, in the scene in a way, and yet out of it. The theater is provided with a velour house curtain, an **Eisenvorhang** and battens for sound and scrim curtains.

There is a small orchestra pit in the **Kleines Haus** with an adjustable floor which can be established at any height by means of motor-driven spindles. When the floor is at stage level it is used as a forestage. When it is at auditorium floor level 40 extra seats can be placed on it raising the seating capacity from the usual 534 to 574. When lowered below auditorium floor level, a small orchestra can be accommodated to accompany musical revues or chamber operas.

On the main stage an area 10 meters by 10 meters can be tilted toward the audience by means of screw jacks. Over the stage are 18 scenery battens and four large cyclorama or backdrop battens. The **Rollenboden** (gridiron) is so close to the roof steel (an economy measure) that there is insufficient head room to work on it. Consequently, the loft blocks are suspended underneath it and to service them a movable, cantilevered bridge 2 meters below the **Rollenboden** runs up and downstage on two steel tracks. It is also used as a light bridge.

There are 100 lighting circuits controlled from an offstage platform 2.5 meters above the stage floor in the portal zone. The master control console, however, is located on the movable tormentor tower so the operator can see the stage lighting. As in the **Grosses Haus**, the dimmer units are magnetic amplifiers.

A demountable turntable with a diameter of 12 meters can be used on either the large or the small stage. In the floor positions at which it might be used — that is, on the full-stage wagons or in the center of the main stage areas — there are metal cylinders into which can be inserted the hub of the turntable. It is 16.67 centimeters high and is turned by a rubber drive wheel controlled by a servo motor at a remote location. Three men can assemble the turntable and put the floor on it in 90 minutes.

In both houses, provision is made for the hard of hearing. Through several stage microphones, the performance is broadcast into the auditorium where it is picked up by antennas located in the floor and ceiling. With a small transistor hearing aid, a deaf person can listen to the performance from any location in the house.

There are several workshops located between the two stages. Two large freight elevators connect the stages with work spaces and storage areas. Administrative offices are also located between the theaters. Rehearsal rooms for ballet, chorus, orchestra and company run-throughs are separated from each other for acoustical reasons by intervening storage and work rooms. All scenery, costumes and properties are constructed and painted on the premises and after being used in the initial performance season are stored for use in future seasons.[31]

The **Staatstheater Kassel** receives an annual subsidy from both the city of Kassel and the state of Hesse. The following table summarizes, in millions of German marks, the financial growth of the two-theater complex from 1959 through 1968.

Calendar Year	Total Expense	Box Office and Other Income	Subsidy, City of Kassel	Subsidy, State of Hesse	Ratio of Subsidy to Expense
1959	5.683	1.549	1.966	2.168	72%
1960	4.928	1.445	1.686	1.797	72%
1961	7.057	1.998	2.424	2.635	71%
1962	7.543	1.955	2.671	2.917	73%
1963	8.394	1.999	3.063	3.332	76%
1964	9.085	1.914	3.420	3.751	79%
1965	9.888	1.891	3.800	4.197	81%
1966	10.359	1.875	4.072	4.412	84%
1967	10.543	2.256	3.978	4.309	82%
1968	10.983	2.069	4.275	4.639	80% [32]

There seems to be little resistance to the idea of subsidies for the theater on the part of the people of Kassel. Now and then, after an experimental piece, one might hear a remark in the lobby to the effect, "For **this** we pay taxes?" but, generally speaking, there is no objection in principle. In fact, there has even been talk within the theater administration about the possibility of letting in free anyone who wants to come, thus calling for a 100 percent subsidy. This situation remains for the future, however.

[31]"Die neuen Theater der Stadt Kassel"; Ernst Brundig, "Baubeschreibung," and Dipl.-Ing. Manfred Weidner, "Die Technik der Buehnen," **Buehnentechnische Rundschau,** LIII (December 1959), pp. 9-18; Hanns Goepfert, "Prospektzuege fuer wahlweise Handbetrieb oder elektrischen Antrieb," BTR LVI (April, 1962), pp. 22-24.

[32]Walter Olbrich, "Die wirtschaftliche Entwicklung des Staatstheaters Kassel in den letzten 10 Jahren," **Kasseler Theaterzeitung** (Januar-Februar 1968) p. 2.

SUBSIDIES FOR THE THEATER

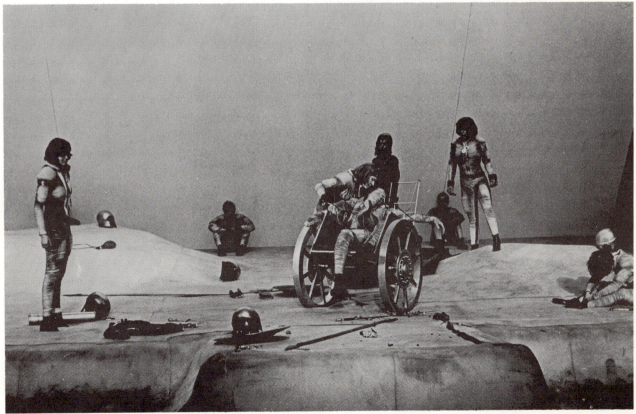

Kleist's *Penthesilea* in modern dress.

Photos by Kaspar Seiffert for the STAATSTHEATER KASSEL

A fanciful version of Aristophanes'
Lysistrata.

Photos by Sepp Baer for the
STAATSTHEATER KASSEL

SUBSIDIES FOR THE THEATER

Kleist's *Das Kaethchen von Heilbronn.*

The children's play *Klaus Klettermaus und die andern Tiere im Hackebackewald* **by Thorbjoern Egner.**

Pavel Kohout's circus play *August August, August.*

STATE THEATERS

Two scenes from Oedoen von Horváth's play of post World War I Germany *Sladek, der schwarze Reichswehrmann.*

Photos by Sepp Baer for the STAATSTHEATER KASSEL

Deutsche Oper Berlin

One of the largest state theaters in West Germany is the **Deutsche Oper Berlin**, formerly the **Staedtische Oper** of Berlin-Charlottenburg. Since moving into its handsome new house on Bismarckstrasse in 1961, the reputation of this organization has been steadily enhanced by its devotion to the very highest standards of production of both opera and ballet, together with its enlightened policy of commissioning and performing new works and staging other new works which either have not been performed at all or are unknown in Germany. This commitment to both the past and the future of the opera as an art form is indispensable to its development. Today's composers require uncommon encouragement to devote years of creative energy to a work for the lyric theater which, under present circumstances in many countries, would have upon completion only a slight chance of a first class production.

The repertory for 1968-69 discloses a remarkable variety of fare for the operagoer and the balletomane:

OPERAS

Claudio Monteverdi	Die Kroenung der Poppea
Wolfgang A. Mozart	Die Entfuehrung aus dem Serail
	Die Hochzeit des Figaro
	Don Giovanni
	Così fan tutte
	Die Zauberfloete
Domenico Cimarosa	Die heimliche Ehe
Ludwig van Beethoven	Fidelio
Carl Maria von Weber	Der Freischuetz
Albert Lortzing	Der Wildschuetz
Jacques Offenbach	Hoffmanns Erzaehlungen (New production)
Richard Wagner	Der fliegende Hollaender
	Tannhaeuser
	Lohengrin
	Das Rheingold
	Die Walkuere
	Siegfried
	Goetterdaemmerung
	Tristan und Isolde
	Die Meistersinger von Nuernberg
	Parsifal
Giuseppe Verdi	Simone Boccanegra (New production)
	Macbeth
	Rigoletto
	Der Troubadour
	La Traviata
	Ein Maskenball
	Don Carlos
	Otello
	Falstaff
Modest Mussorgski	Boris Godounow
Georges Bizet	Carmen
Giacomo Puccini	Tosca (New production)
	La Bohème
	Madame Butterfly
	Turandot
Claude Debussy	Pelléas et Mélisande
Richard Strauss	Salome
	Elektra
	Der Rosenkavalier
	Die Frau ohne Schatten
	Capriccio
Hans Pfitzner	Palestrina
Alban Berg	Wozzeck
	Lulu
Arnold Schoenberg	Moses und Aron
Igor Strawinsky	The Rake's Progress
Leoš Janáček	Die Ausfluge des Herrn Broucek (New production)
Carl Orff	Catulli carmina
	Carmina burana
Gottfried von Einem	Dantons Tod
Luigi Dallapiccola	Odysseus (Ulisse) (World Première)
Hans Werner Henze	Elegie fuer junge Liebende
	Der junge Lord
	Die Bassariden

BALLETS

Antonio Vivaldi	
John Cranko	L'Estro Armonico
Adolphe Adam	
Antony Tudor	Giselle
Peter Tschaikowsky	
Kenneth MacMillan	Dornroeschen
Peter Tschaikowsky	
George Balanchine	Ballet-Imperial
Peter Tschaikowsky	
Kenneth MacMillan	Schwanensee
Igor Strawinsky	
Frederick Ashton	Scènes de Ballet
Igor Strawinsky	
Michael Fokine	
John Cranko	Der Feuervogel
Igor Strawinsky	
Kenneth MacMillan	Olympiade
Serge Prokofieff	
Antony Tudor	Gala Performance
Edgar Varèse	
Tatjana Gsovsky	Labyrinth der Wahrheit
Johann Sebastian Bach	
Brian MacDonald	Aimez-vous Bach?
Maurice Ravel	
Kenneth MacMillan	Valses nobles et sentimentales
Anton von Webern	
John Cranko	Opus 1
Frank Martin	
Kenneth MacMillan	Las Hermanas
Bohuslav Martinu	
Kenneth MacMillan	Anastasia
Arthur Bliss	
Kenneth MacMillan	Diversions
Boris Blacher	
Tatjana Gsovsky	Hamlet
Matyas Seiber	
Kenneth MacMillan	The Invitation
Dmitri Schostakowitsch	
Kenneth MacMillan	Concerto
Malcolm Arnold	
Kenneth MacMillan	Solitaire
Andrzej Panufnik	
Kenneth MacMillan	Kain und Abel (World Première)

A total of 55 operas and 21 ballets is a sizable repertory for any house during a single season. By comparison, the Metropolitan Opera Association in New York, a company of about the same size and of international reputation, offered the public 23 operas and no ballets during the same 1968-69 season. The difference in production capacity between the two theaters unquestionably lies in the realm of the subsidies — the German house received 79 percent of its budget in the form of a public subsidy while the American house had to content itself during the same period with a private subsidy of only 20 percent of its budget.

The personnel of the **Deutsche Oper Berlin** were as follows:

Generalintendant, stage directors, conductors, choreographers, **Dramaturgen** and other members of the artistic staff	44
Principal singers	46
Ballet corps	59
Chorus	120
Orchestra	143
Stagehands, prop men, painters, carpenters, electricians, makeup men and other technical personnel	345
Administrative personnel	67
House personnel	98
Total size of the company	923 [33]

[33] **Theaterstatistik 1968-69**, p. 5. Of this total, 278 employees were women.

STATE THEATERS

Some of the world famous composers, conductors, stage directors, choreographers and managers who have been actively associated with this theater are Bruno Walter, Heinz Tietjen, Carl Ebert, Mary Wigman, Igor Strawinsky, Karl Boehm, Boris Blacher and Rudolf Bing.

The two tasks to which the artistic leadership of this theater addresses itself — maintaining on the stage the best of the old and encouraging what it can of the new — are reflected in the annual repertories. From Monteverdi to Dallapiccola, works of the past and present are continually available for public scrutiny. New productions of the older works, in which everything — music, staging, costuming, scenery, lighting — is carefully restudied in relation to the intentions of the composer and the librettist, form a significant part of every season's schedule, a recent example of interest being the new production Wieland Wagner conceived for his grandfather's music drama **Lohengrin.**

Both of Alban Berg's immensely difficult operas, **Wozzeck** and **Lulu** were in the 68-69 repertory at the same time, continuing and fulfilling a tradition begun in 1925 when the world première of **Wozzeck** took place in Berlin.

The size of the ballet company reflects the European practice of supporting dance within the organizational structure of the opera house, or in a multi-theater complex, in the **Grosses Haus.** The American system is to establish ballet companies as separate entities which makes them hard to support since their activities are limited. When attached to a large theater doing opera, musicals and scenic cantatas the dancers can be used in a variety of productions in addition to their own individual programs. Some of the most imaginative and exciting productions in the 68-69 repertory of the **Deutsche Oper Berlin** were Carl Orff's scenic cantatas **Catulli carmina** and **Carmina burana** which were staged by Gustav Rudolf Sellner and choreographed by Peter Darrell. Settings and costumes were by Teo Otto, the conductor was Eugen Jochum and the chorus director was Walter Hagen-Groll.

Carl Orff's scenic cantatas *Catulli carmina* (above) and *Carmina burana* (below).

Photos by Ilse Buhs for the DEUTSCHE OPER BERLIN

Operas which have been commissioned by the theater, given their first performances anywhere and their first German performances make up a small but very significant part of the repertory of the theater each year. Since 1961, the record is as follows:

YEAR	WORK
1961	**Alkmene,** by Giselher Klebe; commissioned—world première
1962	**La Atlántida** by Manuel de Falla; first production in Germany
1963	**Oreste** by Darius Milhaud; world première of entire work
1964	**Montezuma** by Roger Sessions; world première
1965	**Der junge Lord** by Hans Werner Henze; commissioned—world première
1966	**Amerika** by Roman Haubenstock-Ramati; world première
1968	**Odysseus (Ulisse)** by Luigi Dallapiccola; commissioned—world première
1969	**200,000 Taler** by Boris Blacher; commissioned—world première

These operas are not very well known in America. The Klebe **Alkmene**, which is based on Kleist's **Amphitryon**, is a sensitive setting of the well known story of the seduction of the virtuous Alkmene by Jupiter who is disguised as her husband Amphitryon. The opera is not easy to sing or play — the music is composed in the idiom of Schoenberg and Webern — but in performance it provides good roles for the three principals and satisfying comic possibilities for the counterpart triangle of the servants Cleanthis, Sosias and Mercury. In fact all of Klebe's work in the operatic form is stageable and exciting when performed on the stage, especially his **Die Raeuber** (based on the Schiller play), **Die Ermordung Caesars** (after Shakespeare) and his continuation of the Figaro story, set a few years after the start of the French Revolution, **Figaro laesst sich scheiden,** a charming musical version of the play by Oedoen von Horváth.

Manuel de Falla labored over his last opera **La Atlántida** for some twenty years. It was unfinished at his death and was put into performance condition by the Spanish composer and conductor Ernesto Halffter. The work was first performed at La

German Information Center

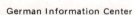
Manuel de Falla's *La Atlántida.*

Scala in Milan in June, 1962 and at the **Deutsche Oper Berlin** in October of the same year for the first time in Germany. A scenic cantata in form, **La Atlántida** is a setting of an epic poem by Jacinto Verdaguer on the subject of the coming of Columbus to the New World and the civilizing mission of Catholic Spain. The work requires a large chorus which conveys much of the musical interest, a few soloists, a narrator and several dancers who pantomime on the stage actions which are being narrated and expressed musically by chorus and orchestra. The musical style evokes the classical age of 16th and 17th century Spanish polyphony and exhibits a consistently refined and elegant feeling for the stirring text.

The production of **La Atlántida** by the stage director Gustav Rudolf Sellner and the scene designer Michel Raffaelli provided extensive visual diversity to compensate for the lack on stage of dramatic action. Mythological animals paraded about, the scenery itself possessed a degree of mobility and a dragon danced nimbly to its death, all amid projected effects of fire and mist.

The form of the scenic cantata — a dramatic spectacle for orchestra, chorus, solo singers and dancers who mime actions which are depicted in musical passages — has enjoyed something of a revival on the contemporary European stage. Some of the earliest experiments with the lyric theater were composed in this form, for example, Cavalieri's **Rappresentazione di anima e di corpo** (1600) and Monteverdi's **Il combattimento di Tancredi e di Clorinada** (1624). Modern examples, in addition to the Carl Orff pieces mentioned above, are Gian-Carlo Menotti's **The Unicorn, the Gorgon and the Manticore** and Leonard Bernstein's **Mass.**

German Information Center

World première of *Alkmene* **by Giselher Klebe.**

STATE THEATERS

Another work of tremendous size which requires very large musical ensembles in performance is Darius Milhaud's musical setting of Paul Claudel's translation of the **Oresteia** trilogy of Aeschylus. The three parts of Milhaud's **Orestie** — which correspond to the three sections of the Greek original — are **Agamemnon** (1913), **Les Choéphores** (1915) and **Les Eumenides** (1922). The work was nearly ten years in composition and, although some parts of the trilogy were staged and some performed in the concert hall, it was more than forty years after he began work on the opera that Milhaud finally saw the entire trilogy staged at the **Deutsche Oper Berlin** in April of 1963.

The stage director and designer were again the team of Sellner and Raffaelli. Some of the work was danced, some spoken and some sung by chorus and soloists. The role of Athene, composed for three voices, was amplified. Again, the form is that of a massive scenic cantata which heavily taxes the musical and financial resources of any theater organization undertaking to produce it.

The well known American composer Roger Sessions also worked on an opera — **Montezuma** — for over twenty years before seeing its first performance at the **Deutsche Oper Berlin** in April of 1964. The music is composed to a text by Giuseppe Antonio Borgese which concerns the complex relationships, viewed from something of a distance, between the Spanish conquistadors led by Hernando Cortés and the Aztec nation led by Montezuma. Both leaders desire peace but a state of war to the end is maintained due to the hatreds and bitterness of their followers. At length, Montezuma is killed by his own people to prevent the advent of peace between the Spaniards and the Aztecs. Thematically, the opera obviously has something to say to contemporary American audiences.

Montezuma contains a good portion of spoken dialogue, possibly an influence of the scenic cantatas, and the composer's richly polyphonic music possesses power and originality. In the Aztec scenes a somewhat expanded percussion section is required including celesta, xylophone, bells, rattles, and a collection of Mexican wooden drums.

The following season, the theater produced an opera which it had commissioned from Hans Werner Henze, a composer already well established through the success of such pieces as his **Das Wundertheater** (1948), **Boulevard Solitude** (1952), **Koenig Hirsch** (1956), **Der Prinz von Homburg** (1960) and **Elegie fuer junge Liebende** (1961). The new opera was entitled **Der junge Lord** and was set to a text by Ingeborg Bachmann which was in turn derived from a story by Wilhelm Hauff entitled **Der Scheik von Allessandria**. The plot of **Der junge Lord** turns on the visit to a small German town of a "young lord" from England who captivates everyone with his imperious manner, his indifference to the niceties of polite society and his exotic speech, which consists chiefly of violent exclamations, proverbs and quotations from Goethe. The social elite of the town adore him and a fetching belle even falls in love with him. He is something new to imitate, a primitive, something genuine in the midst of so much that is artificial, trivial, and well — **false**. At the end, the young lord is disclosed to be an intelligent ape and is led away by the circus director who has trained him to perform for polite society.

The satire on present day mores is telling and bitter, in the manner of Swift. One is reminded of the American phenomenon which the writer Tom Wolfe has described as "radical chic", in which a party is given by the best people for a group of needy radicals whose announced purpose in life is to destroy society. The fun lies in watching the militants smashing up the furniture, liberating the servants and throwing the guests into the swimming pool.

Henze's music for **Der junge Lord** is much more tonal than is the music for his previous operas as befits the musical setting for a satirical comedy. In addition to a medium-sized cast the work calls for a children's chorus and several non-singing circus performers for one scene. Henze and his librettist planned the opera in close cooperation with Gustav Rudolf Sellner and his associates at the **Deutsche Oper**. The work is hard to perform but, over the years, has proved to be worth the effort. It has been done in many German houses, in Eastern European countries — where it can be staged as a satire on capitalist imperialism — in London and in Houston, Texas. A complete recording has been prepared by soloists and ensembles of the **Deutsche Oper** under the musical direction of Christoph von Dohnanyi.

World première of *Der junge Lord* **by Hans Werner Henze at the** *Deutsche Oper Berlin.*

SUBSIDIES FOR THE THEATER

Operas which have been commissioned by the theater, given their first performances anywhere and their first German performances make up a small but very significant part of the repertory of the theater each year. Since 1961, the record is as follows:

YEAR	WORK
1961	**Alkmene,** by Giselher Klebe; commissioned—world première
1962	**La Atlántida** by Manuel de Falla; first production in Germany
1963	**Oreste** by Darius Milhaud; world première of entire work
1964	**Montezuma** by Roger Sessions; world première
1965	**Der junge Lord** by Hans Werner Henze; commissioned—world première
1966	**Amerika** by Roman Haubenstock-Ramati; world première
1968	**Odysseus (Ulisse)** by Luigi Dallapiccola; commissioned—world première
1969	**200,000 Taler** by Boris Blacher; commissioned—world première

These operas are not very well known in America. The Klebe **Alkmene,** which is based on Kleist's **Amphitryon,** is a sensitive setting of the well known story of the seduction of the virtuous Alkmene by Jupiter who is disguised as her husband Amphitryon. The opera is not easy to sing or play — the music is composed in the idiom of Schoenberg and Webern — but in performance it provides good roles for the three principals and satisfying comic possibilities for the counterpart triangle of the servants Cleanthis, Sosias and Mercury. In fact all of Klebe's work in the operatic form is stageable and exciting when performed on the stage, especially his **Die Raeuber** (based on the Schiller play), **Die Ermordung Caesars** (after Shakespeare) and his continuation of the Figaro story, set a few years after the start of the French Revolution, **Figaro laesst sich scheiden,** a charming musical version of the play by Oedoen von Horváth.

Manuel de Falla labored over his last opera **La Atlántida** for some twenty years. It was unfinished at his death and was put into performance condition by the Spanish composer and conductor Ernesto Halffter. The work was first performed at **La**

Manuel de Falla's *La Atlántida.*

Scala in Milan in June, 1962 and at the **Deutsche Oper Berlin** in October of the same year for the first time in Germany. A scenic cantata in form, **La Atlántida** is a setting of an epic poem by Jacinto Verdaguer on the subject of the coming of Columbus to the New World and the civilizing mission of Catholic Spain. The work requires a large chorus which conveys much of the musical interest, a few soloists, a narrator and several dancers who pantomime on the stage actions which are being narrated and expressed musically by chorus and orchestra. The musical style evokes the classical age of 16th and 17th century Spanish polyphony and exhibits a consistently refined and elegant feeling for the stirring text.

The production of **La Atlántida** by the stage director Gustav Rudolf Sellner and the scene designer Michel Raffaelli provided extensive visual diversity to compensate for the lack on stage of dramatic action. Mythological animals paraded about, the scenery itself possessed a degree of mobility and a dragon danced nimbly to its death, all amid projected effects of fire and mist.

The form of the scenic cantata — a dramatic spectacle for orchestra, chorus, solo singers and dancers who mime actions which are depicted in musical passages — has enjoyed something of a revival on the contemporary European stage. Some of the earliest experiments with the lyric theater were composed in this form, for example, Cavalieri's **Rappresentazione di anima e di corpo** (1600) and Monteverdi's **Il combattimento di Tancredi e di Clorinada** (1624). Modern examples, in addition to the Carl Orff pieces mentioned above, are Gian-Carlo Menotti's **The Unicorn, the Gorgon and the Manticore** and Leonard Bernstein's **Mass.**

World première of *Alkmene* **by Giselher Klebe.**

Another work of tremendous size which requires very large musical ensembles in performance is Darius Milhaud's musical setting of Paul Claudel's translation of the **Oresteia** trilogy of Aeschylus. The three parts of Milhaud's **Orestie** — which correspond to the three sections of the Greek original — are **Agamemnon** (1913), **Les Choéphores** (1915) and **Les Eumenides** (1922). The work was nearly ten years in composition and, although some parts of the trilogy were staged and some performed in the concert hall, it was more than forty years after he began work on the opera that Milhaud finally saw the entire trilogy staged at the **Deutsche Oper Berlin** in April of 1963.

The stage director and designer were again the team of Sellner and Raffaelli. Some of the work was danced, some spoken and some sung by chorus and soloists. The role of Athene, composed for three voices, was amplified. Again, the form is that of a massive scenic cantata which heavily taxes the musical and financial resources of any theater organization undertaking to produce it.

The well known American composer Roger Sessions also worked on an opera — **Montezuma** — for over twenty years before seeing its first performance at the **Deutsche Oper Berlin** in April of 1964. The music is composed to a text by Giuseppe Antonio Borgese which concerns the complex relationships, viewed from something of a distance, between the Spanish conquistadors led by Hernando Cortés and the Aztec nation led by Montezuma. Both leaders desire peace but a state of war to the end is maintained due to the hatreds and bitterness of their followers. At length, Montezuma is killed by his own people to prevent the advent of peace between the Spaniards and the Aztecs. Thematically, the opera obviously has something to say to contemporary American audiences.

Montezuma contains a good portion of spoken dialogue, possibly an influence of the scenic cantatas, and the composer's richly polyphonic music possesses power and originality. In the Aztec scenes a somewhat expanded percussion section is required including celesta, xylophone, bells, rattles, and a collection of Mexican wooden drums.

The following season, the theater produced an opera which it had commissioned from Hans Werner Henze, a composer already well established through the success of such pieces as his **Das Wundertheater** (1948), **Boulevard Solitude** (1952), **Koenig Hirsch** (1956), **Der Prinz von Homburg** (1960) and **Elegie fuer junge Liebende** (1961). The new opera was entitled **Der junge Lord** and was set to a text by Ingeborg Bachmann which was in turn derived from a story by Wilhelm Hauff entitled **Der Scheik von Allessandria**. The plot of **Der junge Lord** turns on the visit to a small German town of a "young lord" from England who captivates everyone with his imperious manner, his indifference to the niceties of polite society and his exotic speech, which consists chiefly of violent exclamations, proverbs and quotations from Goethe. The social elite of the town adore him and a fetching belle even falls in love with him. He is something new to imitate, a primitive, something genuine in the midst of so much that is artificial, trivial, and well — **false**. At the end, the young lord is disclosed to be an intelligent ape and is led away by the circus director who has trained him to perform for polite society.

The satire on present day mores is telling and bitter, in the manner of Swift. One is reminded of the American phenomenon which the writer Tom Wolfe has described as "radical chic", in which a party is given by the best people for a group of needy radicals whose announced purpose in life is to destroy society. The fun lies in watching the militants smashing up the furniture, liberating the servants and throwing the guests into the swimming pool.

Henze's music for **Der junge Lord** is much more tonal than is the music for his previous operas as befits the musical setting for a satirical comedy. In addition to a medium-sized cast the work calls for a children's chorus and several non-singing circus performers for one scene. Henze and his librettist planned the opera in close cooperation with Gustav Rudolf Sellner and his associates at the **Deutsche Oper**. The work is hard to perform but, over the years, has proved to be worth the effort. It has been done in many German houses, in Eastern European countries — where it can be staged as a satire on capitalist imperialism — in London and in Houston, Texas. A complete recording has been prepared by soloists and ensembles of the **Deutsche Oper** under the musical direction of Christoph von Dohnanyi.

German Information Center

World première of *Der junge Lord* **by Hans Werner Henze at the** *Deutsche Oper Berlin.*

SUBSIDIES FOR THE THEATER

The following year the theater again produced a work which had received no previous stage performances, **Amerika,** by Roman Haubenstock-Ramati, a composer interested in modern methods of composition who has also made an interesting musical version of Samuel Beckett's **Spiel.** His opera **Amerika** is based on the novel of the same title by Franz Kafka. A somewhat allegorical piece, it explores the loneliness of the foreigner in a new country through a musical medium of considerable difficulty.

The stage director was Deryk Mendel and the scene designer Michel Raffaelli who created a series of cubicles on three levels suggesting the isolation the characters feel from one another. Once again, as in **Der Prozess,** one of Kafka's melancholy stories proved its efficacy for adaptation to the contemporary lyric theater.

One of the most remarkable operas commissioned by the **Deutsche Oper Berlin** was Luigi Dallapiccola's **Odysseus** which was given its world première by the opera house on the Bismarckstrasse September 29, 1968. The work was awaited with anticipation by both critics and public as the reputation of this Italian musician as a gifted composer of opera was everywhere firmly established.

The leading idea of all of Dallapiccola's work in this most demanding of the theatrical forms has been that of the struggle of man against something stronger than himself. In his ballet **Marsyas** he depicts the struggle of the faun Marsyas, the bringer of the art of music to man, against the might of Apollo. For having challenged the god, Marsyas is crushed. In **Der Gefangenen** the hero is shown to be in a contest with the Holy Inquisition. He is allowed to entertain hope of escape from his prison but, at the end, when a friar seems to be assisting him in his hopes he discovers that he has been tricked by the Grand Inquisitor who leads him to his funeral pyre. In the morality piece **Job,** the hero directs penetrating questions to God. He regrets his sins and learns that he can still save himself although everything else is gone.

In **Odysseus,** however, the hero does not struggle with an external force but rather with himself, with the enigma of his own identity. Throughout his life he has endeavoured to observe and study the secrets of nature. His controlling passion, which both the goddess Kalypso and the sorceress Kirke hear him murmur in his sleep, has been "To look and be astonished, and to look again." But the revenge which Poseidon seeks against the Greeks for their wanton destruction of the city which he laid out himself — Troy — manifests itself in the person of Odysseus by a gradual falling away of the hero's knowledge of himself.

In the scene in Hades his mother turns away from him, unable to recognize her son. As she departs, loneliness grips him — the loneliness so well known in our own times. He asks the Shades who he is and they reply that he is Crying, Tears, Suffering, Regret and Depression. "Who are you and where do you come from?" the Lotus-Eaters ask of Odysseus, but he is unable to reply.

Kirke starts him on the road to recovery by providing him with both a sense of sin and a desire — finally — to return to Ithaka, his homeland. The suitors ask him the same question and when he is silent one of them replies for him that he is **Niemand** — No One. Poseidon has achieved his revenge. He has chained Odysseus with **Niemand.** The hero strings his bow, however, and kills the suitors for his wife's hand. He is now free to return to the sea. In the final scene we see him again aboard his ship, but alone. Nothing is left but worthless syllables. . .a word, perhaps, as in the beginning. A flicker of lightning discloses to him the possibility of the existence of God, and the opera comes to an end.

Dallapiccola draws on both Homer and Dante for his libretto. The Italian poet leaves Odysseus in Purgatory because the hero comes before Christ in time. But the composer hints that the hero may enter Paradise after all. Other sources for the story are some verses from Tennyson and Hoelderlin, Thomas Mann's **Joseph und seine Brueder,** Gerhart Hauptmann's **Der Bogen des Odysseus** and James Joyce's **Portrait of the Artist as a Young Man** from which the composer derived the words **Immer! Niemand!** as associated with Odysseus in the Hades scene. The motto for the entire opera, which is inscribed on the final page of the orchestra score, is a fragment from the **Confessions of St. Augustine** which Dallapiccola discovered written on the wall of the railroad station in Westport, Connecticut: FECISTI NOS AD TE ET INQUIETUM EST COR NOSTRUM, DONEC REQUIESCAT IN TE.[34]

Dallapiccola became preoccupied with the musical possibilities of the great Greek legend in 1941-42 while he was making a transcription of the orchestration of Monteverdi's **Il Ritorno d'Ulisse in patria.** He worked on his own version of the material off and on for nearly thirty years, completing first the text in a prologue and two acts and then composing a musical setting of great restraint and subtlety. Opportunities for "big" musical effects abound in his text but he carefully avoids them in favor of extreme understatement. The music does not sound especially "Italianate" but has, instead, a rather international flavor to it. Perhaps this stems from the fact that the composer was born in Trieste, that Adriatic crossroads of Italian, Austrian, German and Slavic cultures.

The Berlin production was staged by Gustav Rudolf Sellner and designed by Fernando Farulli. Lorin Maazel conducted the orchestra and the chorus master was Walter Hagen-Groll.

[34]Luigi Dallapiccola, "Zum Libretto Meiner Oper **Odysseus (Ulisse)," Opern Journal** (Oktober, 1968) pp. 7-10. "You have created this for yourself and our hearts are restless until they find their rest in you." (Put there by Bill Buckley?)

DEUTSCHE OPER BERLIN—Ilse Buhs

World première of *Odysseus* by Luigi Dallapiccola.

Still another opera which had been commissioned by the theater, Boris Blacher's **200,000 Taler** was given its world première September 25, 1969. Derived from a story by Sholem Aleichem it recalls in mood and style the milieu of the popular musical play **Fiddler on the Roof.** The story is concerned with the family of a Jewish tailor living in a town in the Ukraine which wins 200,000 talers in a lottery, spends the money with gleeful abandon for two weeks and then discovers that there had been a printing error in the published announcement and they were not the winners after all. The family has discovered in the meantime that money is the root of much evil and is glad enough to have it all taken away.

For the composer, the charm of this material lay in its many human touches which are common to peoples everywhere. Even a Jewish family living in the East is not remote from us if we look beneath the surface of local custom and habit. Blacher also noted in the story various signs of the powers which were to shake our century — changes in social structure, racial hatred, the antipathy of happiness to materialism. The story is simple enough to acquire in the musical theater the characteristics of a fable and it is expressed, therefore, with a certain naiveté of language and musical means. The future is suggested by contrapuntal devices in the music which predict some of the harsher realities of our times; for example, during the happy ending, inhuman march rhythms predict the future of the young lovers. Thus, the opera becomes not a mere realistic picture of Jewish life in Russia at the turn of the century but rather a picture of a higher reality, which is implicit in the story.[43]

The work should find its place in many theaters as it is musically distinguished, thematically interesting and does not require a chorus, ballet or excessively large orchestra. The Berlin production was staged by Gustav Rudolf Sellner with scenery and costumes by Ita Maximowna. The orchestra was conducted by Heinrich Hollreiser.

[35]Boris Blacher, "Zu meiner Oper 200,000 **Taler,**" **Opern Journal** (Oktober, 1969) p. 9.

As is the case with most of the new German opera houses, the **Deutsche Oper Berlin** possesses an adequate physical plant in which to stage 75 operas and ballets a year and build the scenery, costumes and properties for new productions of five or six operas and an equal number of ballets at the same time. It was completed in September of 1961 after five years of construction work and cost DM 27.44 million, most of which was provided by the state of Berlin with some assistance from the **Bundesrepublik.**

The auditorium seats 1,903 spectators. The usual proscenium width is 14.50 meters and the height is 8 meters. The stage is 28 meters wide and 19 meters deep and the area over the stage reaches to a height of 27.50 meters. The depth of the rear stage is 23 meters. There is a Linnebach cyclorama which winds up on either of two cones stage left and right and the following equipment for flying scenery:

25 standard battens	300 kg capacity	hand operated
25 standard battens	300 kg capacity	electrically operated
6 backdrop battens	300 kg capacity	hand operated
5 backdrop battens	500 kg capacity	electrically operated
2 horizon battens	750 kg capacity	electrically operated
6 spot lines	300 kg capacity	electrically operated

The electrically operated battens can move at speeds from zero to 1 meter per second.

The stage area consists of 6 stage lifts, each of which is 18 meters wide and 3 meters deep. The first four are single-decked and the last two double-decked. They travel from 3 meters above the stage to 3 meters below and can be stopped anywhere between in increments of 0.17 meters. When a side stage wagon is in place on the main stage the lifts are usually lowered 0.17 meters to bring the wagon level down to stage level. When this can't be done an equalizer lift downstage of the six main lifts can be raised up to cover the face of the wagon. It slants down to floor level in a distance of 1.6 meters.

Also included in the scene shifting equipment are two side-stage wagons and a rear-stage wagon. The stage right wagon is in three independent sections which, when ganged together, form a wagon 18 meters by 14 meters in size. The floors of these three wagons can be raked. The stage left wagon is also in three sections and has a total size of 18 meters by 9 meters. The rear wagon is 18 meters square and carries a turntable with a diameter of 17.4 meters.

The side and rear stages can be sealed off from the main stage by electrically operated acoustical curtains. In addition to the **Eisenvorhang,** there is a decorated house curtain operated electrically on a **Scherenzug,** a scene curtain, a full stage scrim and another sound curtain, all of which hang parallel to the footlights in the portal zone. The orchestra pit consists of four lifts, all double-decked, so that the three closest to the stage can be used as a forestage while the remaining unit can be used for a small orchestra if so desired. All lifts run from stage level to 3 meters below stage level.

DEUTSCHE OPER BERLIN—Ilse Buhs

World première of Boris Blacher's 200,000 Taler.

SUBSIDIES FOR THE THEATER

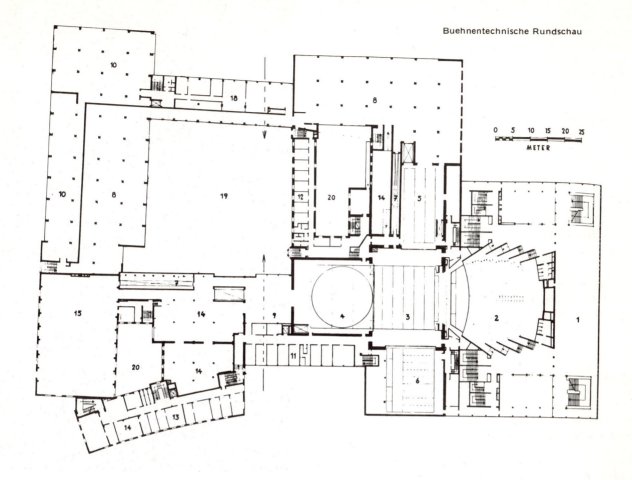

DEUTSCHES OPERNHAUS BERLIN-CHARLOTTENBURG

Grundriß und Schnitt für den endgültigen Ausbau — Bühnengeschoß
Architekt: Dipl.-Ing. Fritz Bornemann

1 Großes Foyer	8 Magazine für Kulissen	14 Magazine°
2 Zuschauerraum Parkett	9 Montageraum	über
3 Hauptbühne°	über	14 Probesaal
4 Hinterbühne	9 Ballettsäle	15 Tischlerei°
über	10 Magazin für Kostüme	16 Schlosserei
4 Große Probebühne	über	17 Malsaal
5 Seitenbühne rechts°	8 u. 10 Großer Malsaal	18 Schneidereien
6 Seitenbühne links	11 Damengarderoben	19 Parkplatz
7 Prospekt-Lager°	12 Herrengarderoben°	20 Hof
	13 Verwaltung°	

°) Bestandteile des alten Hauses

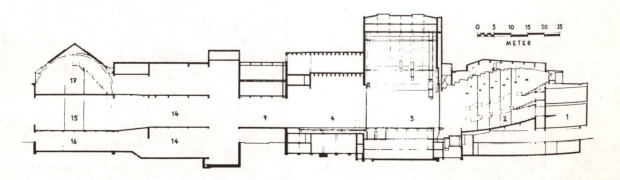

Floor plan and section of the *Deutsche Oper Berlin*.

To accommodate the lighting equipment there are slots in the auditorium ceiling and at the auditorium sides and the following apparatus over the stage:

One portal bridge, double-decked, which can be raised electrically to a height of 8 meters above the stage. This bridge establishes the proscenium height.

Two portal tormenter towers which can be moved by hand to establish proscenium widths between 11 meters and 14 meters.

One lighting bridge, double-decked, which can be raised electrically to a height of 20.0 meters above the stage.

One lighting platform used for cyclorama floods which can be raised electrically to a height of 22.0 meters above the stage.

Two lighting battens for borderlights and some spotlights used for back and side lighting which can be raised electrically to a height of 25.5 meters above the stage.

At the time the theater was opened, the lighting apparatus installed in the auditorium and over the stage consisted of the following:

4 Footlight strips in four colors with 100 watt lamps.

1 Portal borderlight in four colors with 200 watt lamps.

5 Stage borderlights in four colors with 200 watt lamps.

200 Spotlights with low-voltage lamps, 100 to 500 watts, 12 volts to 110 volts, 20 of which are equipped with remote control color changers for four colors each.

220 Spotlights and ellipsoidal floodlights which operate on normal voltage in sizes from 500 to 3,000 watts.

6 Spotlights with air-cooled Xenon-arc lamps of 2,000 watts apiece.

52 Cyclorama floods each with 3 fluorescent tubes at 40 watts each.

100 Special instruments for lighting the stage including a number of units which produce ultra-violet light.

46 Effect machines of various kinds.

The lighting control console is located in a room at the rear of the auditorium and consists of 240 control units.[36]

The **Deutsche Oper Berlin** receives its principal subsidy from the state of Berlin with occasional additional amounts from the federal government of West Germany. The following amounts are in millions of German Marks.

Calendar Year	Total Expense	Box Office and other Income	Subsidy, State of Berlin	Subsidy, Federal Government	Ratio of Subsidy to Expense
1967	25.130	5.348	19.782		78%
1968	27.074	5.618	21.056	0.400	79%
1969	27.794	5.178	22.616		81%
1970	35.785	6.367	27.698	1.720	82% [37]

Bayerische Staatstheater

Another of the important German state theater organizations is the **Bayerische Staatstheater**, which is located in Munich, capital city of the state of Bavaria and home of the **Oktoberfest**, Europe's most ribald folk festival, held annually in late September and October on the **Theresienwiese**. The organization consists of four separate theaters, the **Theater am**

"The Dance of the Seven Veils" from *Salome* by Richard Strauss.

Die Frau ohne Schatten by Richard Strauss and Hugo von Hofmannsthal.

[36]"Die neue Deutsche Oper in Berlin-Charlottenburg"; Werner Krueger, "Die maschinentechnischen Anlagen," and Bruno Warsinski, "Die elektrischen Starkstromanlagen," **Buehnentechnische Rundschau** LV (Dezember 1961) pp. 20-26.

[37]**Theaterstatistik** 1967-68, 1968-69, 1969-70, and 1970-71, p. 27.

Mozart's *Cosi fan tutte* in the *Cuvilliéstheater*.

The royal box of the *Cuvilliéstheater*.

Detail of the decoration in the auditorium.

View of the stage from the auditorium.

Gaertnerplatz, seating 963, which is used for the production of operettas and musical comedies and a three-theater complex located in and near the former **Residenz** of the Kings of Bavaria, the **Staatsoper-Nationaltheater**, seating 2,120, which is used for the production of opera and ballet, the **Staatsschauspiel-Residenztheater**, seating 1,059 which is used for the production of plays and the **Altes Residenztheater (Cuvilliéstheater)**, seating 525 when it is used for the production of plays and 462 when an opera is being performed. The **Cuvilliéstheater** does not have its own company but is operated by the **Staatsschauspiel** if a play is being done in it and by the **Staatsoper** when it houses an opera.

The **Cuvilliéstheater** is the oldest theater still in regular use in Germany. It was erected between 1751 and 1753 during the reign of the Elector Maximilian III Joseph from the design of the French architect François de Cuvilliés. Constructed of linden wood from the forests of Murnau in the Bavarian Alps, the theater was opened on October 12, 1753 with Ferrandini's musical setting of the Metastasio opera text **Catone in Utica**. The first performance of Mozart's **Idomeneo**, also composed to a text in the style of Metastasio, was given on January 29, 1781.

The theater was not used continuously for public performances. During the early decades of the nineteenth century it served as a warehouse for the storage of stage scenery from other theaters in the city but in the latter part of the century it was restored to its original state, electric lights were installed in 1883 and in 1896 it was equipped with the first revolving stage in Europe, designed by Carl Lautenschlaeger.

The theater was badly damaged by bombing attacks on Munich during World War II but because the interior had been dismantled and stored away it was possible to put it all back together again. On June 12, 1958 it opened once more with a production of Mozart's **Die Hochzeit des Figaro**, an event which was part of the celebration of the 800th anniversary of the founding of the city of Munich. Since then it has been used regularly for the production of operas by Mozart, Pergolesi, Rossini, Paisiello and others as well as for plays which are suited to the intimacy of the theater, such as Molière's **Der Geizige**. It also stands as an elegant monument to a celebrated era in European theatrical history.

STATE THEATERS

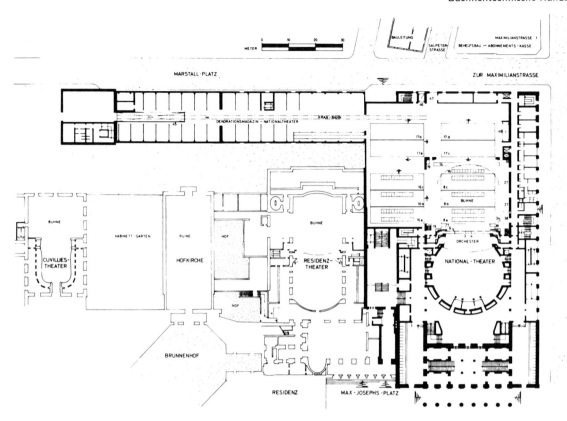

GRUNDRISS DER BETRIEBSANLAGE DER DREI BAYERISCHEN STAATSTHEATER, BAUSTUFE 1963

Erläuterungen zum Grundriß:

1. Eiserner Vorhang
2. Seitlich teilbarer Raff-Vorhang
3. Souffleurraum
4. Raum für Abendregie bei Gastspielen usw.
5. Spezial-Schalldämmvorhang
6. hydr. Vorhangzüge mit seitlicher Führung
7. Portaltürme und Portalbrücke
8a bis 8c Hub- und schrägstellbare Podien
9. Verriegelungseinrichtung
10. Kupplungseinrichtung
11. Krantischversenkung
12. Steuerpult für die Podien
13. Maschinengalerien
14. Prospekthebebühne

15. Versenkungsschieber
16a bis 16c Bühnenwagen in zwei Richtungen verfahrbar mit Versenkungstafeln
17a bis 17d Bühnenwagen in zwei Richtungen verfahrbar mit fugenlosem Fußboden für Ballett
19. Steuerpulte für Bühnenwagen und Podien auf der Bühne
20. Montagezüge auf der Seitenbühne
21. Dekorationszüge auf der Hinterbühne
22. eiserne Schallschutzvorhänge mit hydr. Antrieb
24. Arbeitsgalerien
25. Beleuchtungsgalerien
26. hydraulische Züge
27. Handzüge
30. Horizontbeleuchtungsbrücken

31. Oberlicht- und Scheinwerfergestelle
32. feste Stege für Flugwerke und Effekte
33. begehbarer Schnürboden für Steck- und Einfadenzüge
34. Rollenboden
36. Rauchschieber
37. Rauchhaube
38. Lichtstell- und Speicherwarte
39. Meisterpult für Bühnenlichtregelung
40. Ela-Regelung
41. Scheinwerferstände im Zuschauerraum
42. hydr. verfahrbare Scheinwerferwagen
43. hebbarer Zuschauerraum-Lüster
44. Fahrschienen für Laufkatzen im Dek.- Magazin und Seitenbühne
45. Hebebühne hydr. für Dekorations-Fahrzeuge

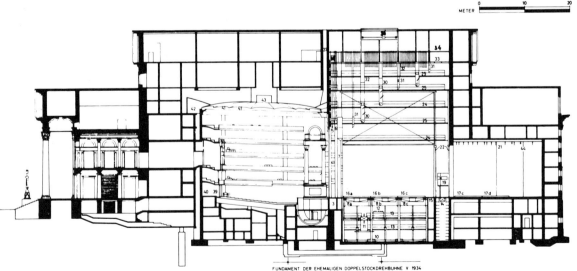

Schnitt durch das Nationaltheater 1963

Ground plan of the *Cuvilliestheater*, **the** *Residenztheater* **and the** *Nationaltheater* **in Munich. Below: Section through the middle of the** *Nationaltheater*.

Ausgegeben: München, 22. Mai 1970

Nachdruck auch im Auszug mit Quellenangabe verboten!

Nr. 38

SPIELPLAN DER BAYERISCHEN STAATSTHEATER

für die Zeit vom 24. Mai bis einschließlich 2. Juni 1970

Nr. 38

STAATSOPER – NATIONALTHEATER

Datum	Zeiten	Vorstellung	Proben	Raum
Sonntag **24.** Mai	18 22 19½ 22	**Tannhäuser** von Dohnanyi, Lehmann Silja, Berthold, Freedmann, Schneider, Tentrop, Haubold, Evangelatos, Böhme, Esser, Prey, Hoffmann, Nöcker, Lenz, Auer **ALTES RESIDENZTHEATER (Cuvilliés-Theater)** **GASTSPIEL** **NEDERLANDS DANS THEATER**	Vorm. **Nederlands Dans Th.** techn. Einrichtg.	Bü. Cuv.-Th.
Montag **25.** Mai	19½ 21½	**NATIONALTHEATER** **Ballett Romeo und Julia** Linz, Cranko/Preisser	10 **Schwanensee** mit Klavier 10 **Widersp. Zähmung,** Orchester allein 10 **Entführung** mit Klavier 17 **Entführung** mit Klavier	Bü. Nat.-Th. Prinzreg. Foyer Cuv.-Th. Probü. Bü. Cuv.-Th.
Dienstag **26.** Mai	19 gegen 22½	Geschlossene Vorstellung **Schwanensee** Kuntzsch, Cranko/Preisser	**Ballett,** techn. Probe 10 **Widersp. Zähmung** Orchester allein 10 **Entführung** mit Klavier 17 **Entführung,** Ensembleprobe	Bü. Nat.-Th. Prinzreg. Foyer Bü. Cuv.-Th.
Mittwoch **27.** Mai	20 22	**GASTSPIEL WÜRTT. STAATSTHEATER STUTTGART** **Der Widerspenstigen Zähmung** Stolze, Cranko	Vorm. **Widersp. Zähmung** techn. Einrichtung 12–14 **Widersp. Zähmung,** Durchlaufprobe mit Klavier ab 14 T und Bel. **Entführung,** techn. Probe 10 **Entführung,** Orchester allein	Bü. Nat.-Th. Bü. Nat.-Th. Bü. Cuv.-Th. Prinzreg. Foyer
Donnerstag **28.** Mai	19 gegen 22½	**Schwanensee** Kuntzsch, Cranko/Preisser mit Lilla Partay und Cyril Atanassoff a. G.		
Freitag **29.** Mai	19 gegen 22½	Geschlossene Vorstellung **Don Carlos** (Originalsprache) Patané, Arnold-Paur Kirschstein, Fassbaender, Hellmann, Schneider, Fahberg, Florei, Lazaro, Braun, Hotter, Paweletz, Tessényi (2), Freundorfer, Knapp, Sapell, Auer, Wichartz	Technik 10 **Entführung** mit Orchester anschl. **Entführung,** Bel.	Bü. Nat.-Th. Bü. Cuv.-Th.
Samstag **30.** Mai	18 22	**Tannhäuser** von Dohnanyi, Lehmann Silja, af Malmborg, Freedmann, Schneider, Tentrop, Haubold, Evangelatos, Böhme, Kozub, Prey, Hoffmann, Nöcker, Lenz, Auer	Technik 10 **Entführung** mit Orchester anschl. **Entführung,** T. u. Bel.	Bü. Nat.-Th. Bü. Cuv.-Th.
Sonntag **31.** Mai	19 gegen 22½	**7. Sonntag-Platzmiete rot und beschr. Kartenverk.** **Don Carlos** (Originalsprache) Patané, Hartleb Bjoner, Fassbaender, Hellmann, Schneider, Fahberg, Florei, Lazaro, Braun, Hotter, Paweletz, Tessényi (2), Freundorfer, Knapp, Sapell, Auer, Wichartz		
Montag **1.** Juni	19 22½	**Die Hochzeit des Figaro** (Originalsprache) Kuntzsch, Rennert Kirschstein, Berthold, Schädle, Wewezow, Schneider, Haubold, Evangelatos, Engen, Grumbach, Kusche, Thaw, Proebstl, Fehenberger	10 **Tannhäuser** mit Klavier 10 **Entführung** mit Orchester Kostüm	Bü. Nat.-Th. Bü. Cuv.-Th.
Dienstag **2.** Juni	19 22	**Ein Maskenball** (Originalsprache) Hager, Haase Bjoner, Topper, Steffek, Lazaro, Tipton, Sapell, Peter, Proebstl, Klarwein, Walter	10 **Tannhäuser** mit Orchester 10 **Entführung,** Hauptprobe mit Orchester	Bü. Nat.-Th. Bü. Cuv.-Th.

STAATSSCHAUSPIEL – RESIDENZ-THEATER

Datum	Zeiten	Vorstellung	Proben	Raum
24. Mai	19½ 22¾	**5. Vorstellung Sonntag-Abonnement Serie rot** **Maria Stuart** Laerum 13 Page: Steffen		
25. Mai	19½ 21¾	**6. Vorstellung Montag-Abonnement Serie grün** **Der Fächer** Schwab 6 Conte: Kiessner	**Der Kirschgarten** **Fächer** **Coriolan**	Bü. Res.-Th. nach Ansage nach Ansage
26. Mai	19½ 21¾	**6. Vorstellung Dienstag-Abonnement Serie blau** **Der Fächer** Schwab 7	**Der Kirschgarten** **Coriolan**	Bü. Res.-Th. nach Ansage
27. Mai	19½ 22¾	**Maria Stuart** Laerum 14 Page: Am Rhein	**Der Kirschgarten** **Coriolan**	Bü. Res.-Th. nach Ansage
28. Mai	19½ 22¾	**7. Vorstellung Donnerstag-Abonnement Serie blau** **Maria Stuart** Laerum 15	**Der Kirschgarten** **Coriolan**	Bü. Res.-Th. nach Ansage
29. Mai	19½ 21¾	**6. Vorstellung Freitag-Abonnement Serie rot** **Der Fächer** Hempelt 8	**Der Kirschgarten** **Coriolan**	Bü. Res.-Th. nach Ansage
30. Mai	19½ 21¾	**6. Vorstellung Samstag-Abonnement Serie rot** **Der Fächer** Schwab 9	**Der Kirschgarten** **Coriolan**	Bü. Res.-Th. nach Ansage
31. Mai	19½ 22¾	**7. Vorstellung Sonntag-Abonnement Serie gelb** **Maria Stuart** Laerum 16		
1. Juni	19½ 22¾	**6. Vorstellung Montag-Abonnement Serie rot** **Maria Stuart** Laerum 17	**Der Kirschgarten** **Coriolan**	Bü. Res.-Th. nach Ansage
2. Juni	19½ 22¾	**6. Vorstellung Dienstag-Abonnement Serie rot** **Maria Stuart** Laerum 18	**Der Kirschgarten** **Coriolan**	Bü. Res.-Th. nach Ansage

STAATSTHEATER AM GÄRTNERPLATZ

Datum	Zeiten	Vorstellung	Proben	Raum
24. Mai	19½ 22½	Preise GS **Hoffmanns Erzählungen** Weder, Lorenz, Koch 79 Chryst, Görgen, Goller, Hartung, Klug, Nerius, Puhlmann, Ball, Ecker, Fürst, Gerlach-Rusnak, Kogel, Kotzerke, Lichtenfeld, Malta, de Ridder, Roßmann		
25. Mai	19½ 21¾	**6. Platzmiete-Vorstellung gelb u. freier Verkauf** **Encores / Yolimba** Preise S Killmayer, Baur, Lorenz, Morasch, Borowitza, Ohl 5 Briner, Chryst, Ebnet, Ehrensperger, Görgen, Nerius, Puhlmann, Ball, Brennicke, Ecker, Fürst, Gerlach-Rusnak, Gorter, Gruber, Kotzerke, Kraemmer, Malta, Mayer, Palos, Rosvaenge — Barth, Heimerer, Schwaarz, Bazan, Braun, Frazier, Gauder, Grötzsch, Herzog, Papp, Weich	10 **Waffenschmied** mit Klavier 10 **Waffenschmied,** Orchesterprobe	Bühne Probebühne
26. Mai	19½ 22¼	Preise S **Der Opernball** Mahlke, Lorenz 56 Barth, Ebnet, Ehrensperger, Kunig-Rinach, Müller, Orén, Pascal, Puhlmann, Ball, Braun, Ecker, Friedauer, Gerlach-Rusnak, Grötzsch, Kotzerke, Palmer, Weich	10 **Waffenschmied** mit Klavier 10 **Waffenschmied,** Orchesterprobe	Bühne Probebühne
27. Mai	19½ 21¾	Preise A **Der Arzt wider Willen** Koch, Rostock 68 Chryst, Görgen, Ortbauer, Brennicke, Ecker, Friedrich, Fürst, Kogel, Louca, Schaidler, Stanek	10 **Waffenschmied** mit Klavier 10 **Waffenschmied,** Orchester-Sitzprobe Chor und Ballett frei	Bühne Probebühne
28. Mai	19½ 22½	Preise GS **Rusalka** Rennert, Lorenz, Koch, Morasch 14 Barth, Briner, Ehrensperger, Görgen, Hartung, Klug, Nerius, Orén, Grötzsch, Gruber, Malta, de Ridder, Wilsing		
29. Mai	19½ 21¾	**6. Platzmiete-Vorstellung orange u. freier Verkauf** **Encores / Yolimba** Preise S Killmayer, Baur, Lorenz, Morasch, Borowitza, Ohl 6 Briner, Chryst, Ebnet, Ehrensperger, Görgen, Nerius, Puhlmann, Ball, Brennicke, Ecker, Friedrich, Fürst, Gerlach-Rusnak, Gorter, Gruber, Kotzerke, Kraemmer, Mayer, Palos, Rosvaenge — Barth, Heimerer, Schwaarz, Bazan, Braun, Frazier, Gauder, Grötzsch, Herzog, Papp, Weich	10 **Waffenschmied,** mit Orchester	Bühne
30. Mai	19½ 22½	Preise S **Die lustige Witwe** Rennert, Lorenz 31 Biebl, Briner, Ebnet, Ehrensperger, Kunig-Rinach, Nerius, Ball, Brennicke, Ecker, Friedauer, Fürst, Gerlach-Rusnak, Kotzerke, Kraemmer, Lichtenfeld, Louca, Thaw, — Barth, Müller, Bazan, Braun, Frazier, Gauder, Weich	10 **Waffenschmied** mit Klavier 10 **Margarete,** Orch.-Sitzprobe	Bühne Probebühne
31. Mai	19½ 22	Preise S **Margarete** Kord, Lorenz, Mahlke, Morasch 47 Barth, Heimerer, Klug, Nerius, Bazan, Braun, Fürst, Gerlach-Rusnak, Grötzsch, Malta, de Ridder, Wilsing		
1. Juni	19½ 22¼	Preise S **Der Barbier von Sevilla** Weder, Rostock, Koch 33 Chryst, Görgen, Ball, Friedrich, Gerlach-Rusnak, Kogel, Kraemmer, Malta, Mayer, Schaidler	10 **Waffenschmied,** mit Orchester	Bühne
2. Juni	19½ 21¾	Preise GS **Pique Dame** Kord, Lorenz, Koch, Morasch 18 Barth I., Klug, Ball, Esser H., Friedrich, Fürst, Gerlach-Rusnak, Hoyem, Louca, Wilsing	10 **Waffenschmied,** Dek.- und Beleuchtg.-Probe 10 **Waffenschmied,** Orchester-Sitzprobe	Bühne Probebühne

SOLOPROBEN SIEHE TÄGLICHEN PROBENPLAN!

In Vorbereitung
Nationaltheater
14. Juli 1970 **Die Zauberflöte**
26. Juli 1970 **Oedipus Rex und Ballett**
Altes Residenztheater (Cuv.-Th.)
17. Juli 1970 **Capriccio**
21. Juli 1970 **Die Entführung aus dem Serail**

Musikal. Leitung: Rafael Kubelik, Gunther Rennert; Michael Gielen, Hans Hartleb John Cranko
Inszenierung: Ferdinand Leitner, Rudolf Hartmann; Hans Schmidt-Isserstedt, Gunther Rennert

In Vorbereitung:
Residenztheater
20. Juni 1970 **Der Kirschgarten** — Inszenierung: Rudolf Noelte
Mitte Juli 1970 **Coriolan** — Inszenierung: Hans Hollmann

In Vorbereitung:
11. Juni 1970 **Der Waffenschmied**
Inszenierung: Wolfgang Blum
Musikalische Leitung: Ulrich Weder

Jedes Mitglied ist verpflichtet, den täglich um 13 Uhr erscheinenden Arbeitsplan einzusehen.

Bei eingetretener Unpäßlichkeit oder Krankheit ist es für jedes Mitglied — gleichviel ob dasselbe an dem betreffenden Tag beschäftigt ist oder nicht — unbedingte Pflicht, dem Betriebsbüro **sofort schriftliche Mitteilung** zu machen. Listen festgelegt, bis das Mitglied sich schriftlich wieder **dienstfähig** Die Krankheitsdauer eines Mitgliedes wird so lange angenommen und in den **gemeldet hat. Schriftliche Wiederanmeldung ist unerläßlich.**

Druck: J. Gotteswinter, München

Production schedule for the *Nationaltheater*, the *Staatsschauspiel* and the *Theater am Gaertnerplatz* from May 24 through June 2, 1970.

The **Nationaltheater** — the opera house — was built in 1811 to designs by Karl von Fischer. It burned down in 1822, was restored, was hit by bombs in 1943 and restored once again to its original exterior appearance. On November 21, 1963 it reopened with a gala performance of **Die Frau ohne Schatten** by Richard Strauss and Hugo von Hofmannsthal, followed two nights later by a second festive performance of Richard Wagner's **Die Meistersinger von Nuernberg.**

Although the outward appearance of this handsome building on Max-Joseph-Platz is much the same as always, the interior of the auditorium has been altered somewhat and the stage equipment is completely new. The house seats 2,111 and has a proscenium width of up to 16 meters and a height of up to 13.50 meters. In addition to the main stage there is a two-section side stage and a conventional rear stage. The floor of the main stage consists of three lifts each 6 meters deep and 20 meters wide. They may be raised and lowered hydraulically and the floors can be slanted to form a raked stage. There are 7 stage wagons available for shifting scenery horizontally each of which is 6 meters by 20 meters. The lighting console provides remote control over 320 magnetic amplifier dimmers which in turn control the intensities of 272 incandescent stage lighting instruments, 28 low-voltage cyclorama units employing fluorescent tubes and 20 Xenon arc units.

This great opera house employs a company and mounts an annual repertory of about the same size as does the **Deutsche Oper Berlin.** It too has commissioned interesting new operas and maintains an important ballet company.

German Information Center

Auditorium of the *Nationaltheater*, Munich.

NATIONALTHEATER—Sabine Toepffer

Bernd Alois Zimmermann's *Die Soldaten* at the *Nationaltheater*.

NATIONALTHEATER—Rudolf Betz

The **Bayerisches Staatsschauspiel,** or **Neues Residenztheater** was built in the years 1948-1951 on the site of the old theater which, when restored, was placed in a different location in the **Residenz.** The new theater was opened on January 28, 1951 with a performance of **Der Verschwender** by Ferdinand Raimund. The auditorium seats 1,059, the proscenium width is variable between 8 and 14 meters, the height between 4.50 and 8 meters, and the stage is 18 meters wide and 20 meters deep.

Included in the stage equipment are two Linnebach cycloramas, a 16-meter turntable and a lighting layout which is standard for a medium-sized stage in Germany. Although intended primarily for the performance of plays, the theater is also equipped with a small orchestra pit in which can be performed incidental music for a spoken drama or accompaniment for a chamber opera.

A typical year's repertory in the **Staatsschauspiel** — for the season of 1970-71 — is as follows:

Johann Wolfgang Goethe	Faust, Erster Teil
Friedrich Schiller	Maria Stuart
William Shakespeare	Troilus und Cressida
	Was ihr wollt
Ben Jonson	Volpone
Carlo Goldoni	Der Faecher
Anton Tschechow	Der Kirschgarten
Oedoen von Horváth	Italienische Nacht
Eugene O'Neill	Alle Reichtuemer der Welt
Tankred Dorst	Toller
Arnold Wesker	Die Kueche
Peter Hacks	Omphale

During the following season the **Staatsschauspiel** performed Anouilh's bitterly humorous **Das Orchester.** Seldom has Anouilh so ruthlessly explored the anguish of the artist who has failed to accomplish anything of worth as he does in this moody one-act play. The girls in the orchestra suffer from broken hopes; both

SUBSIDIES FOR THE THEATER

life and art have disappointed them and at the end, when the leading singer and performer on the cello has shot herself, a piece of cheap salon music becomes a requiem for a shattered human being.

The plays planned for the **Cuvilliéstheater** were Lessing's **Minna von Barnhelm** and Goethe's **Clavigo**. The theater makes an effort ot achieve a balance between productions of the classics of dramatic literature, modern works of stature and plays from the avant-garde. An example of the first category is Goldoni's **Der Faecher** which was directed with a sure instinct for Italian comedy by Eberhard Pieper with scenery by H. W. Lenneweit and costumes by Elisabeth Urbancic. Many modern classics have been staged in this theater of which Paul Claudel's **Der Seidene Schuh**, directed by Hans Lietzau with scenery and costumes by Juergen Rose was an especially interesting example.

German Information Center

BAYERISCHES STAATSSCHAUSPIEL MÜNCHEN
RESIDENZTHEATER
BÜHNENGRUNDRISS   M 1:100

Ground plan of the stage of the *Bayerisches Staatsschauspiel.*

Der Seidene Schuh **by Paul Claudel in the** *Staatsschauspiel.*

The orchestra assembled

Viola

Clarinet

Second violin.

Pianoforte

Cello and leading singer.

Das Orchester by Jean Anouilh in
the Staatsschauspiel.

Double bass and conductor

Photos by Rudolf Betz for the BAYERISCHES STAATSSCHAUSPIEL

STATE THEATERS

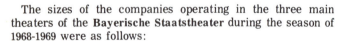
Molière's *Der Geizige* in the *Cuvilliéstheater*.

Two scenes from Genet's *Die Zofen* in the *Staatsschauspiel*.

Photos by Rudolf Betz for the
BAYERISCHES STAATSSCHAUSPIEL

The sizes of the companies operating in the three main theaters of the **Bayerische Staatstheater** during the season of 1968-1969 were as follows:

	National-theater	Staatstheater am Gaertnerplatz	Bayer. Staats-schauspiel
Generalintendant, stage, musical and dance directors, **Dramaturgen** and other artistic personnel	45	22	23
Principal singers	42	29	
Actors and actresses			27
Ballet dancers	59	29	
Chorus singers	102	41	
Orchestra players	137	65	
Stage and technical personnel	342	133	152
Administrative personnel	44	18	19
House personnel	164	56	80
TOTALS	935	393	301
Number of women in each company	294	142	92 [38]

[38] Theaterstatistik 1968-69, p. 5.

The **Bayerische Staatstheater** received the following subsidies, in millions of German marks, during the calendar year 1970:

	National-theater	Staatstheater am Gaertnerplatz	Cuvilliés & Bayer. Staats-Schauspiel
Total expense	30.108	10.240	8.966
Box office and other income	9.262	2.201	1.882
Subsidy, state of Bavaria	15.517	8.039	7.084
Subsidy, city of Munich	5.080		
Subsidy, outside of Munich	0.249		
Total Subsidy	20.846	8.039	7.084
Ratio of subsidy to expense	69%	78%	79% [39]

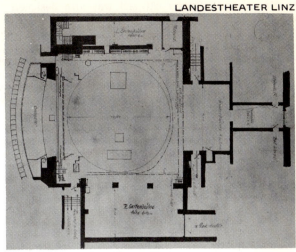

LANDESTHEATER LINZ

Plan of the stage of the *Grosses Haus*.

Landestheater Linz

Austria's state theaters are located in the capital cities of the various **Laender**. Among them, the **Landestheater Linz** provides a good example of the extent of professional theater available to the inhabitants of a medium-sized Austrian city, the population of which was 205,619 on March 1, 1970.

The history of the Danube city of Linz can be traced officially back to Roman times when the settlement was called Lentia, a name first recorded in 410 B.C. The city grew in importance as traffic along the Danube increased. Many churches were established, among which the **Martinskirche** is the oldest surviving building in Austria, dating from before 799. During the fifteenth century the Emperor Frederick III made Linz his **Residenz** and during the baroque era the city enjoyed a period of expansion marked by the erection of many beautiful buildings, some of which still stand.

The astronomer Johannes Kepler resided in Linz and completed there his **Harmonices mundi** which was first printed in 1619. During the theatrical season of 1966-67, the **Landestheater** staged in the **Grosses Haus** the first Austrian production of Paul Hindemith's opera on the subject of Kepler, **Die Harmonie der Welt.**

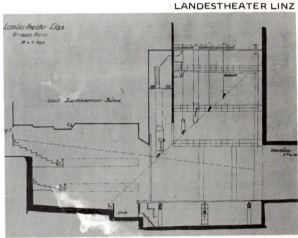

LANDESTHEATER LINZ

Section through the stage and auditorium of the *Grosses Haus*.

Mozart composed his Linz Symphony here in 1783, Bruckner was an organist in Linz from 1855 to 1868 and in 1863 the journalist and playwright Hermann Bahr was born in the city. Another Austrian who went to high school in Linz and wandered its streets and byways dreaming of becoming a painter or an architect was Adolf Hitler.

Unlike Vienna, Salzburg or Innsbruck, the city of Linz was not the site of a permanent court, and the origins of its theater tradition lie rather in the activities of its sixteenth and seventeenth century schools. Between 1578 and 1595, a classics professor at the protestant **Landschaftschule**, Georg Calaminus, wrote a number of plays in Latin which were performed in the school. One of them, **Rudolphus et Ottocarus**, served Grillparzer as inspiration for some portions of his own **Koenig Ottokars Glueck und Ende.** Later, in 1608, the tradition of Jesuit plays in Linz began with pieces attacking the Protestant Reformation in the north. The Jesuits made use of perspective scenery and presented some of their productions before the Emperor Ferdinand III during the Thirty Years War.[40]

[39] **Theaterstatistik 1970-71**, p. 27.

[40] Franz Pfeffer, "Linzer Theater," **Oberoesterreich: Landschaft, Kultur, Wirtschaft, Fremdenverkehr, Sport** (3. Jahr, Heft ¾, Winter 1953-54, Festnummer 150 Jahre Landestheater Linz) pp. 12-20.

The year 1803 marks the beginning of the modern theater tradition in Linz when a new theater was planned for the city after a disastrous fire required that a major civic building project be undertaken. The theater was established on the location of the present **Landestheater**, which was rebuilt after World War II. As is the case with almost all Austrian and German theaters, the **Landestheater Linz** operates two theater buildings, a **Grosses Haus** for the performance of operas, ballets and musicals and a **Kammerspiele** which is used primarily for the production of spoken drama.

The **Grosses Haus**, which seats 756, was designed by Clemens Holzmeister and opened December 20, 1958 with a production of **Arabella** by Richard Strauss and Hugo von Hofmannsthal. The proscenium opening is 9.60 meters wide and 7.0 meters high while the stage occupies an area 21 meters wide by 23 meters deep. The control console for the stage lighting equipment consists of 120 potentiometers which activate an equal number of electronic dimmers. The system was installed by the **Allgemeine Elektricitaets Gesellschaft**. The orchestra pit will accommodate upwards of 75 musicians.

STATE THEATERS

sixty-three

The **Kammerspiele** seats 421 and was also designed by Professor Holzmeister. It opened September 28, 1957 with a production of **Paulus unter den Juden** by Franz Werfel which was directed by Fred Schroer. The proscenium opening is 7.60 meters wide and 6.0 meters high while the stage is 14 meters wide and 15 meters deep. The **Kammerspiele** also has a small orchestra pit which will hold 45 musicians. The lighting console is equipped with 90 controls which activate remotely located magnetic amplifier dimmers, a system installed by **Siemens, A. G.** The two theaters operate subscription systems and are served by 16 **Besucherorganisationen** which have over 7,000 members.

The size of the company of the **Landestheater Linz** during the season of 1969-70 was as follows:

Intendant, Dramaturgen, musical, stage and dance directors and their assistants	22
Stage, costume and lighting designers	6
Singers: Soloists	35
Chorus	36
Actors and actresses	39
Dancers	14
Stage managers and prompters	8
Orchestra musicians	81
Technical directors	26
Technical personnel	74
House personnel	56
TOTAL	397

During the season 1969-70, the repertory in the two houses was as follows:

GROSSES HAUS

OPERAS	Mozart	Die Entfuehrung aus dem Serail
	Rossini	La Cenerentola
	Bizet	Carmen
	Verdi	Othello
	Tschaikowsky	Pique Dame
	Janáček	Jenufa
	Puccini	Gianni Schicchi
	Bartók	Herzog Blaubarts Burg
OPERETTAS	Suppé	Boccaccio
	Lehár	Zigeunerliebe
	Abraham	Victoria und ihr Husar
MUSICAL	Lerner/Loewe	My Fair Lady
PLAYS	Shakespeare	Ein Sommernachtstraum
	Brecht	Leben des Galilei
JUGENDSPIEL	Bassewitz	Peterchens Mondfahrt

KAMMERSPIELE

PLAYS	Schiller	Kabale und Liebe
	Nestroy	Der Talisman
	Feydeau	Der Floh im Ohr
	Pirandello	Heinrich IV
	Hay	Haben
	Kesselring	Arsen und Spitzenhaeubchen
	Shaffer	Komoedie im Dunkeln
	Linney	Armer alter Fritz
	Klinger	Die Helena des Euripides (World première)
	Albee	Wer hat Angst vor Virginia Woolf?
	Hacks	Amphitryon
	Duerrenmatt	Play Strindberg
	Behr	Ich liebe die Oper (Austrian première)
JUGENDSPIEL	Kleist	Der zerbrochene Krug
BALLETS	Hindemith	Die vier Temperamente
	Strawinsky	Die Geschichte vom Soldaten

As is usual in the German-language theater, the **Landestheater Linz** concerns itself with both the masterworks of the past and the newest experiments of the younger generation of playwrights. It is of interest that the theater administration staged several performances of Kleist's classic comedy **Der zerbrochene Krug** for audiences of students from the high schools of Linz and other nearby towns. Students thus learn the theater classics of their language both from the pages of books and from live performances in the theater.

Another classic, which was in the regular repertory, was Johann Nestroy's **Der Talisman**, a farce with music by Adolf Mueller as revised by Adolf Scherbaum. The production was staged by Alfred Stoegmueller and the small orchestra was conducted by Wolfgang Rot. This popular work was derived from a French source, the vaudeville comedy **Bonaventure** by the team of Duperty and F. de Courcy which was first performed in Paris at the **Théâtre du Vaudeville** in January of 1840. Although an adaptation of another work for the theater (the practice was common at the time) **Der Talisman** was marked with Nestroy's unique theatrical flair as was shown shortly after the opening when a translation of the original work was produced at a rival theater, but quickly closed.

The Nestroy-Mueller version opened in December of 1840 in the **Theater an der Wien** and ran for 110 performances, quite a record for the time. It was Nestroy's 42nd work for the theater. By the time he died, in 1862, he had composed 83 stage works of which 18 were one-act plays.

His writing is marked by a strong sense of irony which enabled him to dramatize situations from perspectives which were contrary to the conventional attitudes of his day. Like the George Bernard Shaw of later times, he strove to present truth on the stage by reversing conventional value patterns thus requiring his audiences to examine all over again their most cherished illusions. Today, his plays are as lively and communicative as they were a century ago, not only as played in their original form but in modern adaptations as well. Heinrich Sutermeister has composed an opera to a text derived from **The Talisman** which is entitled **Titus Feuerfuchs**, after the leading personage of the play. It was first performed in 1958 at Basle. And in America, one of the longest running hit musicals of the twentieth century, **Hello Dolly**, was derived from Thornton Wilder's play **The Matchmaker** which was in turn an adaptation of Nestroy's **Einen Jux will er sich machen.**

Nestroy also enjoyed a remarkable career as an actor. During the 30 years of his professional life in Vienna he played 879 roles, of which the lead in **Der Talisman**, Titus Feuerfuchs, was only the 630th. As in the case of Molière before him and Harold Pinter after, it appears that Nestroy's experiences as an actor in the theater made a significant contribution to his artistry as a playwright.

Among plays in the repertory of the **Landestheater Linz** which were written more recently, Peter Hacks **Amphitryon** deserves some comment. The author has discussed the influences exerted on his version of the story by the versions of Plautus, Molière, Dryden and Kleist. He thinks that the central question of the Amphitryon legend is our response to the appearance of a god among us who is disguised as another human being and behaves as we do. One can regard him as a comic adventurer and laugh at him, as did Molière and Dryden. But one can also take Jupiter seriously, as have Plautus and Kleist — and the author of this latest variation on an endlessly recurring theme. Jupiter here becomes the personification of all the aspirations to which man is susceptible, a veritable image of perfection, like Tarzan among the apes. But mankind does not enjoy the presence of

SUBSIDIES FOR THE THEATER

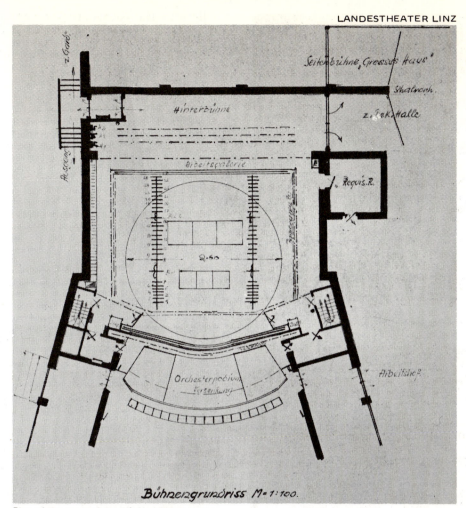

Plan of the stage of the *Kleines Haus*.

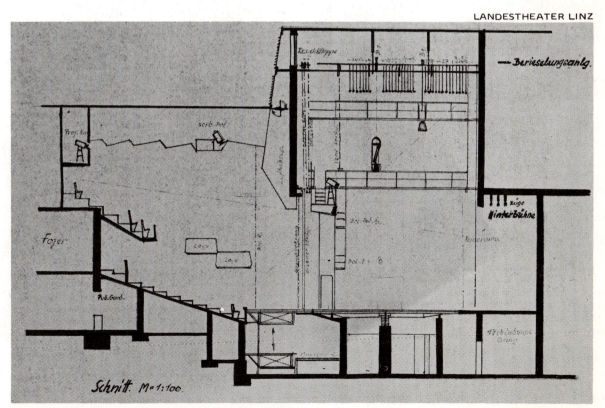

Section through the stage and auditorium of the *Kleines Haus*.

Scenes from *Der Talisman*, by Johann Nestroy.
Photos by Martin Schindelar for the LANDESTHEATER LINZ

He wrote plays in his spare time and in 1955 his **Die Eroeffnung des indischen Zeitalters** was first performed by the Munich **Kammerspiele**. For this play he received a prize from the city of Munich. In the same year he travelled to East Berlin where he joined the Berliner Ensemble and became one of Bertolt Brecht's associates. He worked for some years as a **Dramaturg** at the **Deutsches Theater** (the first home of the Berliner Ensemble) and in 1956 won the Lessing Prize. His plays from this period in his life, most of which were first performed at the **Deutsches Theater**, include **Der Mueller von Sanssouci, Die Sorgen und die Macht, Der Frieden** (after Aristophanes), **Die schoene Helena** (after Offenbach) and **Moritz Tassow**. His **Amphitryon** was first performed in 1968 by the **Deutsches Theater in Goettingen**.

In 1961 he lost his position with the **Deutsches Theater** in Berlin because of an ideological dispute with the S.E.D., the East German Communist Party. Recently, he has continued to live in East Berlin where he earns his living as a free lance writer of plays, children's stories and essays.

LANDESTHEATER LINZ—Martin Schindelar

Peter Hacks' play *Amphitryon*.

perfection in its midst for long, and the material takes on aspects of both the serious and the comic. Both Plautus and Kleist keep the serious separated from the comic, Plautus because he believed in the Greek gods, and Kleist because he didn't.[41]

Peter Hacks was born March 21, 1928 in Breslaus. His father was a lawyer. After 1946 he lived in Dachau and studied at the University of Munich. His subjects were sociology, philosophy, modern literature and theater history, and in 1951 he received the degree Doctor of Philosophy.

[41]**Landestheater Linz: Programmheft der Spielzeit 1969-70,** p. 169.

SUBSIDIES FOR THE THEATER

Another author who is gaining recognition through numerous performances of his plays in the German-language theater is the Hungarian playwright Julius Hay, whose **Haben** was in the 69-70 repertory of the **Landestheater Linz**. Born in 1900 in Abony, Hungary to a German engineer father, the future dramatist studied architecture until the revolution of 1919 which broke up the Austro-Hungarian Empire. Hay travelled to Dresden where he became an apprentice scene painter at the **Staatliches Schauspielhaus**, and while there, began writing plays. His first play, **Das neue Paradies**, was produced in Berlin at the **Volksbuehne** in 1932 during the administration of Heinz Hilpert. Another piece, **Gott, Kaiser und Bauer** was performed in Max Reinhardt's **Deutsches Theater** with great success but was banned after Hitler came to power. Hay left Germany, along with other colleagues of the "Class of '33", travelled to Vienna, then to Zuerich and finally to Moscow. When war broke out between Germany and Russia in 1941 he was interned. After the war he returned to Budapest where he took an active part in the intellectual ferment which climaxed in the Hungarian Revolution of 1956. He was sentenced to prison for six years but received an amnesty after serving three years of the term. Today, he lives in Switzerland.

Hay's most famous play is **Haben**, which was written while he was in jail in Vienna between 1934 and 1936 for being a Communist agitator. It was first performed in Budapest in 1945 as the first Hungarian première after the war. The first German production was at the **Volkstheater**, Vienna, in the same year. Later, Hay wrote **Das Pferd**, first performed at the Salzburg Festival of 1964, **Attilas Naechte**, first done at the Bregenz Festival of 1966 and **Der Grossinquisitor** which was given its première in 1968 at the **Theater in der Josefstadt**, Vienna.

Haben owes its inception to Hay's memories of village life in Hungary during his youth. While in Vienna he read of a strange trial which took place in a small Hungarian town. In order to acquire property, two peasant women killed their husbands and a third woman murdered her husband's daughter and grand-daughter. The court tried the women and found them guilty. The third woman committed suicide but the first two served fifteen years each of their life-imprisonment terms, and were then released. Years later, when Hay was again able to travel in Hungary, he visited the village and found the women living the roles of dignified martyrs to the old spirit of capitalism which had ruled their lives in their youth. In his play, the author recounts the trial, but presents his materials in such a way that not only the women but their strivings for **Haben** — for having things, especially property, are placed on trial and found guilty. The lust for property becomes the true criminal in this highly effective didactic piece.[42]

Two other plays of interest in the 69-70 repertory of the **Landestheater Linz** were **Die Helena des Euripides** by Kurt Klinger and **Armer alter Fritz** by the American author Romulus Linney. The Klinger piece is a free adaptation of the Euripides play which was written in 412 B.C., at which point in time the Peloponnesian War had been going on for nearly twenty years. Although concerned with events of the Trojan War, the war which occupied Euripides' contemporaries must have been very much on his mind as he composed his drama and today, the Viet Nam War provides a similar frame of reference for a play on man's oldest recorded activity.

Scenes from *Haben* by Julius Hay.
Photos by Martin Schindelar for the LANDESTHEATER LINZ

42 **Ibid.**, pp. 177-78.

STATE THEATERS

The author was born in 1928 in Linz, was educated there and at the University of Vienna and afterward became a **Dramaturg**, first at Linz, then at the **Duesseldorfer Schauspielhaus.** Then, from 1964 until 1968, he was **Chefdramaturg** at the **Staedtische Buehnen Frankfurt am Main.** Since 1968 he has been a free-lance writer.

Armer alter Fritz was first performed in 1967 at the Mark Taper Forum in Los Angeles to considerable success. It was later performed in New York and in London and the first German-language production was at the **Duesseldorfer Schauspielhaus.** The Austrian première took place at the **Wiener Burgtheater** in November, 1969. The author was born in Philadelphia in 1930, attended Oberlin College and the Yale School of Drama and has been an actor and director in New York. His novel **Slowly, By Thy Hand Unfurled** and his play **Democracy and Esther** have attracted attention in both America and Europe.

The Austrian state theaters are supported by the cities and states in which they are located and, to a lesser extent, by the federal government. The **Landestheater Linz** received the following sums, in millions of Austrian schillings, during the calendar years 1969 and 1970.

	1969	1970
Total Expense	36.364	38.767
Box Office and Other Income	8.588	8.976
Subsidy, Republic of Austria	3.800	4.280
Subsidy, State of Upper Austria	11.285	12.301
Subsidy, City of Linz	11.285	12.300
Special Tax for the Furtherance of Art	1.406	0.910
Total Subsidy	27.776	29.791
Ratio of Subsidy to Total Expense	76%	77% [43]

LANDESTHEATER LINZ—Martin Schindelar

Romulus Linney's *Armer alter Fritz.*

Vereinigte Buehnen Graz

The capital of the Austrian state of **Steiermark** is Graz which, with a population in 1966 of 252,879, is the republic's second largest city. Regarded as an economic gateway to southeast Europe, the city traces its recorded beginnings back to 1115 A.D. Today, the many buildings in the styles of gothic, renaissance and baroque architecture attest to the city's long history. In the fifteenth century it was the **Residenz** of the Emperor Friedrich III and from 1564 to 1619 it was the site of the government of Inner Austria.

It was an Italian, Pietro Mingotti, who contracted for the building of the first opera house in Graz in 1736. It was made of wood and suffered from repeated fires. The first **Nationaltheater** was erected on the **Freiheitsplatz** in 1776 and was considered an excellent theater for its time. The cost of the building and the subsequent support for the company were provided by the Archdukes of Steiermark and the subsidies proved to be generous enough to establish the reputation of the company in the Austrian territories. The most prominent of the early directors of the **Nationaltheater in** Graz was Joseph von Bellomo who had been director of the Weimar Court Theater before Goethe assumed this position. Bellomo came to Graz in 1791, bringing with him a measure of the "Weimar Spirit" which was already spreading to other parts of the German-speaking territories.

The building burned to the ground in 1823 but efforts were begun at once to obtain funds to replace it. Some of the money for the new theater was obtained by selling cannons from the state armaments museum to the King of Naples, and in 1825 the new theater was reopened on the same site. It was here that the two parts of Goethe's **Faust** were performed together for the first time, in 1850, and in 1854, Wagner's **Tannhaeuser** was staged, three years before the Vienna production. By 1952 it was necessary to close the theater as it had become unsafe. A campaign was instituted to raise funds for a complete interior renovation including the installation of modern stage machinery and lighting equipment. With the help of a sizable gift from the American publisher Charles Merill, the theater was once again opened on March 13, 1964 with the first performance of **Paracelsus und der Lerbeer** by the Austrian poet Max Mell.

[43]**Theaterstatistik 1969-70 and 1970-71,** p. 56.

SUBSIDIES FOR THE THEATER

Schauspielhaus Graz.

Interior of the *Schauspielhaus Graz* with the *Eisenvorhang* partly raised.

STATE THEATERS

The **Schauspielhaus** at Graz seats 588 persons. It has a proscenium opening 10 meters wide and a maximum of 7.65 meters high. The main stage is 22 meters wide and 21 meters deep while the side stage is 15 meters square. Scene shifting and lighting equipment include a 14.50 meter-diameter turntable with a built-in lift 3 meters by 10 meters, a full stage Linnebach cyclorama, two lighting bridges and a 100-dimmer lighting control system, the dimming units for which are magnetic amplifiers. There is also a small orchestra pit for chamber operas or plays which require music.

The **Opernhaus** at Graz dates from 1899 when it was opened with performances of Schiller's **Wilhelm Tell** and Wagner's **Lohengrin.** Designed by the Viennese architectural firm of Fellner and Helmer in the baroque style of Fischer von Erlach the house seats 1400 persons and accommodates an orchestra of Wagnerian proportions in the pit. The proscenium opening is 12 meters wide and 7 meters high and the stage is 22 meters square. A large turntable assists the staff in making scene changes and there is a standard-size large house lighting layout available controlled by magnetic amplifier dimmers.

The size of the company at the **Vereinigte Buehnen Graz** during the season 1968-69 was as follows:

Intendant, stage, musical and dance directors, **Dramaturgen** and other artistic personnel	38
Scene, costume and lighting designers	11
Principal singers including guests	38
Actors and actresses including guests	35
Chorus	40
Ballet dancers	20
Orchestral musicians	96
Stagehands, carpenters, property men, painters, electricians and front-of-the-house personnel	188
TOTAL	466

Waagner-Biró, A.G., Vienna

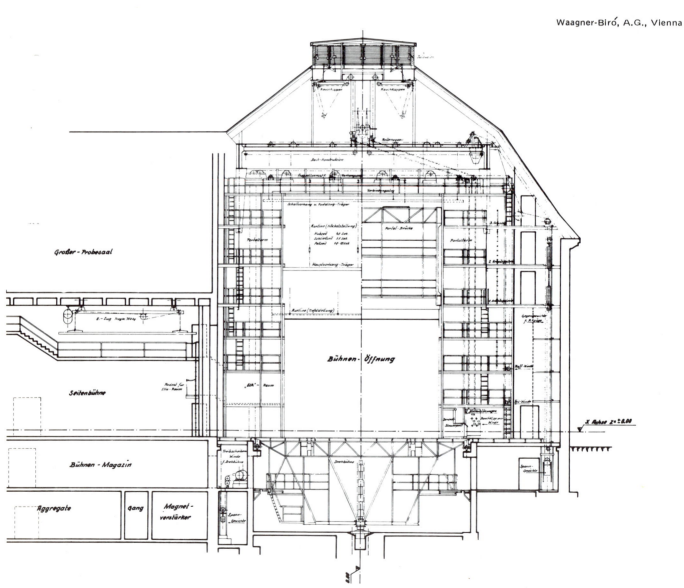

Section through the middle of the main stage and side stage (looking toward the proscenium opening) of the Schauspielhaus Graz.

SUBSIDIES FOR THE THEATER

Turntable of the *Schauspielhaus Graz* under construction. Cyclorama fluorescent units are mounted on the lighting bridges down stage.

Exterior of the *Opernhaus Graz.*

Interior of the *Opernhaus Graz.*

STATE THEATERS

During the season 1969-70 the **Spielplan** for the two theaters was as follows:

OPERAS
New Productions

Richard Wagner	Der fliegende Hollaender
Ernst Krenek	Karl V (Austrian première)
Pietro Mascagni	Cavalleria rusticana
Ruggiero Leoncavallo	Der Bajazzo
Giacomo Puccini	La Bohème
Richard Strauss	Der Rosenkavalier
Albert Lortzing	Zar und Zimmermann
Igor Strawinsky	The Rake's Progress
Giacomo Puccini	Der Mantel
	Gianni Schicchi
Richard Wagner	Rienzi

Restudied Productions

Wolfgang Amadeus Mozart	Così fan tutte
Richard Strauss	Salome

Revivals

Wolfgang Amadeus Mozart	Die Hochzeit des Figaro
	Don Giovanni
Richard Strauss	Capriccio
Nikolai Rimski-Korsakow	Die Legende von der unsichtbaren Stadt Kitesch und der Jungfrau Fewronia
Richard Wagner	Lohengrin
Umberto Giordano	André Chénier
Giacomo Puccini	Tosca
	Madame Butterfly
Carl Maria von Weber	Der Freischuetz

BALLETABEND

OPERETTAS AND MUSICALS
New Productions

Franz Lehár	Die lustige Witwe
Fred Raymond	Maske in Blau
Carl Zeller	Der Vogelhaendler
Leo Fall	Madame Pompadour
Alexander Breffort and Marguerite Monnot	Irma la Douce (In the Schauspielhaus)

Revivals

Franz Lehár	Paganini
Franz von Suppé	Boccaccio
Frederick Loewe	My Fair Lady

REHEARSAL STAGE
New Productions

Samuel Beckett	Glueckliche Tage
	Spiel
Arthur Kopit	Oh Vater, armer Vater, Mutter hing dich in den Schrank, und ich bin ganz krank
Harold Pinter	Der Hausmeister

Revival

Peter Handke	Kaspar

PLAYS IN THE *SCHAUSPIELHAUS*
New Productions

Molière	Don Juan
Neil Simon	Barfuss im Park
Oedoen von Horváth	Zur schoenen Aussicht (World première)
Carlo Goldoni	Mirandolina
Elias Canetti	Hochzeit (Austrian première)
Johann Wolfgang von Goethe	Torquato Tasso
Sean O'Casey	Juno und der Pfau
Johann Nestroy	Der Faerber und sein Zwillingsbruder
Paul Claudel	Das harte Brot (Austrian première)
Pierre Barillet and Jean-Pierre Grédy	Kaktusbluete
Anton Tschechow	Platanow
Gotthold Ephraim Lessing	Minna von Barnhelm
Edward Albee	Alles im Garten
Arthur Schnitzler	Komtesse Mizzi
	Grosse Szene
Rolf Hochhuth	Soldaten

A Children's Play for Christmas

Revivals

Anton Tschechow	Drei Schwestern
Max Mell	Jeanne d'Arc
Arthur Miller	Der Preis

seventy-two

Among the plays in the 69-70 repertory one of the most interesting was **Zur schoenen Aussicht** by the neglected German playwright Oedoen von Horváth. He was born in Fiume, on the Adriatic, in 1901 of a typical Austro-Hungarian ancestry — Croatian, Czech, Hungarian, German — and, in the restless mood of the times, was educated in Budapest, Pressburg and Vienna. In 1920 he began studying theater with Professor Kutscher in Munich and also began writing short stories and plays. His father supported his writing career as he moved about from a room near a graveyard in Schwabing to a farm his parents owned in Murnau. His first play **Die Bergbahn** (1927) had a modest success in Berlin and the publishing house of Ullstein began to support his writing in return for rights to his plays. **Zur schoenen Aussicht** was his second play and was not performed at the time he wrote it. Other of his pieces for the theater are as follows:

1928	Sladek, der schwarze Reichswehrmann
1930	Italienische Nacht
	Geschichten aus dem Wiener Wald (Kleist Prize)
1931	Kasimir und Karoline
1932	Glaube, Liebe, Hoffnung

Hitler's rise to power drove Horváth into exile first in Austria, then Hungary and finally via Switzerland to Amsterdam and Paris. During the years 1933 through 1938 he worked on more plays, among them **Don Juan kommt aus dem Krieg, Figaro laesst sich scheiden, Ein Dorf ohne Maenner, Der juengste Tag** and **Pompeji.**

Horváth has observed that his plays have been misunderstood to some extent partly because he himself had the mistaken notion that they would be clear to the public in performance without the help of any explanations provided by the author. He thought that he could dramatize a synthesis of irony and realism, thus creating a special mood in his plays which the audience would recognize as his own. In this he considered that he was only partly successful.

His aim was to develop his characters in the direction of an ever expanding awareness, a recognition of heightened consciousness which is achieved in the play through the dialogue sequences and not through the action. He felt that a dramatic scene — the clash of two temperaments — could hold the audience's interest because they would recognize that a person can be changed by a verbal encounter with another person of a different background and personality. His plays depend to a considerable degree on this kind of dramatic action and their effectiveness is likely not to register well on audiences which are accustomed merely to watching stage activity and not to listening to the nuances of tone and emphasis in the exchange of carefully shaped dialogue.

Horváth thought of drama as falling into three general categories, the theater of entertainment, the didactic theater and the aesthetic or art theater. All three forms have in common, however, the power of depicting reality more clearly than can any other form of art. People go to the theater to indulge their antisocial drives and then achieve satisfaction from the temporary purgation of these antisocial instincts from their persons — by watching with deep satisfaction a rape or a murder, for instance. He found it strange that people go to the theater to see a man killed but such is the way of dramatic art. In his own plays, Horváth attempts to disturb the usual audience feeling of sympathy for the killing and in so doing has made his plays unpopular with the public.[44]

[44]Oedoen von Horváth, "Meine Stuecke und mein Publikum," **Vereinigte Buehnen Graz: Programmheft Nr. 5 der Spielzeit 1969-70,** pp. 3, 6.

Four scenes from Oedoen von Horváth's *Zur schoenen Aussicht.*

Photos by Lohr Egon for the VEREINIGTE BUEHNEN GRAZ

STATE THEATERS

Zur schoenen Aussicht is the name of a hotel on the crossroads of two tourist routes. Times are bad. There is only one guest to be served by the manager, the waiter, the chauffeur and the wine steward. The guest is worth the trouble, however. A wealthy woman who has travelled much in the world, Ada Freifrau von Stetten keeps the hotel from going bankrupt. Reminiscent of the later figure of the Alte Dame in Duerrenmatt's **Der Besuch der alten Dame**, she has made a habit for many years of buying and selling men of all kinds — skiers, racing drivers, actors, Don Juans — and in explaining all this, she sets the thematic mood of the play.

A young girl from the outside world, Christine, enters the hotel with the illusion that Strasser, the owner, and father of her unborn child will indeed marry her as she has been led to believe. She has persuaded herself that Strasser is not a cad at all but simply has not received her letters. Everyone is amused by her and the brother of the baroness, who has come to cadge some money from her, suggests a plan which should enable Strasser to get rid of her. All the men present will pretend that they too have had affairs with her and that poor Strasser therefore shouldn't be held responsible for the new baby. The plan works and Christine is reduced to a state of helpless desperation. She tries to scream but can't. She falls to her knees before Strasser, kisses his hand and begs him not to believe these liars. He says he thinks she is lying.

Later she realizes the truth about people. And the men feel as though they had been seen through. She then tells the hotelman that she had come to help him with his business. She has just turned 21 and is now eligible to receive an inheritance from her aunt in the amount of 10,000 marks. She wished to give this money to Strasser.

All at once things are changed — changed utterly. The men become very attentive. They discover their love for little children. Each one thinks he might be — after all — the father. During a ghostly ballet arguments over the money continue, and Christine prepares to leave to make her own way in the world. She suspects that there is a God — but you can't depend on Him much. He helps once in a while but most people have to learn to get along without Him.[45] She goes.

This interesting early work sets the tone for much of Horváth's later work. Ironic without being sentimental, he achieves a delicate blend of comedy and seriousness in his plays and in so doing makes several succinct contributions to the tragi-comic dramatic format which came to dominate the playwriting of the period directly before and after the Second World War. His dialogue is filled with subtlety and nuance and political phrases often signal the situation of the times as when the chauffeur in **Zur schoenen Aussicht** suggests that what is needed is a new war and colonies.

Klaus Mann has left some impressions of Horváth when he met him in Amsterdam. Horváth talked of "strange accidents," of "grotesque diseases" and "secret investigations." He thought streets were dangerous and could do bad things to one. He was hounded by hallucinations, intuitions of a curious kind, feelings that he might be a clairvoyant and other manifestations of the spirit world. He was not, however, an hysteric or a pedantic lover of the occult. He was robust, healty, an enthusiastic talker and a man who had stood up to the Nazis as long as he could.

He went to Paris from Amsterdam in 1938 to work out details of a film contract with Robert Siodmak. Before leaving, he went to a fortune teller to inquire if his film would ever be finished. To this question she replied, oracle-wise, that in Paris he would have the greatest adventure of his life. After signing the contract he emerged from the office of the film company on the Champs-Elysées and began walking along the beautiful, tree-lined avenue. A sudden storm came up. The wind whipped the trees about and a branch from one snapped off, fell and struck the playwright on the back of the neck, killing him. As Mann puts it, the man who had entertained no fear of the Nazis was guillotined by a limb from a peaceful Parisian tree.

The repertory at the **Vereinigte Buehnen Graz** is a sound blend of the classical, the new and the thought-provoking in drama and opera. There is little reason to doubt that the management of this vigorous Austrian state theater takes with some seriousness the exhortation expressed in a verse from Schiller's **Die Kuenstler** which appears on the facade of the **Opernhaus**:

"Der Menschheit Wuerde ist
    in Eure Hand gegeben,
Bewahret Sie!
Sie sinkt mit Euch,
Mit Euch wird sie sich heben."[46]

A summary of box office and related income, subsidies and total budget for the calendar years 1969 and 1970 follows. Amounts are in millions of Austrian schillings.

	1969	1970
Total Expense	54.988	55.912
Box Office and Other Income	10.380	10.395
Subsidy, Republic of Austria	5.234	5.565
Subsidy, State of Steiermark	19.687	19.976
Subsidy, City of Gras	19.687	19.976
Total Subsidy	44.608	45.517
Ratio of Subsidy to Expense	81%	81% [47]

[45]"Es gibt einen lieben Gott, aber auf den ist kein Verlass. Er hilft nur ab und zu, die meisten duerfen verrecken."

[46]Mankind's worth is placed in your hand,
Protect it!
It sinks with you,
With you will it stand.

[47]**Theaterstatistik 1969-70 and 1970-71**, p. 56.

SUBSIDIES FOR THE THEATER

Kaspar **by Peter Handke.**

Two scenes from Arthur Miller's *Der Preis.*

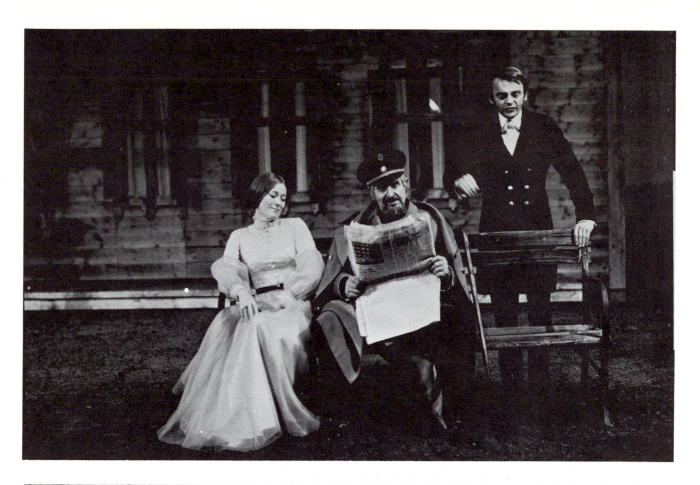

Two scenes from Chekhov's *Drei Schwestern.*

Photos by Lohr Egon for the VEREINIGTE BUEHNEN GRAZ

SUBSIDIES FOR THE THEATER

Two scenes from *Cappricio* by Richard Strauss.

Photos by Lohr Egon for the VEREINIGTE BUEHNEN GRAZ

STATE THEATERS

Two scenes from *Boccacio* by Franz von Suppé.

Photos by Lohr Egon for the VEREINIGTE BUEHNEN GRAZ

SUBSIDIES FOR THE THEATER

Two scenes from *Paganini* by Franz Lehár.

Photos by Lohr Egon for the VEREINIGTE BUEHNEN GRAZ

Tiroler Landestheater

The capital of the Austrian state of Tirol is Innsbruck, an energetic city of 113,768 (1969) which is surrounded on all sides by towering mountain peaks. During the fourteenth century Innsbruck and the Tirol became part of the Hapsburg domains. The future Emperor Frederick III was born there in 1415 and by 1500 the city had become an important center of humanistic studies.

In 1653 the first regular theater, the **Comediehaus**, was built in Innsbruck by Christoph Gump which was the scene, the following year, of the first performance of Marc Antonio Cesti's **Cleopatra**. By 1656 English comedians were performing works by Shakespeare and other English authors in a large hall of the **Hofburg**, the Hapsburg summer residence in Innsbruck. In 1786 the theaters of Innsbruck received their first genuine state subsidy in the amount of 2,000 Gulden and soon afterward the theaters were reorganized as national theaters under the protection of the government. A new theater was built in 1846 at a cost of 40,000 Gulden which opened on April 19th with **Ein deutscher Krieger** by Eduard Bauernfeld. In 1893 it was fitted out with hydraulic lifts and electric lights for the stage in three colors; other items of machinery gradually added were a **Rundhorizont** and movable lighting bridges. The stage equipment was thoroughly redesigned between 1961 and 1967 and once more the **Tiroler Landestheater**, on November 17, 1967, opened its doors to the public with a gala performance of Ferdinand Raimund's **Alpenkoenig und Menschenfeind**.

The spare, modernistic auditorium provides seats for 793 persons and standing room for 30 more. The architect for the project was Dipl.-Ing. Eric Boltenstern of Vienna. The work rooms and storage areas which were added to the original building were planned by Ing. Robert Schuler of Innsbruck.

The stage and work spaces are 77 meters long from north to south (the north-south line runs parallel to the footlights with north toward the audience left) and 38.5 meters wide. Underneath the main work areas are storage spaces for scenery and properties. The north side of the work area includes a painting studio with 350 square meters of floor area and a balcony 5.5 meters high from which one can observe the perspective of a backdrop which has been painted on the studio floor with long-handled brushes. German painting crews seldom make use of the American device of the paint frame, possibly because the paint sometimes runs at an awkward spot when the canvas is being painted vertically. On the south side of the main stage are administrative offices, rehearsal rooms and the entry way. Beyond the stage are more work rooms and stock rooms. A large freight elevator 9 meters by 2 meters is used to convey materials from the storage rooms in the basement to the side stage area and, above, to the painting studio. It has a lifting capacity of 2 German tons.

The main stage is 25 meters wide by 15 meters deep. The proscenium width is variable between 7 and 10 meters and the height is usually set at 9 meters. A turntable on the main stage with a diameter of 14 meters accommodates a large stage lift 4 meters by 8 meters. The lift will sink to 3.66 meters below stage level and rise to a height of 1.83 meters above. It travels in steps of 167 millimeters each, the height of the stage wagons which will fit over the lift. When a wagon is in place the lift is lowered 167 millimeters to make the wagon flush with the stage level. The turntable revolves at a speed of 0.8 meters per second.

Tiroler Landestheater.

SUBSIDIES FOR THE THEATER

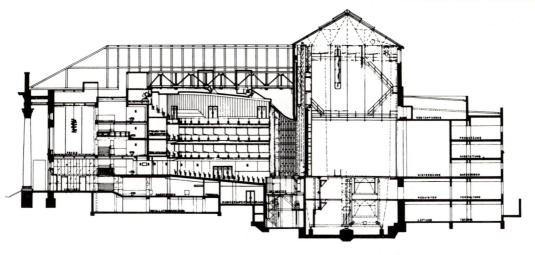

DAS TIROLER LANDESTHEATER IN INNSBRUCK
nach dem Umbau. Schnitt und Grundriß M 1 : 500

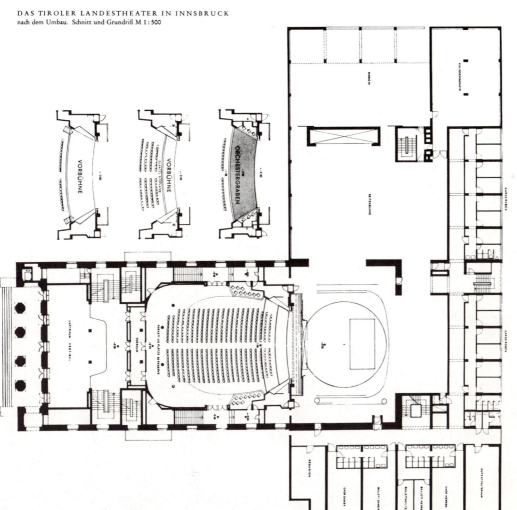

Plan and elevation of the *Tiroler Landestheater.*

View of the auditorium of the *Tiroler Landestheater.*

View from the auditorium toward the stage.

There are sound curtains which isolate the side stage and rear stage and a curtain used to cut off sound between the stage and auditorium in addition to the house curtain. An Eisenvorhang is installed in the usual position for an Austrian theater. There are 55 scene battens operated on the double purchase method from two work galleries. The stage lighting equipment, bridges and control apparatus are standard for a medium-sized house and the orchestra pit will accommodate 70 musicians.[48]

The **Kammerspiele** of the **Tiroler Landestheater** seats 364 persons. It was designed by Dipl.-Ing. Franz Baumann of Innsbruck and was opened on December 1, 1959 with a performance of Grillparzer's **Ein Traum ein Leben**. The proscenium arch is 7 meters wide by 3.70 meters high while the stage is 15.90 meters wide by 8.50) meters deep.

The size of the company at the **Tiroler Landestheater** is as follows:

Intendant, stage, musical and dance directors, designers **Dramaturgen** and administration	34
Principal singers	31
Actors and actresses	27
Chorus singers (sometimes augmented by extras)	37
Ballet dancers	20
Orchestral musicians	64
Stagehands, carpenters, property men, painters, electricians and other technical personnel	75
House Personnel	21
TOTAL	309

During the season of 1969-70 the **Spielplan** for the **Grosses Haus** and the **Kammerspiel** of the **Tiroler Landestheater** was as follows:

GROSSES HAUS
New Productions

Plays	Grillparzer	Weh dem, der luegt
	Gogal	Der Revisor
	Brecht	Herr Puntila und sein Knecht Matti
	Goethe	Faust I
Operas	Egk	Die Verlobung in San Domingo (first performance in Austria)
	Mozart	Die Zauberfloete
	Wagner	Tannhaeuser
	Verdi	Don Carlos
	Strauss	Feuersnot
	Bizet	Carmen
	Donezetti	Don Pasquale
Operettas	Strauss	Wiener Blut
	Kálmán	Die Csárdásfuerstin
	Lehár	Land des Laechelns
Musical Play	Loewe	My fair Lady
Ballet	Salmhofer	Oesterreichische Bauernhochzeit

Revivals

Play	Anouilh	Beckett oder die Ehre Gottes
Operas	Wagner	Die Meistersinger von Nuernberg
	Verdi	Aida
	Offenbach	Hoffmanns Erzaehlungen
Operettas	Strauss	Die Zigeunerbaron
	Kuenneke	Der Vetter aus Dingsda

KAMMERSPIELE

Regular Subscription	Jonson	Volpone
	Mihura	Katzenzungen
	Nestroy	Fruehere Verhaeltnisse Der Zeitvertreib
	Miller	Der Preis
	Shakespeare	Zwei aus Verona
Special Subscription	Frisch	Biografie-ein Spiel
	Hildesheimer	Das Opfer Helena (first performance in Austria)
	Kopit	Oh Vater, armer Vater

There were also three special productions in the workshop area which can be converted to an arena stage on occasion. The season was rounded out by four guest productions.

The first performance in Austria of Werner Egk's **Die Verlobung in San Domingo** presented the Innsbruck theatergoing public with an opportunity to assess the quality of the latest opera by one of the most popular and prolific composers of the German speaking area of Europe. A brief summary of Egk's biography follows.

1901	born in Auchesheim, Bavaria on May 17.
1919	studied composition with Carl Orff.
1932	composed a radio opera — Columbus
1935	his opera **Die Zaubergeige** first performed at Frankfurt am Main with many subsequent productions.
1938	his opera **Peer Gynt** first performed in Berlin.
1939	his ballet **Joan von Zarissa** first performed in Berlin.
1948	his ballet **Abraxas** first performed in Munich.
1949	appointed Director of the Hochschule fuer Musik in Berlin.
1955	his opera **Irische Legende** after Yeats first performed at the Salzburg Festival.
1957	his opera **Der Revisor**, based on Gogol's play, first performed at the Schwetzingen Festival.
1963	his opera **Die Verlobung in San Domingo** first performed in Munich.

Egk's latest opera is derived from a story of the same title by Heinrich von Kleist. The setting is the island of San Domingo during the slave uprising of 1803. A young French officer seeks food and shelter at a house in the jungle. Unknown to the officer the house is owned by one of the Negro leaders of the rebellion, Congo Hoango. His wife and daughter intend to lure the Frenchman and some of his associates into staying at the house until the return of Hoango at which time they will be murdered. The daughter, Jeanne, falls in love with the officer and tries to save him but he misunderstands her actions and shoots her. A prologue and an interlude which Egk added to the original story depict an argument between a white man and a black man over the episodes of the story. Egk seems to be saying that whites and blacks must learn to live together or they will shoot each other, as in the story.

Egk began to think seriously about setting this violent tale to music after he had visited San Domingo in 1959. He stood before the cathedral, which contains some relics of Columbus himself, and began to conceive the slave rebellion of 1803 as a poetic symbol for the decline and fall of that which the spirit of 1492 had begun. The walls were crumbling and grass grew over the cannon emplacements which still pointed toward the sea. Egk was able to see the things which Kleist had had to imagine. He saw the actual documents which proclaimed the revolution in Haiti, signed by the legendary King, Henri Christophe. He devised a musical scheme which he thought could express the stirring material and the opera was finished four years later.[49]

---

[48] Carl Maria Michel, "Das neue Haus," **Theater in Innsbruck** (Verlaganstalt Tyrolia, 1967), pp. 62-64.

[49] Tiroler Landestheater: Programmheft Nr. 1, Grosses Haus, Spielzeit 1969-70, p. 6.

The manner of meeting the annual budget for the calendar years 1969 and 1970 at Innsbruck follows. Monetary amounts are in millions of Austrian schillings.

	1969	1970
Total Expense	32.981	37.768
Box Office and Other Income	9.675	9.022
Subsidy, Republic of Austria	4.246	5.844
Subsidy, State of Tirol	9.530	11.451
Subsidy, City of Innsbruck	9.530	11.451
Total Subsidy	23.306	28.746
Ratio of Subsidy to Expense	71%	76% [50]

[50]Theaterstatistik 1969-70 and 1970-71, p. 56.

Goethe's *Faust, Part I.*

Werner Egk's *Die Verlobung in San Domingo.*

SUBSIDIES FOR THE THEATER

Biografie—ein Spiel **by Max Frisch.**

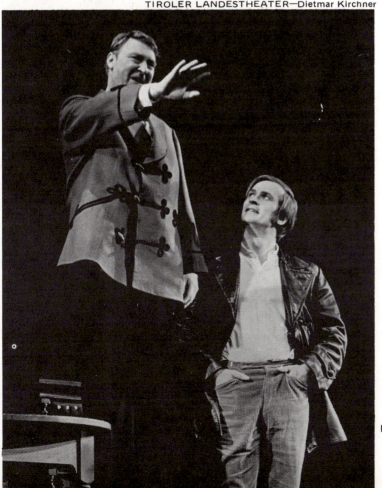

Brecht's *Herr Puntila und sein Knecht Matti.*

Municipal Theaters

Some of the best theater organizations in the German-language area of Europe are supported principally by subsidies supplied by the governments of the cities in which they are located. In some cases, extra subsidies are provided by the state or the federal government — or both — but the largest sums are contributed by the **Rechtstraeger**, the city council concerned. The size of these municipal theaters ranges from some of the largest and most heavily subsidized organizations to some of the smaller companies in Germany and Austria. Three examples (1968-69):

	Buehnen der Stadt Koeln	Wuppertaler Buehnen	Theater der Stadt Bonn
Intendant, Dramaturgen, stage, musical and dance directors, stage, costume and lighting designers, and other artistic personnel	41	34	26
Principal male and female singers	40	27	15
Actors and actresses	48	34	29
Ballet dancers	34	28	23
Chorus singers	74	38	37
Technical director, stagehands, carpenters, painters, electricians and other technicians	331	181	125
Administrative personnel	49	27	9
House personnel	86	61	43
Total size of company	703	430	307
Population of city	854,084	412,943	133,764

The orchestras which play for the operas and operettas given in these theaters are respectively the **Guerzenich-Orchester** of Koeln (113), the **Staedtische Orchester** of Wuppertal (87) and the **Orchester der Beethovenhalle** of Bonn (77). These orchestras give concerts in addition to playing in the orchestra pits of the theaters and are handled as separate administrative units.[51]

One of the most impressive theater structures in the German-language area of Europe is the complex in Koeln, which consists of a **Grosses Haus** and an adjoining **Schauspielhaus**, designed by Arch. Dr.-Ing. e.h. Wilhelm Riphahn and Prof. Dipl.-Ing. Walther Unruh.

The architectural concept of the building is unusual — spacious, elegant, and functional — and yet, not reminiscent of the usual theater shape with its high stage house at the rear. Two large wings extend up on either side of the stage house of the **Grosses Haus** while, in the case of the **Schauspielhaus**, the roof over the auditorium and lobby is high enough so that the stage house does not seem out of proportion to the rest of the structure. The auditorium of the **Grosses Haus** is equally imaginative with its functional seating and its light, airy flying balconies, while the lobby area establishes its own mood of elegance and spaciousness.

The **Grosses Haus** was opened on May 18, 1957. The proscenium width is usually set at 13.50 meters while the height is usually 9.50 meters. The main stage is 26 meters wide and 22 meters deep. There are side stages and a **Hinterbuehne** with three turntables attached to it.

Interior of the auditorium of the *Grosses Haus*.

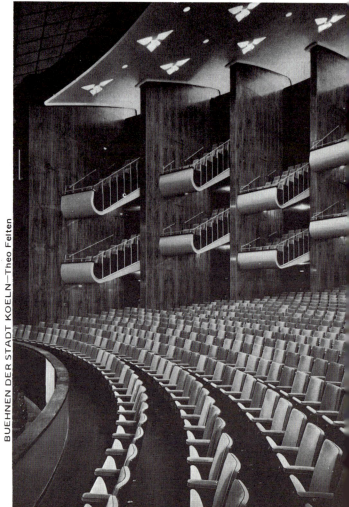

BUEHNEN DER STADT KOELN—Theo Felten

[51] **Theaterstatistik 1968-69**, pp. 6, 7, 8, 40, 41.

View of the *Buehnen der Stadt Koeln,* with the cathedral to the rear.

The main foyer of the *Grosses Haus.*

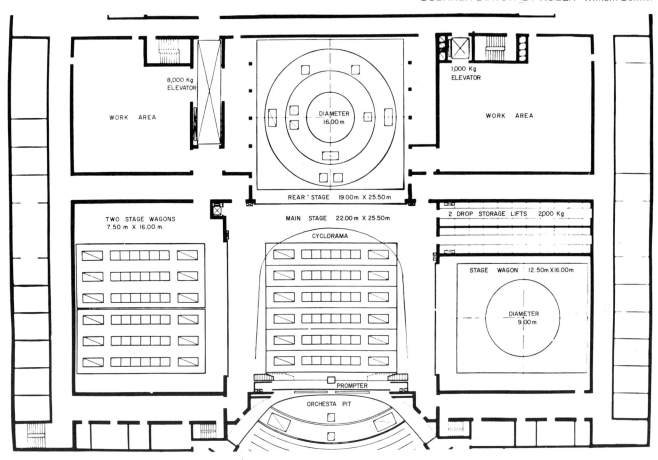

Ground plan of the main stage, side stages and rear stage of the *Grosses Haus.*

Maschinenfabrik Wiesbaden, G.m.b.H.

Scenery mounted on the rear wagon revolving stage unit at the *Grosses Haus.* The wagon carrying the turntable is being moved between the rear stage and the main stage.

SUBSIDIES FOR THE THEATER

Further, the new **Schauspielhaus** at Wuppertal which opened on September 24, 1966 with a production of Lessing's **Nathan der Weise** and the new complex at Bonn which opened on May 5, 1965 with a production of the **Oresteia** of Aeschylus are theater structures entirely within the spirit of modern theater architecture.

There follows a record of box office and other income, subsidies and total budget for these three German municipal theaters for the calendar year of 1970. Monetary amounts are expressed in millions of German marks.

	Buehnen der Stadt Koeln	Wuppertaler Buehnen	Theater der Stadt Bonn
Total Expense	28.009	13.383	10.702
Box Office and Other Income	4.626	2.601	1.745
Subsidy, State of North Rhine-Westphalia	0.350	0.095	0.050
Municipal Subsidy	22.510	10.487	8.722
Radio-TV Subsidy	0.475	0.200	0.185
Other Subsidy	0.048		
Total Subsidy	23.383	10.782	8.957
Ratio of Subsidy to Expense	83%	80%	84% [52]

[52] **Theaterstatistik** 1970-71, p. 27.

Fried. Krupp Maschinen- und Stahlbau, Rheinhausen

View of the stage right tormentor, the right side of the main lighting bridge and the counterweight lines of the *Theater der Stadt Bonn.*

MUNICIPAL THEATERS

Fried. Krupp Maschinen- und Stahlbau, Rheinhausen

Rack and pinion drive assemblies used to raise and lower stage lifts in the *Theater der Stadt Bonn.*

One-ton constant speed hoisting winch used for the raising and lowering of a lighting batten in the *Theater der Stadt Bonn.* The winch is designed to provide a smooth run with careful starts and stops so as not to unduly jar the lighting equipment mounted on the batten.

Fried. Krupp Maschinen- und Stahlbau, Rheinhausen.

Thirty-ton hoisting winch in the *Theater der Stadt Bonn* used to raise and lower the main lighting bridge.

German Information Center

THEATER DER STADT BONN—Foto Stuckmann

Mozart's baroque opera *Idomeneo* **as staged at the** *Theater der Stadt Bonn.*

Italienische Nacht by Oedoen von Horváth.

SUBSIDIES FOR THE THEATER

The most decentralized theaters in the German-language area of Europe, financially speaking, are those which receive their chief support from their municipalities. This situation suggests a parallel situation in America at the present time in which several cities have begun to show some interest in supporting their own professional theaters. For this reason, a close study of three of the German municipal theaters should be of some interest. These will be the **Staedtische Buehnen Frankfurt am Main**, the **Nationaltheater Mannheim** and the **Staedtische Buehnen Nuernberg-Fuerth**.

Staedtische Buehnen Frankfurt am Main

The area around the Main river known today as Frankfurt on the Main (to distinguish it from Frankfurt on the Oder, in East Germany) was settled at least as far back as the Stone Age but it was not until 794 A.D. that the name of the city appeared on an official document proclaiming a synod convened by Charlemagne. During the Carolingian period the city became famous for its trade fairs, something for which it is still noted today.

During the 9th century the Church of St. Bartholomew became the scene of the election of the Kings of Germany and in 1352 Frankfurt was established as the place of election and coronation of all kings and emperors of the German territories by proclamation of Charles IV. In 1372 Frankfurt was declared a free Imperial city, a status it held until it was annexed by Prussia in 1866. It was seriously damaged during the Second World War but was rebuilt and now supports a population in excess of 700,000.

The tradition of being a "free Imperial city" had a special effect on the development of art and literature in Frankfurt. The city itself supported the fine arts, in the absence of a series of royal patrons, and today this tradition manifests itself in the form of one of the finest theater complexes in the western world, a complex supported almost exclusively by municipal taxes.

The **Theaterinsel**, or theater island, in the middle of downtown Frankfurt consists of three buildings in one — an **Oper**, a **Schauspiel** and a **Kammerspiel**. The opera house was opened on Christmas, 1951, and seats 1,430. The **Schauspiel**, seating 911, and the **Kammerspiel**, seating 200, were opened respectively on December 14th and December 21st of 1963. The **Generalintendant**, Harry Buckwitz, felt at the time that there were advantages to having a theater complex surrounded by city traffic, that he was a supporter of theater for the people, open to everyone, and that a theater should not be situated in a kind of ivory tower cut off from pedestrian traffic by parking lots. It should be, instead, an easy matter for people to walk by the building, read the playing schedules for the three theaters and look at the photographs of recent productions mounted in the lobby display windows.[53]

After the destruction of the Frankfurt theaters during the war it was decided to leave the shell of the opera house standing and to rebuild a new complex on the site of the former **Schauspielhaus**. The new structure would accommodate opera, classical drama and new, experimental works for the theater while the famous old opera house could eventually be remodelled as a concert hall.

Hauptwacheplatz **in Frankfurt am Main with the** *Cafe Hauptwache.*

Buehnentechnische Rundschau

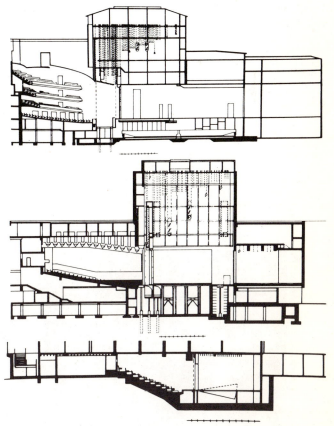

Sections through the center of the theaters.
Oper **at top,** *Schauspiel* **middle and** *Kammerspiel* **at bottom.**

[53]Walter Huneke, "Die 'Theaterinsel' in Frankfurt a. Main," **Buehnentechnische Rundschau** LVIII (Februar 1964), p. 9.

MUNICIPAL THEATERS

The two principal theaters of the *Staedtische Buehnen Frankfurt am Main*. The *Schauspiel* is to the left, the *Oper* right.

The new opera house was built on the site and within the walls of the old **Schauspielhaus** under the direction of Professor Adolf Linnebach, who acted as theater consultant, and the architectural firm of Apel, Letocha and Rohrer. Linnebach was presented with several problems in designing a suitable scene shifting apparatus for a large opera house on this particular site. The walls of the **Schauspielhaus**, which had to be used as an economy measure, did not permit enough width for side stages or a rear stage, thus ruling out the use of large, full-stage wagons. Further, double-decked lifts were found to be out of the question due to the level of the Main River in that area of the city. The only thing left in addition to stage battens was the turntable, and Linnebach designed a very large one — 38 meters in diameter. It is big enough to handle four regular-sized opera settings at once. A smaller turntable was fitted onto the large

one, the diameter of which is 16 meters. For plays, which are sometimes done in the large house, the small turntable can be pulled out over the raised orchestra lift and used to shift scenery in a thrust stage position.

The proscenium opening is 13 meters wide and 9 meters high, while the total stage area is 40 meters by 40 meters. The lighting installation is controlled by a console of 240 dimmer units and the orchestra pit is large enough to accommodate 85 musicians.

The next step in the Frankfurt theater complex was the construction of a large scenery design and storage wing which was added to the side and rear of the main opera stage. This important element of the structure was built during the years 1954 and 1955. A decision then was made by the Frankfurt City Council to complete the project by adding a play house and a chamber theater to the opera house-storage units. The financing was handled by means of municipal bonds, and it is of interest that the city of Frankfurt am Main has one of the highest levels of bonded indebtedness in postwar Germany — over DM 1,000 per capita.

In order to establish a feeling of unity in the new complex, a common lobby area was developed for both the **Oper** and the **Schauspiel**. Marc Chagall was commissioned to paint wall murals for the lobby and the sculptor Zoltan Kemeny created a ceiling sculpture for the 120-meter long foyer.

The most interesting feature of the **Schauspiel** is the fact that it is designed to provide either a proscenium style relationship between stage and auditorium or, by the outward movement of the side walls of the house, a free-flow atmosphere so that stage and auditorium seem to blend into one architectural space. The top portion of each side wall is hinged at a point corresponding to the terminus of the fourteenth row on each side of the auditorium. When parallel, the side walls provide an open space between them of 25 meters; when drawn together, the opening is 14 meters. The movable portions of the side walls also carry lighting slots used for front-of-the-house lighting equipment. The rest of this equipment is located in beams in the ceiling which have movable cover panels in front of them. The panels are opened before a production and kept closed afterward.

The two positions of the side walls of the house require a certain amount of flexibility backstage to accommodate either proscenium or thrust stage productions. The lighting bridge is on tracks which run perpendicular to the footlights. It can be moved to any position from up to down stage. The tormentor towers move with the bridge and can be adjusted to provide any width between 25 meters and 14 meters.

View of the two principal theaters from the outside. The *Oper* is to the right, the *Schauspiel* left. One huge lobby area serves both theaters. The *Kammerspiel* is underneath the *Schauspiel*.

STAEDTISCHE BUEHNEN FRANKFURT AM MAIN

The *Schauspiel* from the outside.

Maschinenfabrik Wiesbaden, G.m.b.H.

Auditorium of the *Schauspiel.* The side walls can be moved in and out. A director's work desk is set up in the middle of the house.

Buehnentechnische Rundschau

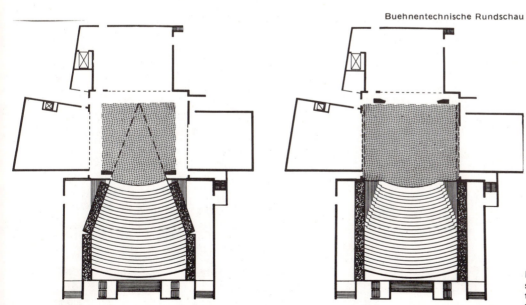

Drawing showing the movable side walls in closed position to the left, and in open position to the right.

MUNICIPAL THEATERS

The theater is provided with an iron curtain, house curtain, sound curtain and full-stage scrim. The orchestra lifts are in three sections which are designed so that it is possible to use them to form wide steps which lead from the stage out into the house in one arrangement, and in another, to accommodate a 60-piece orchestra for chamber operas and plays with music.

Associated with the main stage are two large side stages and a rear stage. Several sizes and shapes of wagons can be joined together into many combinations to carry scenery on and off from right, left and rear of the main stage. There are four lifts installed in the main stage each 2 meters deep and 10 meters wide. They are operated by hydraulic pressure and can run from 0.66 meters above the stage floor to 4.50 meters below it. When a wagon occupying the full stage is in place they can be lowered 0.166 meters (the height of the wagons) to bring wagon level down to stage level. A drop cut lift 19 meters wide and 1.5 meters deep is situated upstage. It is used to lower rolled up backdrops to a storage area beneath the upstage area and to pick up backdrops needed for the next production. Overhead, there are 44 battens for raising and lowering scenery which are driven by means of hydraulic power.

The **Kammerspiel** is designed as an intimate theater seating 200 which is used for the production of works by young playwrights performed and staged by young actors and directors. The stage is 13 meters wide. There is a forestage 11 meters wide and the overall height of the ceiling over the stage is 5 meters. The stage can be raked either up or down, depending on the needs of the production. A small orchestra pit will accommodate 10 musicians. The portal towers can be removed so that auditorium and stage may be melded into one playing-viewing space. Instead of stage battens, 78 spot lines have been installed over the stage which can handle all kinds of scenery pieces, curtains, light pipes or side masking units. Each rope can lift 100 kilograms of weight. These spot lines can be combined into groups and run electrically at the same speed or any spot line can be run by itself.

Taken altogether, the **Staedtische Buehnen Frankfurt am Main** consist of three stages and their respective auditoriums, four rehearsal rooms, one ballet hall, a chorus rehearsal hall and all the necessary workshops, storage areas and supply centers required for an annual production schedule which keeps three theaters busy ten months out of the year. A functional, organic building, the Frankfurt theater complex provides a standard against which other municipal theater structures everywhere can be judged.[54]

During the season 1968-69 season, the size of the Frankfurt ensemble was as follows:

Generalintendant, Dramaturgen, directors,

designers and other artistic personnel	48
Principal male and female singers	37
Actors and actresses	46
Ballet dancers	28
Chorus singers	64
Theater orchestra	100
Technical director, stagehands, carpenters,	
painters, electricians and other technical personnel	364
Administrative personnel	49
House personnel	129
Total size of company	865
Number of women in the company	255 [55]

[54] Ibid., pp. 9-11.
[55] Theaterstatistik 1968-69, p. 6.

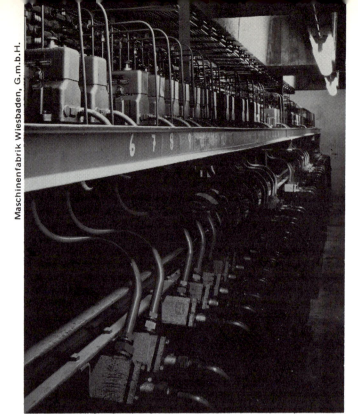

Maschinenfabrik Wiesbaden, G.m.b.H.

Pipes and control valves used in the hydraulic-control batten system installed in the *Schauspiel* at Frankfurt am Main. Electromagnetic control units are above the center I-beam and cutoff valves are below.

The principal parts of the hydraulic batten system are: 1. Plunger, 2. Batten, 3. Control lever, 4. Main valve, 5. Electromagnetic prime valve, 6. Electromagnetic bypass valve, 7. Cutoff valve, 8. Control handle, 9. Handle for Group Control, 10. Height indicator, 11. Brake connector, 12. End switch, 13. Emergency switch. The control valves are opened and closed by electromagnets thus permitting remote electrical control from the fly gallery. Several battens can be grouped together and since the liquid pressure is the same on each plunger, the battens will move at exactly the same speed.

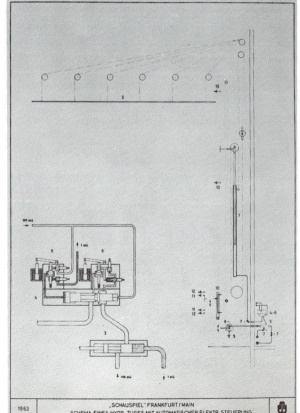

The repertory of the **Staedtische Buehnen Frankfurt Am Main** during the season of 1968-1969 was as follows:

NEW PRODUCTIONS	PERFORMANCES	ATTENDANCE	AVERAGE PERCENT CAPACITY
Oper			
Mozart, **Die Zauberfloete**	29	38,245	92.2
Honegger, **Johanna auf dem Scheiterhaufen**	15	13,068	60.9
Verdi, **Rigoletto**	21	24,881	82.9
Debussy, **Pelléas et Mélisande**	7	6,228	62.2
Prokofieff, **Der feurige Engel**	7	7,581	88.4
Operetta			
Milloecker, **Der Bettelstudent**	8	9,869	86.3
Ballet			
Tschaikowskij, **Der Nussknacker**	19	24,030	88.4
Corelli/Schust/Penderecki			
Kammertanzabend im Kammerspiel	9	1,159	64.4
Schauspiel			
Goethe, **Goetz von Berlichingen**	51	38,318	82.5
Macourek, **Das Susannchenspiel**	47	30,123	70.4
deRojas/Terron, **Celestina**	34	29,182	94.2
Adrien, **Sonntags am Meer**	24	13,744	62.9
Shakespeare, **Koenig Richard der Zweite**	25	17,212	75.6
Williams, **Camino Real**	34	22,682	73.2
Aristophanes, **Die Acharner**	7	4,809	75.4
Feydeau, **Der Floh im Ohr**	7	4,385	68.8
Stelter, **Pitt und Finchen**	25	17,406	76.4
Kammerspiel			
van Itallie, **Amerika, hurra!**	66	12,934	98.0
Sperr, **Landshuter Erzaehlungen**	41	6,438	78.5
Pinter, **Die Heimkehr**	39	6,763	86.7
Mueller, **Philoktet**	23	4,069	88.5
Walser, **Die Zimmerschlacht**	39	7,302	93.6
Brock, **Unterstzuoberst**	9	1,760	97.8
Hacks, **Amphitryon**	10	1,925	96.3
REVIVALS			
Oper			
Beethoven, **Fidelio**	7	7,215	72.1
Berlioz, **Fausts Verdammnis**	11	9,515	60.5
Bizet, **Carmen**	8	9,700	84.8
Borodin, **Fuerst Igor**	13	13,407	72.1
Humperdinck, **Haensel und Gretel**	7	7,279	72.7
Mozart, **Die Entfuehrung aus dem Serail**	8	9,623	84.1
Mozart, **Die Hochzeit des Figaro**	8	8,134	71.1
Puccini, **La Bohème**	4	3,981	69.6
Puccini, **Madame Butterfly**	7	7,049	70.4
Puccini, **Tosca**	6	5,790	67.5
Rossini, **La Cenerentola**	15	14,766	68.9
Smetana, **Die verkaufte Braut**	12	13,716	79.9
Strauss, **Der Rosenkavalier**	6	6,702	78.1
Strauss, **Salome**	2	1,836	64.2
Verdi, **Aida**	6	6,509	75.9
Verdi, **La Traviata**	16	17,486	76.4
Wagner, **Der fliegende Hollaender**	2	2,108	73.7
Wagner, **Tannhaeuser**	3	3,428	79.9
Weber, **Der Freischuetz**	5	5,674	79.4
Operetta			
Strauss, **Die Fledermaus**	23	27,758	84.4
Zeller, **Der Vogelhaendler**	10	11,722	82.0
Ballett			
Adam, **Giselle**/			
Barber, **Souvenirs**	17	14,018	57.7
Schauspiel			
Hochhuth, **Soldaten**	14	10,297	80.7
Schoenthan, **Der Raub der Sabinerinnen**	45	36,247	88.4
Stoppard, **Rosenkrantz und Gueldenstern sind tot**	28	17,815	69.8
Kammerspiel			
Orton, **Beute**	47	7,598	80.8

Maschinenfabrik Wiesbaden—G.m.b.H.

Fly gallery for control of the hydraulic batten system at the *Schauspiel*, **Frankfurt am Main. The position of the control handle determines the speed of the moving batten. Height indicators show the positions of the battens as they travel between the floor of the stage and the gridiron.**

MUNICIPAL THEATERS

Among the new productions of opera given in Frankfurt during this season, **Der feurige Engel**, which some critics regard as Prokofieff's masterpiece for the lyric theater, is of interest because it has not been performed very often since it was completed in 1928. The source of the text is a Gothic novel of the same title by the Symbolist poet Waleri Brjussow.

Against a sixteenth-century German background of late medieval superstition, religious fanaticism, magic, deviltry and witchcraft the opera dramatizes the story of the life and death of a hypersensitive woman who, under the influence of intense religious fervor, believes that she has had a holy encounter with a fiery angel, Madiel. The encounter was not physical, however, because physical love is sinful and Renata is to become a saint. He has promised to come near her now and then, however, in human form.

Much later, as the opera begins, Renata has come to believe that a certain Count Heinrich is the human incarnation of her fiery angel but, after spending some time with her during which she feels overwhelmed by the spell of love, he turns away from her and departs. She falls ill while trying by every desperate means open to her — magic, incantations, necromancy — to bring Heinrich back to her.

In the grip of this consuming love sickness Renata meets Ruprecht, who is on his way home from a mercenary expedition to Mexico. He discovers her writhing on the floor, apparently possessed by demons, the victim of a struggle within her body between good angels and evil angels. She recovers somewhat and finds herself attracted to Ruprecht. When he attempts to make love to her, however, she refuses him, telling him that she belongs to Count Heinrich. Under the spell of her love sickness, Ruprecht agrees to protect her without touching her and to accompany her on her search for her fiery angel.

The two travel together to Koeln where she thinks they may find him. She studies forbidden books provided her by the bookseller Glock. Ruprecht is willing to give up his soul to assist her to achieve her great desire and they engage in a ceremony to conjure up spirits from the nether regions. Mysterious noises seem to herald the imminent approach of Count Heinrich but when they look, no one is outside. A moment later, the bookseller Glock appears with more forbidden writings. At his suggestion, Ruprecht visits the famous philosopher and doctor of necromancy Agrippa von Nettesheim in the hope of enlisting his help in solving the mystery of good and evil which vie for possession of the maiden Renata. While he is gone Renata again finds Count Heinrich. He repulses her advances, however, as he believes her to be a witch. She demands of Ruprecht that he challenge Heinrich to a duel. Ruprecht agrees but suddenly, seeing Heinrich at the window of his house, she becomes convinced once again that he is indeed her angel, Madiel, and forbids Ruprecht to harm him.

In the duel, Ruprecht is badly wounded. Renata now promises herself to him and enters a convent to await his recovery. Inside the convent, the nuns soon begin to behave as though possessed by demons. A representative of the Holy Inquisition appears to determine the cause of this sudden outbreak of hysteria and places Renata on trial. In an orgiastic final scene, the Inquisitor determines that Renata has copulated with the devil and sentences her to be burned at the stake.

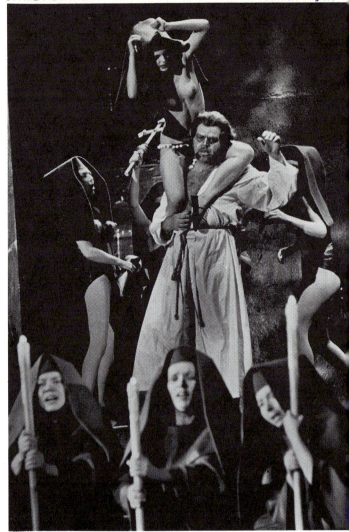

Der feurige Engel **by Sergei Prokofieff**

of surprising opinions. The finale of his second piano sonata called to one critic's mind the vision of a mammoth herd of buffalo thundering over an Asiatic plateau. The pianist had fingers of steel, wrists of steel, biceps and triceps of steel. The discussion might as well have been about a prizefighter as a pianist. Sometimes he walked angrily through New York's Central Park thinking bitterly about the great orchestras which played the same works over and over and displayed only faint interest in new music, a condition which hasn't changed noticeably in 50 years. He concluded that America was not grown up enough for new music and that he would have to go home again.[56]

Prokofieff was in America in 1918 to give some concerts. This period of his life was filled with discouragement. An exile from his own country, he found the musical life of America to be excessively conservative and the New York music critics capable

[56]Serge Prokofieff, "Die Entstehungszeit des 'Feurigen Engels'," **Staedtische Buehnen Frankfurt am Main: Programmheft Nr. 17, Oper, Spielzeit 1968-69,** p. 258.

In 1919, after the failure of **The Love for Three Oranges** in Chicago, Prokofieff immersed himself in the novel **Der feurige Engel** which had been published by Brjussow in 1908. The sixteenth-century setting attracted him and he thought he was now ready to treat the frivolous **Hexenmusik** of **Three Oranges** in a more serious and penetrating manner. He wrote the libretto himself and in 1922 he settled down in the Bavarian Alps near the site of the Oberammergau **Passionspiel** to compose the music. He began the instrumentation in Paris in 1926 and finished it in 1927. A year later, Sergei Koussevitsky conducted a concert version of some excerpts from the opera in Paris but it was not until 1955, two years after Prokofieff's death, that the first stage production of the work was mounted in Venice.

This remarkable opera displays some of Prokofieff's most convincing music for the theater, a score of great psychological subtlety and insight which is acknowledged everywhere it is performed as one of the significant achievements of twentieth-century opera. Along with Prokofieff's other stage works, **The Gambler, Semyon Kotko, The Duenna, The Story of a Real Man, The Love for Three Oranges,** and **War and Peace,** it deserves more hearings in America than it has so far received.

One of the novelties of this same season was an experiment in non-dialogue communication by Bazon Brock called **Unterstzuoberst.** An abstract rendering of the longings of those underneath to achieve positions above, and the desires of those above to relinquish their responsibilities and relax at the bottom of the heap, the play explores the communicative possibilities of pantomimic activity, sound effects and the often repeated words "oben" and "unten" which make up the dialogue. The author, who suggests that as the theater moves into the future the initials "B.B." may soon signal the ideas of Bazon Brock instead of those of Bertolt Brecht, attempts in this piece to stimulate sense perception in his audiences by all communicative devices at the disposal of modern man. The class war is thus dramatized in carefully planned and timed mass movements, sounds, noises, hisses, and a few words which are often distorted considerably. There are words in this kind of theater, but not dialogue as it is known in the traditional theater. A new form of playwriting is here under development. The play is not an imitation of reality but reality itself — the immutable reality of sight, sound and feeling.[57]

Another didactic play on the subject of the international class struggle, performed during the preceding season, was **Viet Nam Diskurs** by Peter Weiss. The action of this piece is quite well described by the complete title: **Diskurs ueber die Vorgeschichte und den Verlauf des lang andauernden Befreiungskrieges in Viet Nam als Beispiel fuer die Notwendigkeit des bewaffneten Kampfes der Unterdrueckten gegen ihre Unterdruecker sowie ueber die Versuche der Vereinigten Staaten von Amerika die Grundlagen der Revolution zu vernichten.**[58] The author gives credit in the program to Juergen Horlemann for assistance with the research

Unterstzuoberst **by Bazon Brock.**

which went into the preparation of this discourse on the Viet Nam matter. The discussion is carried out by speakers who bear numbers in place of names; as in **Unterstzuoberst,** characterization is sacrificed to polemic.

On the subject of the modern technique of the documentary theater, Peter Weiss holds that discussion and the exchange of opinion are essential parts of our day-to-day lives. Newspapers and television intrude on our thoughts all day and the documentary theater has become a necessary antidote to the onesidedness of the mass media which are controlled, after all, by the dominating interest groups. One must ask of a **newspaper** or TV commentator, "What is being kept from us? Whom does the censorship serve? What groups profit if certain episodes of a social nature are modified, changed, or idealized?" These questions refer to the editing of news.

In connection with the deliberate falsification of information, other questions present themselves. "Why would an historical personage, an episode of history, an attitude toward a minority group be stricken from a nation's consciousness? What class of society tends to hide the past? And how are these suppressions of truth and falsifications of history inserted into the minds and hearts of a people?"

[57]Bazon Brock, "Zum Tatbestand," **Staedtische Buehnen Frankfurt am Main: Programmheft Nr. 19, Kammerspiel, Spielzeit 1968-69,** pp. 290-300.

[58]Discourse on the Background and the Proceedings of the Long-Drawn-Out War of Independence in Viet Nam; as an Example both of the Necessity for an Armed Struggle of the Oppressed against their Oppressors and of the Attempts of the United States of America to Exterminate the Groundwork of the Revolution.

MUNICIPAL THEATERS

STAEDTISCHE BUEHNEN FRANKFURT AM MAIN—Guenter Englert

Finally, in connection with deliberate lies which have no basis whatever in actual occurrences, one asks, "What are the consequences of historical deception? How does one recognize a present situation which is built on lies? What difficulties does one encounter in finding out the truth? What influential organizations, what power groups will do anything in order to suppress the truth?"

In spite of the fact that mass communication brings us news from all parts of the world the full significance of events which will determine our future for years to come is concealed from us. Only the event is presented — never its meaning. Information available to the people in office, which could give us the key to what is going on, is not made public.

The documentary theater can be an antidote to all this. Subjects for this kind of theater might be the deaths of Patrice Lumumba, Kennedy, Che Guevara, a massacre in Indonesia, the inside deals made during the Geneva Conference, or the preparations of the U.S. government to carry on war in Viet Nam. The documentary theater opposes the artificial darkness under which the powerful hide their manipulations. It sets itself against the tendency of the mass media to envelop the public in a vacuum of deafness and dumbness.

That is to say, the documentary theater finds itself in the same situation as the interested citizen who wants to find out for himself the pertinent information. But his hands are tied. At last, he takes the only course open to him: the course of open protest. As the people gather spontaneously in the streets and raise their signs for all to read, so the documentary theater presents a reaction against present circumstances with the purpose of clarifying them.

The documentary theater is biased. Its presentations lead to a judgment. For such a theater, objectivity is out of the question because a call for moderation and understanding is bound to be the cry of those who don't wish to lose their advantage. The aggression of the United States against Cuba, the Dominican Republic and Viet Nam can only be regarded as onesided crimes. In depicting pillaging and genocide, a technique of black and white drawing is required. The powerful must not be shown in an attitude of conciliation — there must be no white in the black. Americans must be depicted as all black and the only possible position for the audience must be one of solidarity for the side of the plundered.

The documentary theater may assume the form of a tribunal. It is not an imitation of an actual investigation. It does not strive for the authenticity of a court in Nuernberg, or an Auschwitz trial in Frankfurt, or a hearing in the American Senate but it can bring up the issues and the questions that are raised in these rooms in a new way by disclosing the gap between the various points of view, a gap which perhaps was not made clear in the original trial, investigation or hearing.

The people who are represented appear in an historical context. As we observe their deeds we also observe the forces which made them what they are. We watch as they are hammered out of history, and in addition to what they have already done we note the repercussions of their acts which are still to come in the future. Everything superfluous is cut out; all that remains is the true, unvarnished presentation of the problem. Gone are the moments of surprise, the local color, the sensational. In their place is that which has universal validity.

In the documentary theater the audience can enter into the action in a way which is not possible in a genuine courtroom. The public can be made to sympathize with either the prosecutor or the defendant. It can be made to see the complexities of a situation. It can also be made to adopt a totally unsympathetic attitude toward the proceedings.

ninety-eight

The documentary theater is against a theater which wallows in its own inability to find meaning, against a theater which has for its main theme its **own** frustration and anger. Instead, the documentary theater seeks those alternatives which reality hides, but which can be seen in the theater.[59]

The production of this controversial piece at Frankfurt was directed by Harry Buckwitz, designed and costumed by Gunilla Palmstierna-Weiss and choreographed by Jean Soubeyran. Incidental music was composed by Peter Schat.

STAEDTISCHE BUEHNEN FRANKFURT AM MAIN—Guenter Englert

Viet Nam Diskurs **by Peter Weiss.**

During the season of 1969-70 one of the most interesting items in the repertory was Milko Kelemen's opera **Der Belagerungszustand**, the text for which was derived from the play **L'etat de siège** by Albert Camus. The first performance of this opera in Frankfurt was on April 22, 1970. The stage director was Ulrich Erfurth and the musical director was Gabor Oetvoes.

Camus regarded this play, which he wrote in 1948, as his most characteristic work for the stage. It dramatizes the unplanned but hope-filled revolt of everyday people against a brutal dictatorship which is symbolized in the character called the Plague. The plot of the play is concerned with the relationships between the simple quest for happiness desired by the lovers Victoria and Diego and the craze for order displayed by the Plague. The scene of this allegory is Cadiz under the Franco dictatorship, but the Plague stands for all dictators, everywhere. He stands both for the sickness inherent in

[59]Peter Weiss, "Notizen zum dokumentarischen Theater," **Staedtische Buehnen Frankfurt am Main: Programmheft Nr. 39, Schauspiel, Spielzeit 1967-68,** pp. 2-3.

SUBSIDIES FOR THE THEATER

mankind and for the power which can crush the individual spirit; he represents both self-guilt and the collective urge to overcome evil. As man strives for happiness and self-realization he loses interest in society at large and closes his eyes to the evils which surround him. Order and security take on the status of natural rights because they make possible the personal happiness of the individual. A cry goes up for "law and order." But the illusion of a perfect security system within an indifferent human order is already the first indication of the approach of the Plague.

In response to the query, why Spain — why not Eastern Europe as a setting for this piece, Camus has stated that he needed a convenient model for a totalitarianism of both right and left to show that the police state grows from the desire of the common people to suppress dissent. In his search for security, man invites the Plague of oppression into his house and freedom dies of the disease of order.[60]

The operatic version by Milko Kelemen brings together the most dramatic scenes of the Camus play. The Plague is announced by the noise, played over the theater's sound system of an unlucky comet whooshing over the city. He represents the incarnation of disease, a cancerous growth in a decadent society which manifests itself in the form of dictatorship and oppression.

The Plague invades the city and exerts pressure on a government which is inactive out of a belief in the efficacy of optimism. The government quiets the populace in the name of the magic word "security" and finally, as the nature of the Plague becomes apparent, it quits the city and leaves the people to their suffering. Fear, indecision and the egotism of the middle class combine to build the groundwork for the dictatorship of the Plague. Only the lovers, Victoria and Diego, and the nihilist, Nada, make any effort to resist the Plague. Diego struggles to overcome his fear and in doing so, he experiences a growing power within himself. He becomes the one who stands up against tyranny — the rebel, the underground hero. In a final effort to establish absolute power the Plague threatens to kill Victoria, but his plan fails in the face of Diego's courage. Diego dies willingly in place of Victoria and by this act, he frees the city. In the last scene, however, Nada sees the earlier government returning and with it the possibility of a restoration of the old balance of power of a corrupt society.

Milko Kelemen employs a many-sided musical apparatus to dramatize the psychological struggles of those who confront the Plague. In addition to electronic music, the composer makes use of **Sprechgesang**, wide-ranging intervals in the vocal lines, a chorus which is often divided into many parts and is called on to whisper and shout as well as sing, and an orchestra which provides a very wide range of instrumental color and contrast. Live music meshes with recorded music in a manner intended to prevent the audience from knowing the difference. The musical element is always transparent, however; it interprets without covering up the text.

Kelemen is one of the most prolific of the younger European composers. He was born in 1924 in Croatia, studied composition first in Zagreb with Stjepan Sulek and later in Paris with Olivier Messiaen and Darius Milhaud. After displaying some interest in folk music and neo-classicism Kelemen began studying with Wolfgang Fortner in Freiburg where he developed a technique of his own involving the use of tone clusters. In 1961 he became president of the Zagreb Festival for new Music. He became

interested in Camus's novel **The Plague** when he came across a passage describing a woman who had waited all night for her husband's return and upon asking, "Where is my husband?" was told not to worry, that he had been taken, along with some others who were yelling, to be deported. Years earlier, Kelemen's own father had failed to return home and he recalled how his own mother had rushed into the street saying over and over in a distraught voice, "Where is my husband?" At this, the composer ceased to regard Camus as merely a famous author and thinker who had won the Nobel Prize for literature. He came to feel a sense of kinship with the outlook and philosophy of Camus, a kind of self-identification with the Frenchman's ethically colored existentialism. The questions asked in the novel and the later play on the same subject were universal questions which continue to demand answers, now and in the forseeable future. The composer tried to find new means of expression for these timeless ideas. He turned away from the developments of the recent past — twelve-tone music, serial techniques, etc. and immersed himself in a kind of subconscious composition which could convey to the audience the meanings of the Camus play.[61]

The total budget, subsidy and box office income, in millions of German marks for the **Staedtische Buehnen Frankfurt am Main** during the calendar years 1968, 1969 and 1970 were as follows:

	1968	1969	1970
Total Expense	23.341	25.259	29.285
Box Office Income	6.613	6.276	6.191
Reserves	0.104		1.268
Subsidy, City of Frankfurt	16.624	18.983	21.826
Ratio of Subsidy to Expense	71%	75%	74% [62]

[61]Milko Kelemen, "Warum ich den **Belagerungszustand** komponierte," **Ibid.**, pp. 278-280.

[62]**Theaterstatistik 1968-69, 1969-70, 1970-71**, p. 27.

Amerika, hurra! by Jean-Claude van Itallie.

STAEDTISCHE BUEHNEN FRANKFURT AM MAIN—Guenter Englert

[60]Albert Camus, "Antwort an Marcel," **Staedtische Buehnen Frankfurt am Main: Programmheft Nr. 18, Oper, Spielzeit 1969-70**, p. 275.

MUNICIPAL THEATERS

Johanna auf dem Scheiterhaufen **by Arthur Honegger and Paul Claudel.**

Goethe's *Goetz von Berlichingen.*

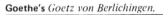

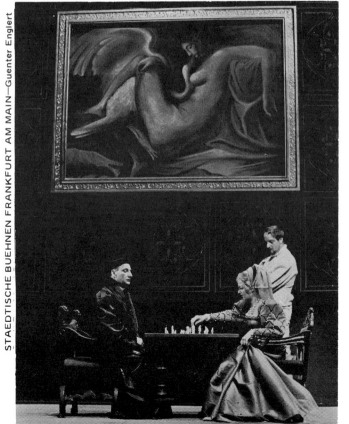

Koenig Lear **by Shakespeare.**

SUBSIDIES FOR THE THEATER

Die Kollektion by Harold Pinter

Play Strindberg by Friedrich Duerrenmatt.

Der Babutz by Felicien Marceau.

Alban Berg's *Lulu.*

one hundred one

STAEDTISCHE BUEHNEN FRANKFURT AM MAIN—Guenter Englert

Das Susannchenspiel **by Milos Macourek.**

German Information Center

The *Friedrichsplatz* in Mannheim.

Nationaltheater Mannheim

The history of the **Nationaltheater Mannheim** provides a useful example of the artistic strength and stability which a performing arts organization can draw from a great tradition. The concept of the permanent, subsidized, non-profit theater run by a salaried **Generalintendant** dates back to the middle years of the eighteenth century in the German-speaking states. The first of the German national theaters was established in Hamburg by Friedrich Loewen in 1767. It was backed by a number of businessmen who lived in Hamburg and was managed by a businessman, Abel Seyler. The acting company was headed by Karoline Neuber and Lessing was persuaded to join the venture as literary advisor and program editor, an event which established in Germany the concept of the **Dramaturg** who advises the **Generalintendant** on the artistic merit of plays being considered for the repertory, translates foreign works and provides a house program which contains a balanced critical view of the play for which it is written. Lessing later published an edited collection of the programs he prepared for the Hamburg company under the title **Hamburgische Dramaturgie**, a major contribution to German dramatic criticism.

Although the vision and energy of the Hamburg businessmen who established this first German national theater must receive due praise, the inability of private enterprise properly to sustain a true national theater manifested itself almost at once when the new theater was forced to close after only two years of operation. The incompatibility of profit and art was duly noted in the German capitals and the next steps to found national theaters were undertaken by the heads of states who were in a position to provide tax-derived subsidies. In Vienna, the Emperor Joseph II reorganized the **Burgtheater** in 1776 into the first German national theater which has performed continuously ever since and in 1777 the **Pfaelzer Kurfuerst** Carl Theodor emulated his example by establishing in Mannheim a **Kurfuerstliche deutsche Schaubuehne** which also has maintained subsequently a continuous existence.

The first **Intendant** at Mannheim was Wolfgang Heribert Reichsfreiherr von Dalberg who managed the theater from 1778 to 1803. On October 7, 1779 he offered the first production of the Mannheim **Nationaltheater**, Goldoni's **Geschwind, eh' es jemand erfaehrt** but he established his reputation for good judgment as an **Intendant** in 1782 when he decided — with some hesitation — to mount the first production of a new play by an unknown writer from Stuttgart — **Die Raeuber**, by Friedrich Schiller. The play had a great success and two years later Dalberg produced both **Die Verschwoerung des Fiesko zu Genua** and **Kabale und Liebe**. Schiller himself became the theater's **Dramaturg** and the company's reputation for quality productions of the plays of Goethe, Lessing, Shakespeare and others was soon unrivalled. In 1803 it became the **Grossherzoglich badisches Hof - und Nationaltheater** and in 1839 it was reorganized once again as Germany's first true municipal theater with primary responsibility for its operation and financing resting with the Mannheim municipal administration. Today, this city of 335,000 persons maintains one of Germany's first theaters.

The original theater which housed the Mannheim company had been a shooting range and arsenal before the architect Lorenzo Quaglio redesigned it in the years 1775-77 into a "Teutschen Komoedienhaus." It served the company well for a number of years, was redesigned in 1853-55 when a second story was added and it was strengthened and made fire resistant in 1934. On September 5, 1943 the new season opened with Weber's **Der Freischuetz** to a sold-out house. Thirty minutes after the conclusion of the performance, air raid sirens sounded, phosphorous bombs struck the theater and by morning it had burned to the ground.

After the war, operations were carried on in a renovated movie house and the **Mozartsaal** in the palace rose garden. But there was never any question of the need to rebuild the structure itself. A saying which Mannheimers attribute to a former **Oberbuergermeister**, "Ehe der Mannheimer sein Theater aufgibt, eher gibt er sein Leben auf,"[63] is possibly true and in 1952, after studying several sites in the city, the **Stadtrat** decided to erect a new **Nationaltheater** on the **Goetheplatz**, not far from the original site on **Schillerplatz**. A Frankfurt architect, Professor Gerhard Weber developed a plan in which two theaters could be accommodated under one roof, the first of its kind in post-war Germany. The large house was intended for operas, ballets and plays with very large casts while the smaller house was designed as either an arena or proscenium theater in which could be staged plays and chamber operas. This double-house plan established a precedent in Germany and Austria which has been followed by many other theatrical organizations planning new theater buidings.

[63]"A Mannheimer would sacrifice his life before he would give up his theater."

German Information Center

View of the *Nationaltheater Mannheim* **on the** *Goetheplatz.*

Maschinenfabrik Wiesbaden, G.m.b.H.

Proscenium of the *Grosses Haus* **at Mannheim.**

The **Grosses Haus** seats 1,200 and has a proscenium opening of 20 meters by 10 meters. The stage can be raked and there are several elevators which operate within a revolving stage of 17 meters diameter. There is a large lighting installation, two Linnebach cycloramas and the orchestra pit will accommodate 90 musicians. This part of the complex was opened on January 13, 1957 with a performance of Weber's **Der Freischuetz** — to continue where things had left off fourteen years before.

The **Kleines Haus** seats 600 in proscenium style and 800 in arena style. Some ideas derived from Walter Gropius's **Totaltheater** are evident in the design of this very flexible theater. For example, the performers can completely surround the audience if the director so desires since there are two large ramps on either side of the audience seating area and space in back allowing 360-degree circulation of the actors around the spectators. This part of the **Nationaltheater Mannheim** was also opened on January 13, 1957 with a performance of Schiller's **Die Raeuber** directed by Erwin Piscator — exactly 175 years after the first performance of the play which established the reputation of both theater and playwright.

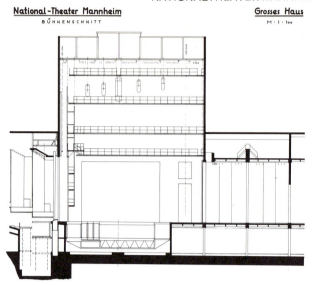

Section through the stage of the *Grosses Haus.*

Floor plan of the stage of the *Grosses Haus.*

View from the stage toward the auditorium of the *Grosses Haus.* Note the doubledecked lighting bridge and the hand follow spots mounted on the movable tormentors.

Maschinenfabrik Wiesbaden, G.m.b.H.

nterior of the *Kleines Haus* with the lighting and sound control rooms at rear. Note the suspended side stages which enable the action of a
lay to flow around the audience on three sides.

NATIONALTHEATER MANNHEIM

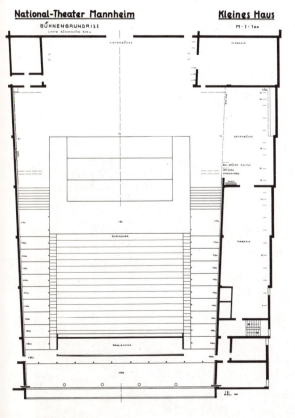

Floor plan of the stage of the *Kleines Haus*. The theater can be
converted to arena or proscenium style production.

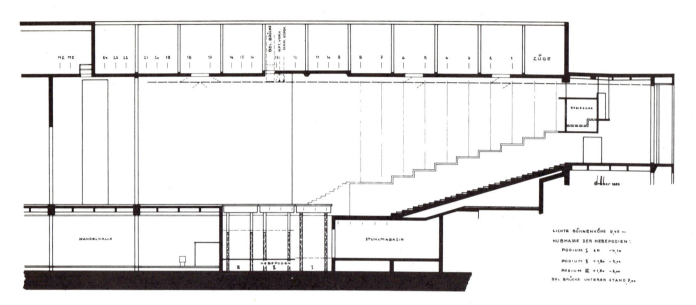

Section through the stage and the auditorium of the *Kleines Haus*.

A production of Schiller's *Die Raeuber* in the *Kleines Haus* directed by Erwin Piscator.
The action flowed between the suspended side stages and the main stage in the middle.

The opening of the new **Nationaltheater** was more than the opening of a new theater building. In the course of its distinguished history this cultural institution has become the very spiritual center of the city of Mannheim, a sanctuary for leisure, imagination and introspection in the midst of a vigorous and expanding industrial establishment.[64]

During the season 1968-69 the ensemble at the **Nationaltheater Mannheim** numbered the following personnel:

Generalintendant, Dramaturgen, directors, designers and other artistic personnel	37
Principal male and female singers	27
Actors and actresses	31
Ballet dancers	14
Chorus singers	46
Theater orchestra	88
Technical director, stagehands, carpenters, painters, electricians and other technical personnel	166
Administrative personnel	22
House personnel	63
Total size of company	494
Number of women in the company	131 [65]

The repertory of the **Nationaltheater Mannheim** during the season 1968-69 was as follows:

MUSICAL WORKS	PERFORMANCES
Operas	
Strauss, **Der Rosenkavalier**	6
Verdi, **Die Macht des Schicksals**	4
Auber, **Fra Diavolo**	6
Gounod, **Margarete**	8
Puccini, **Tosca**	6
Wagner, **Lohengrin**	6
Puccini, **La Bohème**	6
Saint-Saens, , **Samson und Dalila**	7
Klebe, **Die Raeuber**	2
Bizet, **Carmen**	3
Mozart, **Die Zauberfloete**	8
Verdi, **Der Troubador**	4
Smetena, **Die verkaufte Braut**	6
Janáček, **Katja Kabanowa**	2
Mozart, **Don Giovanni**	4
Strauss, **Ariadne auf Naxos**	4
Mascagni, **Cavalleria rusticana**	3
Leoncavallo, **Der Bajazzo**	3
Wagner, **Tristan und Isolde**	2
Klebe, **Jacobowsky und der Oberst**	6
Verdi, **Nabucco**	8
Verdi, **Aida**	7
Nicolai, **Die lustigen Weiber von Windsor**	7
Janáček, **Jenufa**	11
Wagner, **Die Meistersinger von Nuernberg**	5
Verdi, **Ein Maskenball**	7
Strauss, **Capriccio**	5
Bartok, **Herzog Blaubarts Burg**	3
Orff, **Die Kluge**	3
Beethoven, **Fidelio**	1
Strauss, **Salome**	3
Wagner, **Das Rheingold**	1
Tschaikowski, **Eugen Onegin**	9
Wagner, **Die Walkuere**	2
Wolf-Ferrari, **Die vier Grobiane**	8
Wagner, **Parsifal**	1
Rossini, **Die Tuerke in Italien**	11
Puccini, **Madame Butterfly**	5
Pfitzner, **Palestrina**	3
Mozart, **Cosi fan tutte**	4
Cimarosa, **Die heimliche Ehe**	10
Operettas:	
Kuenneke, **Der Vetter aus Dingsda**	19
Heuberger, **Der Opernball**	3
Strauss, **Die Fledermaus**	4
Strauss, **Eine Nacht in Venedig**	10

Musical	
Loewe, **My Fair Lady**	7
Ballets	
Mendelssohn, **Italienische Sinfonie**	
Scheidt, **De profundis**	
Haendel, **Koenig Hirsch**	1
Bach/ Webern, **Ricercare**	
Strawinsky, **Konzert fuer Klavier und Blaeser**	
Ravel, **La Valse**	
Tschaikowski, **Die Erzaehlungen des E.T.A. Hoffmann**	3
Prokofieff, **Cinderella**	11
Wolfgang Lauth, **Dithyrambus, Elektra, Besuchen Sie Griechenland**	7
Lauth, **Jazztime**	
Schubert/ Davis, **Die Arche**	
Lauth, **Totentanz**	8
Spoken Drama	
Hauptmann, **Rose Bernd**	22
Sartre, **Die Fliegen**	25
Ernst Elias Niebergall, **Datterich**	43
Shakespeare, **Der Kaufmann von Venedig**	20
Gogol, **Der Revisor**	13
Brecht, **Der aufhaltsame Aufstieg des Arturo Ui**	24
Kesselring, **Spitzenhaeubchen und Arsenik**	22
Shaw, **Helden**	50
Schiller, **Die Verschwoerung des Fiesko zu Genua**	13
Baldwin, **Blues fuer Mister Charlie**	17
Behan, **Die Geisel**	19
Josef und Karel Čapek, **Aus dem Leben der Insekten**	14
Kleist, **Amphitryon**	19
Shaffer, **Schwarze Komoedie**	18
Peter Handke, **Kaspar**	15
Václav Havel, **Die Benachrichtigung**	9
Martin Walser, **Die Zimmerschlacht**	7
Hermann Stelter, **Pitt und Finchen** (Children's Play)	31

Several German-language theaters have been producing recently the plays of the Czech émigré author Václav Havel and the Mannheim production of his satire **Die Benachrichtigung** caused a good deal of discussion. The play is concerned with a mysterious memorandum which appears one morning on the desk of the manager of a factory. It is written in a new, synthetic language which has been devised by the state bureaucracy to improve the accuracy of inter-office communications. The manager struggles desperately against the bureaucracy in his own organization to obtain a translation of the document. In the process, he is reduced to the status of an office spy who sits in a cubicle between three offices all day watching his former associates. He finally persuades a sympathetic secretary to translate the memorandum for him. It states that the new language has been a failure and is not to be used any longer. He recovers his position as manager of the factory but the secretary is fired.

As in most of Havel's work for the theater, **Die Benachrichtigung** poses a commentary on the mechanization of humanity. Touches of humanizing characterization which could make his work more popular are deliberately eschewed so that mechanization can become the leading performer. Cowardice, power, even indifference, are rendered mechanical, as automatic responses to any given stimulus. Human alienation is built slowly but inexorably out of everyday, banal, but stupidly logical events. An artificial language is dropped into a factory routine causing untold human anguish — an event which has never happened and probably never will happen — yet, such is the logic of it all that the audience is forced to participate, forced to imagine itself confronted by a similar opaque, intangible menace. Jan Grossmann, Havel's first director, has said that it pleased him to hear a member of the audience say after a performance of **Die Benachrichtigung** that he couldn't help laughing, but he experienced cold shivers at the same time.[66]

[64]"Das alte und das neue Haus," **Nationaltheater** 1779-1967, p. 5.

[65]Theaterstatistik 1968-69, p. 7.

[66]Jan Grossmann, "Commentary on Havel," **Nationaltheater Mannheim: Programmheft Nr. 2, Studio, Spielzeit 1968-69.**

MUNICIPAL THEATERS

Václav Havel was born in 1936 in Prague. He worked as a laborer and attended a **Gymnasium** at night from which he received a diploma in 1954. After military service he became a stagehand at the **Theater am Gelaender** in Prague and gradually worked his way up to the position of **Dramaturg**. It was this theater which produced his first plays, **Das Gartenfest** and **Die Benachrichtigung**. Mr. Havel's **Kulturplan** is as follows:

MONDAY	office	rest	movies	sleep
TUESDAY	office	rest	television	sleep
WEDNESDAY	office	rest	movies	sleep
THURSDAY	office	rest	television	sleep
FRIDAY	office	rest	movies	sleep
SATURDAY	office	rest	pleasure	sleep
SUNDAY	sleep	television	television	sleep [67]

The total budget, subsidy and box office income, in millions of German marks, for the **Nationaltheater Mannheim** during the calendar years 1968, 1969 and 1970 were as follows:

	1968	**1969**	**1970**
Total Expense	12.149	13.675	14.713
Box Office and Other Income	3.241	3.567	3.555
Reserves	0.060	0.056	0.063
Subsidy, City of Mannheim	6.490	7.531	7.856
Subsidy, State of Baden-Wuerttemberg	2.351	2.521	3.239
Subsidy, Federal Republic Republic	0.007		
Total Subsidy	8.848	10.052	11.095
Ratio of Subsidy to to Expense	73%	73%	75% [68]

[67] Ibid.

[68] Theaterstatistik 1968-69, 1969-70, 1970-71, p. 27

Two scenes from Werner Egk's opera *Peer Gynt,* after Ibsen.

Photos by Mara Eggert for the
NATIONAL THEATER MANNHEIM

NATIONAL THEATER MANNHEIM
—Foto Mara Eggert

Peter Handke's *Kaspar.*

one hundred eight

Two scenes from Carl Orff's opera *Die Kluge.*

Photos by Mara Eggert for the
NATIONAL THEATER MANNHEIM

Hans Pfitzner's opera *Palestrina.*

Photos by Mara Eggert for the
NATIONAL THEATER MANNHEIM

Blues fuer Mister Charlie **by James Baldwin.**

Josef and Karel Čapek's *Aus dem Leben der Insekten.*

Friedrich Duerrenmatt's adaptation of Shakespeare's *Koenig Johann.*

SUBSIDIES FOR THE THEATER

Staedtische Buehnen Nuernberg-Fuerth

The adjacent cities of Nuernberg and Fuerth, whose 1968 populations were respectively 467,492 and 94,219, provide an example of joint municipal sponsorship of a good-sized theater complex. The **Oper, Schauspiel** and **Kammerspiel** are based in Nuernberg but all items in the repertory are given performances in nearby Fuerth.

Nuernberg possesses a very old tradition of depending on its own resources for survival as a city. Founded about 1050 by the Emperor Henry III for military and political reasons, Nuernberg was under the protection of the Hohenstaufen dynasty until the end of the thirteenth century. With the collapse of the imperial house of Hohenstaufen, however, the military garrison vanished and Nuernberg was left to shift for itself as a free city. The **Stadtrat**, faced with the costs of self defense, embarked on a policy of improving trade and encouraging handicrafts in the hope of earning enough tax revenue to hold the city together. Both aspects of this policy were singular successes.

During the Middle Ages, overland trade in Europe was confined to a few main routes. These ran from the Balkans via Vienna to Antwerp, from Venice via the Brenner Pass to Hamburg, from France via Strasbourg to Prague and from Switzerland to Saxony and Poland. All of these trade routes intersected at Nuernberg making the city a sizable traffic center. By obtaining favorable tax concessions and trade privileges from various kings, princes and other free cities the **Stadtrat** made Nuernberg one of the great trading centers of civilized Europe.

During this period the city also became well known for its artisans and its craft guilds. Farming was not profitable in this area of Germany and the majority of the population worked at fashioning salable goods. By the early 1300's the working of metals had been particularly cultivated. For example, the craftsmen who worked copper and brass were classified as coppersmiths, red coppersmiths and copper and brass founders who, in their turn, were subdivided into moulders, founders, candlestick-makers, pulley-makers, bell-founders, weight-founders, faucet-makers, coppersmith's turners, and so forth. The oldest index of master craftsmen of Nuernberg, dating from 1363, lists 60 different crafts and 1,227 master craftsmen. No other German city developed so many different crafts nor such excellence of artisanship and this feeling for fine quality soon manifested itself in a flowering of the fine arts in the city, especially of painting and sculpture during the decades before and after 1500. The altars from the workshop of Michael Wolgemut, the woodcarvings of Veit Stoss, the brass works of Peter Vischer and his sons and the paintings of Albrecht Duerer found their way to all parts of the civilized world.

Science, literature and music also flourished at this time. Philipp Melancthon founded one of the first Gymnasiums in Germany in 1526 and Nuernberg was also the home of the society of master singers, the most prominent representative of which was the poet Hans Sachs. Throughout its subsequent history, the city of Nuernberg has been noted for its hospitality to the fine and performing arts.

The present theater complex in Nuernberg consists of an **Oper** (opened in 1905), a **Schauspiel** (opened in 1959) and a **Kammerspiel** (opened in 1962) all of which, together with shops and storage facilities, occupy a large area on Richard-Wagner-Platz, just outside the remainder of the wall which surrounded the old quarter of the city. The **Oper**, which was damaged during the war but restored and reopened in 1945, seats 1,456. It has a proscenium opening 11.40 meters wide and 7.50 meters high and the main stage area occupies a space 18.50 meters by 16.50 meters. There is a **Rundhorizont**, a double-decked lighting bridge in the stage portal zone, a large

The Albrecht Duerer House in Nuernberg.

cyclorama lighting bridge equipped with fluorescent lighting units, six borderlights, 120 spotlights, eight large scene projectors and footlights. This lighting layout is controlled by a console which activates 200 magnetic amplifier dimmers.

The **Schauspiel** seats 924, has a proscenium opening 9.50 wide by 6.50 meters high, a main stage 20 meters wide by 14.80 meters deep and ancillary stage spaces at the sides and rear. Cyclorama and lighting apparatus are similar in scope to what is installed in the **Oper**; the control console for the lighting layout activates 140 magnetic amplifier dimmers. The **Kammerspiel** is located in the **Schauspiel** building. It seats 197, has a proscenium opening 11.50 meters wide by 4.0 meters high, a stage area 11.50 meters wide and 10.50 meters deep and scene shifting and lighting equipment adequate for a small, experimental theater. The theater in which the company performs in Fuerth dates from 1902 and seats 988 persons.[69]

[69] **Deutsches Buehnen Jahrbuch 1969**, p. 426.

MUNICIPAL THEATERS

During the season 1968-69 the ensemble at the **Staedtische Buehnen Nuernberg-Fuerth** included the following personnel:

Generalintendant, Dramaturgen, directors,
designers and other artistic personnel 49
Principal male and female singers 39
Actors and actresses 39
Ballet dancers 27
Chorus singers 52
Theater orchestra 86
Technical director, stagehands, carpenters, painters,
electricians and other technical personnel 235
Administrative personnel 38
House personnel 65
Total size of company 630
Number of women in the company 190[70]

The repertory planned for the season of 1969-70 was as follows:

OPERAS (OPER)
New Productions
Haendel   Agrippina
Mozart   Die Entfuehrung aus dem Serail
Cimarosa   Die heimliche Ehe
Weber   Der Freischuetz
Donizetti   Lukrezia Borgia
Wagner   Lohengrin
Verdi   La Traviata
Wolf-Ferrari   Die vier Grobiane
Orff   Carmina burana and Catulli carmina
Nono   Intolleranza

Revivals
Mozart   Don Giovanni
                 Die Zauberfloete
Lortzing   Zar und Zimmermann
Wagner   Tristan und Isolde
                 Die Meistersinger von Nuernberg
Verdi   Die Macht des Schicksals
                 Othello
Humperdinck   Haensel und Gretel
Puccini   La Bohème
                 Madame Butterfly
Strauss   Der Rosenkavalier
Busoni   Arlecchino
Leoncavallo   Der Bajazzo
Yung   Traeume

OPERETTAS AND MUSICALS
New Productions
Strauss   Die Fledermaus
Milloecker   Gasparone
Kálmán   Die Csardasfuerstin
Siegel   Charley's Tante
Carste/Flatow   Rampenlicht (world première)

Revivals
Milloecker   Der Bettelstudent
Lehár   Die lustige Witwe
Fall   Madame Pompadour
Herman   Hallo, Dolly!

BALLET
Revivals
Petrassi   Der Wahnsinn des Orlando
Rimsky-
Korsakow   Scheherazade

PLAYS (SCHAUSPIEL)
New Productions
Shakespeare   Macbeth
Molière   Der eingebildete Kranke
Kleist   Amphitryon
Gogol   Die Heirat
Ibsen   Die Wildente
Brecht   Mann ist Mann
Horváth   Geschichten aus dem Wienerwald
Sperr   Landshuter Erzaehlungen
Frisch   Biografie
Terson   Zicke-Zacke
Duerrenmatt   Koenig Johann
Wassermann   Der Mann von La Mancha

[70]**Theaterstatistik 1968-69**, p. 7.

one hundred twelve

Revivals
Albee   Alles im Garten
Macalpine   Tom Jones
Feydeau   Der Floh im Ohr
Christie   Zehn kleine Neger

PLAYS (KAMMERSPIEL)
New Productions
Orton   Seid nett zu Mr. Sloane
Arrabal   Der Architekt und der Kaiser von Assyrien
Walser   Die Zimmerschlacht
Schmidt/Jones   I do, I do (Das musikalische Himmelbett)

Revivals
Albee   Wer hat Angst vor Virginia Woolf . . .?
Anderson   Du weisst doch, dass ich dich nicht verstehen kann,
                 Liebling, wenn das Wasser laeuft
Orton   Beute
Duerrenmatt   Play Strindberg

THEATER OF YOUTH
Twaine/Bremer   Huckleberry Finn
Franz   Linksherumrechtsherum

The Nuernberg production of Luigi Nono's **Intolleranza 70**, which was given its first performance at Venice ten years earlier under the title **Intolleranza 60**, aroused considerable discussion and controversy. An opera on the general subject of man's intolerance of man in our day, Nono has employed for this modern **Gesamtkunstwerk** all the available resources of the contemporary lyric theater — solo voices, choruses which sing live mixed together with choral numbers which have been previously tape-recorded, a large orchestra and some spoken dialogue. The setting is simply a platform backed by a large motion picture screen on which are projected various scenes of violence and intolerance picked at random from the headlines of yesterday's newspapers.

Subtitled in the original Italian "Azione Scenica," the opera follows the trials and sufferings of an immigrant who, because of the lack of work available and social injustice on every hand, leaves his own country (Italy) and travels to a foreign country to find work. He is overcome by homesickness, however, and, with some fellow workers, leaves his job to return home. On the way he accidentally becomes a member of a demonstration, is beaten by the police, arrested, tortured and sent to a concentration camp. He escapes and finally arrives in Italy only to discover the same conditions which drove him away from the foreign country. A devastating flood causes many people to lose their jobs and immigrate to a foreign country but the hero remains behind. His experiences have led him to conclude that one must stay where one is and try to effect changes for the better as best he can.

The stage directors for the Nuernberg production, Wolfgang Weber and Peter Heyduck considered that they were obliged to set aside traditional conceptions of operatic staging and try to realize the work on the stage in its own terms. The figures in the opera, the immigrant, a woman, a tortured man, an Algerian and a companion are neither persons nor theatrical characters in the usual sense but rather exemplary drawings of people, sketches, mere objects of political, social and psychological situations. The demonstrations are likewise abstractions, intended to suggest the concept of demonstrating all over the world, against intolerance of the right and intolerance of the left, against oppression, lack of freedom and dictatorship.

Nono's musical technique for expressing this stage material consists of collage-like mixtures of orchestral sound with natural voices on which are superimposed voices distorted by means of microphones and voices which have already been

SUBSIDIES FOR THE THEATER

recorded and can be played into the auditorium through loud speakers. Tone rows and music of chance techniques underlie the musical structure. The result is a conscious building of a certain kind of non-realistic realism, an inner logic which is nevertheless at the opposite end of the aesthetic realm from the old agitprop theater of the thirties. Nono's theater manages to be both political and human at the same time.[71]

Luigi Nono was born in 1924 in Venice. He studied serial techniques with Arnold Schoenberg and Anton von Webern and later, under the influence of John Cage, experimented with methods of composing by chance. He considered himself an "engaged" composer, engaged, that is, in the worldwide struggle of the masses against capitalist imperialism. He attended lectures delivered by the founder of the Italian Communist Party, Antonio Gramsci, and devoted his music to the cause in such works as **Il canto sospeso** (1956) which sets to music the last letters of various European revolutionaries who have been sentenced to death, a choral work on the subject of the bombing of Guernica by the French poet Paul Eluard, and numerous settings of poems by the Spanish martyr to Franco, Federico Garciá Lorca. Nono has sought to write music for the workers, the ordinary people without education. His **La fabbrica illuminata** contains at the end a discussion about the piece between the composer and some workers in a factory.

Nono has turned his back on the conception of opera as an important edifice in the cultural skyline of the Establishment. Opera must speak to today's audiences or disappear into the limbo of museum opera houses. **Intolleranza 70** is set to a text by Angelo Maria Rippelino with further additions arranged by Yaak Karsunke from the poems of Brecht, Eluard and Majakowski. The ultimate triumph of justice and freedom seems to be the underlying thematic concept of the text and the music.

Nono's opera has been compared to Bernd Alois Zimmermann's **Die Soldaten** in that both works employ all the means of modern expression to convey to the audience an apocalyptic vision of that contemporary life which is under the dark shadow of atomic annihilation and military mass destruction. But while there is in Zimmermann's opera a general pessimism in the face of a decaying world situation Nono attempts to force his audiences to view the situations of social injustice, war, concentration camps, torture and racism and, by so doing, actively take up the struggle to eliminate these blights from the earth. The choruses in the opera particularly contribute to a feeling of optimism by offering humanitarian alternatives in elaborate spoken and sung tableaux.

Intolleranza 70 is not a "beautiful" work. It expresses the ugly, the inhuman, the pestilential quality of modern life. But in so doing it evokes the possibility of conquering evil and building a better world. In this sense, it is a work of hope.[72]

Luigi Nono's opera *Intolleranza 70.*

Photos by Lajos Keresztes for the
STAEDTISCHE BUEHNEN NUERNBERG-FUERTH

The total budget, subsidy and box-office income, in millions of German marks, for the **Staedtische Buehnen Nuernberg-Fuerth** during the calendar years 1968 and 1969 were as follows:

	1968	1969
Total Expense	14.978	16.327
Box Office and Other Income	3.125	2.823
Reserves	0.053	0.333
Subsidy, City of Nuernberg	9.400	10.651
Subsidy, City of Fuerth	0.400	0.400
Subsidy, State of Bavaria	2.000	2.120
Total Subsidy	11.800	13.171
Radio of Subsidy to Total Expense	79%	81% [73]

[71]Wolfgang Weber and Peter Heyduck, "Intentionen," **Staedtische Buehnen Nuernberg-Fuerth, "Intolleranza 70" Programmheft**, p. 5.

[72]Wolf-Eberhard von Lewinski, "Engagiertes Musiktheater: Luigi Nono und sein Stueck **Intoleranza**," **ibid.**, pp. 5-9.

[73]**Theaterstatistik 1968-69**, p. 27.

MUNICIPAL THEATERS

Two scenes from Isang Yung's opera *Traeume.*

Photos by STAEDTISCHE BUEHNEN NUERNBERG-FUERTH

Lorca's tragedy *Bernarda Albas Haus.*

Toller **by Tankred Dorst.**

SUBSIDIES FOR THE THEATER

Die Meistersinger **by Richard Wagner.**

MUNICIPAL THEATERS

Conclusions

The famous literary expatriate Henry James once described America as "a great unendowed, unfurnished, unentertained and unentertaining continent," but there is no need for the conditions which prompted this harsh judgment to continue indefinitely. The example of the European theater indicates plainly that institutions supported by tax monies can provide the public with ten-month seasons of good theater at a reasonable box-office price and can encourage the composition of new works of dramatic art, a condition essential to the survival of the theater. The Europeans have placed the responsibility for the health of the performing arts in their countries on all the people, by means of taxation, and experience shows that in the case of both government and art, the people can be depended on to look out for their own best interests.

In America, however, we place the burden of support for the performing arts primarily on the wealthy, concerned, private individual. The result of this policy is that the support becomes highly capricious, even unreliable. For example, the Metropolitan Opera Association, one of America's leading repertory theaters, has had many a close call in its history. More than once it has been on the verge of bankruptcy but has been bailed out at the last minute by private contributions. If the Met could count on tax support in place of charity, it could stabilize its finances, lower ticket prices, and produce more new operas than it does at present. As things are, the deficit can be allowed to reach only that sum of money in a given year which the trustees think can be met by private fund raising. This sum fluctuates considerably, as a look at the deficits in relation to number of performances shows:

Year	Annual Expense (in millions)	Number of Performances	Deficit (in millions)	Ratio of Subsidy Expense
1958	$6.3	234	$0.6	9%
1959	6.5	234	0.5	8%
1960	6.8	236	0.8	12%
1961	7.2	239	0.9	12%
1962	7.1	235	0.9	13%
1963	8.4	237	1.4	16%
1964	8.9	244	1.8	20%
1965	9.9	252	1.9	19%
1966	15.8	289	4.9	31%
1967	21.3	303	7.0	33%
1968	16.9	301	3.5	21%
1969	17.4	285	3.5	20%
1970	16.0	201	5.9	37% [74]

Such dramatic shifts in the amount of the annual deficit keep the Metropolitan's management in a constant state of traumatic insecurity. Opera runs a deficit everywhere, of course, the only difference between American and European houses being the

[74]Metropolitan Opera Association, Inc., **Annual Report**: 1969-70 (New York, 1970) p. 21.

manner in which the deficit is made up: in Europe the subsidy is paid out of taxes while in the United States the subsidies are contributed haphazardly by private individuals and business out of a sense of charitable obligation.

For example, the cost of running the Metropolitan for the 1968-69 season was $17.4 million. The income from ticket sales and other sources, such as program advertising, fees for radio broadcasts, etc.) amounted to $13.9 million. The deficit of $3.5 million, amounting to 20 per cent of the budget, was contributed by friends of the Metropolitan Opera Association. By way of contrast, the **Deutsche Oper Berlin**, a company about the same size as the Met which gave 273 performances of opera and 42 of ballet during their 1968-69 season, operated on a budget of DM 27.0 million. Of this amount, the box office (and other sources) provided DM 5.6 million while the federal government of West Germany and the state of Berlin contributed a subsidy of DM 21.4 milion. The subsidy was thus about 80 per cent of the budget, as compared to the Met's 20 per cent subsidy.

This remarkable difference in percentage of subsidy explains a good deal. Ticket prices at European theaters of the first rank are much lower, proportionally, than are the Metropolitan's prices. More importantly, however, the much larger subsidies allow European theaters to perform new works of operatic art, a practice necessary to the continued existence of the form. New operas are not likely to draw 95 per cent to 98 per cent of house capacity, of course, and since the general manager is expected to achieve this capacity routinely in order to hold his annual deficit to something close to 20 per cent of his budget, the Met has fallen short of its responsibility to its public. Where in this theater's recent schedules are the works of such established composers of modern opera as Werner Egk, Carl Orff, Hans Werner Henze, Francis Poulenc, Karl Amadeus Hartmann, Boris Blacher, Luigi Dallapiccola, Hans Pfitzner, Krzysztof Penderecki, Bernd Alois Zimmermann, Sergei Prokofieff, Ferruccio Busoni, Wolfgang Fortner, Idelbrando Pizzetti, Luigi Nono, Othmar Shoeck, Heinrich Sutermeister, Dmitri Shostakowicz, Leoś Janáček, Frederick Delius, Arnold Schoenberg, Paul Hindemith, Darius Milhaud, Giselher Klebe, Ernst Krenek, Bohuslav Martinu, Gian Francesco Malipiero, Frank Martin, Béla Bartók, Gunther Schuller, Alberto Ginastera and Milko Kelemen? Operas by these composers are not done very often by the Met — if at all — nor are they likely to be in the forseeable future until New York City, the State of New York, and the United States government accept the responsibility of supporting the nation's leading theater in a manner commensurate with its international reputation. It is high time, in fact, for responsible governing units all over the country to come to the aid of America's desperate theater, opera and ballet companies.

Glossary

Alle Reichtuemer der Welt . . . O'Neill's **More Stately Mansions**
alt . . . old
Amt . . . office, position, department
Arsen und Spitzenhaeubchen . . . Kesselring's **Arsenic and Old Lace**
Bajazzo, Der . . . Leoncavallo's **Pagliacci**
Bauhaus . . . German school of architecture founded by Walter Gropius
Besucherorganisation . . . patrons of a theater who are organized into a group
Betriebsdirektor . . . director of the theater department responsible for day-to-day operations, such as planning rehearsal schedules, taking care of visiting artists, etc.
Bundestheater . . . federal theaters
Bundestheaterverwaltung . . . organization which administers the Austrian federal theaters
Chefdisponent . . . chief clerk
Chefdramaturg . . . chief literary advisor to the **Intendant**
Chefredakteur . . . editor-in-chief
Deutsch . . . German
Deutschland . . . Germany
Dipl.-Ing . . . engineer by diploma
Disponent . . . clerk
Domplatz . . . open space in front of a cathedral
Dramaturg . . . literary advisor to the **Intendant**
Dramaturgen . . . plural of **Dramaturg**
Dramaturgin . . . feminine of **Dramaturg**

Eisenvorhang . . . iron safety curtain
Empfindliches Gleichgewicht . . . Albee's **A Delicate Balance**
Fast ein Poet . . . O'Neill's **A Touch of the Poet**
Felsenreitschule . . . riding academy at Salzburg. The spectators sat in "boxes" carved out of the rocky face of a mountain
Festspiel . . . festival play
Festspielhaus . . . theater at Bayreuth in which Wagner's festival music dramas are performed
Gebaeudeverwaltung . . . administration of theater buildings
Geizige, Der . . . Molières **The Miser**
Geliebter Luegner . . . Kilty's **Dear Liar**
Gemaeldegalerie . . . art museum
Generalintendant . . . general director of a large theater complex
Gerettet . . . Bond's **Saved**
Gesamtkunstwerk . . . unified art work for the stage
Gespenster . . . Ibsen's **Ghosts**
Glueckliche Tage . . . Beckett's **Happy Days**
gnaedige Frau . . . a well-born lady
Grosses Haus . . . large theater or auditorium
Hausmeister, Der . . . Pinter's **The Caretaker**
heilige Johanna, Die . . . Shaw's **Saint Joan**
Heimkehr, Die . . . Pinter's **The Homecoming**
Herausgeber . . . editor
Hinterbuehne . . . rear stage
Hofburg . . . the Imperial palace in Vienna
Hofrat . . . a government advisor, at present, usually an honorary title
Hoftheater . . . court theater
Intendant . . . director of a theater complex
Intendanten plural of **Intendant**

Kammerspiel . . . chamber play; theater in which experimental pieces with small casts are performed
Komoedie im Dunkeln . . . Shaffer's **Black Comedy**
Kleines Haus . . . small theater or auditorium
Kroenung der Poppea, Die . . . Monteverdi's **L'Incoranazione di Poppea**
Kueche, Die . . . Wesker's **The Kitchen**
Kuenste . . . fine arts
Kuenstler . . . artist
Land . . . state
Landesregierung . . . state administration
langen Tages Reise in die Nacht, Eines . . . O'Neill's **Long Day's Journey into Night**
Leitmotiv . . . a musical phrase repeated and developed during the course of an opera
Leitmotive . . . plural of **Leitmotiv**
Leiter . . . leader, or director
Leuchtkunst . . . the art of stage lighting
Liebhaber, Der . . . Pinter's **The Caretaker**
Lied . . . song
Macht des Schicksals, Die . . . Verdi's **La forza del destino**
Mantel, Der . . . Puccini's **Il tabarro**
Margarethe . . . Gounod's **Faust**
Maskenball, Ein . . . Verdi's **Un ballo in maschera**
Mond fuer die Beladenen, Ein . . . O'Neill's **A Moon for the Misbegotten**
Musikverein . . . society for the performance of works of musical art
Nationaltheater . . . national theater; state theater
Nussknacker, Der . . . Tschaikovski's ballet **The Nutcracker**
O Wildness . . . O'Neill's **Ah, Wilderness**
Oberbaurat . . . a government advisor
Opernhaus . . . opera house
Oesterreich . . . Republic of Austria
Purpurstaub . . . O'Casey's **Purple Dust**
Preis, Der . . . Arthur Miller **The Price**
Presse . . . the press, newspapers
Pressebuero . . . press office
Rechtstraeger . . . agency which owns and operates a theater
Redoutensaal . . . large room in the **Hofburg** in which the Vienna **Staatsoper** stages chamber operas
Residenztheater . . . theater in the residential buildings of the rulers of a state, nation, country or empire
Ringstrasse . . . a series of streets in Vienna forming a ring around the old quarter of the city
Rollenboden . . . gridiron over the stage
Rundhorizont . . . stage cyclorama
Rundfunk . . . radio
Schauspiel . . . drama; theater in which spoken drama is performed
Scherenzug . . . two pantagraph-like devices which contract and expand like an accordion, carrying the two halves of an act curtain with them
Schlosstheater . . . theater in the castle at Schoenbrunn
Schriftleiter . . . editor
Schwanensee, Der . . . Tschaikovski's ballet **Swan Lake**
Schwarze Komoedie . . . Schaffer's **Black Comedy**
Schwestern, Drei . . . Chekhov's **The Three Sisters**
Seidene Schuh, Die . . . Claudel's **The Silken Slipper**
Seltsames Zwischenspiel . . . O'Neill's **Strange Interlude**

Sommernachtstraum, Ein . . . Shakespeare's **A Midsummer Night's Dream**

Spiel . . . Beckett's **Play**

Spielleiter . . . director of spoken drama; stage director for a musical or an opera

Spielplan . . . schedule of productions for a given period of time

Spielplaene . . . plural of **Spielplan**

Staatstheater . . . state theater; federal theater

Staedtische Buehnen . . . municipal theaters, city theaters

Stadtrat . . . city council

Strasse, Die . . . Elmer Rice's **Street Scene**

Trauer muss Elektra tragen . . . O'Neill's **Mourning Becomes Electra**

Verfremdungseffekt . . . effect of psychical distance between the audience and the performers in a theatrical production

Vergangenheitsbewaeltigung . . . an intellectualized understanding of past events of history

Verwaltung . . . administration

Warte, bis es dunkel ist . . . Knott's **Wait until Dark**

Warten auf Godot . . . Beckett's **Waiting for Godot**

Werbung . . . advertising

Wer hat Angst vor Virginia Woolf? . . . Albee's **Who's Afraid of Virginia Woolf?**

Wickelkonen . . . wrapping cones used to roll up a full stage cyclorama

Widerspenstigen Zaehnung . . . Shakespeare's **The Taming of the Shrew**

Zeitung . . . newspaper

Zofen, Die . . . Genet's **The Maids**

Appendix

A TYPICAL MONTH'S ACTIVITY IN THE EUROPEAN PROFESSIONAL THEATER: PRODUCTION SCHEDULES FROM A CROSS-SECTION OF THE GERMAN-LANGUAGE THEATERS, MID-MAY TO MID-JUNE, 1970.

The posters announcing the production schedules of a number of German, Austrian and Swiss theaters, from which the following photographs were made, were kindly furnished by Dr. Karl Richter, Redakteur, **Buehnen der Stadt Koeln.**

Stadttheater '69 70
Aachen

Generalintendant Peter Massmann

MAI/JUNI

Großes Haus				Kammerspiele/Nachtstudio		Voranzeigen	
Volpone oder Der Fuchs Komödie von Ben Jonson/Robert Gillner	Ltg.: Gillner, Stevens, Grams, Stein Mitw.: Iwanowitsch, Schink / Cohra, Hartmann, Kranz, La Doux Mahnert, Wilhelm, Wolff u. a.	19.30 bis 21.30	**23** Samstag	NACHTSTUDIO **Die Nacht der Mörder** von José Triana	PREMIERE Ltg.: Hildebrandt, Stevens 22.00 Mitw.: Bauer, Lienstädt, bis Luxem 23.15 Freier Verkauf	6., Samstag **BLICK VON DER BRÜCKE** 6., Samstag **HOFFMANNS ERZÄHLUNGEN** 6., Samstag **DER FISCHZUG/ DIE KLEINBÜR- GERHOCHZEIT**	19.30 Uhr, Christl. Abendl. Jugend 2 und Freier Verkauf 19.30 Uhr, Christl. Abendl. 2 u. 3 und Freier Verkauf 20.00 Uhr, Kammerspiele, Bühne Sa und Freier Verkauf
ROLF WANKA in Endspurt Ein biographisches Abenteuer von Peter Ustinov	Ltg.: Wagner, Engel, Grams Mitw.: Blume, Lienstädt, Schink, Schmidt/Cohra, La Doux, Mahnert, Musäus, Wilhelm	15.00 bis 17.00	**24** Sonntag	Des großen Erfolges wegen **O Susana** „Die schrecklichen jungen Mädchen" Komödie von Alfonso Paso	Ltg.: Hildebrandt, Stevens, Grams 20.00 Mitw.: Lienstädt, bis Sparnholt, Schink, 22.00 Schmidt/Cohra. La Doux, Freier Verkauf	7., Sonntag **BLICK VON DER BRÜCKE** 8., Montag **HOFFMANNS ERZÄHLUNGEN** 8., Montag **DER FISCHZUG/ DIE KLEINBÜR- GERHOCHZEIT**	20.00, Freier Verkauf 19.30 Uhr, Mo I-Abo und Freier Verkauf 20.00 Uhr, Kammerspiele, Christl. Abendl. 10. R, Ring/V u. Fr. Verk.
Aus der Arbeit des Balletts Training - Choreographie - Aufführung	Ltg.: Schnitzler, Massmann, Schrempp, Grams Mitw.: Greta Gutmann, Karin Wiegand/Srblalav Balac, Jens Sand, Peter Schnitzler und das verstärkte Ballett des Aachener Stadttheaters Freier Verkauf	20.00 bis 22.00					
Arabella Lyrische Komödie von Hofmannsthal/Strauss	Ltg.: Kaufmann, Massmann, Munz, Grams, Martin Mitw.: Franssen, Hinz, Krummel, Knoll, Lodge, Wormsdad, Zambelly / Böhme, Van Gemert, Suchsdorf, Thiessen, Tripp, Vogt, Waller u. a. Mo II-Abo u. Freier Verkauf	19.30 bis 22.15	**25** Montag	Des großen Erfolges wegen **O Susana** „Die schrecklichen jungen Mädchen" Komödie von Alfonso Paso	Besetzung siehe 24. 5. 20.00 bis Freier Verkauf 22.00	9., Dienstag **Gastspiel Royal Ballet** 9., Dienstag **DER FISCHZUG/ DIE KLEINBÜR- GERHOCHZEIT**	20.00, Freier Verkauf 20.00 Uhr, Kammerspiele, Christl. Abendl. 10. R, Ring/V u. Fr. Verk.
PREMIERE **Hoffmanns Erzählungen** Phantastische Oper von Jacques Offenbach	Ltg.: Martin, Wodehind, Munz, Grams, Schnitzler Mitw.: Hinz, Krummel, Jacobs, Vesterling, Wormsdad, Zambely/Böhme, Van Gemert, Jochem, Maurer, Suchsdorf, Thiessen, Tripp, Vogt, Zimmermann DI II-Abo und Freier Verkauf	19.30 bis 22.00	**26** Dienstag	**Der Fischzug/ Die Klein- bürgerhochzeit** Einakter von Bertolt Brecht	Ltg.: Wagner, Stevens, Grams, Stein 20.00 Mitw.: Iwanowitsch, bis Schink/Burschewski, 21.50 La Doux, Musäus, Theuring, Schwab u. a. Bühne DI u. Fr. Verkauf	10., Mittwoch **BLICK VON DER BRÜCKE** 10., Mittwoch **DER ARCHITEKT UND DER KAISER VON ASSYRIEN**	19.30, Bühne 4 und Freier Verkauf 22.00 Uhr, Nachtstudio Freier Verkauf
Arabella Lyrische Komödie von Hofmannsthal/Strauss	Besetzung siehe 25. 5. 20.00 Bühne 9 und Freier Verkauf 22.45		**27** Mittwoch			11., Donnerstag **ENDSPURT** 12., Freitag **BLICK VON DER BRÜCKE**	19.30, Christl. Abendl. 5 und Freier Verkauf 19.30, Christl. Abendl. 4 u. Freier Verkauf
Hoffmanns Erzählungen Phantastische Oper von Jacques Offenbach	Besetzung siehe 26. 5. 19.30 bis Bühne 1 und Freier Verkauf 22.00		**28** Donnerstag			13., Samstag **HOFFMANNS ERZÄHLUNGEN** 13., Samstag **DER FISCHZUG/ DIE KLEINBÜR- GERHOCHZEIT**	19.30, Sa-Abo. und Freier Verkauf 20.00 Kammerspiele, Sa-Abo. und Freier Verkauf
Volpone oder Der Fuchs Komödie von Ben Jonson/Robert Gillner	Besetzung siehe 23. 5. 19.30 Christl. Abendland 6 und bis Freier Verkauf 21.30		**29** Freitag			14., Sonntag **Ballett-Matinee** 14., Sonntag **VOLPONE ODER DER FUCHS** 14., Sonntag **VOLPONE ODER DER FUCHS**	11.00 Uhr Freier Verkauf 15.00 Sonntagnachmittags-Abo Bühne 11 und Freier Verkauf 19.30, Bühne 6 und Freier Verkauf
ROLF WANKA in Endspurt Ein biographisches Abenteuer von Peter Ustinov	Besetzung siehe 24. 5. 19.30 Bühne 5, Christl. Abendl. 7 und bis Freier Verkauf 21.30		**30** Samstag	**Die Nacht der Mörder** von José Triana	NACHTSTUDIO Besetzung siehe 23. 5. 22.00 bis Freier Verkauf 23.15	15., Montag **HOFFMANNS ERZÄHLUNGEN** 15., Montag **PARADIES AUF ERDEN**	19.30, Mo II-Abo, Jugend-Abo. und Freier Verkauf 20.00, Kammerspiele, Bühne 1 und Freier Verkauf
Hallo, Dolly! (Hello, Dolly!) Musical von Michael Stewart und Jerry Herman	Ltg.: Höfs. Stein, Herzeux, Martin, Schnitzler Mitw.: Aebach, Hohmann, Prössing, Vesterling, Worell/ Burkhardt, Niemeyer, Scholl, Schwab u. a. Bühne 3 und Freier Verkauf	15.00 bis 17.45	**31** Sonntag	Einmaliges Gastspiel des **Royal Ballet** The Royal Opera House, Covent Garden, London mit **Schwanensee** von Peter Tschaikowski am 9. Juni 1970 um 20.00 Uhr — Siehe Sonderplakat —		16., Dienstag **BLICK VON DER BRÜCKE** 17., Mittwoch **ARABELLA** 18., Donnerstag **DER BETTEL- STUDENT** 18., Donnerstag **PARADIES AUF ERDEN** 19., Freitag **BLICK VON DER BRÜCKE**	19.30, DI II-Abo. und Freier Verkauf 19.30, Bühne 7 und Freier Verkauf 19.30, Christl. Abendl. 8 und Freier Verkauf 20.00, Kammerspiele, Bühne 1 und Freier Verkauf 19.30 Uhr, Bühne 8 und Freier Verkauf
Hoffmanns Erzählungen Phantastische Oper von Jacques Offenbach	Besetzung siehe 26. 5. 20.00 bis Freier Verkauf 22.30						
Keine Vorstellung			**1** Montag				
Blick von der Brücke Drama von Arthur Miller	Ltg.: Köhler, Munz, Grams Mitw.: Bauer, Schmidt / La Doux, Mahnert, Niemeyer, Theuring u. a. DI I-Abo, Jugend-Abo u. Fr. Verkauf	19.30 bis 22.00	**2** Dienstag			Vorverkauf 6 Tage vor der Aufführung montags bis samstags 11—13 und 17—19 Uhr sonn- und feiertags 11—12.30 Uhr	
Blick von der Brücke Drama von Arthur Miller	Besetzung siehe 2. 6. 20.00 Mi-Abo, Jugend-Abo und bis Freier Verkauf 22.30		**3** Mittwoch	**Der Architekt u. der Kaiser von Assyrien** von Fernando Arrabal	NACHTSTUDIO PREMIERE Ltg.: Wagner, Stevens, 22.00 Grams, Schaefan bis Mitw.: Prochnow, Ueding 23.15 Freier Verkauf	Telefonische Bestellungen von 11.30—13.00 Uhr und von 17.30—19.00 Uhr unter 2 13 51 u. 3 72 11 Abonnementsbüro Theaterstraße 1—3: montags bis freitags 11—13 und 16—18 Uhr Vorbestellte Karten müssen 10 Minuten vor Beginn der Vorstellung abgeholt sein.	
Volpone oder Der Fuchs Komödie von Ben Jonson/Robert Gillner	Besetzung siehe 23. 5. 19.30 Do-Abo u. Freier Verkauf bis 21.30		**4** Donnerstag			Sonntag, 24. Mai 1970, 20.00 Uhr, Großes Haus Sonntag, 14. Juni 1970, 11.00 Uhr, Großes Haus **Aus der Arbeit des Balletts** Training - Choreographie - Aufführung	
Hoffmanns Erzählungen Phantastische Oper von Jacques Offenbach	Besetzung siehe 26. 5. 20.00 bis Fr-Abo und Freier Verkauf 22.30		**5** Freitag	**Der Architekt u. der Kaiser von Assyrien** von Fernando Arrabal	NACHTSTUDIO Besetzung siehe 3. 6. 22.00 bis Freier Verkauf 23.15	Programm: Ballett-Suite von Johann Sebastian Bach „Geschlossene Gesellschaft" nach Jean-Paul Sartre von Mathieu Nölis „Boléro" von Maurice Ravel Ausführende: Die Solisten und das verstärkte Ballett des Stadttheaters Aachen Leitung: Peter Schnitzler, Peter Massmann, Reinhard Schrempp	

one hundred twenty-one

STÄDTISCHE BÜHNEN
AUGSBURG 1969·70

STADTTHEATER   **KOMÖDIE**   **MARIONETTENTHEATER**

Freitag
29
Mai

20.00—22.15 Uhr; Beschränkter Verkauf · Jugendring A   Preise B 3.50 bis 13.50 DM

Der Graf Ory ZUM LETZTEN MALE IN DIESER SPIELZEIT

Oper von Gioacchino Rossini
Leitung: Voigt, Ebert, Karén, Keim-Strauß, Nowowiejski
Mitwirkende: Hempel, Karén, Menzel, Petersen; Bentrup, Finke, Kirschner, Matthias, R. Straub

---

Samstag
30
Mai

20.00—22.45 Uhr; Freier Verkauf · Platzmiete M   Preise C 3.— bis 11.50 DM
Preise C 3.— bis 11.50 DM

Die heilige Johanna ZUM LETZTEN MALE

Dramatische Chronik von George Bernard Shaw
Leitung: Eisel, Schmückle, Keim-Strauß
Mitwirkende: Röder, Seida, Bergler, Borns, Dittmann, G. Ebert, Engst, Götzfried, Heim, Jantsch,
Laugwitz, Meinhardt, Meyer, Michell, Peter, Reichelt, v. Roëll, Schulzki, Wäsche, Walther, Wehnert,
Zeller, Ziemann

Sonntag
31
Mai

20.00—22.45 Uhr; Freier Verkauf · Theater-Gem. 10   Preise B 3.50 bis 13.50 DM

Gräfin Mariza ZUM LETZTEN MALE

Operette von Emmerich Kálmán
Leitung: Hirsch, Juzek, Müller, Keim-Strauß, Nowowiejski, Goese
Mitwirkende: Briner a. G., Conradi, Peschka, Petersen; Bentrup, Graml, Schulzke, Schwarz,
Walther, Weaving a. G. · Liebhauser, Dietrich, Kaiser; Schmidt, Akin, Svoboda

11.00—12.45 Uhr; Freier Verkauf   Preise 1.50 bis 4.— DM

Kaspar

Sprechstück von Peter Handke
Leitung: Kleinseibeck, Grell/Warnecke (Klasse Prof. Heinrich, München)
Mitwirkende: Pichler; Beurle, Engst, Götzfried, Peter, v. Roëll, Schulzki

---

Montag
1
Juni

20.00—21.30 Uhr; Beschränkter Verkauf · Konzertmiete I; Theater-Gem. 74, 76
Preise B 3.50 bis 13.50 DM

X. Symphonie-Konzert
Ludwig van Beethoven
MISSA SOLEMNIS

Leitung: HANS ZANOTELLI
Solisten: AGNES GIEBEL, URSULA GUST,
HANS-DIETER ELLENBECK, HEINZ KLAUS ECKER
PHILHARMONISCHER CHOR AUGSBURG (Einstudierung: Hannsthomas Nowowiejski)

20.00—22.00 Uhr; Freier Verkauf · Theater-Gem. 35, 36   Preise 3.50 bis 7.— DM

Die Lokomotive

Lustspiel von André Roussin
Leitung: Eisel, Zircher, Keim-Strauß
Mitwirkende: Kubus, Menzel, Seida; Laugwitz, Meyer, Reichelt

Dienstag
2
Juni

20.00—21.30 Uhr; Freier Verkauf · Konzertmiete III; Theater-Gem. 77; Volksbühne-Gr. 22
Preise B 3.50 bis 13.50 DM

X. Symphonie-Konzert
Ludwig van Beethoven
MISSA SOLEMNIS

Leitung: HANS ZANOTELLI
Solisten: AGNES GIEBEL, URSULA GUST,
HANS-DIETER ELLENBECK, HEINZ KLAUS ECKER
PHILHARMONISCHER CHOR AUGSBURG (Einstudierung: Hannsthomas Nowowiejski)

20.00—22.00 Uhr; Freier Verkauf · Theater-Gem. 52   Preise 3.50 bis 7.— DM

Die Lokomotive

Lustspiel von André Roussin
Leitung: Eisel, Zircher, Keim-Strauß
Mitwirkende: Kubus, Menzel, Seida; Laugwitz, Meyer, Reichelt

Mittwoch
3
Juni

Keine Vorstellung

Donnerstag
4
Juni

Keine Vorstellung

Vorschau:

6. 6. Die Dreigroschenoper NEUINSZENIERUNG

7. 6. Die Dreigroschenoper

Eingt. Konzertmiete III
6. 6. VI. Kammer-Konzert (Nachholung vom 3. 4. 70)
Augsburger Kammermusikvereinigung

7. 6. Kaspar 11.00 Uhr ZUM LETZTEN MALE

7. 6. Die Entführung aus dem Serail 19.30 Uhr
GASTSPIEL IM STADTTHEATER INGOLSTADT

VORVERKAUF Stadttheater, Komödie, Kleiner Goldener Saal:
jeweils 2 Tage vor dem Vorstellungstag in der Kassenhalle des Stadttheaters, an Wochentagen von 10—13 Uhr, an Sonn- und Feiertagen von 11.30—13 Uhr.
Abendkasse eine halbe Stunde vor Beginn der Vorstellung. Telefonische Vorbestellungen an Wochentagen von 11—13 und 17—19 Uhr, an Sonn- und Feiertagen von 11.30—13 Uhr unter Nr. 2 84 85.

Druck: Joh. Walch, Augsburg, Zeugplatz

one hundred twenty-two

the ater

der Stadt Baden-Baden

Die schöne Helena

Operette für Schauspieler von Peter Hacks, Musik von Jacques Offenbach
Premiere am Freitag, 8. Mai 1970, 20.15 Uhr

Premiere am Freitag, 15. Mai 1970, 20.15 Uhr
Schauspiel von Marguerite Duras

Ganze Tage in den Bäumen

Spielplan-Kalender Mai 1970

8 Freitag, 20.15–22.15 Uhr, Premiere
Die schöne Helena
P und freier Verkauf, DM 3,– bis 15,–

9 Samstag, 20.15–22.15 Uhr
Die schöne Helena
SA und freier Verkauf, DM 3,– bis 15,–

10 Sonntag, 20.15–23.00 Uhr – Letzte Vorstellung
Die hl. Johanna der Schlachthöfe
VB und freier Verkauf, DM 3,– bis 15,–

11 Montag – Keine Vorstellung

12 Dienstag, 20.15–22.15 Uhr
Die schöne Helena
VB und freier Verkauf, DM 3,– bis 15,–

13 Mittwoch, 20.15–22.00 Uhr
Leonce und Lena
MF und freier Verkauf, DM 3,– bis 12,–

14 Donnerstag – Keine Vorstellung
Gastspiel in Speyer mit
Die schöne Helena

15 Freitag, 20.15–22.00 Uhr, Premiere
Im Kontrastprogramm
Ganze Tage in den Bäumen
Freier Verkauf, DM 3,– bis 12,– (VB 50%)

16 Samstag, 20.15–22.15 Uhr
Die schöne Helena
Freier Verkauf, DM 3,– bis 15,–

17 Sonntag, 20.15–22.45 Uhr – Letzte Vorstellung
Die Kaktusblüte
Freier Verkauf, DM 3,– bis 12,–

18 Montag, 20.15–22.00 Uhr
Leonce und Lena
Freier Verkauf, DM 3,– bis 12,–

19 Dienstag, 20.15–22.15 Uhr
Die schöne Helena
D und freier Verkauf, DM 3,– bis 15,–

20 Mittwoch, 20.15–22.15 Uhr
Die schöne Helena
M und freier Verkauf, DM 3,– bis 15,–

Ernst Koelblin KG Baden-Baden

21 Donnerstag, 20.15–22.15 Uhr
Die schöne Helena
DO und freier Verkauf, DM 3,– bis 15,–

22 Freitag – Keine Vorstellung

23 Samstag, 20.15 Uhr, Gastspiel
Tagebuch eines Wahnsinnigen
Städt. Bühne Heidelberg
Geschlossene Vorstellung

24 Sonntag, 20.15–22.15 Uhr
Die schöne Helena
SO und freier Verkauf, DM 3,– bis 15,–

25 Montag – Keine Vorstellung

26 Dienstag – Keine Vorstellung
Gastspiel in Böblingen mit
Der tolle Tag

27 Mittwoch, 20.15–22.15 Uhr
Die schöne Helena
MF und freier Verkauf, DM 3,– bis 15,–

28 Donnerstag – Keine Vorstellung

29 Freitag, 20.15–22.45 Uhr, Premiere
Der Wald
P und freier Verkauf, DM 3,– bis 15,–

30 Samstag, 20.15–22.45 Uhr
Der Wald
SA und freier Verkauf, DM 3,– bis 15,–

31 Sonntag, 15.00–16.45 Uhr
Leonce und Lena
SN, VB und freier Verkauf, DM 3,– bis 10,–

20.15–22.00 Uhr
Leonce und Lena
VB und freier Verkauf, DM 3,– bis 12,–

Auf dem Spielplan

Leonce und Lena
Lustspiel von Georg Büchner
Inszenierung: Günther Penzoldt
Bühnenbild und Kostüme: Katharina Witte

Heidi Berndt, Jutta Kästel, Lieselotte Prinz; Jan Aust,
Günther Backes, Karlheinz Büchi, Thomas Frey,
Werner Haindl, Manfred Hilbig, Rolf Hübner,
Gerhard Remus, Willi Schneider

Vorverkauf im Theater:
Dienstag bis Samstag von 10–13 und 16–18 Uhr; Sonntag von 11–13 Uhr; Tel. 27 52 60

Die schöne Helena
Operette für Schauspieler
von Peter Hacks, Musik von Jacques Offenbach
Inszenierung: Hannes Tannert
Bühnenbild und Kostüme: Hartmut Krügener
Musikalische Leitung: Werner v. Overheidt

Heidi Berndt, Sibylle von Eicke, Heide Eudenbach, Suzanne
Geyer, Jutta Kästel, Maria Majewski, Lieselotte Prinz,
Angelika Schneider; Peter Uwe Arndt, Günther Backes,
Karlheinz Büchi, Kurt Eichmann, Thomas Frey, Werner
Haindl, Alexander Höller, Manuel Armin Höhne, Rolf
Hübner, Gerhard Marcel, Hermann Röbeling, Willi
Schneider, Gian-Fadri Töndury, Peter Zeiller

Die Kaktusblüte
Komödie von Pierre Barillet und Jean-Pierre Grédy
Inszenierung: Hannes Tannert
Bühnenbild und Kostüme: Hartmut Krügener

Heidi Berndt, Carola Erdin, Charlotte Klinger;
Thomas Frey, Manfred Hilbig, Rolf Hübner, Hermann
Röbeling

Die hl. Johanna der Schlachthöfe
von Bertolt Brecht
Inszenierung: Günther Penzoldt
Bühnenbild und Kostüme: Hartmut Krügener

Barbara v. Annenkoff, Heidi Berndt, Sibylle von Eicke,
Carola Erdin, Suzanne Geyer, Jutta Kästel, Charlotte
Klinger, Lieselotte Prinz, Angelika Schneider; Peter Uwe
Arndt, Peter Arnold, Jan Aust, Günther Backes, Richard
Bohne, Karlheinz Büchi, Kurt Eichmann, Thomas Frey,
Werner Haindl, Manfred Hilbig, Manuel Armin Höhne,
Alexander Höller, Rolf Hübner, Gerhard Remus, Hermann
Röbeling, Willi Schneider, Arnulf Schumacher,
Gian-Fadri Töndury

Ganze Tage in den Bäumen
Schauspiel von Marguerite Duras
Inszenierung, Bühnenbild
und Kostüme: Michael Haneke

Suzanne Geyer, Annette Roland; Karlheinz Büchi,
Gerhard Remus

Der Wald
Komödie von Alexander Ostrowskij
Inszenierung: Rolf Hübner
Bühnenbild und Kostüme: Heinz Küpferle

Carola Erdin, Jutta Kästel, Annette Roland; Günther
Backes, Richard Bohne, Thomas Frey, Werner Haindl,
Manfred Hilbig, Alexander Höller, Gert Keller, Hermann
Röbeling

Basler Theater

Spielplan 29.5.—8.6.70

Stadttheater   Vorverkauf Telefon 24 19 65

Fr. 29. Mai 20.00 - 22.20 Uhr Fr. Abo. Nit. 179	**Einen Jux will er sich machen** von J. Nestroy Musik. Leitung: Czeipek; Regie: Davy; Ausstattung: Zimmermann mit Duhan, Gautschy, Koch, Melles, Renn, Stolle, Ziegler; Berger, Chen, Früh, Hofmann, Imbsweiler, Knapp, Kronlachner, Messerli, Pflegerl, Popp, Reinbacher, Rittermann, Ruf, Russius, Ryser
Sa. 30. Mai 20.00 - 22.30 Uhr	**Der Zigeunerbaron** von Johann Strauss Musik. Leitung: Czeipek; Regie: Holliger; Ausstattung: Schäfer; Choreographie: Knütter
So. 31. Mai 20.00 - 22.30 Uhr	Zum letzten Mal **Falstaff** von Giuseppe Verdi Musik. Leitung: Maurer; Regie: Markun; Ausstattung: Zimmermann; Chorleitung: Keuerleber mit Schuler, Sindik, Szirmay, Todorova; Bastian, Funken, Hanak, Henn, Kruse, Popp, Schwanbeck; Theaterchor
Mo. 1. Juni 20.00 - 22.30 Uhr Nit. 180	**Romeo und Julia** von Sergej Prokofieff Musik. Leitung: Rodmann; Choreographie: Sertic; Ausstattung: Mai mit Naranda, Häusel, Albus, Frei, Pellmont, Sagon, Heyde, Kunz; Zschach, Knütter, Hoppmann, Samm, Spoerli, Izrailowski, Kleiber, Keiser; Damen und Herren des Balletts
Di. 2. Juni 20.00 - 22.20 Uhr TGA	**Einen Jux will er sich machen** von J. Nestroy (Besetzung wie 29. Mai)
Mi. 3. Juni 20.00 - 22.30 Uhr Nit. 181	**Romeo und Julia** von Sergej Prokofieff (Besetzung wie 1. Juni)
Do. 4. Juni 20.00 - 22.30 Uhr Nit. 182	**Fidelio** von Ludwig van Beethoven Musik. Leitung: Löwlein; Regie: Schramm; Ausstattung: Schäfer; Chorleitung: Keuerleber mit Henn; Mc Jntyre, Diakov, Funken, Hanak, Jung, Kramp, Kruse, Mayall; Theaterchor
Fr. 5. Juni 20.00 - 22.20 Uhr Fremd. Abo. Nit. 183	**Einen Jux will er sich machen** von J. Nestroy (Besetzung wie 29. Mai)
Sa. 6. Juni 20.00 Uhr Prem. Abo.	**Die vier Grobiane** von E. Wolf-Ferrari Musik. Leitung: Löwlein; Regie: Babst; Ausstattung: Schäfer mit Berger, Gilhofer, Henn, Sindik; Diakov, Funken, Kramp, Kruse, Mayall, Simon
So. 7. Juni 20.00 - 22.20 Uhr Th. Verein-Abo. Nit. 184	**Einen Jux will er sich machen** von J. Nestroy (Besetzung wie 29. Mai)
Mo. 8. Juni 20.00 - 22.30 Uhr Nit. 185	Zum vorletzten Mal **Romeo und Julia** von Sergej Prokofieff (Besetzung wie 1. Juni)

Komödie   Vorverkauf Telefon 23 79 75

Fr. 29. Mai 20.15 - 21.50 Uhr Fr. Abo. Nit. 266, 267	**Des Ruzante Rede, so er vom Schlachtfeld kommen** von Ruzante Regie: Engels; Ausstattung: Schäfer mit Schoon; Holzner, Kunath, Scheibli **Die Paduanerin** von Ruzante Regie: Engels; Ausstattung: Schäfer mit Schoon; Holzner, Kunath, Peyer, Scheibli
Sa. 30. Mai 20.15 - 22.00 Uhr	**Mandragora** von Machiavelli Regie: Menzel; Ausstattung: Schäfer mit Renn, Thommen, Ziegler; Früh, Habich, Imbsweiler, Kronlachner, Peyer
So. 31. Mai 20.15 - 22.40 Uhr Nit. 268, 269	Nur noch 3 Vorstellungen **Warten auf Godot** von Samuel Beckett Regie: Bauer; Ausstattung: Meyer mit Beckmann, Brogle, Gogel, Kronlachner, Spirgi
Mo. 1. Juni 20.15 Uhr	6. Montag-Abend **Wo's Mühlenrad am Bach sich dreht** (Die Schweiz im Schullesebuch) von Paul Schorno
Di. 2. Juni 20.15 - 21.50 Uhr Di. Abo. Nit. 270, 271, 272	**Des Ruzante Rede, so er vom Schlachtfeld kommen** von Ruzante **Die Paduanerin** von Ruzante (Besetzung wie 29. Mai)
Mi. 3. Juni 20.15 - 22.00 Uhr Th. Verein-Abo. Nit. 273, 274	**Mandragora** von Machiavelli (Besetzung wie 30. Mai)
Do. 4. Juni 20.15 - 21.50 Uhr Do. Abo. + TGA Nit. 275, 276	Zum vorletzten Mal **Des Ruzante Rede, so er vom Schlachtfeld kommen** von Ruzante **Die Paduanerin** von Ruzante (Besetzung wie 29. Mai)
Fr. 5. Juni 20.15 - 21.50 Uhr ACV-Abo. + freier Verkauf Nit. 277	Zum letzten Mal **Des Ruzante Rede, so er vom Schlachtfeld kommen** von Ruzante **Die Paduanerin** von Ruzante (Besetzung wie 29. Mai)
Sa. 6. Juni 20.15 - 22.00 Uhr	**Mandragora** von Machiavelli (Besetzung wie 30. Mai)
So. 7. Juni 20.15 - 21.30 Uhr Komb. Abo. Nit. 278, 279, 280	Zum letzten Mal **Grosser Wolf** von Harald Mueller Regie: Babst; Bild: Mai mit Bihler, Hoffmann, Koll, Kummli, Mattèrn, Peter, Peyer, Steck
Mo. 8. Juni 20.15 - 22.40 Uhr Nit. 281, 282	Zum vorletzten Mal **Warten auf Godot** von Samuel Beckett (Besetzung wie 31. Mai)
Telefonische Spielplanvorschau	**22 09 10**

Vorverkauf

Öffnungszeiten: werktags 10.00 -12.30 Uhr
und 15.00 -18.45 Uhr; sonntags 10.30 -11.45 Uhr.
Schriftliche Bestellungen für alle
angezeigten Vorstellungen.
Billettvorverkauf
an der Kasse und telefonische Bestellung
jeweils nur 5 Tage vor der betreffenden Aufführung
(inkl. Vorstellungstag).

DEUTSCHE OPER BERLIN

30. Mai bis 10. Juni 1970

Sonnabend 30. Mai 19.30 bis nach 22.15 Uhr Runde III vom 21.4.	**La Traviata** (in italienischer Sprache) Beschränkter Kartenverkauf Preisgruppe B Oper in 3 Akten von Francesco Maria Piave · Musik von Giuseppe Verdi	Leitung: Maazel — Sellner — Sanjust — Hagen-Groll Damen: Weathers, Wisniewska, Mikes Herren: Alva, Murray, Mercker, Dicks Röhrl, Sardi, Barrera, Clam, Weber
Sonntag 31. Mai 18.00 bis nach 22.30 Uhr Runde I vom 10.4.	**Tristan und Isolde** Preisgruppe B von Richard Wagner	Leitung: Zanotelli — W. Wagner — Hagen-Groll Damen: Kuchta, Caporale Herren: Beirer, Greindl, Feldhoff, McDaniel Krebs, Vantin, Koffmane
Montag 1. Juni 20.00 — 22.00 Uhr Runde I	**Ballettabend** Preisgruppe A **Opus I** (Musik: A. Webern) **Episodes** (Musik: A. Webern) **When summoned** (Musik: M. Subotnick) **Susi Cremecheese** (Musik: F. Zappa)	Leitung: Lawrence — Cranko — Balanchine — Evans — Kresnik Damen: Seymour a.G., Carli, Kesselheim, Jahnke, Evdokimova Radamm, Binner, Dubois Herren: Beelitz, Holz, Kapuste, Frey, Job, Barra, Dimitrievitch
Dienstag 2. Juni 20.00 — 21.45 Uhr Runde I	**Elektra** Preisgruppe A Tragödie in 1 Akt · Musik von Richard Strauss	Leitung: Kraus — Völker — Reinking Damen: Kuchta, Caporale, Weathers, Tasset, Little-Augustithis Mikes, Oelke, Weiss, Otto, Dzakis, Noel Herren: Stewart, Melchert, Lang, van Dijk, Weber
Mittwoch 3. Juni 20.00 bis nach 22.00 Uhr Runde I	**200 000 Taler** Preisgruppe A Oper in 3 Bildern und einem Epilog nach Scholem Alejchem von Boris Blacher	Leitung: Hollreiser — Sellner — Maximowna Damen: Mödl, Weiss, Mikes — Herbeth Herren: Reich, Haefliger, Feldhoff, Neralić, Krukowski Mercker, van Dijk, Koffmane, Frenzel
Donnerstag 4. Juni 19.00 — 22.15 Uhr Runde I	**Don Giovanni** (in italienischer Sprache) Beschränkter Kartenverkauf Preisgruppe A Oper in 2 Akten · Musik von Wolfgang Amadeus Mozart	Leitung: Patané — Ebert — Wakhevitch — Hagen-Groll Damen: Weathers, Wyckoff, Köth Herren: Stewart, Haefliger, Neralić, Sardi, Lang
Freitag 5. Juni 20.00 bis gegen 22.15 Uhr Runde I	Carl Orff Preisgruppe A **Catulli carmina / Carmina burana** Lieder des Catull Gesänge aus Benediktbeuren	Leitung: Jochum — Sellner/Darrell — Otto — Hagen-Groll Damen: Thomaz — Cito, Jahnke, Kohavi, Dubois, Peters, Karol Herren: Haefliger, Vantin, Fortune, Krukowski Beelitz, Holz, Kapuste, Dimitrievitch, Bohner, Job
Sonnabend 6. Juni 18.30 — 22.30 Uhr Runde III vom 20.4.	**Tannhäuser** Beschränkter Kartenverkauf Preisgruppe B Große Romantische Oper in 3 Akten von Richard Wagner	Leitung: Patané — Kelch — Hill — Hagen-Groll — Reinholm Damen: Norman a.G., Little-Augustithis, Jasper Iseler, Tettenborn, Profé, Wonneberger Herren: Beirer, Greindl, Fortune, Mercker, Lang van Dijk, Röhrl
Sonntag 7. Juni 19.30 — 22.00 Uhr Runde I	Neuinszenierung Preisgruppe B **Ariadne auf Naxos** Beschränkter Kartenverkauf Oper in einem Aufzug und einem Vorspiel · Musik von Richard Strauss	Leitung: Jochum — Sellner — Svoboda — Skalicky Damen: Lear, Gayer, Ligendza, Otto, Wagner, Weiss Herren: Melchert, Feldhoff, Hering, Barrera, Krebs, Clam Koffmane, McDaniel, Driscoll, van Dam, Vantin
Montag 8. Juni 19.30 bis nach 22.15 Uhr Runde II	**Fidelio** Beschränkter Kartenverkauf Preisgruppe A Oper in 2 Akten · Musik von Ludwig van Beethoven	Leitung: Jochum — Sellner — Reinking — Hagen-Groll Damen: Kuchta, Köth Herren: Beirer, von Halem, Neralić, Greindl Mercker, McDaniel, Weber
Dienstag 9. Juni 19.30 — 22.45 Uhr Runde II	BALLETTABEND **Apollon musagète** (Musik von Igor Strawinsky) Preisgruppe A **Labyrinth der Wahrheit** (Musik von Edgar Varèse) **Solitaire** (Musik von Malcolm Arnold) **Le Corsaire** (Musik von Ricardo Drigo) **Aimez-vous Bach?** (Musik von Johann Sebastian Bach)	Leitung: Lawrence — Balanchine — Gsovsky/Aratym MacMillan — Petipa — MacDonald Damen: Seymour a.G., A. Holmes a.G., Kesselheim, Cito Jahnke, Evdokimova, Radamm, Dubois Herren: D. Holmes a.G., Beelitz, Kapuste, Holz, Frey, Marcus Dimitrievitch, Bohner, Job
Mittwoch 10. Juni 19.30 — 22.00 Uhr Runde II	**Ariadne auf Naxos** Beschränkter Kartenverkauf Preisgruppe B Oper in einem Aufzug und einem Vorspiel · Musik von Richard Strauss	Leitung: Jochum — Sellner — Svoboda — Skalicky Damen: Lear, Gayer, Ligendza, Otto, Wagner, Weiss Herren: Melchert, Feldhoff, Hering, Barrera, Krebs, Clam Koffmane, McDaniel, Driscoll, van Dam, Vantin

DEUTSCHE OPER BERLIN · CHARLOTTENBURG, BISMARCKSTRASSE 34-37 · GENERALINTENDANT G. R. SELLNER
Vorverkauf von 10-14 Uhr und 1 bis 1/2 Stunde vor Beginn der Vorstellung, ab Sonntag für Donnerstag bis Sonntag;
ab Donnerstag für Montag bis Mittwoch (Sonntag und Donnerstag keine telefonischen Bestellungen) Telefon: Billettkasse 344449, Verwaltung 340181

Druck: G. Kalesse, Berlin 62 · Entwurf: W. Reinking

WEST-BERLINER BÜHNEN

one hundred twenty-six

Komödie
Kurfürstendamm 206 · Telefon 881 38 93

Täglich 20 Uhr (außer montags)
Deutsche Erstaufführung
Auf und davon
Komödie v. Peter Yeldham · Deutsch: Nina Adler-Ursuliak

Vorverkauf täglich 10–12 und ab 18.30 Uhr an der Theaterkasse (Tel 88 38 93) und an den bekannten Vorverkaufsstellen

Theater am Kurfürstendamm
Kurfürstendamm 209 · Telefon 881 24 89

Täglich 20 Uhr · 30. Mai 18 · 21 Uhr
Deutsche Erstaufführung
Vier Fenster zum Garten
Komödie von Pierre Barillet und Jean Pierre Grédy · Deutsch von Charles Regnier

tribüne
am Ernst-Reuter-Platz · Telefon 34 26 00

Täglich 20 Uhr (außer montags)
Ich bin nicht der Eiffelturm
Komödie von Ecaterina Oproiu · Deutsch: Josefina Czollek

29. Mai, 1. 5. Juni täglich 10 Uhr
NEUES JUGENDTHEATER
Der Schatz von Ba Ba Lu
Jugendstück von Norbert Langer · Regie Norbert Langer

Berliner Theater
Nürnberger Straße 50–52 · Telefon 24 24 44

Täglich 20 Uhr · 2. Juni · 50 ×
Staatsbesuch
The Sleeping Prince · von Terence Rattigan · Deutsch: A. u. P. Capell

Schaubühne am Halleschen Ufer
Hallesches Ufer 32 · Tel. 16 30 16, 18 17 66

Täglich 20 Uhr (außer 1, 7, 8, 9 Juni)
Das Knochenhaus

Forum-Theater
Kurfürstendamm · Ecke Knesebeckstraße 881 79 47

Täglich 20 Uhr
Der Selbstmörder
von Nikolai R. Erdmann

Berliner Kammerspiele
Tel. 391 55 43 · Theater der Jugend Alt-Moabit 99

Der fliegende Teppich

Theater des Westens
Kantstraße 12 · Telefon 32 11 12 / 31 70 51

Täglich 20 Uhr
Die Csardasfürstin
von Emmerich Kálmán

Vaganten-Bühne
Kantstraße 12a (am Zoo) · Telefon 312 45 29

Geschlossene Gesellschaft
von Jean-Paul Sartre

1. Juni 20 Uhr
Romeo und Jeanette
von Jean Anouilh

Die Aula

Mooney's Wohnwagen

Biedermann und die Brandstifter
von Max Frisch

Deutsche Oper Berlin
Bismarckstraße · Kasse 34 44 49 · Vorstellung 34 01 81

Freitag 29.
19.30 Uhr
Die Entführung aus dem Serail

30. Mai
La Traviata

31. Mai Sonntag
Tristan und Isolde
von Richard Wagner

1. Juni Montag
Ballett modern
Elektra

2. Juni
200.000 Taler

3. Juni Mittwoch
Tannhäuser

4. Juni Donnerstag
Don Giovanni

5. Juni Freitag
Carl Orff Catulli carmina / Carmina burana

6. Juni Sonnabend
Ariadne auf Naxos

7. Juni Sonntag
Fidelio

8. Juni Montag
Ballettabend

9. Juni Dienstag
Sergej Obraszow

Schiller-Theater Werkstatt
Bismarckstraße 110 · Telefon 31 06 61

Schiller-Theater
Bismarckstraße 110 · Telefon 31 06 61

Faust II
Der Floh im Ohr
Kabale und Liebe
Emilia Galotti
Des Teufels General
Katharina Knie
Der Frieden
Yvonne, Prinzessin von Burgund

Schloßpark-Theater
Steglitz, Schloßstraße 48 · Telefon 791 12 13

Freunde und Feinde
Gespenster
Der Floh im Ohr
Change
Haus Herzenstod
Hidalla
Das letzte Band von Samuel Beckett

Freie Volksbühne
Berlin 15, Schaperstraße 24 · Telefon 881 37 42

Play Strindberg
von Friedrich Dürrenmatt

Tabula rasa
von Carl Sternheim

Renaissance-Theater
Hardenbergstraße 6 · Tel. 312 42 02 / 312 28 87

Gastspiele und Liebe

Hebbel-Theater
Stresemannstraße 29 · Telefon 18 22 12

Play Strindberg
von Friedrich Dürrenmatt

Tabula rasa
von Carl Sternheim

Schauspielhaus Hansa
391 44 60 · Berliner Volkstheater · Alt-Moabit 48

Tabula rasa
von Carl Sternheim

Herr im Haus bin ich

Tabula rasa
von Carl Sternheim

Panik bei Tag

ⓘ Theater mit Schwerhörigenanlage

Berner Theater

Stadttheater

Direktor: Volker Glaser

2. Juni Dienstag
Caligula
Schauspiel von Albert Camus

3. Juni Mittwoch
Zum letztenmal
Die Geschichte von Aucassin und Nicolette
Oper von Erdmann Warnke

4. Juni Donnerstag
Caligula
Schauspiel von Albert Camus

5. Juni Freitag
Zum letztenmal
Liebe für Liebe
Komödie von William Congreve

6. Juni Samstag
Zum 25. Mal
Die Fledermaus
Operette von Johann Strauss

7. Juni Sonntag
Don Carlos
Oper von Giuseppe Verdi

8. Juni Montag
Vergessene Kostbarkeit
Schwänke von Albert Camus

Einführungsabend
Titus

Voranzeige
16. Juni Dienstag
Premiere
Titus

Spielplan
von 9. bis 16. Juni

Unsere Theaterbesucher finden Parkmöglichkeiten im **Rathaus-Parking**

atelier theater

Direktion: Ernst Ernsthoft

Montag, 1. Juni
Letzte Vorstellung
Kurt Tucholsky Rheinsberg

Schweizer Erstaufführung
Kinder des Schattens
Komödie von Karl Wittlinger

theater am käfigturm

Festival Theater am Geländer, Prag

8. Premiere
Montag
Timon von Athen — Schauspielgruppe
von William Shakespeare

9. Dienstag
Premiere
Der Knopf — Pantomimengruppe
von Ladislav Fialka

10. Mittwoch
Westliche Erstaufführung
Die Rache einer russischen Waise — Schauspielgruppe

11. Donnerstag
Der Weg — Pantomimengruppe
von Ladislav Fialka

12. Freitag
Westliche Erstaufführung
Der Kaiser und der Architekt — Schauspielgruppe

13. Samstag
Premiere
Pantomime am Geländer — Pantomimengruppe

14. Sonntag
Westliche Erstaufführung
Die Rache einer russischen Waise — Schauspielgruppe

Beginn aller Vorstellungen 20.30 Uhr

kleintheater kramgasse 6

Direktion: Thomas Nydas
Schweizer Erstaufführung

Abaelard und Héloïse

Spuk — Spott — Groteske

Robert Musil

François Lilienfeld — neues Programm

z.B. Mikis Theodorakis

die Rampe

Kramgasse 56. Leitung: Bernhard Stettenmann

Nur 4 Vorstellungen
1./4./5. und 6. Juni, je 20.30 Uhr

Höhe 493

Werner Lässer

Vietnam ist unser Nachbar. Geographisch, politisch, moralisch. Vietnam ist auch unser Kriegsschauplatz. Am Beispiel des Vietnamkrieges zeigt der Autor die Unmenschlichkeit des Krieges überhaupt.

one hundred twenty-seven

Städtische Bühnen Bielefeld

Stadttheater   Theater am Alten Markt

---

20 — 22.40 Uhr | Platzmiete **S**₁₂ und freier Verkauf | **Samstag 30** Mai | **20 — 21.45 Uhr** ERSTAUFFÜHRUNG | Freier Verkauf

Cosi fan tutte
Komische Oper von Wolfgang Amadeus Mozart
Henke — Hosenfeldt — Gruner a. G. — Zimmermann
Barnett, Höbel, Reppel
Constantino, Rosendorff, Schulte

ANDORRA
Schauspiel von Max Frisch
Schneider a. G. — Plänker — Schulz
de Vries, Funke, Klimm, Pusch
Böhre, Cremer, Gehrmann, Günther, Hoffmann, Korn,
Radloff, Starcke-Brauer, Wolff

---

20 — 22.20 Uhr | Freier Verkauf | **Sonntag 31** Mai | **20 Uhr** | Freier Verkauf

Annie get your gun
Musical von Irving Berlin
Henke — Spongler — Hosenfeldt — Steigerwald — Zimmermann — Schulz
Christ, Mayer, Neuhaus, Umlauf
Baasner, Cremer, Frings, Gerhardt, Götze, Misserre, Radloff, Skoludek, Wege
Werkowska, Wolf — Geisendörfer, Neven-Zelic

GASTSPIEL DER STÄDTISCHEN BÜHNEN ESSEN
anläßlich der Tage des zeitgenössischen Theaters
MARIE IM PELZ
von Shuji Terayama
Deutsch von Manfred Hubricht

---

20 — 22.30 Uhr | Geschlossene Vorstellung für die Volksbühne „E" blau „F" rot Abschnitt 10 | **Montag 1** Juni | **20 — 21.45 Uhr** | Geschlossene Vorstellung für den Jugendkulturring

Macbeth
Oper von Giuseppe Verdi
Dress — Weber a. G. — Heyduck a. G. — Schulz — Zimmermann
Höbel, Schürmann, Seidler-Winkler, Zimmermann
Assmann, Capellmann, Fiorito, Kassel, Miserre, Petrov

Andorra
Schauspiel von Max Frisch

---

20 — 22.45 Uhr | Platzmiete **A**₁₃ und freier Verkauf | **Dienstag 2** Juni | **20 — 21.45 Uhr** | Platzmiete **E**₁₂ und freier Verkauf

Der Wüstling
(THE RAKE'S PROGRESS)
Oper von Igor Strawinsky
Dress — Kindermann — Plänker — Zimmermann — Geisendörfer
Höbel, Lorek, Promonti
Fiorito, Kassel, Miserre, Panzner, Petrov
Haiden - Fahrer, Muhar

Andorra
Schauspiel von Max Frisch

---

20 Uhr EINMALIGES GASTSPIEL | Freier Verkauf | **Mittwoch 3** Juni | **20 — 21.45 Uhr** | Platzmiete **F**₁₁ und freier Verkauf

AUS MANGEL AN BEWEISEN
Schauspiel von Giulio del Torre
mit Hilde Krahl und Hannes Messemer
BERLINER TOURNEE   SIEHE SONDERPLAKAT

KONZERT DES PHILHARMONISCHEN ORCHESTERS IN BAD OEYNHAUSEN

Andorra
Schauspiel von Max Frisch

---

20 — 22.45 Uhr | Platzmiete **G**₁₂ und freier Verkauf | **Donnerstag 4** Juni | **11.30 — 13.15 Uhr** | Geschlossene Vorstellung

Cosi fan tutte
Komische Oper von Wolfgang Amadeus Mozart
Ferrando: Wolfram Assmann

Andorra
Schauspiel von Max Frisch

20 — 21.45 Uhr | Platzmiete **C**₁₁ und freier Verkauf

Andorra
Schauspiel von Max Frisch

| | **Freitag 5** Juni | **20 Uhr** | Freier Verkauf

Keine Vorstellung

GASTSPIEL DER STÄDTISCHEN BÜHNEN DORTMUND
anläßlich der Tage des zeitgenössischen Theaters
AMERIKA, HURRA!
Drei Einakter von Jean-Claude van Itallie

---

20 — 22.45 Uhr GASTSPIEL ULRICH GENTZEN ZUM LETZTEN MALE | Freier Verkauf | **Samstag 6** Juni | **20 — 21.45 Uhr** | Platzmiete **Z**₁₂ und freier Verkauf

Mein Freund Bunbury
Ein Musical von Helmut Bez und Jürgen Degenhardt
Musik von Gerd Natschinski
Henke — Stelter — Herrmann a. G. — Steigerwald a. G. — Geisendörfer — Zimmermann
Bachmann, Christ a. G., Höbel, Mayer, Seydewitz, Werkowska, Wirth u. a.
Baasner, Capellmann, Frings, Gerhardt, Miserre, Skoludek, Wege u. a.

Andorra
Schauspiel von Max Frisch

---

20 — 22.20 Uhr | Freier Verkauf | **Sonntag 7** Juni | **20 — 21.40 Uhr** | Freier Verkauf

Annie get your gun
Musical von Irving Berlin

Der eingebildete Kranke
Komödie von Molière
Reinke — Plänker — Hasenpusch — Mors
Jelisch, Vetsch, de Vries
Böhre, Gehrmann, Günther, Korn, Röhr, Starcke-Brauer, Steig, Weisser

---

Montag, 8. 6. Keine Vorstellung
Dienstag, 9. 6. Cosi fan tutte JKR u. FK
Mittwoch, 10. 6. Keine Vorstellung
Donnerstag, 11. 6. Der Wüstling **C**₁₃
(The Rake's Progress)
Freitag, 12. 6. Keine Vorstellung
Samstag, 13. 6. Der Vogelhändler (Premiere)
Sonntag, 14. 6. Gastspiel münchener antitheater

IN VORBEREITUNG:

PREMIEREN:

Der Vogelhändler
Operette von Carl Zeller

(13. Juni 1970 - Stadttheater)

Montag, 8. 6. Andorra 11.30 Uhr (Geschl. Vorst.)
Die Heiratsurkunde VB
Dienstag, 9. 6. Andorra **A**₁₁
Mittwoch, 10. 6. Andorra 11.30 Uhr (Geschl. Vorst.)
Andorra **B**₁₁
Donnerstag, 11. 6. Andorra **G**₁₁
Freitag, 12. 6. Andorra **D**₁₁
Samstag, 13. 6. Gastspiel Staatstheater Braunschweig
Sonntag, 14. 6. Andorra **So**₁₁

VORVERKAUF nur werktags: Für Vorstellungen im Stadttheater von 10.30 bis 13.00 Uhr und von 17.00 Uhr bis ½ Stunde vor Beginn der Vorstellung. Für Vorstellungen im Theater am Alten Markt von 10.30 bis 13.00 Uhr und von 17.00 bis 18.30 Uhr an der Kasse im Stadttheater. An Sonn- und Feiertagen Verkauf nur für die jeweilige Abendvorstellung eine Stunde vor Beginn. Montag geschlossen. Telefonische Kartenvorbestellungen nur über direkten Postanschluß 6 87 87. Vorbestellte Karten sind bis 13.00 Uhr des Vorstellungstages abzuholen, für Sonn- und Feiertage bis 18.30 Uhr des Vortages.
Druck: Sievert & Sieveking

one hundred twenty-eight

SCHAUSPIELHAUS·BOCHUM
HANS SCHALLA

SCHAUSPIELHAUS

DONNERSTAG
21. Mai
20.00 — 23.15 Uhr
Aufführung des Musiktheaters im Revier, Gelsenkirchen
MY FAIR LADY
Nach G. B. Shaws „Pygmalion" und dem Film von Gabriel Pascal — Bochumer Symphoniker
Bach von A. J. Lerner, Musik von F. Loewe — Deutsch von R. Gilbert
Inszenierung: Scheffler / Roth / Meyer / Kottner / Asbeck / Kim
Darsteller: Döltzsch, Goll, Kaufhold, Kleiber — Cahoy, Dani, Edwards, Finkelberg, Krüger, Lucon, Sraurwald, Zell
Ballett: Hislatscheva, Lichtenthäler, Serrano — Damen und Herren des Balletts

Theaterring Bochum — Gruppe II und freier Verkauf — Preise I

FREITAG
22. Mai
20.00 — 22.30 Uhr
DER RAUB DER SABINERINNEN
Schwank von Franz und Paul von Schönthan
Inszenierung: Zeiner / Steiger / Szalla / von Troeck
Darsteller: Manjan, Papula, Schanzara, Zietsche — Clausen, Ehlers, Jacobsen, Schick, Schloese, Uttendörfer

Theaterring Bochum — Gruppe IV und freier Verkauf — Preise I

SONNABEND
23. Mai
20.00 — 23.15 Uhr
Aufführung des Musiktheaters im Revier, Gelsenkirchen
MY FAIR LADY
Nach G. B. Shaws „Pygmalion" und dem Film von Gabriel Pascal — Bochumer Symphoniker

Außer Vormiete — Preise I

SONNTAG
24. Mai
20.00 — 23.15 Uhr
Aufführung des Musiktheaters im Revier, Gelsenkirchen
MY FAIR LADY
Nach G. B. Shaws „Pygmalion" und dem Film von Gabriel Pascal — Bochumer Symphoniker

Theaterring Bochum — Gruppe VII und freier Verkauf — Preise I

MONTAG
25. Mai
20.00 — 22.30 Uhr
DER RAUB DER SABINERINNEN
Schwank von Franz und Paul von Schönthan

Theaterring Bochum — Gruppe VIII und freier Verkauf — Preise I

DIENSTAG
26. Mai
20.00 — 22.30 Uhr
DER RAUB DER SABINERINNEN
Schwank von Franz und Paul von Schönthan

Theaterring Bochum — Gruppe IX und freier Verkauf — Preise I

MITTWOCH
27. Mai
20.00 — 22.45 Uhr
ZUM ERSTEN MAL
GUERILLAS
Tragödie von Rolf Hochhuth
Inszenierung: Schalla / Szalla / von Troeck / Seimert
Darsteller: Alvo, Amos, Violet, Watz, Fork — Adler, Arnswald, Borek, Cossarili, Dorner, Gassen, Hauer, Heinz, Hochhuth, Hradek, Kluss, Kahl, Leuthen, Mack, Söder, Snikach, Steib, Sterzenbach, Strehlen, Trefenstrunner, Amswar-Boodu

Vormiete L 12. Vorstellung und freier Verkauf — Preise I

DONNERSTAG
28. Mai (Fronleichnam)
20.00 — 22.00 Uhr
12. HAUPTKONZERT
WOLFGANG AMADEUS MOZART: Symphonie Nr. 23 in D-dur, KV. 181 — Ausführende: Bochumer Symphoniker
JEAN SIBELIUS: Konzert für Violine und Orchester in d-moll, op. 47 — Solist: Ricardo Odnoposoff, Violine, Wien
DIMITRI SCHOSTAKOWITSCH: Symphonie Nr. 9 in Es-dur, op. 70 — Leitung: Othmar M. F. Mága

Konzertreihe A — Preise 4., 5., 6., 7., 8.— DM — Schülerkarten nur an der Abendkasse

FREITAG
29. Mai
20.00 — 22.00 Uhr
WIEDERHOLUNG 12. HAUPTKONZERT

Konzertreihe B — Preise 4., 5., 6., 7., 8.— DM — Schülerkarten nur an der Abendkasse

SONNABEND
30. Mai
20.00 — 22.15 Uhr
Aufführung des Musiktheaters im Revier, Gelsenkirchen
BLUTHOCHZEIT
Oper von Wolfgang Fortner — Bochumer Symphoniker
Inszenierung: Romansky / Roth / Meyer / Asbeck / Kluss
Darsteller: Döltzsch, Dominguez, Estlinbaum, Goll, Green, Griesenbach, Heitbrink, Karrusch, Kleiber, Kolbkowski, Schröder, Schubert, Schulte-Grewe, Weberling — Braun, Cahoy, Ehrich, Faubltich, Finkelberg, Hocke, Kunzmann, Thompson, Zell — Damen und Herren des Balletts

Vormiete E 12 Vorstellung und freier Verkauf — Preise I

SONNTAG
31. Mai
20.00 — 22.30 Uhr
DER RAUB DER SABINERINNEN
Schwank von Franz und Paul von Schönthan

Theaterring Bochum — Gruppe II und freier Verkauf — Preise I

MONTAG
1. Juni
20.00 — 22.15 Uhr
Aufführung des Musiktheaters im Revier, Gelsenkirchen
BLUTHOCHZEIT
Oper von Wolfgang Fortner — Bochumer Symphoniker

Vormiete A 13. Vorstellung und freier Verkauf — Preise I

DIENSTAG
2. Juni
20.00 — 22.45 Uhr
GUERILLAS
Tragödie von Rolf Hochhuth

Kulturgemeinde Witten — Serie A und freier Verkauf — Preise I

MITTWOCH
3. Juni
20.00 — 22.45 Uhr
GUERILLAS
Tragödie von Rolf Hochhuth

Kulturgemeinde Witten — Serie B und freier Verkauf — Preise I

DONNERSTAG
4. Juni
20.00 — 22.45 Uhr
GUERILLAS
Tragödie von Rolf Hochhuth

Vormiete F 14. Vorstellung und freier Verkauf — Preise I

FREITAG
5. Juni
20.00 — 22.30 Uhr
DER RAUB DER SABINERINNEN
Schwank von Franz und Paul von Schönthan

Theaterring Bochum — Gruppe VII und freier Verkauf — Preise I

SONNABEND
6. Juni
20.00 — 22.30 Uhr
Aufführung des Musiktheaters im Revier, Gelsenkirchen
DER TROUBADOUR
Oper von Giuseppe Verdi
Inszenierung: Möls./ Roth / Meyer / Asbeck — Orchester der Stadt Gelsenkirchen
Darsteller: Döltzsch, Hönig, Schubert — Becker, Brodowka, Ristow, Stauren, Thompson, Ziemann

Vormiete E 13. Vorstellung und freier Verkauf — Preise I

KAMMERSPIELE

DONNERSTAG
21. Mai
20.00 — 22.30 Uhr
VICTOR ODER DIE KINDER AN DER MACHT
Bürgerliches Schauspiel von Roger Vitrac in der Einrichtung von Jean Anouilh — Deutsch von Hella Kralewski
Darsteller: Drüge, Hänsch, Keyssler, Stein, Twiesselmann — Adler, Arnswald, Hauer, Heinz, Schmidt

Vormiete Serie I 7. Vorstellung und freier Verkauf — Preise: 3,50; 5,50; 8.— DM

FREITAG
22. Mai
20.00 — 22.30 Uhr
VICTOR ODER DIE KINDER AN DER MACHT
Bürgerliches Schauspiel von Roger Vitrac in der Einrichtung von Jean Anouilh — Deutsch von Hella Kralewski

Vormiete Serie V 8. Vorstellung und freier Verkauf — Preise: 3,50; 5,50; 8.— DM

SONNABEND
23. Mai
20.00 — 22.15 Uhr
ZUM ERSTEN MAL
AUF UND DAVON
Komödie von Peter Yeldham — Deutsch von Nino Adler und Ursula Lyn
Inszenierung: Steiger / Fritzsche / Boensing
Darsteller: Gorden, Siemers, Stein — Borner, Groth, Küttemeyer, Mikolet

Außer Vormiete — Preise: 3,50; 5,50; 8.— DM

SONNTAG
24. Mai
20.00 — 22.15 Uhr
GARTEN DER LÜSTE
von Fernando Arrabal — Deutsch von Kurt Klinger — Inszenierung: de Boer / Szalla / Andriassen / Seimert
Darsteller: Amm, Garten, Rigauer, Sterzenbach

Außer Vormiete — Preise: 3,50; 5,50; 8.— DM

MONTAG
25. Mai
20.00 — 22.30 Uhr
VICTOR ODER DIE KINDER AN DER MACHT
Bürgerliches Schauspiel von Roger Vitrac in der Einrichtung von Jean Anouilh — Deutsch von Hella Kralewski

Vormiete Serie VI 9. Vorstellung und freier Verkauf — Preise: 3,50; 5,50; 8.— DM

FREITAG
29. Mai
20.00 — 22.15 Uhr
GARTEN DER LÜSTE
von Fernando Arrabal — Deutsch von Kurt Klinger

Vormiete Serie IV 8. Vorstellung und freier Verkauf — Preise: 3,50; 5,50; 8.— DM

SONNABEND
30. Mai
20.00 — 22.15 Uhr
CHANGE
von Wolfgang Bauer — Bearbeitung von Gerd Heinz und Volker Lirock — Inszenierung: Heinz / Kühl
Darsteller: Amm, Arnswald, Drüge, Gorden — Bonesch, Violet, Wolff — Arnswald, Clausen, Gorbers, Hauer, Kilbinger, Kluss, Lirock, Orlus, Söder, Steib, Weiss

Außer Vormiete — Preise: 3,50; 5,50; 8.— DM

MONTAG
1. Juni
20.00 — 22.15 Uhr
AUF UND DAVON
Komödie von Peter Yeldham — Deutsch von Nino Adler und Ursula Lyn

Theaterring Bochum — Gruppe Ia und freier Verkauf — Preise: 3,50; 5,50; 8.— DM

DIENSTAG
2. Juni
20.00 — 22.15 Uhr
AUF UND DAVON
Komödie von Peter Yeldham — Deutsch von Nino Adler und Ursula Lyn

Theaterring Bochum — Gruppe Ib und freier Verkauf — Preise: 3,50; 5,50; 8.— DM

MITTWOCH
3. Juni
20.00 — 22.15 Uhr
AUF UND DAVON
Komödie von Peter Yeldham — Deutsch von Nino Adler und Ursula Lyn

Theaterring Bochum — Gruppe III a und freier Verkauf — Preise: 3,90; 5,50; 8.— DM

DONNERSTAG
4. Juni
20.00 — 22.15 Uhr
AUF UND DAVON
Komödie von Peter Yeldham — Deutsch von Nino Adler und Ursula Lyn

Theaterring Bochum — Gruppe III b und freier Verkauf — Preise: 3,50; 5,50; 8.— DM

FREITAG
5. Juni
20.00 — 22.15 Uhr
ZUM LETZTEN MAL
CHANGE
von Wolfgang Bauer — Bearbeitung von Gerd Heinz und Volker Lirock

Außer Vormiete — Preise: 3,50; 5,50; 8.— DM

SONNABEND
6. Juni
20.00 — 22.30 Uhr
ZUM LETZTEN MAL
VICTOR ODER DIE KINDER AN DER MACHT
Bürgerliches Schauspiel von Roger Vitrac in der Einrichtung von Jean Anouilh — Deutsch von Hella Kralewski

Vormiete Serie III 8. Vorstellung und freier Verkauf — Preise: 3,50; 5,50; 8.— DM

Aufführungen in Gelsenkirchen: GROSSES HAUS: DER RAUB DER SABINERINNEN: 21. MAI, 20.00 UHR, 23., 24. MAI, 6. JUNI, 19.30 UHR / HOKUSPOKUS: 30. MAI, 19.30 UHR
KLEINES HAUS: AUF UND DAVON: 27. MAI, 20.00 UHR

Mai/Juni

22
Freitag
20.00 - ca. 23.00 Uhr

Die Zauberflöte
Oper von Wolfgang Amadeus Mozart   Freier Verkauf

23
Samstag
19.30 - ca. 21.45 Uhr

Erstaufführung:
Italienische Nacht
von Ödön von Horvath
. Abonnement A und freier Verkauf

24
Sonntag
19.30 - ca. 23.15 Uhr

Der Rosenkavalier
Oper von Richard Strauss   Volksbühne

25
Montag
20.00 - ca. 21.30 Uhr

Der zerbrochene Krug
Lustspiel von Heinrich von Kleist   Theatergemeinde
Gastspiel in Solingen: Die Zauberflöte

26
Dienstag
19.30 - ca. 23.15 Uhr

Der Rosenkavalier
Volksbühne

27
Mittwoch
19.30 - ca. 21.45 Uhr

Italienische Nacht
Freier Verkauf

28
Donnerstag
19.30 - ca. 21.45 Uhr

Maria di Rohan
Oper von Gaetano Donizetti
Theatergemeinde

29
Freitag
19.30 - ca. 21.45 Uhr

Italienische Nacht
Abonnement A und freier Verkauf

30
Samstag
19.30 - ca. 23.15 Uhr

Der Rosenkavalier
Volksbühne

31
Sonntag
19.30 - ca. 21.00 Uhr

Der zerbrochene Krug
Theatergemeinde und freier Verkauf

2
Dienstag
19.30 - ca. 21.45 Uhr

Italienische Nacht
Abonnement A und freier Verkauf

3
Mittwoch
20.00 - ca. 22.15 Uhr

Maria di Rohan
Theatergemeinde

4
Donnerstag
19.30 - ca. 21.45 Uhr

Italienische Nacht
Abonnement A und freier Verkauf
Gastspiel in Solingen: Ein Maskenball

THEATER BREMEN

Landestheater Darmstadt

Theater im Schloß

Die Geburtstagsfeier

von Harold Pinter
Nau durchgesehene
Fassung nach der
Übersetzung von
Willy H. Thiele

Juni 1970
4 Donnerstag
20.00–22.15 Uhr
Miete, Stio. K
Regie:, Schmelz
Preise: Pik.

Einmaliges Gastspiel
Freier Verkauf

**Mazedonisches
Nationalballett**

Die Ohrider Legende
Impressionen
Das Lied der Lieder

Geo. Konitzerkz:
Kessmar, Thelen.

Stadthalle

Mai 1970
31 Tango
Sonntag
22.00–22.30 Uhr
Miete Z
und Freiverkauf
Preise B

Schauspiel von
Slawomir Mrozek
Deutsch von
Ludwig Zimmerer

Neuenfels, Barth:
Gusmer, Kayssler,
Thelen:

Brockert, Sauer:
Vietsch, Vogler

Juni 1970
2 Tango
Dienstag
19.30–22.00 Uhr
Miete H 1
und Freiverkauf
Preise X

Schauspiel von
Slawomir Mrozek
Deutsch von
Ludwig Zimmerer

Neuenfels, Barth:
Gusmer, Kayssler,
Thelen:

Brockert, Sauer:
Vietsch, Vogler

Freier Verkauf – Einmaliges Gastspiel

5 Mazedonisches
Nationalballett (Skopje)
Freitag
20.00–22.00 Uhr
Preise:
DM 4,5–20,10

Die Ohrider Legende·
Impressionen·
Das Lied der Lieder

Zum vorletzten Mal

6 Tango
Samstag
19.30–22.00 Uhr
Miete Z
und Freiverkauf
Preise B

Schauspiel von
Slawomir Mrozek
Deutsch von
Ludwig Zimmerer

Neuenfels, Barth:
Gusmer, Kayssler,
Thelen:

Brockert, Sauer:
Vietsch, Vogler

Gastspiele

Schweinfurt

Mai 1970
31 Die Hochzeit
des Figaro
Sonntag
18.00–22.15 Uhr

Komische Oper in 4 Akten
von Lorenzo da Ponte
Musik von
Wolfgang Amadeus Mozart

Dreesen, Horfeuble,
Krogs, Kühn, Schäfer,
Berg, Morris, Reber,
Roberts, v. Stein:

Grambach, Krogs,
Kühn, Maran, Schäfer,
Schmautz

Leverkusen

Juni 1970
8 Tango
Montag
20.00–22.30 Uhr

Schauspiel von
Slawomir Mrozek
Deutsch von
Ludwig Zimmerer

Neuenfels, Barth:
Gusmer, Kayssler,
Thelen:

Brockert, Sauer:
Vietsch, Vogler

9 Tango
Dienstag
20.00–22.00 Uhr

Schauspiel von
Slawomir Mrozek
Deutsch von
Ludwig Zimmerer

Neuenfels, Barth:
Gusmer, Kayssler,
Thelen:

Brockert, Sauer:
Vietsch, Vogler

Orangerie

Mai 1970
29 Die Ratten
Premiere
Freitag
19.30–22.15 Uhr
Miete SP
und Freiverkauf
Preise I

Berliner
Tragikomödie
von
Gerhart Hauptmann

Heilmann, Pick, Regie:,
Ronnenwett, Sauer:,
Schierschel, Schneider,
Schlott, Vietsch

30 Wind in den Zweigen
des Sassafras
Samstag
19.30–22.00 Uhr
Miete S
und Freiverkauf
Preise II

Kamerastücke von
Obaldia
Deutsch von Eugen Helmle

Pick, Mercino, Kayssler,
v. Stein, Brockert, Sauer:

Schierschel, Schneider

31 Wind in den Zweigen
des Sassafras
Sonntag
19.30–22.00 Uhr
Miete S
und Freiverkauf
Preise II

Kamerastücke von
Obaldia
Deutsch von Eugen Helmle

Pick, Mercino, Kayssler,
v. Stein, Brockert, Sauer:

Schierschel, Schneider

Juni 1970
1 Die Ratten
Montag
19.30–22.15 Uhr
Volksbühne
Miete
und Freiverkauf
Preise I

Berliner
Tragikomödie
von
Gerhart Hauptmann

Heinz, Gräber, Bachem,
Gusmer, Kühn, Kayssler,
Pick, Preißler,
v. Stein, Brockert:

Heilmann, Pick, Regie:,
Ronnenwett, Sauer:,
Schierschel, Schneider,
Schlott, Vietsch

2 Simon Boccanegra
Dienstag
19.30–22.00 Uhr
Miete X
und Freiverkauf
Preise II

Oper in einem Prolog
und drei Bildern
von Giuseppe Verdi
Deutsch von
Nies Stemmeriz

Dreesen, Ditzka, Barth,
Gusmer, Kühn,
Gaden, Schäfl, Morris,
Roberts, Andersson,

Kühn, Schäfer, Schmautz,
Walters

Zum 26. und vorletzten Mal

3 Wind in den Zweigen
des Sassafras
Mittwoch
19.30–22.00 Uhr
Miete S
und Freiverkauf
Preise II

Kamerastücke von
Obaldia
Deutsch von Eugen Helmle

Pick, Mercino, Kayssler,
v. Stein, Brockert, Sauer:

Schierschel, Schneider

4 Martha
Donnerstag
19.30–22.15 Uhr
Miete X
und Freiverkauf
Preise I

Oper in vier Akten
von Friedrich Flotow
Musik von
Friedrich von Flotow

Dreusch, Gitzk, Gaden,
Schäfl, Bachem, Morris:

Schäfer, Schmautz,
Stumm, Walters

5 Die Ratten
Freitag
19.30–22.15 Uhr
Miete D
und Freiverkauf
Preise I

Berliner
Tragikomödie
von
Gerhart Hauptmann

Heinz, Gräber, Bachem,
Gusmer, Kühn, Kayssler,
Pick, Preißler,
Mettor, Müller, Preißler,
v. Stein, Brockert:

Heilmann, Pick, Regie:,
Ronnenwett, Sauer:,
Schierschel, Schneider,
Schlott, Vietsch

6 Martha
Samstag
19.30–22.15 Uhr
Miete X
und Freiverkauf
Preise I

Dreusch, Gitzk, Gaden,
Schäfl, Bachem, Charbert,
Bachem, Morris:

Kühn, Schäfer,
Schmautz,
Stumm, Walters

Zum vorletzten Malin diesen Spielzeit

7 Die Hochzeit
des Figaro
Sonntag
19.30–22.00 Uhr
Miete X
und Freiverkauf
Preise I

Komische Oper in 4 Akten
von Lorenzo da Ponte
Musik von
Wolfgang Amadeus Mozart

Dreesen, Horfeuble,
Barth, Gaden, Schäfl,
Morris, Reber, Roberts,
Röberg, v. Stein:

Krogs, Kühn, Maran,
Schäfer, Schmautz, Stumm

THEATER BREMEN

Theater im Schloß

Stadthalle

Mai 1970

31 Tango
Schauspiel von
Slawomir Mrozek
Deutsch von
Ludwig Zimmerer

Sonntag
22.00–23.30 Uhr
Miete E
und Freiverkauf
Preise E

Neuenfels, Barth,
Gaesner, Kayssler,
Thelen.

Beudert, Sauer,
Vietsch, Vogler.

Juni 1970

2 Tango
Schauspiel von
Slawomir Mrozek
Deutsch von
Ludwig Zimmerer

Dienstag
19.30–21.00 Uhr
Miete H
und Freiverkauf
Preise E

Neuenfels, Barth,
Gaesner, Kayssler,
Thelen.

Beudert, Sauer,
Vietsch, Vogler.

Freier Verkauf · Einmaliges Gastspiel

**5 Mazedonisches
Nationalballett (Skopje)**
Zum vorletzten Mal

Freitag
20.00–22.00 Uhr
DM 4,1–20,10

»Die Ohrider Legende«
»Impressionen«
»Das Lied der Lieder«

6 Tango
Schauspiel von
Slawomir Mrozek
Deutsch von
Ludwig Zimmerer

Samstag
18.30–20.00 Uhr
Miete E
und Freiverkauf
Preise E

Neuenfels, Barth,
Gaesner, Kayssler,
Thelen.

Beudert, Sauer,
Vietsch, Vogler.

Gastspiele

Schweinfurt

Mai 1970

**31 Die Hochzeit
des Figaro**

Sonntag
19.30–22.15 Uhr

Komische Oper in 4 Akten
von Lorenzo da Ponte
Musik von
Wolfgang Amadeus Mozart

Drewanz, Herfurth,
Barth, Goden, Schäßl,
Borth, Goden, Müller,
Roberts, v. Stein.

Grunbach, Sauer,
Kuhn, Maran, Schäßler,
Schmann.

Leverkusen

Juni 1970

8 Tango
Schauspiel von
Slawomir Mrozek
Deutsch von
Ludwig Zimmerer

Montag
20.30–22.30 Uhr

Neuenfels, Barth,
Gaesner, Kayssler,
Thelen.

Beudert, Sauer,
Vietsch, Vogler.

9 Tango
Schauspiel von
Slawomir Mrozek
Deutsch von
Ludwig Zimmerer

Dienstag
20.30–22.30 Uhr

Neuenfels, Barth,
Gaesner, Kayssler,
Thelen.

Beudert, Sauer,
Vietsch, Vogler.

Juni 1970

4 Die Geburtstagsfeier
von Harold Pinter
Neu durchgesehene
Fassung nach der
Übersetzung von
Willy H. Thiem

Dienstag
20.00–22.15 Uhr
Miete Sdd. X
und Freiverkauf
Preise Sdd.

Grässer, Pick,
Riegler, Schmeißer.

Einmaliges Gastspiel
Freier Verkauf

Mazedonisches
Nationalballett

Die Ohrider Legende
Impressionen
Das Lied der Lieder

Orangerie

Mai 1970

Premiere

29 Die Ratten
Berliner
Tragikomödie
von
Gerhart Hauptmann

Freitag
19.30–22.15 Uhr
Miete F
und Freiverkauf
Preise II

Hennig, Gröbbel, Boehm,
Gaesner, Kayssler,
Mettler, Müller, Prellbek,
v. Stein, Beudert.

Heilmüll, Pick, Riegler,
Rosmanowski, Sauer,
Scheurmhof, Schneider,
Schütt, Vietsch.

**30 Wind in den Zweigen
des Sassafras**

Sonntag
19.30–22.00 Uhr
Miete H I
und Freiverkauf
Preise II

Konzertverein von
René de Obaldia
Deutsch von Eugen Helmlé

Pick, Maccino, Kayssler,
Kölmann, Mettler, Pick,
Rosmanowski, Sauer.

Scheurahof, Schneider.

**31 Wind in den Zweigen
des Sassafras**

Sonntag
18.30–17.30 Uhr
und Freiverkauf
Preise II

Konzertverein von
René de Obaldia
Deutsch von Eugen Helmlé

Pick, Maccino, Kayssler,
Kölmann, Mettler, Pick,
Rosmanowski, Sauer.

Scheurahof, Schneider.

Juni 1970

1 Die Ratten
Berliner
Tragikomödie
von
Gerhart Hauptmann

Montag
19.30–22.15 Uhr
Volksbühne
Miete M
und Freiverkauf
Preise II

Hennig, Gröbbel, Boehm,
Gaesner, Kayssler,
Mettler, Müller, Prellbek,
v. Stein, Beudert.

Heilmüll, Pick, Riegler,
Rosmanowski, Sauer,
Scheurmhof, Schneider,
Schütt, Vietsch.

2 Simon Boccanegra

Dienstag
19.30–22.00 Uhr

Oper in vier Akten
von Giuseppe Verdi
Deutsch von
Hans Swarowsky

Drewanz, Goden, Borth,
Goden, Schütt, Moran,
Battini, Ambrosius.

Neuenfels, Schmann,
Welker.

Zum 25. vorletzten Mal

**3 Wind in den Zweigen
des Sassafras**

Mittwoch
19.30–22.00 Uhr
Miete B
und Freiverkauf
Preise II

Konzertverein von
René de Obaldia
Deutsch von Eugen Helmlé

Pick, Maccino, Kayssler,
Kölmann, Mettler, Pick,
Rosmanowski, Sauer.

Scheurahof, Schneider.

4 Martha

Donnerstag
20.00–22.15 Uhr
Miete A
und Freiverkauf
Preise II

Oper in vier Akten
von W. Friedrich
Musik von
Friedrich von Flotow

Drayth, Gluck, Goden,
Schütt, Bathius, Roberts.

Schäffer, Schmann,
Storm, Welker.

5 Die Ratten
Berliner
Tragikomödie
von
Gerhart Hauptmann

Freitag
19.30–22.15 Uhr
Miete F
und Freiverkauf
Preise II

Hennig, Gröbbel, Boehm,
Gaesner, Kayssler,
Mettler, Müller, Prellbek,
v. Stein, Beudert.

Heilmüll, Pick, Riegler,
Rosmanowski, Sauer,
Scheurmhof, Schneider,
Schütt, Vietsch.

6 Martha

Sonntag
19.30–21.45 Uhr
Miete K
und Freiverkauf
Preise II

Oper in vier Akten
von W. Friedrich
Musik von
Friedrich von Flotow

Drayth, Gluck, Goden,
Schütt, Bathius, Charlott.

Kuhn, Schmann,
Storm, Welker.

Zum vorletzten Male dieser Spielzeit

**7 Die Hochzeit
des Figaro**

Sonntag
19.30–22.00 Uhr
Miete H II
und Freiverkauf
Preise II

Komische Oper in 4 Akten
von Lorenzo da Ponte
Musik von
Wolfgang Amadeus Mozart

Drewanz, Herfurtha,
Barth, Goden, Schäßl,
Borth, Goden, Müller,
Morris, Rabmann, Rober,
Roberts, v. Stein.

Krogs, Kuhn, Moran,
Schäffer, Schmann, Storm.

Landestheater Darmstadt

one hundred thirty-two

Städtische Bühnen Dortmund

Künstlerischer Leiter der Oper Wilhelm Schüchter
Künstlerischer Leiter des Schauspiels Gert Omar Leutner

GROSSES HAUS
HANSASTRASSE

KLEINES HAUS
HILTROPWALL

MONTAG 1 JUNI

Dortmunder Männergesangverein
SIEHE SONDERPLAKAT
20.00 Uhr

Der Froschkönig
Märchenspiel von Hermann Wandersleb

Die fliegende Kuh (Piriluoh...!)
Eine blutige Idylle in drei Akten
von Jean Cierves und
Guillaume Hanoteau
Musik: Jean Wiener

DIENSTAG 2 JUNI

Tristan und Isolde
Oper von Richard Wagner
19.30—22.45 Uhr
Freier Verkauf
ab 25. 5.
und BSW
Preise von
3,60—16,60 DM

Der Froschkönig
Partner ■
Premiere
10 Beispiele von Renke Korn
Leitung: Borchardt, Stahl, Hutterli, Schnitzer

Der Autofriedhof
Stück von Fernando Arrabal
Deutsch von Klaus Fischer

STUDIO Kleines Haus Hiltropwall, 4. Stock

MITTWOCH 3 JUNI

Die Zauberflöte
Oper von Wolfgang Amadeus Mozart
18.00—21.00 Uhr
Freier Verkauf
ab 28. 5.

Mutter Courage und ihre Kinder
Eine Chronik aus dem
Dreißigjährigen Krieg
von Bertolt Brecht
Musik: Paul Dessau

DONNERSTAG 4 JUNI

Die Hochzeit des Figaro
Oper von Wolfgang Amadeus Mozart
19.30—23.00 Uhr
Freier Verkauf
und Vormieta W
Preise von
3,60—16,60 DM

Mutter Courage und ihre Kinder
Eine Chronik aus dem
Dreißigjährigen Krieg
von Bertolt Brecht

Die fliegende Kuh (Piriluoh...!)
Eine blutige Idylle in drei Akten
von Jean Cierves und
Guillaume Hanoteau

FREITAG 5 JUNI

Maske in Blau
Operette von Fred Raymond
19.30—21.45 Uhr
Freier Verkauf
ab 28. 5.
Preise von
3,60—16,60 DM

Der Balkon
Schauspiel von Jean Genét
Zum letzten Male

Gastspiel in Bielefeld: Amerika, Hurra!

SAMSTAG 6 JUNI

Die Zauberflöte
Oper von Wolfgang Amadeus Mozart
19.30—22.00 Uhr
Freier Verkauf
ab 30. 5.
Preise von
3,60—16,60 DM

Die fliegende Kuh (Piriluoh...!)
Eine blutige Idylle in drei Akten
von Jean Cierves und
Guillaume Hanoteau
Musik: Jean Wiener
Einmaliges Gastspiel
Franz-Josef Degenhardt singt seine Lieder

SONNTAG 7 JUNI

Die lustige Witwe
Operette von Franz Lehár
19.30—22.00 Uhr
Freier Verkauf
ab 30. 5.
Preise von
3,60—16,60 DM

Der Autofriedhof
Stück von Fernando Arrabal
Deutsch von Klaus Fischer

STUDIO Kleines Haus Hiltropwall, 4. Stock

Spielplanvorschau

Vorverkaufsstellen

Spielplanvorschau

Düsseldorfer Schauspiel-haus

Karl Heinz Stroux

Großes Haus		Kleines Haus

Abonnement 12
Ausverkauft

20.00 bis 22.45 Uhr

Ein Sommernachtstraum
(A Midsummer Night's Dream)
von William Shakespeare
in der neuen deutschen Übersetzung von Erich Fried

Evelyn Balser   Veronika Bayer   Resa Liebenow   Bettina Lindtberg   Brigitte Schneider   Hildburg Schmidt
Wolfgang Arps   Richard Elias   Wolfgang Forester   Wolfgang Haußner   Günter Hörner   Christoph Hofrichter
Arthur Jaschke   Karl-Heinz Martell   Manfred Poethe   Siegfried Siegert   Hermann Weisse
Stefan Wigger   Klaus Zimmermann

Inszenierung und Ausstattung: Jean-Pierre Ponnelle   Musik: Eberhard Schöner

Freitag
5.
Juni

Die kahle Sängerin
(La cantatrice chauve)
Anti-Stück von Eugène Ionesco   –   Deutsch von Serge Stauffer

20.00 bis 22.15 Uhr

Jakob oder Der Gehorsam
(Jacques ou la soumission)
Naturalistische Komödie von Eugène Ionesco
Aus dem Französischen übertragen von Erica de Bary und Claus Bremer

Maria Alex   Eva Böttcher   Susanne Flury   Birgid Füllenbach   Marianne Holke
Hilde Mikulicz   Anne Stegmann
Peter Franke   Werner Meyer   Heinrich Ortmayr   Alf Pankarter   Dieter Wernecke

Inszenierung: Eugène Ionesco   Ausstattung: Jean-Pierre Ponnelle

Abonnement 4 B
und beschränkter Verkauf

Preise DM 3,– bis DM 18,–

20.00 bis 22.15 Uhr

Beschränkter Verkauf

Preise DM 4,50 bis DM 20,–

20.30 bis 22.30 Uhr

Der Biberpelz
Eine Diebskomödie von Gerhart Hauptmann

Christiane Hammacher   Heidemarie Hatheyer   Johanna Liebeneiner   Annemarie Schmid
Dom de Beern   Helmut Everke   Marius Flachsmann   Wolfgang Grünebaum   Gunther Malzacher
Otto Rouvel   Frank Robert Schneider   Waldemar Schütz

Inszenierung: Karl Heinz Stroux   Ausstattung: Pit Fischer

Samstag
6.
Juni

Theatergemeinde
Volksbühne
und beschränkter Verkauf

Preise DM 3,– bis DM 18,–

20.00 bis 22.15 Uhr

Abonnement 18
und beschränkter Verkauf

Preise DM 4,50 bis DM 20,–

20.00 bis 22.45 Uhr

Zum letzten Mal

Dantons Tod
Drama von Georg Büchner

Evelyn Balser   Veronika Bayer   Susanne Flury   Birgid Füllenbach   Nicole Heesters   Elvira Hofer
Bettina Lindtberg   Hilde Mikulicz   Ingeborg Welrich
Dom de Beern   Helmut Everke   Peter Franke   Joachim Gehrmann   Wolfgang Grünebaum   Wolfgang Haußner
Christoph Hofrichter   Arthur Jaschke   Gunther Malzacher   Manfred Poethe
Joachim Peters   Wolfgang Reichmann   Otto Rouvel   Frank Robert Schneider   Waldemar Schütz   Dieter Wernecke

Inszenierung: Karl Heinz Stroux   Ausstattung: Wilfried Minks   Musik: Edward Artol

Sonntag
7.
Juni

Jan de Blieck zeigt in Verbindung mit dem British Council

The Theatre Machine
Caught in the Act
(Ertappt bei der Handlung)

Ben Benison   Roddy Maude-Roxby   Richardson Morgan   Anthony Trent

Inszenierung: Keith Johnstone

Freier Verkauf

Preise DM 4,50 bis DM 18,–

20.00 bis 22.15 Uhr

Volksbühne

20.00 bis 22.45 Uhr

Ein Sommernachtstraum
(A Midsummer Night's Dream)
von William Shakespeare
in der neuen deutschen Übersetzung von Erich Fried

Evelyn Balser   Veronika Bayer   Resa Liebenow   Bettina Lindtberg   Brigitte Schneider   Hildburg Schmidt
Wolfgang Arps   Richard Elias   Wolfgang Forester   Wolfgang Haußner   Günter Hörner   Christoph Hofrichter
Stefan Wigger   Klaus Zimmermann

Inszenierung und Ausstattung: Jean-Pierre Ponnelle   Musik: Eberhard Schöner

Montag
8.
Juni

Die kahle Sängerin
(La cantatrice chauve)
Anti-Stück von Eugène Ionesco   –   Deutsch von Serge Stauffer

Jakob oder Der Gehorsam
(Jacques ou la soumission)
Naturalistische Komödie von Eugène Ionesco

Maria Alex   Eva Böttcher   Susanne Flury   Birgid Füllenbach   Marianne Holke
Hilde Mikulicz   Anne Stegmann
Peter Franke   Werner Meyer   Heinrich Ortmayr   Alf Pankarter   Dieter Wernecke

Inszenierung: Eugène Ionesco   Regiemitarbeit: Stephan Stroux   Ausstattung: Jean-Pierre Ponnelle

Beschränkter Verkauf

Preise DM 3,– bis DM 18,–

20.00 bis 22.15 Uhr

Abonnement 13
und freier Verkauf

Preise DM 4,50 bis DM 20,–

20.00 bis 22.30 Uhr

Der Biberpelz
Eine Diebskomödie von Gerhart Hauptmann

Christiane Hammacher   Heidemarie Hatheyer   Johanna Liebeneiner   Annemarie Schmid
Dom de Beern   Helmut Everke   Marius Flachsmann   Wolfgang Grünebaum   Gunther Malzacher
Otto Rouvel   Frank Robert Schneider   Waldemar Schütz

Inszenierung: Karl Heinz Stroux   Ausstattung: Pit Fischer

Dienstag
9.
Juni

Die Augenbinde
Schauspiel von Siegfried Lenz

Resa Liebenow   Wolfgang Arps   Günter Hörner   Karl-Heinz Martell   Arthur Mentz
Werner Meyer   Siegfried Siegert

Inszenierung: Richard Münch   Ausstattung: Pit Fischer

Abonnement 5 B
und freier Verkauf

Preise DM 3,– bis DM 18,–

20.00 bis 22.15 Uhr

Abonnement 14
und freier Verkauf

Preise DM 4,50 bis DM 20,–

20.00 bis 22.30 Uhr

Der Biberpelz
Eine Diebskomödie von Gerhart Hauptmann

Heidemarie Hatheyer   Johanna Liebeneiner   Annemarie Schmid   Ingeborg Welrich
Dom de Beern   Helmut Everke   Marius Flachsmann   Wolfgang Grünebaum   Gunther Malzacher
Otto Rouvel   Frank Robert Schneider   Waldemar Schütz

Inszenierung: Karl Heinz Stroux   Ausstattung: Pit Fischer

Mittwoch
10.
Juni

Die Augenbinde
Schauspiel von Siegfried Lenz

Resa Liebenow   Wolfgang Arps   Günter Hörner   Karl-Heinz Martell   Arthur Mentz
Werner Meyer   Siegfried Siegert

Inszenierung: Richard Münch   Ausstattung: Pit Fischer

Abonnement 6 B
und beschränkter Verkauf

Preise DM 3,– bis DM 18,–

20.00 bis 21.15 Uhr

Abonnement 15
und freier Verkauf

Preise DM 4,50 bis DM 20,–

20.00 bis 22.00 Uhr

Die letzten Vorstellungen

Triumph des Todes oder Das große Massakerspiel
(Jeu de massacre)
Ein Stück von Eugène Ionesco   –   Deutsch von Lore Kornell

Evelyn Balser   Veronika Bayer   Susanne Flury   Birgid Füllenbach   Nicole Heesters   Bettina Lindtberg
Hilde Mikulicz   Ingeborg Welrich
Helmut Everke   Wolfgang Grünebaum   Wolfgang Haußner   Christoph Hofrichter   Gunther Malzacher
Manfred Poethe   Joachim Peters   Otto Rouvel   Waldemar Schütz

Inszenierung: Karl Heinz Stroux / František Miska   Ausstattung: Jacques Noël
Musik: Michael Dress   Choreographie: José Gomez

Donnerstag
11.
Juni

Die Augenbinde
Schauspiel von Siegfried Lenz

Resa Liebenow   Wolfgang Arps   Günter Hörner   Karl-Heinz Martell   Arthur Mentz
Werner Meyer   Siegfried Siegert

Inszenierung: Richard Münch   Ausstattung: Pit Fischer

Abonnement 7 B
und beschränkter Verkauf

Preise DM 3,– bis DM 18,–

20.00 bis 21.15 Uhr

Abonnement 16
und freier Verkauf

Preise DM 4,50 bis DM 20,–

20.00 bis 22.00 Uhr

Freitag
12.
Juni

Die Augenbinde
Schauspiel von Siegfried Lenz

Resa Liebenow   Wolfgang Arps   Günter Hörner   Karl-Heinz Martell   Arthur Mentz
Werner Meyer   Siegfried Siegert

Inszenierung: Richard Münch   Ausstattung: Pit Fischer

Abonnement 8 B
und beschränkter Verkauf

Preise DM 3,– bis DM 18,–

20.00 bis 21.15 Uhr

Freier Verkauf

Preise DM 4,50 bis DM 30,–

20.00 bis 22.45 Uhr

Die herrschende Klasse
(The Ruling Class)
Eine Baroke Komödie von Peter Barnes   Deutsche Fassung von Martin Esslin

Birgid Füllenbach   Christiane Hammacher   Elvira Hofer   Tatjana Iwanow
Peter Hommen   Heinrich Ortmayr   Alf Pankarter   Joachim Peters   Günther Pritz   Wolfgang Reichmann
Walter Taub   Edgar Walther   Dieter Wernecke

Inszenierung: Geoffrey Reeves   Ausstattung: John Gunter   Choreographische Gestaltung: Elmar Gehlen

Samstag
13.
Juni

Die Augenbinde
Schauspiel von Siegfried Lenz

Resa Liebenow   Wolfgang Arps   Günter Hörner   Karl-Heinz Martell   Arthur Mentz
Werner Meyer   Siegfried Siegert

Inszenierung: Richard Münch   Ausstattung: Pit Fischer

Theatergemeinde
Volksbühne
und freier Verkauf

Preise DM 3,– bis DM 18,–

20.00 bis 21.15 Uhr

Freier Verkauf

Preise DM 4,50 bis DM 30,–

20.00 bis 22.15 Uhr

Coriolan
Trauerspiel von William Shakespeare
Deutsche Fassung von Gerhard Klingenberg

Angela Salloker   Brigitte Schneider   Christine Weber
Hanns Otto Ball   Adolf Dell   Richard Elias   Marius Flachsmann   Wolfgang Forester   Benjamin Gassmann
Hansjakob Göttelmyhoff   Florentin Groll   Peter Gruber   Peter Hommen   Justus Ineska   Peter Kuiper
Bernhard Letizky   Rolf Mälders   Alf Pankarter   Dieter Ruge   Edgar Walther   Frank Robert Schneider
Hermann Weisse   Klaus Zimmermann

Inszenierung und Bühnenbild: Gerhard Klingenberg   Kostüme: Günter Walbeck   Musik: Peter Fischer

Sonntag
14.
Juni

Die Augenbinde
Schauspiel von Siegfried Lenz

Resa Liebenow   Wolfgang Arps   Günter Hörner   Karl-Heinz Martell   Arthur Mentz
Werner Meyer   Siegfried Siegert

Inszenierung: Richard Münch   Ausstattung: Pit Fischer

Abonnement 17 B
und beschränkter Verkauf

Preise DM 3,– bis DM 18,–

20.00 bis 21.15 Uhr

Theatergemeinde

20.00 bis 22.45 Uhr

Die herrschende Klasse
(The Ruling Class)
Eine Baroke Komödie von Peter Barnes   Deutsche Fassung von Martin Esslin

Birgid Füllenbach   Christiane Hammacher   Elvira Hofer   Tatjana Iwanow
Peter Hommen   Heinrich Ortmayr   Alf Pankarter   Joachim Peters   Günther Pritz   Wolfgang Reichmann
Walter Taub   Edgar Walther   Dieter Wernecke

Inszenierung: Geoffrey Reeves   Ausstattung: John Gunter   Choreographische Gestaltung: Elmar Gehlen

Montag
15.
Juni

Die Augenbinde
Schauspiel von Siegfried Lenz

Resa Liebenow   Wolfgang Arps   Günter Hörner   Karl-Heinz Martell   Arthur Mentz
Werner Meyer   Siegfried Siegert

Inszenierung: Richard Münch   Ausstattung: Pit Fischer

Theatergemeinde
Volksbühne
und freier Verkauf

Preise DM 3,– bis DM 18,–

20.00 bis 21.15 Uhr

Vorverkauf für die Vorstellungen von Dienstag bis Montag jeweils ab SAMSTAG der vorhergehenden Woche

Vorverkaufskasse SCHAUSPIELHAUS: Täglich 10–13.30 und 17–20. Samstags und sonntags nur 10–13.30. Telefonische Bestellungen: Kasse Großes Haus: Ruf 35 66 00 –
Kasse Kleines Haus: Ruf 35 66 96 von 10–13.30 und 16–19. Samstags und sonntags nur 10–13.30.
Das ABONNEMENTSBÜRO ist geöffnet: montags–freitags 9.30–13.30, samstags 9.30–12, Ruf 36 38 38. Telefonische Spielplanauskünfte Ruf 1 15 16.
Weitere Vorverkaufsstellen: Düsseldorf: VERKEHRSVEREIN am Hauptbahnhof; HEINERSDORFF in der Flingerpassage; Reisebüro im Kaufhaus HORTEN; Reisebüro UNITOUR;
Gerresheim: Gerresheimer Reisebüro, Benderstraße 106; Garath: Reisebüro UNITOUR; Krefeld: Verkehrsverein; Köln: Theaterkasse im KAUFHOF.

Die Eintrittspreise verstehen sich zuzüglich DM 0,50 für gesetzliche Altersversorgung der Künstler und Garderobe.

Hochdruck Düsseldorf

Einlaß für Zuspätkommende ist jeweils nur in der Pause möglich.

Düsseldorf
Opernhaus

Theatergemeinschaft
Düsseldorf-Duisburg

Duisburg
Stadttheater

Keine Vorstellung

Freitag
29
Mai

19³⁰ Ende 22.00 Uhr Abonnement Serie 24

La Traviata
In italienischer Sprache

Oper von Giuseppe Verdi

Dirigent: Schaub   Brockhaus   Caspari   Zara
Inszenierung: Ducreux
Bühnenbild
und Kostüme: Malclès   Allen   Delorko   Kahlstorf   Kosnowski
  Ollendorf   Slabbert   Tagger   Radinger   Rietjens
Chor: Staude
Choreographie: Nilanowa   Nilanowa   Berger

19³⁰ Ende 22.45 Uhr Abonnement Serie 7 Aufrufvorstellung

Arabella
Oper von Richard Strauss

Dirigent: Quennet   Beckmann   Caspari   Walker   Zara   Zarou
Inszenierung: Völker
Bühnenbild: Businger   Beckles   Harper a. G.   Kosnowski
Kostüme: Diettrich   Rintzler   Roar   Slabbert
Chor: Schulz   Dohmen   Lorenz   Rietjens   Wagner

Samstag
30
Mai

19³⁰ Ende nach 22.15 Uhr

Zar und Zimmermann
Komische Oper von Albert Lortzing

Dirigent: Palla   Dürler   Eckenstein
Inszenierung: Hess
Bühnenbild: Soherr   Appel   Braunsteiner   Hoyem
  Runge   Schweikart   Wimberger
Kostüme: Kisaling   Lohenstein   Ziethen
Soherr: Szewczuk
Chor: Schulz
Choreographie: Mazalova

14³⁰ Ende gegen 17.30 Uhr

Die Fledermaus
Komische Oper von Johann Strauß

Dirigent: Schneider   Ehret-Bachmann a. G.   Gramatzki a. G.
Inszenierung: Petzold   Zelles   Rothe
Bühnenbild: Soherr   Beckles   Curzi   Gester
Kostüme: Diettrich   Juhani   Ollendorf   Taub
Choreographie: Walter   Rossack   Delavalle
Chor: Schulz

Sonntag
31
Mai

19³⁰ Ende gegen 22.30 Uhr Abonnement W

Die Fledermaus
Komische Oper von Johann Strauß

Dirigent: Schaub   Engelskamp   Marheineke a. G.   Schmidt   Yakar
Inszenierung: Petzold   Appel   Götz   Ollendorf
Bühnenbild: Soherr   Runge   Steinbach a. G.   Taub
Kostüme: Diettrich
Choreographie: Walter   Deppisch   Vondruska
Chor: Schulz

19³⁰ Ende gegen 22.00 Uhr Abonnement Serie 1

Titus
Oper von Wolfgang Amadeus Mozart

Dirigent: Schaub   Dürler   Mathes   Puleston
Inszenierung: Reinhardt
Bühnenbild: Wendel   Delorko   Holley   Wimberger
Kostüme: Kappel
Chor: Schulz

Montag
1
Juni

19³⁰ Ende nach 22.15 Uhr Abonnement Serie 2

Hoffmanns Erzählungen
Phantastische Oper von Jacques Offenbach

Dirigent: Schneider   Brockhaus   Caspari   Pettersen
Inszenierung: Herlischka   Sokorska   Walker   Sörmsen
Bühnenbild: Soherr   Götz   Juhani   Lohenstein   Meven   Rintzler
Kostüme: Halmen   Schweikart   Slabbert   Ziethen   Schaeter
Chor: Schulz
Pantomime: Till

Dienstag
2
Juni

19³⁰ Ende gegen 22.45 Uhr Abonnement Serie 3

Die Zauberflöte
Oper von Wolfgang Amadeus Mozart

Dirigent: Schneider   Dreis   Einarson   Engelskamp   Lasser
Inszenierung: Reinhardt   Marsh   Puleston   Walker   Zara   Zinkler
Bühnenbild: Wendel
Kostüme: Kappel   Diekmann   Ernest   Gester   Hoyem
Chor: Staude   Ridderbusch   Runge   Schüttler   Tyl   Wimberger

Mittwoch
3
Juni

19³⁰ Ende gegen 22.30 Uhr Abonnement Serie 4

Die Fledermaus
Komische Oper von Johann Strauß

Dirigent: Schaub   Engelskamp   Schmidt   Yakar   Zelles
Inszenierung: Petzold   Beckles   Gester   Juhani
Bühnenbild: Soherr   Kollo   Ollendorf   Krüger a. G.
Kostüme: Diettrich
Choreographie: Walter   Scott   Buzek
Chor: Schulz

Donnerstag
4
Juni

19³⁰ Ende gegen 22.15 Uhr Abonnement Serie 22

Jenufa
Oper von Leos Janacek

Dirigent: Quennet   Bak   Dreis   Dürler   Eckenstein   Hey
Inszenierung: Herlischka   Kniplova   Pettersen   Zinkler   Schaarschmidt
Bühnenbild: Soherr   Allen   Fehn   Götz   Holley
Kostüme: Erler
Chor: Schulz

Freitag
5
Juni

19³⁰ Ende gegen 21.15 Uhr Abonnement Serie 18 Aufrufvorstellung

Salome
Musikdrama von Richard Strauss

Dirigent: Schneider   Caspari   Dunn   Hey   Schröder-Feinen
Inszenierung: Völker   Appel   Delorko   Diekmann   Ernest
Bühnenbild   Holley   Kosnowski   Roar   Schüttler
und Kostüme: Bignens   Schweikart   Slabbert   Wimberger   Schaefer

Samstag
6
Juni

19³⁰ Ende gegen 22.30 Uhr Abonnement Serie 11 Aufrufvorstellung

Die Fledermaus
Komische Oper von Johann Strauß

Dirigent: Schneider   Schmidt   Yakar   Zelles   Rothe
Inszenierung: Petzold   Beckles   Gester   Juhani
Bühnenbild: Soherr   Kollo   Ollendorf   Taub
Kostüme: Diettrich
Choreographie: Walter   Rossack   Delavalle
Chor: Schulz

Sonntag
7
Juni

19³⁰ Ende gegen 23.00 Uhr Abonnement S

Die Hochzeit des Figaro
Oper von Wolfgang Amadeus Mozart

Dirigent: Schaub   Beckmann   Brockhaus   Dreis
Inszenierung: Reinhardt   Dürler   Engelskamp   Zinkler
Bühnenbild
und Kostüme: Bignens   Appel   Brunsmeier   Diekmann
Chor: Staude   Rintzler   Roar   Schweikart

Keine Vorstellung

Montag
8
Juni

Gesamtgastspiele
der Deutschen Oper am Rhein
beim Festival in Helsinki
im Nationaltheater
und
beim Festival in Kopenhagen
im Königlichen Opernhaus
vom 26. bis 29. Mai 1970

Titus
Der Freischütz
L'infedeltà delusa
in Helsinki am 26., 27. und 28. Mai

Der Rosenkavalier
Moses und Aron
in Kopenhagen am 28. und 29. Mai

Regelung des Kartenverkaufs, Eintrittspreise usw. siehe Sonder-Wochenspielpläne des Opernhauses Düsseldorf (Tel. 13151) und des Stadttheaters Duisburg (Tel. 334097)

BÜHNEN DER STADT ESSEN

Generalintendant
Dr. Erich Schumacher

Opernhaus

DIE HOCHZEIT DES FIGARO
Musikalische Leitung: Rainer Koch — Inszenierung: Paul Hager — Bühnenbild und Kostüme: Leni Bauer-Ecsy — Chöre: Josef Krepela
Choreographie: Boris Pilato/Anton Vujanic — Carol Bauer, Marita Dübbers, Köthe Graus, Doris Herbert,
Sakiko Kanamori, Rudolf Holtenau, Horst Hüskes, Hans Nowack, Dan Richardson, Heinrich Semmelrath, Hugo Zinkler

Komische Oper von Wolfgang Amadeus Mozart	Samstag,	30. 5.	19.30-23.00	Essener Theaterring und freier Verkauf Preis A

MY FAIR LADY
Musikalische Leitung: Leo Plettner — Inszenierung: Werner Saladin — Bühnenbild: Philipp Blessing — Kostüme: Haidi Schürmann
Chöre: Josef Krepela — Choreographie: Boris Pilato/Anton Vujanic
Renate Fack, Anni Körner, Gabriele Marti, Anneliese Rehse, Regine Vergeen, Michael Enk, Robin Fairhurst, Horst Fechner, Werner Gaefke,
Matthias Gnädinger, Friedrich Gröndahl, Ulrich Hielscher, Wolfgang Hofmann, Horst Hüskes, Rolf Sebastian

Musical von Alan Jay Lerner und Frederik Loewe	Sonntag,	31. 5.	19.30-22.40	Freier Verkauf, Sonderpreise

DIE MÖWE
Inszenierung: Kazimierz Dejmek — Bühnenbild und Kostüme: Hans Aeberli
Ilse Anton, Christa Bernhardt, Hildegard Jacob, Brigitte Lebahn, Peter Danzeisen, Michael Enk, Friedrich Gröndahl,
Alfred Hansen, Hermann Motschach, Rolf Sebastian

von Anton Tschechow In der Übertragung des slawischen Seminars der Universität Kiel	Montag,	1. 6.	19.30-21.35	Essener Theaterring und freier Verkauf Preis I

DON PASQUALE
Musikalische Leitung: Rainer Koch — Inszenierung: Paul Hager — Bühnenbild und Kostüme: Hans Aeberli — Chöre: Josef Krepela
Doris Herbert, Romano Emili, Hans-Walter Bertram, Ulrich Hielscher, Karl-Heinz Lippe

Komische Oper von Gaetano Donizetti	Dienstag,	2. 6.	19.30-22.10	Kulturring RWE und freier Verkauf Preis I

KISS ME KATE
Musikalische Leitung: Alfons Nowacki — Inszenierung: Claus Leininger — Ausstattung: Erwin W. Zimmer — Choreographie: Boris Pilato/Anton Vujanic
Brigitte Lebahn, Ute Meinhardt, Regine Vergeen, Werner Brunn, Peter Danzeisen, Fritz Doege, Werner Gaefke,
Matthias Gnädinger, Friedrich Gröndahl, Wolfgang Hofmann, Uli Krohm, Hermann Lause, Wolff Lindner, Rolf Sebastian, Manfred Zapatka,
Tanzsolisten: Adele Zurhausen, Christa Piroch, Vanja Bourgoudjieva, Janez Samec, Damen und Herren des Balletts

Musical von Samuel und Bella Spewack Musik und Gesangstexte von Cole Porter Deutsch von Günter Neumann	Mittwoch,	3. 6.	20.00-22.40	Geschlossene Vorstellung

DER FREISCHÜTZ
Musikalische Leitung: Gustav König — Inszenierung: Paul Hager — Bühnenbild: Paul Walter — Kostüme: Ursula Inge Amann — Chöre: Josef Krepela
Choreographie: Boris Pilato/Anton Vujanic
Doris Herbert, Sakiko Kanamori, Marita Napier, Robin Fairhurst, Luis Glocker, Ulrich Hielscher, Hans Walter Hirt, Rudolf Holtenau,
Karl-Heinz Lippe, Hans Nowack

Romantische Oper von Carl Maria von Weber	Donnerstag,	4. 6.	19.30-22.40	Kulturring Essener Jugend und freier Verkauf Preis A

DON PASQUALE
Komische Oper von Gaetano Donizetti	Freitag,	5. 6.	19.30-22.10	Vormiete IV und freier Verkauf Preis I

KISS ME KATE
Musical von Samuel und Bella Spewack Musik und Gesangstexte von Cole Porter Deutsch von Günter Neumann	Samstag	6. 6.	19.30-22.10	Essener Theaterring und freier Verkauf Preis A

DIE HOCHZEIT DES FIGARO
Komische Oper von Wolfgang Amadeus Mozart	Sonntag,	7. 6.	19.30-23.00	Essener Theaterring und freier Verkauf Preis A

Humboldtaula

DER FLOH IM OHR
Inszenierung: Georg Montfort — Bühnenbild und Kostüme: Fritz Riedl
Christa Bernhardt, Eva Garg, Annemarie Saul, Nina Skaletz, Brigitte Weckelmann, Rudolf Cornelius, Michael Enk, Alfred Hansen, Hans-Walter Hirt,
Hermann Motschach, Rainer Pigulla, Theo Pöppinghaus, Hans Wehrl, Bernhard Willert

Schwank von Georges Feydeau	Samstag,	30. 5.	19.30-22.1f.	Essener Theaterring

DAS ORCHESTER
Inszenierung: Dieter Dorn — Bühnenbild und Kostüme: Fritz Riedl — Musik: Gerd Luft
Christa Bernhardt, Hildegard Jacob, Brigitte Lebahn, Gabriele Marti, Annemarie Saul, Nina Skaletz, Michael Enk, Rainer Pigulla

DIE KLEINBÜRGERHOCHZEIT
Inszenierung: Dieter Dorn/Jean Soubeyran — Bühnenbild und Kostüme: Fritz Riedl — Musik: Alfons Nowacki
Hildegard Jacob, Gabriele Marti, Ute Meinhardt, Regine Vergeen, Michael Enk, Matthias Gnädinger,
Hermann Lause, Rolf Sebastian, Manfred Zapatka

Konzertstück von Jean Anouilh	Dienstag,	2. 6.	19.30-21.50	Vormiete IX und freier Verkauf
Einakter von Bertolt Brecht				

DAS ORCHESTER
DIE KLEINBÜRGERHOCHZEIT
Konzertstück von Jean Anouilh	Donnerstag,	4. 6.	19.30-21.50	Vormiete IX und freier Verkauf
Einakter von Bertolt Brecht				

DER FLOH IM OHR
Schwank von Georges Feydeau	Freitag,	5. 6.	19.30-22.10	Essener Theaterring und freier Verkauf

DER FLOH IM OHR
	Samstag,	6. 6.	19.30-22.10	Essener Theaterring und freier Verkauf

DIE LEHRLINGE
Inszenierung: Claus Leininger — Ausstattung: Erwin W. Zimmer
Eva Garg, Gabriele Marti, Nina Skaletz, Regine Vergeen, Gerd Baehr, Rudolf Cornelius, Matthias Gnädinger, Gottfried Herbe, Hans-Walter Hirt,
Uli Krohm, Hermann Lause, Rainer Pigulla, Theo Pöppinghaus, Alfred Rupprecht, Hendrik Vögler, Günther Wille, Manfred Zapatka

von Peter Terson	Sonntag,	7. 6.	19.30-22.00	Kulturring Essener Jugend und freier Verkauf

Gastspiel in Bielefeld

MARIE IM PELZ
Inszenierung: Shuji Terayama/Claus Leininger — Bühnenbild und Kostüme: Akira Uno — Musikalische Leitung: Alfons Nowacki
Werner Brunn, Rudolf Cornelius, Peter Danzeisen, Fritz Doege, Hans-Walter Hirt, Peter Hohberger, Hermann Lause, Wolff Lindner, Reinhard Musik,
Rainer Pigulla, Peter Pützer, Günther Wille, Hendrik Vögler

von Shuji Terayama Deutsch von Manfred Hubricht	Sonntag,	31. 5.	20.00-21.15	

Städtische Bühnen Frankfurt am Main

Oper		Schauspiel		Kammerspiel

Der Freischütz Oper von Carl Maria von Weber
19.30—22.30 Uhr Preise 3—20 DM Mai Freitag
Leitung: Otvös, Buckwitz, Schneider-Siemssen, Reiter, Görgen
Meyfarth, Card
Winkler, Nienstedt, Missenhardt, Weiler, Slembeck, Wolinski,
Lange, Rummel, Kreuzer

20.30—22.00 Uhr Preise 4—16 DM Freitag-Abonnement C Patronatsverein (22)
Play Strindberg
August Strindberg's Totentanz arrangiert von Friedrich Dürrenmatt
Leitung: Olszewski, Heyduck, Harnisch
Schroth / Böse, Kutschera

20.00—22.15 Uhr Preise 4—9 DM
Tschin-Tschin
Komödie von François Billetdoux Deutsch von Meta La Roche
Leitung: Reible, Kistner
Wichmann / Heister, Laubenthal

29

Don Giovanni Oper von Wolfgang Amadeus Mozart
19.30 20.00—22.30 Uhr Preise 3—20 DM Samstag-Abonnement B Samstag
(in italienischer Sprache)
Leitung: Wand, Brecht, Grübler, Brinkmann, Doutreval
Tarres, Card, Lewgowd
Cross, Schwanbeck, Kolk, Schenk, De Kanel

Zum vorletzten Mal 20.00—22.30 Uhr Preise 6—20 DM Samstag-Abonnement A
August August, August
Eine Zirkusvorstellung von Pavel Kohout
Deutsch von Lucie Taubova Musik Jan Fischer
Leitung: Olszewski, Heckroth, Scheffel, Heß
Dahmen, Neff
Dennechaud, Eichhorn, Heister, Nydegger, Hans Richter,
Rueffer, Schweitzer

Im Zirkusprogramm
Zirkus Aramant, Conny-Scheffel-Band, Bora und Tamara,
Buffalo Bill und Partnerin, die 7 Atus, Moses und Sohn,
Illusionisten, Zauberer, Trapezkünstler, Parterre-Akrobaten,
Kunstschützen, Schlangenmenschen, Girls, Girls, Girls:
Tiere, Menschen, Attraktionen

20.00—22.30 Uhr Preise 4—9 DM
Die Kollektion   **Der Liebhaber**
Zwei Einakter von Harold Pinter
Neu durchgesehene Fassung nach der Übersetzung von W. H. Thiem
Leitung: Neuhaus, Kistner Leitung: Olszewski, Kistner
Barth / Benedict, Fiege, Dirichs / Amberger, Benedict
Horst Richter

30

14.00—16.00 Uhr Preise 2,50—15 DM Sonntag-Nachm.-Abonn. C Sonntag
Der feurige Engel Oper von Serge Prokofieff
Leitung: v. Dohnanyi, Kaslik, Svoboda, Skalicky, Brinkmann
Kouba, Schlemm, Baltsa, Maurer, O'Neill, Lewgowd
Constantin, Weiler, Müller, De Kanel, Wolinski, Vökt, Feldmann

Zum vorletzten Mal 13.30—16.30 Uhr Preise 2,50—11 DM Sonntag-Nachm.-Abonn. B
Kabale und Liebe
Ein bürgerliches Trauerspiel von Friedrich Schiller
Leitung: Reible, Heyduck
Dahmen, Dene, Anita Mey, Neff
Fiege, Friedrich, Hoerrmann, Kutschera,
Schweitzer, Stroux, Wageck

31

19.30—22.15 Uhr Preise 3—20 DM
Der Bettelstudent Operette von Carl Millöcker
Leitung: Ramin, Vasil, Heyduck, Meid, Brinkmann, Volk
Stahlman, Lewgowd, Zapf, Silver
Hopferwieser, Slembeck, Stern, De Kanel, Barnard, Herbinger,
Müller, Gorstelle, Knappe, Lange, Schäfer, Schlessl, W. Rühl,
Corps de ballet

Zum letzten Mal 20.00—22.30 Uhr Preise 6—20 DM Sonntag-Abonnement C
August August, August
Eine Zirkusvorstellung von Pavel Kohout Musik Jan Fischer
Besetzung wie am 30. Mai

20.00—22.30 Uhr Preise 4—9 DM
Die Kollektion   **Der Liebhaber**
Zwei Einakter von Harold Pinter
Besetzung wie am 30. Mai

31

Juni Montag
OPERNKASSE GESCHLOSSEN
(Hauptvorverkaufsstelle U-Bahnhof Hauptwache 9-18.30 Uhr geöffnet)

20.00—22.15 Uhr Preise 4—16 DM Montag-Abonnement C
Bürger Schippel Komödie von Carl Sternheim
Leitung: Harnack, Heckroth, Montijn
Barth, A. Mey
Assmann, Böse, Dennechaud, Dorfer, Fiege, Friedrich,
Laubenthal, Minden

20.00—22.00 Uhr Preise 4—9 DM
Der Babutz (Le Babour)
Ein Stück von Feliclen Marceau Deutsch von Lore Kornell
Leitung: Riehle, Heckroth
Hausmann, Heid, Mörger
Dommisch, Düvelsdorf, Mey, Rehfeldt, Retschy

1

20.00—21.45 Uhr Preise 3—20 DM Dienstag-Abonnement D Dienstag
Der Belagerungszustand
Oper von Milko Kelemen nach dem Bühnenstück von Albert Camus
in der Übersetzung von Guido G. Meister
Leitung: Otvös, Erfurth, Grübler, Görgen, Siefert
Cervena, Silver, Zapf / Constantin, Köninger, Müller, Cross, Caban,
Missenhardt, Vökt, De Kanel, Barnard, Wolinski

19.30—22.15 Uhr Preise 4—16 DM Dienstag-Abonnement A
König Lear Tragödie von Shakespeare Deutsch von Wolf Graf Baudissin
Leitung: Schalla, Fritzsche, Montijn, Angelini
Barth, Dene, Engel / Amberger, Assmann, Benedict, Bison,
Dennechaud, Dorfer, Habeck, Hoerrmann, Kolander, Kollek, Lauben-
thal, Minden, Hans Richter, Schweitzer, Stetter, Stroux, Wageck

20.00—22.15 Uhr Preise 4—9 DM Gastspiel
Pepusch
Szenen aus dem Pantominoptikum und Zirkus Makabria
Pantomimen von und mit Peter Siefert

2

19.30—21.45 Uhr Preise 3—20 DM Mittwoch-Abonnement B Mittwoch
Ballettabend mit Marianne Kruuse
Brandenburg 3, Musik v. J. S. Bach, Opus 1, Musik v. A. v. Webern
(Choreographie J. Cranko), Der Feuervogel, Musik v. I. Strawinsky
Leitung: Weigmann, Neumeier, Barra, Zippel
Cordua, Schwaarz, Tobias, Troitzsch
Doutreval, Duse, Neumeier und das Corps de ballet

20.00—22.15 Uhr Preise 4—16 DM Mittwoch-Abonnement D
Play Strindberg
August Strindberg's Totentanz arrangiert von Friedrich Dürrenmatt
Besetzung wie am 29. Mai

20.00—22.15 Uhr Preise 4—9 DM
Tschin-Tschin
Komödie von François Billetdoux
Besetzung wie am 29. Mai

3

20.00—22.15 Uhr Preise 3—20 DM Donnerstag-Abonnement B Donnerstag
Fausts Verdammnis Dramatische Legende von Hector Berlioz
Leitung: Rennert, Neugebauer, Grübler, Brinkmann, Bolender
Schlemm, Wendels
Remedios, Constantin, De Kanel
Haemmig, Heil, Tachangislan / Duse, Herbinger, Ziegler
und das Corps de ballet

19.30—21.45 Uhr Preise 4—16 DM Donnerstag-Abonnement D
Bürger Schippel
Komödie von Carl Sternheim
Besetzung wie am 1. Juni

20.00—22.00 Uhr Preise 4—9 DM
Der Babutz (Le Babour)
Ein Stück von Feliclen Marceau
Besetzung wie am 1. Juni

4

20.00—22.45 Uhr Preise 3—20 DM Freitag Premiere 19.30—21.45 Uhr Preise 6—25 DM Premieren-Abonnement
Die Zauberflöte Oper von Wolfgang Amadeus Mozart
Leitung: Sander, Samjust, Brinkmann
Lewgowd, Sgourda, Meyfarth, Samar, Paustian, O'Neill
Hagenau, Kolk, Slembeck, Weiler, Müller, Wollnski,
De Kanel, Barnard, Feldmann

Die Gräfin von Rathenow
Komödie von Hartmut Lange
Leitung: Moszkowicz, Heyduck, Montijn
Engel, Heid, Kaiser, Knott
Bison, Dommisch, Düvelsdorf, Gavajda, Kollek, Minden,
Rehfeldt, Retschy, Horst Richter, Rueffer

20.00—22.15 Uhr Preise 4—9 DM
Tschin-Tschin
Komödie von François Billetdoux
Besetzung wie am 29. Mai

5

20.00—23.15 Uhr Preise 3—20 DM Samstag-Abonnement D Samstag
Lohengrin Oper von Richard Wagner
Leitung: Otvös, Samjust, Brinkmann
Kirchstein, Mastilovic, Spielhoff, Krewing, Ufer, Nedelko
Winkler, Wolovsky, Schenk, Slembeck, Barnard, Strahl,
Caban, De Kanel

Die Gräfin von Rathenow
Komödie von Hartmut Lange
Besetzung wie am 5. Juni

20.00—22.15 Uhr Preise 4—9 DM
Tschin-Tschin
Komödie von François Billetdoux
Besetzung wie am 29. Mai

6

14.00—16.00 Uhr Preise 2,50—15 DM Sonntag-Nachm.-Abonn. A Sonntag
Der feurige Engel Oper von Serge Prokofieff
Leitung: Geist, Kaslik, Svoboda, Skalicky, Brinkmann
Kouba, Cervena, Baltsa, Maurer, Lewgowd, O'Neill
Constantin, Weiler, Müller, Vökt, De Kanel, Wolinski, Feldmann

7

20.00—22.15 Uhr Preise 3—20 DM Sonntag-Abonnement E 7
Ballettabend mit Marianne Kruuse
Brandenburg 3, Musik v. J. S. Bach, Opus 1, Musik v. A. v. Webern
(Choreographie J. Cranko), Der Feuervogel, Musik v. I. Strawinsky
Leitung: Weigmann, Neumeier, Barra, Zippel
Cordua, Schwaarz, Tobias, Troitzsch
Doutreval, Duse, Neumeier und das Corps de ballet

Gastspiel des Irischen Nationaltheaters The Abbey Theatre Dublin
19.30—22.00 Uhr Preise 6—20 DM Vorverkauf ab 31., für Abonnenten ab 25. Mai
The Hostage (Die Geisel)
von Brendan Behan
Inszenierung Hugh Hunt
In englischer Sprache

20.00—22.30 Uhr Preise 4—9 DM
Die Kollektion   **Der Liebhaber**
Zwei Einakter von Harold Pinter
Besetzung wie am 30. Mai

7

20.00—22.15 Uhr Preise 3—20 DM Montag-Abonnement A Montag
Der Bettelstudent Operette von Carl Millöcker
Leitung: Weigmann, Vasil, Heyduck, Meid, Brinkmann, Volk
Stahlman, O'Neill, Zapf, v. Kienau
Curzi, Köninger, Stern, Barnard, De Kanel, Wolinski, Müller,
Feldmann, Hiebel, T. Rühl, Rummel, Schäfer, W. Rühl, Corps de ballet

Schauspielkasse geschlossen. Karten zur heutigen Kammerspiel-
Vorstellung an der Vorverkaufskasse Oper und Abendkasse
(Hauptvorverkaufsstelle U-Bahnhof Hauptwache 9-18.30 Uhr geöffnet)

20.00—22.30 Uhr Preise 4—9 DM Patronatsverein (23)
Die Kollektion   **Der Liebhaber**
Zwei Einakter von Harold Pinter
Besetzung wie am 30. Mai

8

Dienstag
OPERNKASSE GESCHLOSSEN
(Hauptvorverkaufsstelle U-Bahnhof Hauptwache 9-18.30 Uhr geöffnet)

Zum letzten Mal 20.00—22.30 Uhr Preise 4—16 DM Dienstag-Abonnement B
Der Floh im Ohr (La puce à l'oreille)
Schwank von Georges Feydeau Deutsch von Fred Alten
Leitung: Reible, von Zallinger
Dahmen, Engel, Knott, Mörger, Neff
Böse, Dennechaud, Dommisch, Dorfer, Eichhorn, Friedrich,
Christian Mey, Polixa, Siedhoff, Stetter

20.00—22.30 Uhr Preise 4—9 DM
Die Kollektion   **Der Liebhaber**
Zwei Einakter von Harold Pinter
Besetzung wie am 30. Mai

9

Nächste Premieren
Hoffmanns Erzählungen Oper von Jacques Offenbach (10. Juni)
Der Barbier von Sevilla Oper von Gioacchino Rossini (6. Juli)

Bitte an unsere ABONNENTEN: Warten Sie mit der Einlösung restlicher
Tauschgutscheine
nicht bis zu den letzten Vorstellungen vor den Theaterferien, die in
wenigen Wochen beginnen. Mit dem Ende der Spielzeit werden die
Gutscheine ungültig.

Nächste Premiere (Samstag, 4. Juli)
Kiste — Worte des Vorsitzenden Mao Tse-Tung — **Kiste**
Zwei Stücke von Edward Albee Deutsch von Pinkas Braun

Oper		Schauspiel		Kammerspiel

Kartenverkauf (jeweils 4 Tage vor dem Aufführungstag)
Theaterkassen (Oper Tel. 21 06335), Schauspiel und Kammerspiel (Tel. 21 06435) weiktags
10.30—13.30 Uhr, sonn- und feiertags 11—13 Uhr. Telefonische Kartenbestellungen werktags nur
11.30—13.30 Uhr. Abendkassen (Oper Tel. 21 06335, Schauspiel Tel. 21 06435, Kammerspiel
Tel. 21 06395) eine Stunde vor Vorstellungsbeginn. Über bestellte, bis 30 Minuten vor Beginn
nicht abgeholte Karten wird anderweitig verfügt.
Hauptvorverkaufsstelle U-Bahnhof Hauptwache (Tel. 28 37 38) montags bis freitags
9—18.30 Uhr, samstags 9—15, an verkaufsoffenen Samstagen 9—18 Uhr.
Ludwig J. M. Schäfer, Schweizer Straße 35 (Tel. 62 37 79) montags bis freitags 8—13 und
15—18.30, samstags 10—14 Uhr. Lotterie Beck, Ffm.-Höchst, Bolongarostraße 132
(Tel. 31 64 12) montags bis mittwochs 9—13 und 15—18, donnerstags und freitags 9—18 Uhr.
Reisebüro Nord-West, Nordwestzentrum, an der U-Bahn-Treppe (Tel. 57 60 68)
montags-freitags 9—13 und 14.30—18.30 Uhr, samstags 9—14 Uhr

Druckerei Erich Imbescheid KG, Ffm.

Montag, 29. Juni, 20.00 Uhr, Oper
Gastspiel des Holländischen Nationalballetts
mit

NUREJEW

Abonnementsvorstellungen
vom 10. bis 16. Juni 1970

	OPER	TAG	SCHAUSPIEL
	Prem.	Mittwoch, 10. 6.	
E		Donnerstag, 11. 6.	C
		Freitag, 12. 6.	D
B-Prem.		Samstag, 13. 6.	
		Sonntag, 14. 6.	Nachm. C
B		Sonntag, 14. 6.	F
B		Montag, 15. 6.	
A		Dienstag, 16. 6.	

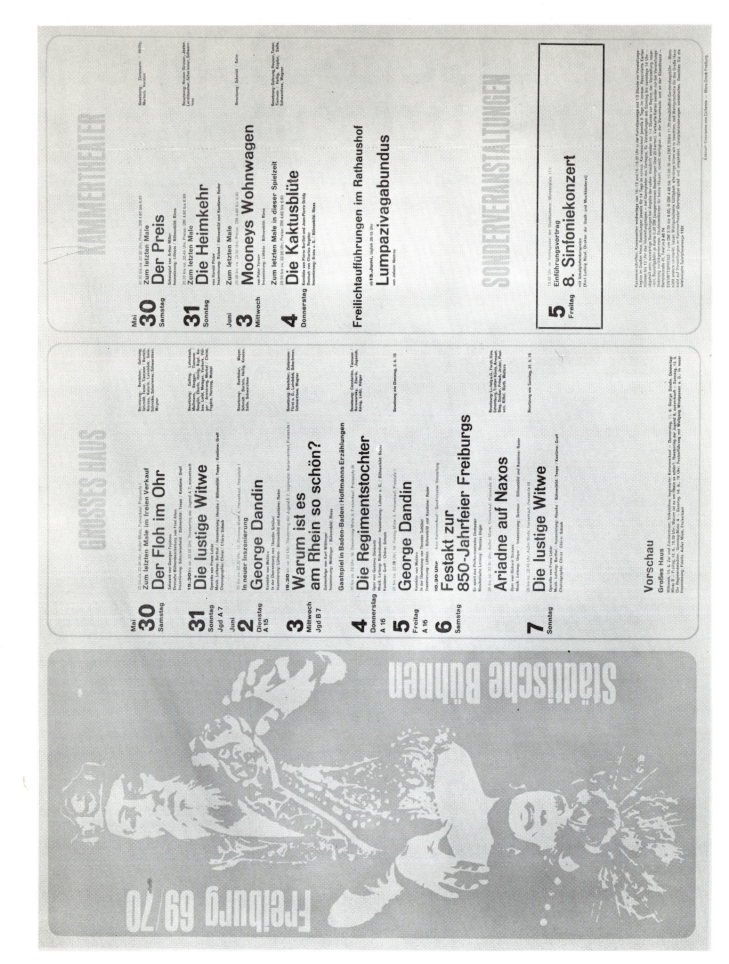

MUSIK THEATER IM REVIER

Stadt Gelsenkirchen

69/70

Großes Haus

Donnerstag 21. 5. Der Raub der Sabinerinnen *
20.00 — 22.30 Uhr
Schwank von Franz und Paul von Schönthan
Leitung: Zeiser / Szalla / van Treeck
Mitwirkende: Marjan, Papula, Schanzara, Zetzsche — Clausen, Ehlers, Jacobsen, Schick, Schlosze, Uttendörfer
Jugendring V und Freiverkauf 3,00 — 10,00 DM

Freitag 22. 5. Der Troubadour
20.00 — 22.30 Uhr
Oper von Giuseppe Verdi
Leitung: Schick / Roth / Meyer / Asbeck
Mitwirkende: Dölitzsch, Kollakowsky, Schubert — Brodawka, Meutsch, Stamm, Thompson, Ristow, Ziemann
Theatergemeinde Ring I und Freiverkauf 4,00 — 12,00 DM

Samstag 23. 5. Der Raub der Sabinerinnen *
19.30 — 22.00 Uhr
Schwank von Franz und Paul von Schönthan
Besuchergemeinde Dorsten und Freiverkauf 3,00 — 10,00 DM

Sonntag 24. 5. Der Raub der Sabinerinnen *
19.30 — 22.00 Uhr
Schwank von Franz und Paul von Schönthan
Theatergemeinde Ring V, Jugendring Buer und Freiverkauf 3,00 — 10,00 DM

Dienstag 26. 5. Undine
20.00 — 22.30 Uhr
Ballett von Frederick Ashton — Musik von Hans Werner Henze
Leitung: Mölich / Klos / Hartmann / Fuchsius
Mitwirkende: Bodart, Fabry, Greiser, Heede, Houkstra, Kreiser, Lichtenthäler, Martinelli, da Rocha, Rodin, Smith, Wacker, v. Zdunowski — Casa, Coss, K. Halatschew, Z. Halatschew, Laraguibel, Martinelli, Russo, Serrano, Wolf — Damen und Herren des Bewegungschores
Miete Weiß A, B, M und Freiverkauf 4,00 — 12,00 DM

Mittwoch 27. 5. Julius Cäsar
20.00 — 22.30 Uhr
Oper von Georg Friedrich Händel
Wiederaufnahme
Leitung: Romansky / Roth / Meyer / Asbeck
▶ Mitwirkende: Kollakowsky, Schubert — Becker, Faulstich, Stamm, Vermeersch, Zell, Ziemann
Miete Blau A, B, M und Freiverkauf 4,00 — 12,00 DM

Donnerstag 28. 5. Undine
19.30 — 22.00 Uhr
Ballett von Frederick Ashton — Musik von Hans Werner Henze
Miete Rosa A, B, M und Freiverkauf 4,00 — 12,00 DM

Freitag 29. 5. Julius Cäsar
20.00 — 22.30 Uhr
Oper von Georg Friedrich Händel
Miete Gelb A, B, M und Freiverkauf 4,00 — 12,00 DM

* Aufführung des Schauspielhauses Bochum

Samstag 30. 5. Hokuspokus *
19.30 — 21.45 Uhr
Ein Reißer von Curt Goetz
Zum letzten Mal
Leitung: Kirchner / Gondolf / van Treeck / Schönbach
Mitwirkende: Dietrich, Papula, Schanzara, Siemers, Fuck — Adler, Barner, Dorner, Hünseler, Jachmann, Kütemeyer, Maecker, Meinhardt, Mikoleit, Schick, Strehlen, Rautenberg
Theatergemeinde Ring IV und Freiverkauf 3,00 — 10,00 DM

Sonntag 31. 5. La Bohème — in italienischer Sprache —
19.30 — 21.45 Uhr
Oper von Giacomo Puccini
Leitung: Romansky / Roth / Hartmann / Asbeck
Mitwirkende: Griesenbach, Schulte-Grewe — Ehrich, Finkelberg, Julian, Ristow, Stamm, Strahlendorf, Vermeersch, Zell
Theatergemeinde Ring III und Freiverkauf 4,00 — 12,00 DM

Dienstag 2. 6. Die vier Grobiane
20.00 — 22.15 Uhr
Oper von Ermanno Wolf-Ferrari
Leitung: Mölich / Roth / Meyer
Mitwirkende: Dobbertin, Karrasch, Kollakowsky, Roth, Schulte-Grewe — Doss, Finkelberg, Hacke, Stamm, Thompson, Zell
Miete Rot A, B, M und Freiverkauf 4,00 — 12,00 DM

Mittwoch 3. 6. Salome
20.00 — 21.45 Uhr
Musikdrama von Richard Strauss
Leitung: Mölich / Roth / Meyer
Mitwirkende: Estlinbaum, Kollakowsky, Schröder, Schubert — Braun, Brencke, Doss, Ehrich, Faulstich, Finkelberg, Hacke, Julian, Kunzmann, Ralew, Stamm, Thompson, Vermeersch.
Theaterring d. Christl. Kulturgem. D, E und Freiverkauf 4,00 — 12,00 DM

Donnerstag 4. 6. Der Troubadour
20.00 — 22.30 Uhr
Oper von Giuseppe Verdi
Besuchergemeinde Gladbeck und Freiverkauf 4,00 — 12,00 DM

Freitag 5. 6. Wiener Blut
20.00 — 23.00 Uhr
Operette von Johann Strauß
Leitung: Scheffler / Liebeneiner / Meyer / Asbeck / Klos
Mitwirkende: Bourda, Griesenbach, Goll, Heigl, Moscheik, Roth — Cuhay, Hüskes, Lichte, Mersch, Odendahl, Pilgrim, Sauerwald, Werner, Zell
Ballett: Kreiser, Lichtenthäler — Halatschew, Serrano
Damen und Herren des Balletts
Miete Orange A, B, M, Theaterring der Christl. Kulturgemeinde A, B, C, und beschränkter Freiverkauf 4,00 — 12,00 DM

Kleines Haus

Mittwoch 27. 5. Auf und Davon *
20.00 — 22.15 Uhr
Komödie von Peter Yeldham
Zum ersten Mal
Deutsch von Nina Adler und Ursula Lyn
Leitung: Steiger / Fritzsche / Boening
▶ Mitwirkende: Garden, Siemers, Stein — Barner, Groth, Kütemeyer, Mikoleit
Miete Grau B, S und Freiverkauf 3,00 — 7,00 DM

AUSWÄRTIGE VORSTELLUNGEN DES MUSIKTHEATERS IM REVIER: 21., 23., 24., 30. MAI UND 1. JUNI IN BOCHUM

Der Vorverkauf beginnt 6 Tage vor dem Tag der Aufführung. Die Theaterkasse in Alt-Gelsenkirchen (Eingangshalle des Großen Hauses) ist geöffnet von Dienstag bis Freitag 9 bis 13 Uhr und 14.30 bis 16 Uhr; Samstag 9 bis 13 Uhr; an Sonn- und Feiertagen 11 bis 13 Uhr. Abendkasse: 1 Stunde vor Vorstellungsbeginn. Telefon 4 29 36. Öffnungszeiten der Theaterkasse in Gelsenkirchen-Buer, Horster Straße 5 (Heimatmuseum): Montag bis Freitag 8 bis 12.30 Uhr und 13 bis 16 Uhr. Telefon 38 43 04. Telefonische Spielplan-Ansage: 1 15 16.

Drei-Linden-Druck 24

one hundred thirty-nine

DEUTSCHES THEATER
IN GÖTTINGEN

LEITUNG GÜNTHER FLECKENSTEIN

Mai 1970

29 **Freitag** 19.45 bis 22.15 Uhr
●
Zum letzten Male
König Johann
nach Shakespeare von Friedrich Dürrenmatt ✱
Regie Helge Thoma / Bühnenbild und Kostüme Wolf Münzner
Andersen – Giller – Maak – Minetti – Monnard – Müller / Bergmann – Bojack – Bongartz – Engel – Geldern – Gilbert
Haas - Jülich - Kollakowsky - Krack - Müller-Elmau - Polscher - Röder - Roland - Sattmann - Schaufuß - Seiffert - Sichler
Weicker

Freier Kartenverkauf

30 **Sonnabend** 19.45 bis ca. 22.15 Uhr
●
Zum ersten Male
Triumph des Todes
von Eugène Ionesco
Deutsch von Lore Kornell
Regie Valentin Jeker / Bühnenbild und Kostüme Gralf-Edzard Habben
Alphons – Giller – Huesges – Lattermann – Monnard – Wiedenmann / Firchow – Geldern – Gilbert – Haas –
Hinzpeter – Kollakowsky – Krack – Meyer – Polscher – Röder – Sattmann – Schaufuß – Sichler – Woesthoff

Premierenabonnement 13
und beschränkter Kartenverkauf

31 **Sonntag** 11.15 bis 12.45
●
Einmalige Wiederaufnahme
Philoktet
von Heiner Müller ✱ / Bühnenbild und Kostüme Gralf-Edzard Habben
Regie Eberhard Müller-Elmau
Haas – Kollakowsky – Sattmann

Freier Kartenverkauf
Preise von 2.10 bis 4.50 DM

19.45 bis 22.15 Uhr
●
Zum unwiderruflich letzten Male
Die Vögel
Komödie von Aristophanes / Deutsch von Wolfgang Schadewaldt ✱
Musik Rudolf Mors
Regie Günther Fleckenstein
Bühnenbild und Kostüme Wolf Münzner / Mitarbeit Gralf-Edzard Habben
Musikalische Leitung Hermann Fuchs / Tänzerische Beratung Marianne Vogelsang
Alphons – Andersen – Christiansen – Giller – Lattermann – Müller – Reisenberger – Stave – Wiedenmann /
Baensch – Bergmann – Ciulli-Chentrens – Engel – Firchow – Gallwitz – Geldern – Gilbert – Haas – Hoffmeister – Jülich -
Kollakowsky – Krack – Müller-Elmau – Polscher – Röder – Roland – Sattmann – Seiffert – Sichler – Weicker – Woesthoff

Freier Kartenverkauf

Juni 1970

1 **Montag** 19.45 bis 21.45 Uhr
Halbe Wahrheiten
Lustspiel von Alan Ayckbourn / Deutsch von Heinz Rudolf
Regie Eberhard Müller-Elmau / Bühnenbild und Kostüme Gralf-Edzard Habben
Alphons – Lattermann – Firchow – Woesthoff

Volksbühne Nr.
1000-1500
und beschränkter Kartenverkauf

2 **Dienstag** 19.45 bis 22.15
Die Millionärin
Eine turbulente Komödie von G. B. Shaw
Regie Eberhard Müller-Elmau / Bühnenbild und Kostüme Wolf Münzner
Lapsien - Monnard - Müller - Bergmann - Bongartz - Geldern - Haas - Röder - Schaufuß

Abonnement D
und freier Kartenverkauf

20.15 bis 22.15
Im Jungen Theater:
Kaspar
Ein Stück von Peter Handke ✱
Regie Dieter Hackemann / Bühnenbild und Kostüme Gralf-Edzard Habben
Giller - Wiedenmann / Firchow - Hinzpeter - Jülich - Kollakowsky - Meyer - Sattmann

Kartenverkauf nur im
Jungen Theater
Preise 3.- bis 6.- DM

3 **Mittwoch** 19.45 bis 22.45
Der Teufel und der liebe Gott
Stück von Jean-Paul Sartre / Deutsch von Eva Rechel-Mertens
Regie Günther Fleckenstein / Bühnenbild und Kostüme Hansheinrich Palitzsch
Alphons - Giller - Minetti - Monnard - Mordo - Müller - Wiedenmann / Bergmann - Bongartz - Ciulli-Chentrens
Firchow - Gallwitz - Geldern - Gilbert - Haas - Jülich - Kollakowsky - Krack - Müller-Elmau - Polscher - Röder - Roland
Sattmann - Schaufuß - Sichler - Weicker - Woesthoff

Abonnement E
und freier Kartenverkauf

4 **Donnerstag** 19.45 bis ca. 22.15 Uhr
Triumph des Todes
von Eugène Ionesco / Deutsch von Lore Kornell

Abonnement F
und freier Kartenverkauf

5 **Freitag** 19.45 bis 22.15 Uhr
Die Millionärin
Eine turbulente Komödie von G. B. Shaw

Abonnement K
und freier Kartenverkauf

6 **Sonnabend** 19.45 bis 21.45 Uhr
Zum vorletzten Male:
Halbe Wahrheiten
Lustspiel von Alan Ayckbourn

In Viersen: König Johann

Freier Kartenverkauf

7 **Sonntag** 20.00 Uhr
●
In der Weender Festhalle:
Das Orchester
Ein Konzertstück von Jean Anouilh
mit anschließender Diskussion

Vorverkauf im Deutschen Theater
Abendkasse der
Weender Festhalle
Preise 2.-, 2.50, 3.-

8 **Montag** 19.45 bis 22.15 Uhr
Die Millionärin
Eine turbulente Komödie von G. B. Shaw

Betriebsabonnement 7
und freier Kartenverkauf

✱ In der Woche deutschsprachiger Autoren

35

Die Theaterkasse ist täglich von 10 bis 13 Uhr und eine Stunde vor Vorstellungsbeginn geöffnet.
An spielfreien Sonntagen bleibt die Kasse geschlossen. Telefonische Vorbestellungen (Telefon
5 94 73) werden während der Kassenstunden entgegengenommen. Vorbestellte Karten werden
am jeweiligen Vorstellungstag nur bis 13 Uhr reserviert.

Vereinigte BÜHNEN GRAZ STEIERMARK

Opernhaus

Geschlossene Vorstellung zum zehnjährigen Bestehen der Stadtwerke AG

15 Freitag
Maske in Blau
Operette von Fred Raymond
Leitung: Goldschmidt, Popp, Johren, Wortenegg, Salez, Schröder
Mitwirkende: Ging a. G., Kalitza – Cerll, Gester, Kepplinger, Krebs, Popp, Sekers, Schweighofer, Torijan, Wollner
19.00 bis nach 22.00 Uhr

Mini Coortss in der Tielpremie
16 Samstag
La Traviata
(in italienischer Sprache)
Oper von Giuseppe Verdi
Leitung: Kojetinsky, Weber, Drobesch, Rosenberger, Brun, Mortony
Mitwirkende: Cortis a. G., Roser, Schubert – Hornik, Hufnagl, Klaus, Krebs, Ognjenović, Peres, Radovan, Schweighofer
19.30 bis ca. 22.45 Uhr – Freie Miete, Theatergemeinschaft
Erhöhte Preise

Zum vorletzten Mal
17 Pfingstsonntag
Der Vogelhändler
Operette von Carl Zeller
Leitung: Cerll, Wortenegg, Johren, Rosenberger, Mortony
Mitwirkende: Daschbacher, Hornik, Voll – Gester, Hufnagl, Ingle, Kepplinger, Laxl, Minich a. G., Popp, Wilde
19.30 bis ca. 22.45 Uhr – Freie Miete, Theatergemeinschaft, Theatorringgemeinde, Theatorring-Jugend
Erhöhte Preise

Conrio Connell Byrne
18 Pfingstmontag
Cavalleria rusticana
Oper von Pietro Mascagni
Der Bajazzo
Oper von Ruggiero Leoncavallo
Leitung: Furrer, Belénfhy, Johren, Piecziio, Schobesweller
Mitwirkende: Kronzell, Kyrioki, Roser – Böhm, Byrne, Hornik, Peres, Polka, Radovan, Wilde
19.30 bis ca. 22.15 Uhr – Freie Miete, Theatergemeinschaft

19 Dienstag
Geschlossen

Mini Coortss in der Tielpremie
20 Mittwoch
La Traviata
(in italienischer Sprache)
Oper von Giuseppe Verdi
Leitung: Kojetinsky, Weber, Drobesch, Rosenberger, Brun, Mortony
Mitwirkende: Cortis a. G., Roser, Schubert – Hornik, Hufnagl, Klaus, Krebs, Ognjenović
19.30 bis ca. 22.45 Uhr – Freie Miete, Theatergemeinschaft

Altisi: Dolton Popović
21 Donnerstag
Der Bajazzo
Oper von Ruggiero Leoncavallo
Cavalleria rusticana
Oper von Pietro Mascagni
Leitung: Furrer, Belénfhy, Johren, Piecziio, Schobesweller
Mitwirkende: Kronzell, Kyrioki, Roser, Schubert – Amez, Byrne a. G., Hornik, Klaus, Popović, Radovan, Wilde
19.30 bis ca. 22.15 Uhr – Freie Miete, Theatergemeinschaft

22 Freitag
Geschlossen

Boron Ochs auf Lerchenau: Karl Ridderbusch a. G.
23 Samstag
Der Rosenkavalier
Komödie für Musik von Hugo von Hofmannsthal
Leitung: Cerny, Hartmann a. G.
Mitwirkende: Fuchs, Kyrioki, Laxli, Mayr, Meyforth, Pfister, Reichel, Klaus, Voll –
Torijan
19.00 bis ca. 23.00 Uhr – Freie Miete, Theatergemeinschaft
Mäßig erhöhte Preise

Schauspielhaus

15 Freitag
Minna von Barnhelm
Lustspiel von Gotthold Ephraim Lessing
Leitung: Szyszkowitz, Schiedel, Wortenegg
Mitwirkende: Greiner, David, Holzer, Juni, Samorovski, Schägenhauf, Urzy, Wessely
19.45 bis ca. 22.15 Uhr – Freie Miete, Theatergemeinschaft, Theatorringgemeinde, Theatorring-Jugend

16 Samstag
Die Kaktusblüte
Lustspiel von Pierre Barillet und Jean-Pierre Grédy
Leitung: Greiner, Wortenegg
Mitwirkende: Lussnigg, Foll, Stohl, Vogel – Eilen, Geschler, Gelzer, Jakob, Juni
19.45 bis nach 22.30 Uhr – Freie Miete, Theatergemeinschaft

17 Pfingstsonntag
Minna von Barnhelm
Lustspiel von Gotthold Ephraim Lessing
Leitung: Szyszkowitz, Schiedel, Wortenegg
19.45 bis ca. 22.15 Uhr – Freie Miete, Theatergemeinschaft

18 Pfingstmontag
Die Kaktusblüte
Lustspiel von Pierre Barillet und Jean-Pierre Grédy
Leitung: Greiner, Wortenegg
19.45 bis nach 22.30 Uhr – Freie Miete – Theatergemeinschaft

19 Dienstag
Die Heiratskomödie
Eine ganz unglaubliche Geschichte von Nikolai Gogol
Leitung: Bicsyoki, Fischer, Piecziio, Schobesweller
Mitwirkende: Gesrk, Heger, Kropola, Lussnigg, Müller, Petry, Schubert, Vogel – Gesshler, Simonischek, Stemeck, Wessely
19.30 bis ca. 22.00 Uhr – Freie Miete, Theatorringgemeinde, Theatorring-Jugend

Probeaufführung
20 Mittwoch
Spiel Ein Akt von Samuel Beckett
Das Orchester Ein Konzertstück von Jean Anouilh
Leitung: Greiner, Schiedel, Drossvwitsch, Krebs
Mitwirkende: Gesrk, Heger, Kropola, Lussnigg, Müller, Petry, Schubert, Vogel – Gesshler
19.45 bis 21.45 Uhr – Theatergemeinschaft
Mürzzuschlag: PLAY STRINDBERG

21 Donnerstag
Die Kaktusblüte
Lustspiel von Pierre Barillet und Jean-Pierre Grédy
Leitung: Greiner, Wortenegg
19.45 bis ca. 22.15 Uhr – Freie Miete, Theatergemeinschaft

Erstaufführung
22 Freitag
Biografie: Ein Spiel
von Max Frisch
Leitung: Greiner, Johren, Wortenegg, Ehl
Mitwirkende: Vogel – Aichholzer, Cerll, Eilen, H. Ch. und W. Flederer, Gelzer, Jakob, Juni, Kohb, Laxl, Molly, Ourth, Samorovski, Schlagenhauf, Schütz, Simonischek, Stemeck, Urzy
19.45 bis 22.15 Uhr – Freie Miete, Theatergemeinschaft-Premieren-Abo, Theatorringgemeinde

23 Samstag
Minna von Barnhelm
Lustspiel von Gotthold Ephraim Lessing
Leitung: Szyszkowitz, Schiedel, Wortenegg
19.45 bis ca. 22.15 Uhr – Freie Miete, Theatergemeinschaft, Theatergemeinschaft-Jugend

Schauspielhaus

Geschlossene Vorstellung für die Raiffeisenkasse
24 Sonntag
Minna von Barnhelm
Lustspiel von Gotthold Ephraim Lessing
Leitung: Szyszkowitz, Schiedel, Wortenegg
14.30 bis ca. 17.15 Uhr

Biografie: Ein Spiel
von Max Frisch
Besetzung wie am 22. Mai
19.45 bis 22.15 Uhr – Freie Miete, Theatergemeinschaft

25 Montag
Minna von Barnhelm
Lustspiel von Gotthold Ephraim Lessing
Besetzung wie am 15. Mai
19.45 bis ca. 22.15 Uhr – Freie Miete, Theatergemeinschaft, Theatergemeinschaft

26 Dienstag
Die Kaktusblüte
Lustspiel von Pierre Barillet und Jean-Pierre Grédy
Leitung: Greiner, Wortenegg
19.45 bis nach 22.30 Uhr – Freie Miete, Theatergemeinschaft, Theatergemeinschaft-Jugend
Eisenerz: DIE HEIRATSKOMÖDIE

Probeaufführung
27 Mittwoch
Spiel Ein Akt von Samuel Beckett
Das Orchester Ein Konzertstück von Jean Anouilh
Leitung: Greiner, Schiedel, Drossvwitsch, Krebs
Besetzung wie am 20. Mai
19.45 bis 21.45 Uhr – Theatergemeinschaft

Zum letzten Mal
28 Donnerstag Fronleichnam
Das harte Brot
Schauspiel von Paul Claudel
Leitung: Bicsyoki, Fischer, Piecziio, Schobesweller
Mitwirkende: Gesrk, Kropola – Cerll, Ourth, Schütz, Stemeck
19.45 bis nach 22.00 Uhr – Freie Miete, Theatergemeinschaft

29 Freitag
Die Kaktusblüte
Lustspiel von Pierre Barillet und Jean-Pierre Grédy
Leitung: Greiner, Wortenegg
19.45 bis nach 22.30 Uhr – Freie Miete, Theatergemeinschaft

30 Samstag
Biografie: Ein Spiel
von Max Frisch
Leitung: Greiner, Johren, Wortenegg, Ehl
Besetzung wie am 22. Mai
19.45 bis 22.00 Uhr – Freie Miete, Theatergemeinschaft, Theatorring-Jugend

31 Sonntag
Die Heiratskomödie
Eine ganz unglaubliche Geschichte von Nikolai Gogol
Leitung: Bicsyoki, Fischer, Piecziio, Schobesweller
15.00 bis ca. 17.30 Uhr

Geschlossene Vorstellung für die Theatergemeinschaft-Jugend
Minna von Barnhelm
Lustspiel von Gotthold Ephraim Lessing
19.45 bis ca. 22.15 Uhr – Freie Miete, Theatergemeinschaft-Jugend, Theatorring-Jugend

Juni 1 Montag

Opernhaus

Zum letzten Mal
Adam: Peter Minich
24 Sonntag
Der Vogelhändler
Operette von Carl Zeller
Leitung: Cerll, Wortenegg, Johren, Rosenberger, Mortony
Besetzung wie am 17. Mai
19.30 bis ca. 22.45 Uhr – Freie Miete, Theatergemeinschaft, Theatorring-Jugend

25 Montag
Geschlossen
Knittelfeld: PAGANINI

Von Bett: Karl Ridderbusch a. G.
26 Dienstag
Zar und Zimmermann
Komische Oper von Albert Lortzing
Leitung: Goldschmidt, Belénfhy, Rosenberger, Mortony, Piecziio, Schobesweller
Mitwirkende: Fuchs, Voll – Drobesch, Hornik, Hufnagl, Ingle, Klaus, Laxtgen, Ognjenović, Ridderbusch a. G.
19.30 bis nach ca. 22.45 Uhr – Freie Miete, Theatergemeinschaft, Theatergemeinschaft-Jugend, Theatorring-Jugend

Erstaufführung
27 Mittwoch
Die Sache Makropulos
Oper von Leos Janáček
Leitung: Klöberlor, Schubert, Gröblor, Schneider
Mitwirkende: Donsler, Kriss, Roser, Schubert – Amez, Fourié a. G., Hornik, Hufnagl, Ingle, Klaus, Peres
19.30 bis ca. 22.15 Uhr – Freie Miete, Theatergemeinschaft

28 Donnerstag Fronleichnam
Madame Pompadour
Operette von Leo Fall
Leitung: Goldschmidt, Zander, Johren, Wortenegg, Rosenberger, Wildorijo
Mitwirkende: Hofer, Kalitza, interzikow, Kyrioki, Reichel, Roth, Schobesweller, Waldmüller, Wostian – Bresch, Gester, Groß, Heger, Hornik, Kepplinger, Krebs, Laxl, Popp, Torijan, Wollner
19.30 bis ca. 22.15 Uhr – Freie Miete, Theatergemeinschaft, Theatergemeinschaft

Boron Ochs auf Lerchenau: Karl Ridderbusch a. G.
29 Freitag
Der Rosenkavalier
Komödie für Musik von Hugo von Hofmannsthal
Leitung: Cerny, Hartmann a. G., Neumann-Spollort, Wortenegg, Rosenberger
Mitwirkende: Donsler, Hornik, Krcis, Laxli, Mayr, Pfister, Reichel, Roser, Voll – Böhm, Schweighofer, Torijan – Cerll, Eilen, H. Ch. und W. Flederer, Gelzer, Jakob, Juni, Kohb
19.00 bis ca. 23.00 Uhr – Freie Miete, Theatergemeinschaft
Mäßig erhöhte Preise

30 Samstag
Maske in Blau
Operette von Fred Raymond
Leitung: Goldschmidt, Popp, Johren, Wortenegg, Salez, Schröder
Besetzung wie am 15. Mai
19.30 bis ca. 22.00 Uhr – Freie Miete, Theatergemeinschaft, Theatorring-Jugend
Mäßig erhöhte Preise

Mini Coortss in der Tielpremie
31 Sonntag
Die Sache Makropulos
Oper von Leos Janáček
Leitung: Klöberlor, Schubert, Gröblor, Schneider
Besetzung wie am 27. Mai
19.30 bis ca. 22.15 Uhr – Freie Miete, Theatergemeinschaft

Mai/Juni 1970 — Kartenverkauf: Tageskasse, Landhaus, Herrengasse 16, Tel. 87-2-89
Montag bis Samstag von 9 bis 14 Uhr, sonn- und feiertags geschlossen — Abendkasse eine halbe Stunde vor Beginn der Vorstellung
Kartenvorverkauf einschließlich Ausgabe der Karten für alle Vorstellungen jeweils eine Woche vor der Aufführung und ab Freitag für die übernächste Woche und
Steorm. Landesdruckerei, Graz – 237.70

one hundred forty-one

Intendant Dr. Hermann Werner

Kartenverkauf für die ganze
Woche jeweils ab Freitag an der
Theaterkasse.
Montags bis samstags von
10 bis 13 Uhr,
dienstags bis freitags zusätz-
lich von 17 bis 18.30 Uhr.
Die Abendkasse wird eine Stunde
vor Vorstellungsbeginn geöffnet.
Telefonische Bestellungen
werktags unter 31131 während
der Vorverkaufszeiten.
Vorverkaufsstellen:
Kaufhof Hagen, Elberfelder Str.
Tel. 32711
Hasper Zeitung, Geschäftsstelle
Tel. 43422/23
Spielplan-Fernsprechdienst der
Bundespost unter 1156 Hagen.

Theater-Gutschein

das schöne Geschenk

für viele Anlässe

Bucentha GmbH Hagen

Juni

Freitag
20.00 – ca. 22.15 Uhr
Abonnement F
u. beschr. Freiverkauf
Preise 3.- bis 11.- DM

5

Zum letzten Mal

Ein Walzertraum
Operette von Oscar Straus

Hofmann, Heinze, Schwarz, Haas, Karras - Eckhold,
Eigen, Freyburger, Kroem, Zorn - D'Aßmann,
Kloss, Pier, Rafalski, Rödiger, Schwarz - Hückel,
Groenendyk, Moesta u. ges. Ballett

Samstag
20.00 – ca. 22.30 Uhr
Freiverkauf
Preise 3.- bis 11.- DM

6

Premiere

Der Zarewitsch
Operette von Franz Lehar

Hofmann, Mauckner, Zuckmayer, Haas, Karras -
Freyburger, Hoffmeister, Prüssing - Drieß,
Dünnebach, Franc, Kloss, Mauckner, Odenkirchen,
Voshart - Ballett-Soli und -Gruppe

Sonntag
19.30 – ca. 22.00 Uhr
Volksbühne A
u. beschr. Freiverkauf
1 Std v. d. Vorstellg.
d. d. Volksbühne

7

Tosca
Oper von Giacomo Puccini

Rockstroh, Désy, Karras, Schwarz - Axarlis,
Stawski - Cicha, D'Aßmann, Dünnebach, Neill,
Rafalski, Sablotzke

Dienstag
20.00 – ca. 22.15 Uhr
Abonnement K
u. beschr. Freiverkauf
Preise 3.- bis 13.- DM

9

Städtische Bühnen Dortmund

Kasimir und Karoline
Volksstück von Ödön von Horváth

Borchardt, Hutterli, Schnitzer - Bunte, Dost, Kessler,
Mitterhauser, Müller - Albrecht, Berg, Behrent,
Bohmert, Hüttmann, Ostermann, Riemer, Rode,
Scheuer, Schneider

Mittwoch
20.00 – ca. 22.30 Uhr
Abonnement L
u. beschr. Freiverkauf
Preise 3.- bis 13.- DM

10

Tosca
Oper von Giacomo Puccini

Scarrone: Drieß
Übrige Besetzung wie am 7. 6

Donnerstag
20.00 – ca. 22.20 Uhr
Abonnement D
u. beschr. Freiverkauf
Preise 3.- bis 13.- DM

11

Don Pasquale
Komische Oper von Gaetano Donizetti

Lehmann, Désy, Zuckmayer, Karras - Müller - Cicha,
D'Aßmann, Dyson, Hollfelder, Klose, Kloss,
Odenkirchen, Rafalski

Freitag
19.45 – ca. 22.05 Uhr
Abonnement C
u. beschr. Freiverkauf
Preise 3.- bis 13.- DM

12

Zum letzten Mal

Tiefland
Musikdrama von Eugen d'Albert

Rockstroh, Dr. Werner, Schwarz, Karras - Axarlis,
Psaropoulou, Stawski, Vladyková, Zorn - Badorek,
D'Aßmann, Rafalski, Sablotzke, Tretás

Samstag
20.00 – ca. 22.30 Uhr
Freiverkauf
Preise 3.- bis 11.- DM

13

Der Zarewitsch
Operette von Franz Lehar

Besetzung wie am 6. 6.

Sonntag
19.30 – ca. 22.00 Uhr
Volksbühne B
u. beschr. Freiverkauf
1 Std v. d. Vorstellg.
d. d. Volksbühne

14

Tosca
Oper von Giacomo Puccini

Besetzung wie am 7. 6.

Dienstag
20.00 – ca. 22.20 Uhr
Abonnement A
und beschr. Freiverkauf
Preise 3.- bis 13.- DM

16

Don Pasquale
Komische Oper von Gaetano Donizetti

Besetzung wie am 11. 6.
Vorverkauf ab 12. 6.

Spielplanvorschau:

Mi. 17. 6. 20.00 Tosca   Abo B
Schweizer Tournee-Theater
Do. 18. 6. 20.00 Herr Lamberthier   Abo M
Fr. 19. 6. 20.00 Don Pasquale   Abo F
Sa. 20. 6. 20.00 Der Zarewitsch   Freiverk.
So. 21. 6. 19.30 Carmen   JR III
Theater am Domhof Osnabrück
Mo. 22. 6. 19.30 Die Schule der Frauen   JR I
Di. 23. 6. 20.00 Don Pasquale   Abo K
Mi. 24. 6. 20.00 Don Pasquale   Abo L

Vorankündigung:

Schweizer Tournee-Theater

Herr Lamberthier
Stück von Louis Verneuil

mit **Sonja Ziemann**

Charles Regnier

Do. 18. 6. 20.00 Uhr   Abo M und beschr. Freiverkauf

Theater an der Berliner Allee Düsseldorf

Barfuß im Park
von Neil Simon

mit Carola Höhn

Fr. 26. 6. 19.45 Uhr   Abo C und beschr. Freiverkauf

Wollen Sie besser informiert werden?

Dann lesen Sie die Hagener Theaternach-
richten - mit Monatsspielplan, Abonnements-
u. Jugendringankündigungen, Informationen,
Interviews und Werkhinweisen.

Erhältlich:

an der Theaterkasse
an den Vorverkaufsstellen:
Kaufhof Hagen, Elberfelder Straße
Geschäftsstelle der Hasper Zeitung
und auswärtigen Vorverkaufsstellen
sowie bei den Hagener Tageszeitungen.

Beachten Sie bitte:

die neueingerichteten Vorverkaufsstellen:

Kaufhof Hagen, Elberfelder Str.
Tel. 32711

Hasper Zeitung, Geschäftsstelle
Tel. 43422/23

Theaterkarten nur für
Freiverkaufs-Vorstellungen

Staats OPER Hamburg

Hamburger Volksbühne – Mitglieds-Nr.: 6451–7350, 9001–9700, 46701–46750
(Gutschein 9)

1 . Juni 1970
Montag,
19.30 Uhr bis 22.15 Uhr
Geschlossene Aufführung
Kein Kartenverkauf

Der Freischütz von Carl Maria von Weber
Leitung: Klee, Gießen, Wenk, Otto, Zimmer, Schmidt-Bohländer
Mitwirkende: Saunders, Thieme, Blankenheim, Fliether, Grundheber, Kloose, Kozub, van Mill, Rakocz, Zimmer

2 . Juni 1970
Dienstag,
19.30 Uhr bis 22.00 Uhr
VTg-Abonnement 1. Folge
und freier Kartenverkauf

Fidelio von Ludwig van Beethoven
Leitung: Ludwig, Rennert, Wenk, Reinking, Schmidt-Bohländer
Mitwirkende: Lang, Popp, Förster, Grundheber, Haage, Hofmann, Kozub, Krause, Wiemann

3 . Juni 1970
Mittwoch,
20.00 Uhr bis 21.45 Uhr
Mittwoch-Abonnement 2. Folge
und freier Kartenverkauf

Der Belagerungszustand von Milko Kelemen
Leitung: Gregor, Hess, Bunzel, Majewski, Schmidt-Bohländer
Mitwirkende: Hetzel, v. Ilosvay, Steiner, Blankenheim, Bunzel, Grundheber, Kloose, Marschner, Melchert, Plate, Ruzdak, Sotin, Wilhelm, Wolansky

4 . Juni 1970
Donnerstag,
19.00 Uhr bis 23.00 Uhr
Donnerstag-Abonnement 2. Folge
und freier Kartenverkauf

Die Frau ohne Schatten von Richard Strauss
Leitung: Ludwig, Schuh, Bunzel, Otto, Erler
Mitwirkende: Bjoner, Dalis, Krüger a.G., Kuchta, Steiner, Troyanos, Usselmann a.G., Blankenburg, Fliether, Kozub, Marschner, Schultz, Wiemann, Wilhelm, Workman

5 . Juni 1970
Freitag,
19.30 Uhr bis 22.00 Uhr
VTg-Abonnement 2. Folge
und freier Kartenverkauf

Cavalleria rusticana von Pietro Mascagni
Leitung: Gregor, Heger, Bunzel, Siercke, Schmidt-Bohländer
Mitwirkende: v. Ilosvay, Lang, Steiner, Fliether, Hartmann
hierauf:

Der Bajazzo von Ruggiero Leoncavallo
Leitung: Gregor, Heger, Bunzel, Siercke, Fellmer
Mitwirkende: Saunders, Cassilly, Förster, Krause, Marschner, Schultz, Wolansky

6 . Juni 1970
Sonnabend,
19.30 Uhr bis 22.30 Uhr
Sonnabend-Abonnement 2. Folge
und freier Kartenverkauf

In italienischer Sprache
Rigoletto von Giuseppe Verdi
Leitung: Janowski, Felsenstein, Wenk, Heinrich, Schmidt-Bohländer
Mitwirkende: v. Ilosvay, Meyer, Page, Scovotti, Thieme, Ahlersmeyer, Förster, Grundheber, Hofmann, Kloose, de Ridder, Ruzdak, Schultz

7 . Juni 1970
Sonntag,
18.00 Uhr bis 21.30 Uhr
Freier Kartenverkauf
Eintrittspreise: DM 4.– bis DM 27.–

Tannhäuser von Richard Wagner
Leitung: Janowski, Meyen, Bunzel, Svoboda, Skalicky, Fellmer
Mitwirkende: Collier, Page, Saunders, Cassilly, Grundheber, Krause, Marschner, Plate, Schultz, Wiemann

---

In italienischer Sprache
8 . Juni 1970
Montag,
19.30 Uhr bis 22.00 Uhr
Freier Kartenverkauf

Nabucco von Giuseppe Verdi
Leitung: Ludwig, Lindberg, Wenk, Siercke, Schmidt-Bohländer
Mitwirkende: Krüger a.G., Tinsley, Troyanos, Hartmann, Marschner, Ruzdak, Schultz, Wiemann

9 . Juni 1970
Dienstag,
19.30 Uhr bis 22.30 Uhr
Dienstag-Abonnement 2. Folge
und freier Kartenverkauf

Der fliegende Holländer von Richard Wagner
Leitung: Ludwig, Wagner, Wenk, Fellmer
Mitwirkende: Bjoner, Boese, Hofmann, Kozub, Wiemann, Wilhelm

In italienischer Sprache
10 . Juni 1970
Mittwoch,
19.30 Uhr bis 22.45 Uhr
Mittwoch-Abonnement 1. Folge
und freier Kartenverkauf
Eintrittspreise: DM 4.– bis DM 27.–

Aida von Giuseppe Verdi
Leitung: Santi, Sanjust, Hartmann, Schmidt-Bohländer
Mitwirkende: Dalis, Hetzel, Krilovci, Cassilly, Haage, Moll, Ohanesian, Wiemann

11 . Juni 1970
Donnerstag,
20.00 Uhr bis 21.45 Uhr
Donnerstag-Abonnement 3. Folge
und freier Kartenverkauf

Der Belagerungszustand von Milko Kelemen
Leitung: Gregor, Hess, Bunzel, Majewski, Schmidt-Bohländer
Mitwirkende: Hetzel, v. Ilosvay, Steiner, Blankenheim, Bunzel, Grundheber, Kloose, Marschner, Melchert, Plate, Ruzdak, Sotin, Wilhelm, Wolansky

12 . Juni 1970
Freitag,
19.00 Uhr bis 22.30 Uhr
Freitag-Abonnement 3. Folge
und freier Kartenverkauf

Die Fledermaus von Johann Strauß
Leitung: Ludwig, Lindberg, Bunzel, Otto, Knepert, Fellmer, Charrat
Mitwirkende: Ahlin, Beckmann, Marheineke, Thieme, Beirer, Blankenheim, Kloose, Marschner, Otto, Storr a.G., Wilhelm

13 . Juni 1970
Sonnabend,
19.30 Uhr bis 22.00 Uhr
Sonnabend-Abonnement 3. Folge
und freier Kartenverkauf

Ariadne auf Naxos von Richard Strauss
Leitung: Ludwig, Wenk, Siercke
Mitwirkende: Ahlin, Bjoner, Marheineke, Scovotti, Thieme, Troyanos, Blankenheim, Cox a.G., Fliether, Grundheber, Mangin, Marschner, Schultz, Unger, Workman, Mandák

14 . Juni 1970
Sonntag,
19.30 Uhr bis 22.00 Uhr
Sonntag-Abonnement
und freier Kartenverkauf

Die Entführung aus dem Serail von Wolfgang Amadeus Mozart
Leitung: Ludwig, Siercke, Wenk, Reinking, Fellmer
Mitwirkende: Algay a.G., Thieme, Mamero, Mangin, Otto, Unger, Wilhelm, Umlandt

---

In Vorbereitung

Uraufführung
Das kommt davon
oder
Wenn Sardakai auf Reisen geht
von Ernst Krenek

Musikalische Leitung: Ernst Krenek
Inszenierung: Leopold Lindtberg
Ausstattung: Rudolf Heinrich

Eintrittspreise: DM 3.– 4,50 6.– 10.– 12.– 15.– 17.– 19.– 21.– 24.– zuzüglich Altersversorgungsabgabe, wenn nicht anders vermerkt. Kartenverkauf: Tageskasse der Staatsoper (Gr. Theaterstr. 35) montags bis freitags 10–18 Uhr, sonnabends 10–14 Uhr, sonn- und feiertags 10–13 Uhr, ferner bei den bekannten Vorverkaufsstellen. Abendkasse (Dammtorstraße Ecke Gr. Theaterstr.) eine halbe Stunde vor Beginn der Aufführung. Beginn des Kartenverkaufs jeweils sechs Tage vor der Aufführung. Telefonische Bestellungen ab 11 Uhr unter 35 15 55. Das Abonnementsbüro (Gr. Theaterstr. 34, 1. Stock) ist montags bis freitags von 9–14 Uhr geöffnet. Vorstellungs- und Besetzungsänderungen vorbehalten. Herausgegeben von der Hamburgischen Staatsoper AG
Christiansdruck

one hundred forty-three

one hundred forty-four

Niedersächsische Staatstheater Hannover G M B H

Intendant der Oper: Reinhard Lehmann   Intendant des Schauspiels: Prof. Franz Reichert

OPERNHAUS

BALLHOF

THEATER AM AEGI

Donnerstag 28. Mai
Reihe W5, VB

Freitag 29. Mai
Reihe W11, VB

Toller
von Tankred Dorst

Samstag 30. Mai
Reihe C3 11, VB

Dienstag 2. Juni
Reihe Ta 11, VB

BALLHOF

Montag 1. Juni 1970, 20.00 Uhr

Großer Wolf (Premiere)

GARTENTHEATER HERRENHAUSEN

Freitag 3. Juni 1970, 20.30 Uhr

Die Vögel (Premiere)

SPIELPLANVORSCHAU

BALLHOF

THEATER AM AEGI

Montag 25. Mai

Die Zauberflöte
Oper von Emanuel Schikaneder · Musik von Wolfgang Amadeus Mozart

Dienstag 26. Mai

Macbeth
Oper von Franceso Maria Piave · Musik von Giuseppe Verdi

Mittwoch 27. Mai

Klein Zack getanzt Zinneber

Donnerstag 28. Mai

Der fliegende Holländer
Romantische Oper von Richard Wagner

Freitag 29. Mai

Rigoletto
Oper von Francesco Maria Piave · Musik von Giuseppe Verdi

Sonnabend 30. Mai

Der Graf Ory

Sonntag 31. Mai

Klein Zack getanzt Zinneber

Montag 1. Juni

Margarete

Dienstag 2. Juni

Die Zauberflöte
Oper von Emanuel Schikaneder · Musik von Wolfgang Amadeus Mozart

---

BALLHOF

Was kam denn da ins Haus

Sozialaristokraten
Komödie von Arno Holz

Wie es euch gefällt

Play Strindberg

Play Strindberg

Play Strindberg

Der Preis

Großer Wolf (Premiere)

Play Strindberg

OPERNHAUS

Schwetzinger Festspiele 1970

Gastspiel der

Niedersächsischen Staatsoper Hannover

mit

Die neugierigen Frauen

Jugend-Matinée

Cavalleria rusticana

Der Bajazzo

SPIELPLANVORSCHAU

OPERNHAUS

Stadttheater Hildesheim

Großes Haus. Marienstraße 6. und Studio-
bühne. Aula der Landestaubstummenschule.
Annenstraße 34. Vorverkauf jeweils ab
Sonntag für die Vorstellungen der folgen-
den acht Tage.

Theaterkasse, Marienstraße 6, geöffnet:
11.00–13.30. sonntags 11.00–13.00 Uhr.
Abendkasse 1 Stunde vor jeder nicht ge-
schlossenen Vorstellung.
Telefon der Theaterkasse (0 51 21) 3 25 66.

April 1970

Mi **1**	20.00–22.00 Ring B	**Die heimliche Ehe** Komische Oper von Domenico Cimarosa	
Do **2**	20.00–22.15 Ring C	**So eine Liebe** Spiel von Pavel Kohout	
Fr **3**	20.00–22.00	**Koeckert-Quartett**	
Sa **4**	20.00–22.40 Ring III	**Die Fledermaus** Operette von Johann Strauß	

Ernst Ritter

Omnibus- und Taxenbetrieb
Gesellschaftsfahrten
Güntherstraße 13 · Telefon 3 53 54

So **5**	20.00–22.40	**Die Fledermaus**	
Mo **6**	20.00–22.10 Volksbühne	**Rigoletto** Oper von Giuseppe Verdi	Zum letzten Male
	20.00–21.15	**Die Stühle** Tragische Farce von Eugène Ionesco	Studiobühne
Di **7**	20.00–22.30 Ring D	**Madame Pompadour** Operette von Leo Fall	Premiere
Mi **8**	20.00–22.15 Ring E	**Landshuter Erzählungen** Stück von Martin Sperr	
Do **9**	20.00–22.15 Ring F	**So eine Liebe**	
Fr **10**	20.00–22.15 Kulturring	**Landshuter Erzählungen**	
Sa **11**	20.00–22.30	**Madame Pompadour**	

Nichts aus dem Dutzend: Kerner-Herrenkleidung

KERNER HERRENKLEIDUNG — HILDESHEIM, ALMSSTRASSE 22

So **12**	11.00–12.15	**Matinée: Vom Expressionismus zum modernen Theater**	
	20.00–22.40	**Die Fledermaus**	
Mo **13**	20.00–22.40 Ring V	**Die Fledermaus**	
Di **14**	20.00–22.15 Ring A	**Landshuter Erzählungen**	
Mi **15**	20.00–22.15 Abo. für junge Menschen	**So eine Liebe**	
Do **16**	20.00–22.40 Ring C	**Die Fledermaus**	
Fr **17**	20.00–22.40 Ring I	**Die Fledermaus**	
Sa **18**	20.00–22.30	**Madame Pompadour**	
	20.00–21.30	**Kleine Morde** Stück von Jules Feiffer	Studiobühne

Bargeldlos zahlen!
Ein Bankkonto ermöglicht, Zahlungen durch Scheck oder Über-
weisung bargeldlos vorzunehmen.
Sie ersparen sich unnötige Wege und gewinnen Zeit.

DRESDNER BANK

Filiale Hildesheim, Almstor 1
Zweigstellen: Schuhstraße 34, Steuerwalder Straße 56 (Nordstadt)

So **19**	15.00–17.00 Ring VI	**Die heimliche Ehe**	
	20.00–22.15	**So eine Liebe**	
Mo **20**	20.00–22.40	**Die Fledermaus**	
Di **21**	20.00–22.30	**Das Land des Lächelns** Operette von Franz Lehár	Einmalige Wiederholung
Mi **22**	20.00–22.15 Ring E	**Ein wahrer Held** Lustspiel von William Synge	Premiere
Do **23**	20.00–22.15 Ring F	**Ein wahrer Held**	
Fr **24**	20.00–22.00 Ring II	**Die heimliche Ehe**	
Sa **25**	20.00–22.40 Ring IV	**Die Fledermaus**	
	20.00–21.15	**Die Stühle**	Studiobühne
So **26**	20.00–22.15	Einmaliges Gastspiel mit Elfe Gerhart und Paul Dahlke **Es ist nie zu spät** Komödie von Sumner Arthur Long In dieser reizenden Komödie geht es um die schlichte Tatsache, daß ein in Ehren ergrautes Ehepaar, das bislang auf eine erwachsene Tochter nebst Gatten herabblicken konnte, völlig unerwartet Nachwuchs- freuden entgegensieht.	
Mo **27**	20.00–22.15 für die Handels- lehranstalt	**So eine Liebe**	Zum letzten Male
Di **28**	20.00–22.30 Ring A	**Madame Pompadour**	
Mi **29**	20.00–22.30 Ring B	**Madame Pompadour**	
Do **30**	20.00–22.15 Ring C	**Ein wahrer Held**	
Fr **1**	20.00–21.30	**Kleine Morde**	Studiobühne
Sa **2**	20.00–22.00 Ring III	**Die heimliche Ehe**	
So **3**	20.00–22.30	**Madame Pompadour**	

Änderungen vorbehalten
Auch bei Ringvorstellungen freier Kartenverkauf

PFALZTHEATER KAISERSLAUTERN

INTENDANT GUNTER KÖNEMANN

Großes Haus | **Kammerbühne** und auswärtige Gastspiele

19.30 – 22.00 Uhr

25. Aufführung

Eine Nacht in Venedig

Operette in 3 Akten von F. Zell und R. Genée
Nach der Fassung von Ernst Marischka und Erich Wolfgang Korngold neu eingerichtet von Günter Könemann u. Charly Schneider
Musik von Johann Strauß

Leitung: Jacoby – Könemann – Hardt – Gripsas-Frühling – Graseck – Nessel
Mitwirkende: Bobra, Kasper, Koch, Stubbe – Federlin, Kurzwell, Matrisch, Nett, Nowak, Quaiser, Schmidt, Sona, Wegener, Burdett-Beasly, Hülsonbeck, Quaim, Schörnig, Kitt, Rapos

Platzmiete III und Freiverkauf
Preistafel I – DM 3,50-9,–

Samstag 23 Mai

Vom 30. Mai bis 6. Juni 1970 bringt das Pfalztheater seine „WOCHE DER ITALIENISCHEN OPER" in dieser Veranstaltungsreihe sehen – mit prominenten Gästen in den Hauptpartien – die Werke „RIGOLETTO" (30. 5.), „LUCIA D'LAMMERMOOR" (31. 5.), „IL CAMPIELLO" (3. 6.), „NORMA" (Gastspiel der zusammenarbeitenden Mainzer Bühne, 4. 6.), „LA TRAVIATA" (5. 6.) und „MADAME BUTTERFLY" (6. 6.) an den Spielplan. An die Theaterkasse beginnt ab heute der Kartenvorverkauf für diese hochwertige Ausländisches Pfalztheaters beim Kaiserslautern für einen Aufführungen am Freitag, den 22. Mai 1970.

19.30 – 22.00 Uhr

Die Räuber

Schauspiel in 5 Akten von Friedrich Schiller

Leitung: Schneider a. G. – Arnemann – Schnell
Mitwirkende: Reschke – Fromiowitz, Grewolla, Härtmann-Knote, Klinkšieck, Korner, Loebel, Matrisch, Patzer, Sidler, Stein, Stephan, Stiel, Straub, Vespermann, Zander-André, Zehnder

Platzmiete
5 (8. Vorst.)
und Freiverkauf
Preistafel II – DM 2,50-7,50

Sonntag 24 Mai

Montag 25 Mai

Gastspiele in Ludwigshafen: (14.00 Uhr u. 20.00 Uhr)
Piroschka

20.00 – 22.45 Uhr

Die Kluge

Die Geschichte von dem König und der klugen Frau von Carl Orff
Leitung: Landenberger – Vokálek z. G. – Arnemann – Schnell
Mitwirkende: Caroll – Brendel, Nett, Nowak, Pola, Skirko, Schmuckert, Wegener, Weis; Grefenkamp, Kitt, Rapos

Cinderella

(Aschenbrödel)
Ballett von Serge Prokofieff
Leitung: Graseck – Landenberger – Hardt – Griosas-Frühling
Mitwirkende: Burdett-Beasly, Dilges, Dow, Hug, Hülsenbeck, Manneck, Matthews, Quaim, Smith, Schneider, Schörnig, Weatherill – Döhler, Grefenkamp, Kitt, Rapos

Platzmiete
D/II (18. Vorst.)
und Freiverkauf
Preistafel I – DM 3,50-9,–

Dienstag 26 Mai

Mittwoch 27 Mai

Gastspiel in Germersheim:
My Fair Lady

19.30 – 22.15 Uhr

Woche der Italienischen Oper
Gastspiel

Urzula Kossut, Württembergische Staatsoper Stuttgart, (Gilda)
Wieslaw Öchman, Staatsoper Hamburg, (Herzog)

Rigoletto

Oper in 3 Akten nach Victor Hugo von F. M. Piave
Musik von Giuseppe Verdi
(in italienischer Sprache)

Leitung: Emmert – Könemann – Hardt – Gripsas-Frühling – Nessel – Graseck
Weitere Mitwirkende: Andrée, Bergfeld, Femar, Stubbe – Brendel, Nowak, Pola, Schmuckert, Skirko, Wegener, Weis; Burdett-Beasly, Hülsenbeck, Quaim – Döhler, Kitt, Rapos

Sonderabonnement I und Freiverkauf
DM 10.00–25.00

Samstag 30 Mai

19.30 21.45 Uhr

Woche der Italienischen Oper
Gastspiel

Lucia Cappellino, Teatro La Fenice di Venezia, San Carlo di Napoli, (Lucia)
Ion Piso, Württembergische Staatsoper Stuttgart, (Edgar)

Lucia di Lammermoor

Tragische Oper in 6 Bildern von Salvatore Cammarano – Deutsch von Joachim Popelka
Musik von Gaetano Donizetti
(in italienischer Sprache)

Leitung: Kämpfel z. G. – Vokálek a. G. – Arnemann – Schnell – Nessel
Weitere Mitwirkende: Femar – Nett, Nowak, Pola, Skirko

Sonderabonnement II und Freiverkauf
DM 10.00–25.00

Sonntag 31 Mai

20.00 – 22.45 Uhr

Ball im Savoy

Operette in 3 Akten von Alfred Grünwald und Fritz Löhner-Beda
Musik von Paul Abraham

Leitung: Landenberger – Kurzwell – Hardt – Schnell – Graseck – Nessel
Mitwirkende: Andrée, Bobra, Clausen, Femar, Maroti, Maruyama-Behnke, Mücke, Schmid, Schmidt – Federlin, Holzhäuser, Kurzwell, Nowak, Quaiser, Sons, Straub, Waniewski; Burdett-Beasly, Dilges, Hülsenbeck, Manneck, Quaim, Schörnig, Weatherill – Döhler, Grefenkamp, Kitt, Rapos

Platzmiete
D/I (19. Vorst.)
und Freiverkauf
Preistafel I – DM 3,50-9,–

Dienstag 2 Juni

In Vorbereitung:

Il Campiello Oper von Ermanno Wolf-Ferrari

Der Diener zweier Herren Komödie von Carlo Goldoni

Spielplan-Vorschau:

Mittwoch, den 3. Juni — Il Campiello (Erstaufführung)
Donnerstag, den 4. Juni — Norma (Sonder-Gastspiel)
Freitag, den 5. Juni — La Traviata
Samstag, den 6. Juni — Madame Butterfly
Sonntag, den 7. Juni — Am zweiten Dienstag im November
Dienstag, den 9. Juni — Il Campiello

Laufende Spielplandurchsage unter Fernsprecher Nr. 11 51

Vorverkauf: Jeweils acht Tage vor der Vorstellung.
Kassenstunden: Dienstag bis Samstag von 11-13 und 17-18 Uhr. Sonn- und Feiertage von 11-13 Uhr. Ferner jeweils eine Stunde vor Beginn der Vorstellung. Vorbestellte Karten werden nur bis eine viertel Stunde vor der Vorstellung reserviert. Telefonische Kartenbestellung unter Nr. 6 90 38.
Rufnummer: Intendant, Verwaltung und Theaterkasse 6 90 86

Druck: Georg Gehringer GmbH., Kaiserslautern

PFALZTHEATER KAISERSLAUTERN

INTENDANT GUNTER KONEMANN

Großes Haus   **Kammerbühne** und auswärtige Gastspiele

WOCHE DER ITALIENISCHEN OPER 30.5. - 6.6. 1970

22.15 Uhr

Gastspiel

Ursula Koszut, Württembergische Staatsoper Stuttgart, (Gilda)
Wieslaw Ochman, Staatsoper Hamburg, (Herzog)

Rigoletto

Oper in 3 Akten nach Victor Hugo von F. M. Piave
Musik von Giuseppe Verdi
(in italienischer Sprache)
Leitung: Emmert – Könemann – Hardt – Gripsas-Frühling – Nessel – Graseck
Weitere Mitwirkende: Andrée, Berghold, Femar, Stubbe – Brendel, Nowak, Pola, Schmuckert, Skirko, Wegener, Weis, Burdett-Beazly, Hülsenbeck, Qualim – Döhler, Kitt, Rapos

Sonderabonnement I
und Freiverkauf
DM 10,00 - 25,00

Samstag 30 Mai

21.45 Uhr

Gastspiel

Lucia Cappellino, Teatro La Fenice di Venezia, San Carlo di Napoli, (Lucia)
Ion Piso, Württembergische Staatsoper Stuttgart, (Edgar)

Lucia di Lammermoor

Tragische Oper in 6 Bildern von Salvatore Cammarano – Deutsch von Joachim Popelka
Musik von Gaetano Donizetti
(in italienischer Sprache)
Leitung: Kämpfer a. G. – Vokálek a. G. – Arnemann – Schnell – Nessel
Weitere Mitwirkende: Femar – Nett, Nowak, Pola, Skirko

Sonderabonnement II
und Freiverkauf
DM 10,00 - 25,00

Sonntag 31 Mai

20.00 – 22.45 Uhr

Ball im Savoy

Operette in 3 Akten von Alfred Grünwald und Fritz Löhner-Beda
Musik von Paul Abraham
Leitung: Landenberger – Kurzweil – Hardt – Schnell – Graseck – Nessel
Mitwirkende: Andrée, Bobra, Claußen, Femar, Maroti, Maruyama-Behnke, Mücke, Schmid, Schmidt – Federlin, Holzhäuser, Kurzweil, Nowak, Quaisor, Sona, Straub, Wisniewski, Burdett-Beazly, Dilges, Hülsenbeck, Mannock, Qualim, Schöniig, Weatherill – Döhler, Grafenkamp, Kitt, Rapos

Platzmiete
D/I (19. Vorst.)
und Freiverkauf
Preisstafel I – DM 3,50-9,–

Dienstag 2 Juni

20.00 – 22.15 Uhr

Erstaufführung

Il Campiello

Komische Oper in 3 Akten nach Carlo Goldoni von Mario Ghisalberti
Musik von Ermanno Wolf-Ferrari
Leitung: Emmert – Könemann – Hardt – Gripsas-Frühling – Nessel
Mitwirkende: del Campo, Femar, Käsper, Stubbe – Brendel, Hensel, Holzhäuser, Nett, Schmuckert, Skirko, Sona

Platzmiete
M (18. Vorst.)
und Freiverkauf
Preisstafel I – DM 3,50-9,–

Mittwoch 3 Juni

20.00 – 22.30 Uhr

Gastspiel der Jugoslawischen Nationaloper Skopje

Norma

Oper in 2 Akten (5 Bildern) von F. Romani
Musik von Vincenzo Bellini
(in italienischer Sprache)
Musikalische Leitung: Aleksandur Lekonski – Inszenierung: Vasil Kortosov – Bühnenbild: Dragulin Awramovski – Kostüme: Helena Patinschajq – Chöre: Ladislav Peridik – Choreographie: Olga Milossvijeva
Mitwirkende: Anastassia Bosikova, Evdolija Dobropoteva, Asna Tupovic-Lisa – Georgi Brnikov, Stojan Gencev, Artur Surmejan

Sonderabonnement III
und Freiverkauf
DM 10,00 - 25,00

Donnerstag 4 Juni

Gastspiel in Eisenberg:
Piroschka

20.00 – 22.45 Uhr

La Traviata

Oper in 3 Akten (4 Bildern)
Text von Francesco Maria Piave
Deutsche Übersetzung von Walter Felsenstein
Musik von Giuseppe Verdi
Leitung: Emmert – Könemann – Hardt – Gripsas-Frühling – Nessel – Graseck
Weitere Mitwirkende: Femar, Lehnert a. G., Maroti – Behnke, Evans, Immig, Nowak, Pola, Schmuckert, Skirko, Wegener, Weis, Hülsenbeck, Qualim, Schöniig – Grafenkamp, Kitt

Volksbühne II
und Freiverkauf
Preisstafel I – DM 3,50-9,–

Freitag 5 Juni

22.00 Uhr

Gastspiel

Els Bolkestein, Deutsche Staatsoper und Komische Oper Berlin, (Butterfly)
René Kollo, Deutsche Oper am Rhein, Düsseldorf, (Linkerton)

Madame Butterfly

Oper in 3 Akten nach D. Belasco von L. Illica und G. Giacosa
Neue deutsche Übertragung von Hans Hartleb
Musik von Giacomo Puccini
(in italienischer Sprache)
Leitung: Emmert – Hartmann-Knira – Arnemann – Gripsas-Frühling – Nessel
Weitere Mitwirkende: Bobra, Femar, Lorentz, Maruyama-Behnke, Stubbe – Immig, Kirchner, Nowak, Pola, Schmuckert, Skirko, Sona

Sonderabonnement IV
und Freiverkauf
DM 10,00 - 25,00

Samstag 6 Juni

Gastspiel in Klingenmünster:
Barfuß im Park

In Vorbereitung:

Der Diener zweier Herren Komödie von Carlo Goldoni

Spielplan-Vorschau:

Sonntag, den 7. Juni	Am zweiten Dienstag im November
Dienstag, den 9. Juni	Il Campiello
Mittwoch, den 10. Juni	Am zweiten Dienstag im November
Freitag, den 12. Juni	Die Kluge / Cinderella
Samstag, den 13. Juni	Ball im Savoy
	Besenbinder (Kammerbühne)
Sonntag, den 14. Juni	My Fair Lady

Laufende Spielplandurchsage unter Fernsprecher Nr. 1151

Vorverkauf: Jeweils acht Tage vor der Vorstellung.
Kassenstunden: Dienstag bis Samstag von 11-13 und 17-18 Uhr. Sonn- und Feiertags von 11-13 Uhr. Ferner jeweils eine Stunde vor Beginn der Vorstellung. Vorbestellte Karten werden nur bis eine viertel Stunde vor der Vorstellung reserviert. Tavernküche-Kartenübersendung unter Nr. 5903/6.
Rufnummer: Intendanz, Verwaltung und Theaterkasse 6903/6.

Druck: Georg Gehringer GmbH., Kaiserslautern

Staatstheater Kassel 3500 Kassel Am Friedrichsplatz 15
Intendanz Tglefon 1 32 13 1 32 14 1 32 15

Öffnungszeiten der Tageskassen:
Dienstag bis Samstag: 10.00 bis 13.30 Uhr und eine Stunde vor Beginn der Vorstellungen
Sonntag von 11.00 bis 12.00 Uhr und eine Stunde vor Beginn der Vorstellungen
Montag vormittag geschlossen; bei Vorstellungen eine Stunde vor Beginn geöffnet
Der Vorverkauf beginnt jeweils 8 Tage (für Abonnenten 10 Tage) vor der Vorstellung und nur an den Vormittagskassen
Telefon Großes Haus 1 58 62, Kleines Haus 1 58 53

Öffnungszeiten des Abonnementsbüros (Telefon 1 58 54)
Di.–Fr. von 10 bis 13.30 Uhr und von 17 bis 18.30 Uhr
Montag und Samstag von 10.00 bis 13.30 Uhr
Sonntag geschlossen

* Für diese Vorstellungen bekommen Schüler, Lehrlinge und Studenten ermäßigte Karten auch im Vorverkauf

● Nach Ansicht der Intendanz für Jugendliche unter 18 Jahren nicht geeignet

Staatstheater Kassel

26 Dienstag Mai
Großes Haus — Keine Vorstellung
Kleines Haus — ▶ Klassiker heute
19.30 bis 21.30 Uhr — Stammsitzmiete A 15 — Preise DM 3,50 bis 9,– — Wahlmiete — ▶ Penthesilea — Ein Trauerspiel von Heinrich von Kleist

27 Mittwoch
Großes Haus — 19.30 bis 21.55 Uhr — Wahlmiete — Preise DM 4,– bis 14,– — Freier Verkauf — Csárdásfürstin 70 — Operette von Emmerich Kálmán · Eine Fritz-Fischer-Inszenierung
Kleines Haus — 19.30 bis 21.30 Uhr — Preise DM 3,50 bis 9,– — Freier Verkauf * ● — Die jämmerliche Tragödie von Titus Andronicus — von William Shakespeare · Deutsch von Claus Bremer und Renate Voss

28 Donnerstag
Großes Haus — 19.30 bis 21.45 Uhr — Premierenmiete M 10 — Jugendkulturring J II-5 — Preise DM 4,– bis 14,– — Freier Verkauf * — Die Möwe
Kleines Haus — 19.30 bis 21.30 Uhr — Wahlmiete — Preise DM 3,50 bis 9,– — Freier Verkauf * — ▶ Penthesilea — Ein Trauerspiel von Heinrich von Kleist · Kasseler Fassung

29 Freitag
Großes Haus — 19.30 bis 22.30 Uhr — Wahlmiete — Preise DM 4,– bis 14,– — Freier Verkauf * — My Fair Lady — Musical nach Bernard Shaws „Pygmalion" von Alan Jay Lerner · Musik von Frederick Loewe
Kleines Haus — 19.30 bis 22.40 Uhr — Wahlmiete — Preise DM 3,50 bis 9,– — Freier Verkauf * — Romeo und Julia — Tragödie von William Shakespeare · Deutsch von Erich Fried

30 Samstag
Großes Haus — 19.30 bis 22.30 Uhr — Wahlmiete — Preise DM 4,– bis 14,– — Freier Verkauf — My Fair Lady — Musical nach Bernard Shaws „Pygmalion" von Alan Jay Lerner · Musik von Frederick Loewe
Kleines Haus — 19.30 bis 22.20 Uhr — Wahlmiete — Preise DM 3,50 bis 9,– — Freier Verkauf * — Kabale und Liebe — Ein bürgerliches Trauerspiel von Friedrich Schiller

31 Sonntag
Kleines Haus — 11.30 bis 13.00 Uhr — ▶ Matinee: Klassiker heute

31 Sonntag
Großes Haus — 19.30 bis 21.45 Uhr — Wahlmiete — Preise DM 4,– bis 14,– — Freier Verkauf * — Nabucco — Oper von Giuseppe Verdi
Kleines Haus — 19.30 bis 22.03 Uhr — Wahlmiete — Preise DM 3,50 bis 9,– — Freier Verkauf — Der Floh im Ohr — Schwank von Georges Feydeau · Deutsch von Fred Alten

1 Montag Juni
Großes Haus — 14.30 bis 17.30 Uhr — Wahlmiete — Preise DM 4,– bis 14,– — Freier Verkauf * — My Fair Lady — Musical nach Bernard Shaws „Pygmalion" von Alan Jay Lerner · Musik von Frederick Loewe
— 19.30 bis 22.30 Uhr — Wahlmiete — Preise DM 3,50 bis 9,– — Freier Verkauf * — My Fair Lady — Musical nach Bernard Shaws „Pygmalion" von Alan Jay Lerner · Musik von Frederick Loewe

2 Dienstag
Großes Haus — 19.30 bis 21.45 Uhr — Jugendkulturring J I-5 — Wahlmiete — Preise DM 4,– bis 14,– — Freier Verkauf * — ▶ Die Möwe — Variationen für Tänzer, Schauspieler und Sänger von Roman Vlad · Text von Anton Tschechow · Fassung: Günter Fischer und Wolfram Frommlet — Besetzung wie am 28. Mai
Kleines Haus — 19.30 bis 21.30 Uhr — Wahlmiete — Preise DM 3,50 bis 9,– — Freier Verkauf * — ▶ Penthesilea — Ein Trauerspiel von Heinrich von Kleist · Kasseler Fassung — Besetzung wie am 28. Mai

3 Mittwoch
Großes Haus — 19.30 bis 22.55 Uhr — Stammsitzmiete B 15 — Wahlmiete — Preise DM 4,– bis 14,– — Freier Verkauf * — Die Macht des Schicksals — Oper von Giuseppe Verdi · Neue Übersetzung von Joachim Popelka und Georg C. Winkler
Kleines Haus — 19.30 bis 21.30 Uhr — Wahlmiete — Preise DM 3,50 bis 9,– — Freier Verkauf * — Hier sind Sie richtig! — Schwank von Marc Camoletti · Deutsch von Gerald und Uta Szyszkowitz

4 Donnerstag
Großes Haus — 19.30 bis 22.00 Uhr — Wahlmiete — Preise DM 4,– bis 14,– — Freier Verkauf * — ▶ Madame Butterfly — Oper von Giacomo Puccini
Kleines Haus — 19.30 bis 22.06 Uhr — Stammsitzmiete C 16 — Wahlmiete — Preise DM 3,50 bis 9,– — Freier Verkauf * — Der Floh im Ohr — Schwank von Georges Feydeau · Deutsch von Fred Alten — Besetzung wie am 31. Mai

Vorschau ▶

Großes Haus
5. Juni, Freitag 19.30 Uhr Kálmán: Csárdásfürstin 70
6. Juni, Samstag 19.30 Uhr Verdi: Die Macht des Schicksals
7. Juni, Sonntag 19.30 Uhr Mozart: Die Entführung aus dem Serail
9. Juni, Dienstag 19.30 Uhr Csárdásfürstin 70
10. Juni, Mittwoch 19.30 Uhr
11. Juni, Donnerstag 19.30 Uhr Lerner, Loewe: My Fair Lady

Kleines Haus
5. Juni, Freitag 19.30 Uhr Molière: Der Geizige
6. Juni, Samstag 19.30 Uhr Kohout: August August, august
7. Juni, Sonntag 19.30 Uhr Camoletti: Hier sind Sie richtig!
9. Juni, Dienstag 19.30 Uhr Feydeau: Der Floh im Ohr
10. Juni, Mittwoch 19.30 Uhr Hier sind Sie richtig!
11. Juni, Donnerstag 19.30 Uhr Tom Sawyers Abenteuer
19.30 Uhr Tom Sawyers Abenteuer

▶ Klassiker heute
Schauspiel-Woche im Kleinen Haus vom 26. bis 31. Mai mit den Klassiker-Aufführungen dieser Spielzeit · Diskussionen nach jeder Aufführung und eine Matinee mit Podiums- und Publikumsdiskussion · Lehrlinge, Schüler und Studenten 50% Ermäßigung · Diskussionen und Matinee: Eintritt frei

Entwurf: Karl Oskar Blase · Druck: Schneider & Weber, Kassel   25

BADISCHES STAATSTHEATER KARLSRUHE

GROSSES HAUS

Freitag **29** Mai	Maske in Blau	Revue-Operette von Fred Raymond
Samstag **30** Mai	Maske in Blau	Revue-Operette von Fred Raymond
Sonntag **31** Mai	Carmen	Oper von Georges Bizet
Sonntag **31** Mai	Maske in Blau	Revue-Operette von Fred Raymond
Montag **1** Juni	Maske in Blau	Revue-Operette von Fred Raymond
Dienstag **2** Juni	Maske in Blau	Revue-Operette von Fred Raymond
Mittwoch **3** Juni	Intermezzo	Zum letzten Male
Donnerstag **4** Juni	Carmen	Oper von Georges Bizet
Freitag **5** Juni	Maske in Blau	Revue-Operette von Fred Raymond
Samstag **6** Juni	Gala-Abend / Tosca	Oper von Giacomo Puccini
Sonntag **7** Juni	Vorkonzert	
Sonntag **7** Juni	Margarete (Faust)	Oper von Charles Gounod
Montag **8** Juni	Neuntes (letztes) Symphoniekonzert	

KLEINES HAUS

Freitag **29** Mai	Amphitryon	Komödie von Peter Hacks
Samstag **30** Mai	Philoktet	Schauspiel von Heiner Müller
Sonntag **31** Mai	Was ihr wollt	Lustspiel von William Shakespeare
Montag **1** Juni	Keine Vorstellung	
Dienstag **2** Juni	Keine Vorstellung	
Mittwoch **3** Juni	Keine Vorstellung	
Donnerstag **4** Juni	Keine Vorstellung	
Freitag **5** Juni	Onkel Wanja	Schauspiel von Anton Tschechow
Samstag **6** Juni	Amphitryon	Komödie von Peter Hacks
Sonntag **7** Juni	Philoktet	Schauspiel von Heiner Müller
Montag **8** Juni	Keine Vorstellung	

Studio „die probebühne"

Magic Afternoon von Wolfgang Bauer

Denk ich an Deutschland in der Nacht

Gala-Abend
Marina Krilovici
Gilbert Py
Thomas Tipton

Tosca
Oper von Giacomo Puccini

Spielplanvorschau

In Vorbereitung

Undine
Der Barbier von Sevilla
Was der Butler sah
Kampfmoral

THEATER

DER STADT

KOBLENZ

INTENDANT H. W. WOLFF

GÖRRES-DRUCKEREI GMBH KOBLENZ

5.5. - 16.5.1970

| Di | 19.30 - 22.00 Uhr | 5. | **Die vier Grobiane** | C 16 und freier Verkauf |

Musikalische Komödie in 3 Akten von Ermanno Wolf-Ferrari — Musikalische Leitung: Sergio Albertini — Inszenierung: Fritz Bockius

| Mi | 19.30 - 21.15 Uhr | 6. | **Schwarze Komödie** | A 16 und freier Verkauf |

Lustspiel von Peter Shaffer — Inszenierung: Wolfgang Regentrop

| Do | 19.30 - 22.00 Uhr Himmelfahrt | 7. | **Schwarzwaldmädel** | freier Verkauf |

Operette in 3 Akten von L. Jessel — Inszenierung: Willi Auerbach — Musikalische Leitung: Heinz Nickisch

| Fr | 19.30 - 22.00 Uhr | 8. | **Die vier Grobiane** | B 16 und freier Verkauf |

Musikalische Komödie in 3 Akten von Ermanno Wolf-Ferrari — Musikalische Leitung: Sergio Albertini — Inszenierung: Fritz Bockius

| Sa | 19.30 - 21.15 Uhr | 9. | **Schwarze Komödie** | G 16 und freier Verkauf |

Lustspiel von Peter Shaffer — Inszenierung: Wolfgang Regentrop

| So | 19.30 - 22.00 Uhr | 10. | **Die vier Grobiane** | Besucherring 2 und freier Verkauf |

Musikalische Komödie in 3 Akten von Ermanno Wolf-Ferrari — Musikalische Leitung: Sergio Albertini — Inszenierung: Fritz Bockius

| Mo | | 11. | Keine Vorstellung | |

Zum letzten Male!

| Di | 19.30 - 21.15 Uhr | 12. | **Schwarze Komödie** | F 16 und freier Verkauf |

Lustspiel von Peter Shaffer — Inszenierung: Wolfgang Regentrop

| Mi | 19.30 - 22.00 Uhr | 13. | **Die vier Grobiane** | D 16 und freier Verkauf |

Musikalische Komödie in 3 Akten von Ermanno Wolf-Ferrari — Musikalische Leitung: Sergio Albertini — Inszenierung: Fritz Bockius

| Do | 19.30 - 22.00 Uhr | 14. | **Schwarzwaldmädel** | E 16 und freier Verkauf |

Operette in 3 Akten von L. Jessel — Inszenierung: Willi Auerbach — Musikalische Leitung: Heinz Nickisch

Zum letzten Male!

| Fr | 19.30 - 22.00 Uhr | 15. | **Die vier Grobiane** | J 16 und freier Verkauf |

Musikalische Komödie in 3 Akten von Ermanno Wolf-Ferrari — Musikalische Leitung: Sergio Albertini — Inszenierung: Fritz Bockius

Zum letzten Male!

| Sa | 19.30 - 22.00 Uhr | 16. | **Schwarzwaldmädel** | H 16 und freier Verkauf |

Operette in 3 Akten von L. Jessel — Inszenierung: Willi Auerbach — Musikalische Leitung: Heinz Nickisch

Ende der Spielzeit 1969/70

Telefonische Bestellungen nur dienstags bis samstags von 9.00 bis 11.00 Uhr (Telefon-Sonderdienst der Theaterkasse) Tel. Nr. 3 46 29 / 2 93 50 / 2 95 50

Kassenstunden:
Dienstags bis samstags von 11.00 bis 14.00 und ab 17.30 Uhr.
An Sonn- und Feiertagen ab 17.30 Uhr.
Bestellte Karten müssen jeweils am Tage vor der Aufführung bis 12.00 Uhr abgeholt werden.
Postüberweisungen auf Postscheckkonto Nr. 183 45 Köln müssen am Tage der Aufführung eingehen.

Bühnen der Stadt Köln

Opernhaus
Spielplanvorschau

Fr 5. Juni	**Giselle**	Musik von Adolphe Adam. Choreographie: Peter Wright
Sa 6. Juni	**Macbeth**	Oper von Giuseppe Verdi
So 7. Juni	**Pariser Leben**	Buffo-Oper von Jacques Offenbach
	Pariser Leben	Buffo-Oper von Jacques Offenbach
Mo 8. Juni	**Samson und Dalila**	Oper von Camille Saint-Saëns
Di 9. Juni	**Ballett-Abend** (Concerto barocco / Intime Briefe / Petruschka)	Musik von Johann Sebastian Bach, Leoš Janáček, Igor Strawinsky
Mi 10. Juni	**Die Zauberflöte**	Oper von Wolfgang Amadeus Mozart
Do 11. Juni	**Das schlaue Füchslein**	Oper von Leoš Janáček
Fr 12. Juni	**Aufstieg und Fall der Stadt Mahagonny**	Oper von Bertolt Brecht. Musik von Kurt Weill

Spielplanvorschau:
- Sonntag 13. Juni — **Tosca**
- Sonntag 14. Juni — **Fidelio**
- Montag 15. Juni — **Der Mantel / Die Kluge**
- Dienstag 16. Juni — **Titus**
- Mittwoch 17. Juni — **Tannhäuser**
- Donnerstag 18. Juni — **Die Zauberflöte**
- 20.00 — **Der Mantel / Die Kluge**
- Freitag 19. Juni — **Das Rheingold**

Schauspielhaus
Spielplanvorschau

Fr 5. Juni	**Der Ritter vom Mirakel**	Komödie von Lope de Vega. Deutsch von Hans Schlegel. Bearbeitung von Otto Tausig
Sa 6. Juni	Gastspiel Irisches Nationaltheater Dublin — The Abbey Theatre **Die Geisel** (The Hostage)	von Brendan Behan
So 7. Juni 11 Uhr	Zum letzten Male **Wallenstein** / Dramaturgisches Studio in der Volkshochschule — Forum: Vortrag Prof. Wolfgang Schadewaldt anläßlich der Aufführung „Die Sieben gegen Theben/Antigone" im Schauspielhaus	von Friedrich Schiller
Mo 8. Juni	**Der Ritter vom Mirakel**	Komödie von Lope de Vega
Di 9. Juni	**Der Ritter vom Mirakel**	Komödie von Lope de Vega
Mi 10. Juni	**Der Ritter vom Mirakel**	Komödie von Lope de Vega
Do 11. Juni	Aischylos **Die Sieben gegen Theben** / Sophokles **Antigone**	
Fr 12. Juni	**Der Ritter vom Mirakel**	Komödie von Lope de Vega

Spielplanvorschau:
- Sonntag 13. Juni — **Der Ritter vom Mirakel**
- Sonntag 14. Juni — Keine Aufführung / **Wallenstein**
- Montag 15. Juni — **Der Ritter vom Mirakel**
- Dienstag 16. Juni — **Der Ritter vom Mirakel**
- Mittwoch 17. Juni — **Die Sieben gegen Theben / Antigone**
- Donnerstag 18. Juni — **Der Ritter vom Mirakel**
- Freitag 19. Juni — **Der Ritter vom Mirakel**

Kammerspiele am Ubierring
Spielplanvorschau

Fr 5. Juni	Gastspiel des berühmten irischen Schauspielers Micheál Mac Liammóir in **The Importance of Being Oscar** (Die Unmöglichkeit Oscar Wilde zu sein)	
Sa 6. Juni	**Der Architekt und der Kaiser von Assyrien**	von Fernando Arrabal. Deutsch von Kurt Klinger
So 7. Juni	Gastspiel des berühmten irischen Schauspielers Micheál Mac Liammóir in **The Importance of Being Oscar** (Die Unmöglichkeit Oscar Wilde zu sein)	
Mo 8. Juni	**Drei Schwestern**	Drama von Anton Tschechow
Di 9. Juni	**Drei Schwestern**	Drama von Anton Tschechow
Mi 10. Juni	**Der Architekt und der Kaiser von Assyrien**	von Fernando Arrabal. Deutsch von Kurt Klinger
Do 11. Juni	**Drei Schwestern**	Drama von Anton Tschechow
Fr 12. Juni	**Drei Schwestern**	Drama von Anton Tschechow

Spielplanvorschau:
- Sonntag 13. Juni — **Drei Schwestern** / **Zicke-Zacke**
- Sonntag 14. Juni — Keine Aufführung
- Montag 15. Juni — **Drei Schwestern**
- Dienstag 16. Juni — **Drei Schwestern** / **Zicke-Zacke**
- Mittwoch 17. Juni — **Der Architekt und der Kaiser von Assyrien**
- Donnerstag 18. Juni — Gastspiel Werner Finck: **Witz als Schicksal** / **Zicke-Zacke**
- Freitag 19. Juni — **Drei Schwestern** / **Zicke-Zacke**

vereinigte städtische bühnen
krefeld mönchengladbach

generalintendant j. fontheim

krefelder haus
april 1970

M	**1**	**Die Entführung aus dem Serail** Singspiel von Wolfgang Amadeus Mozart	20.00 Uhr Theaterring
Do	**2**	**Der Selbstmörder** von Nikolai Robertowitsch Erdmann	20.00 Uhr Stammiete E
Fr	**3**	**Keine Vorstellung**	
Sa	**4**	**Streng geheim** Kriminalkomödie von Arthur Watkyn	20.00 Uhr Stammiete D Blau
So	**5**	Premiere **Carmen** Oper von Georges Bizet	20.00 Uhr Stammiete Grün
Mo	**6**	**Faust I** Tragödie von Johann Wolfgang von Goethe	19.30 Uhr DEW Theaterring
Di	**7**	**Carmen** Oper von Georges Bizet	20.00 Uhr Stammiete B
Mi	**8**	**Play Strindberg** Arrangiert von Friedrich Dürrenmatt	20.00 Uhr Stammiete D
Do	**9**	**Faust I** Tragödie von Johann Wolfgang von Goethe	19.30 Uhr Theaterring
Fr	**10**	**6. Sinfoniekonzert** **Bericht für eine Akademie** von Franz Kafka **Das letzte Band** von Samuel Beckett	20.00 Uhr 20.00 Uhr Studio im Stadttheater
Sa	**11**	**Der Selbstmörder** von Nikolai Robertowitsch Erdmann Einmaliges Gastspiel des spanischen Tanzpaares **Cristal y Manuel Moreno**	19.30 Uhr DEW Theaterring 21.30 Uhr
So	**12**	**Das Land des Lächelns** Operette von Franz Lehár	20.00 Uhr Theaterring
Mo	**13**	**Carmen** Oper von Georges Bizet	20.00 Uhr Stammiete A
Di	**14**	**Faust I** Tragödie von Johann Wolfgang von Goethe	19.30 Uhr Stammiete C
Mi	**15**	**Die Entführung aus dem Serail** Singspiel von Wolfgang Amadeus Mozart	20.00 Uhr Theaterring
Do	**16**	**Martha** Komische Oper von Friedrich von Flotow	20.00 Uhr Stammiete F
Fr	**17**	**Carmen** Oper von Georges Bizet	20.00 Uhr Sonder- vorstellung
Sa	**18**	**Faust I** Tragödie von Johann Wolfgang von Goethe	19.30 Uhr Stammiete Blau
So	**19**	**Carmen** Oper von Georges Bizet	20.00 Uhr Kulturring Dülken
Mo	**20**	**Der Selbstmörder** von Nikolai Robertowitsch Erdmann	20.00 Uhr DEW Theaterring
Di	**21**	**Faust I** Tragödie von Johann Wolfgang von Goethe	19.30 Uhr Stammiete B
Mi	**22**	**Faust I** Tragödie von Johann Wolfgang von Goethe	19.30 Uhr Stammiete D
Do	**23**	**Faust I** Tragödie von Johann Wolfgang von Goethe	19.30 Uhr Stammiete E
Fr	**24**	**Martha** Komische Oper von Friedrich von Flotow	20.00 Uhr Theaterring
Sa	**25**	**Der Selbstmörder** von Nikolai Robertowitsch Erdmann	17.30 Uhr DEW Theaterring
So	**26**	**5. Jugendkonzert** **Feuerwerk** Musikalisches Lustspiel von Erik Charell und Jurg Amstein Musik von Paul Burkhard	11.00 Uhr 20.00 Uhr Theaterring
Mo	**27**	**Das Land des Lächelns** Operette von Franz Lehár	20.00 Uhr Theaterring
Di	**28**	**Das schlaue Füchslein** Oper von Leoš Janáček	20.00 Uhr Theaterring
Mi	**29**	**Faust I** Tragödie von Johann Wolfgang von Goethe	19.30 Uhr Stammiete Weiß
Do	**30**	**Das Land des Lächelns** Operette von Franz Lehár	20.00 Uhr Freier Verkauf

Änderungen vorbehalten!

one hundred fifty-two

Landestheater Linz

Großes Haus   Kammerspiele

Viktoria und ihr Husar Operette von Paul Abraham Leitung: Marik, Steiner, Köttel, Vaughan Mitwirkende: Brehler, Gubitzer, Klippstedt — Eckhardt, Klimesch, Kral, Messany, Selenko, Siesz, Sofka, Wedtgrube, Werner	20—22.30 Uhr Montag-Reihe Freier Verkauf	**Montag** **11.** Mai	Keine Vorstellung (in Bad Hall: Heinrich IV.)
Die Entführung aus dem Serail Zum 25. Male Singspiel von W. A. Mozart Leitung: Lacovich, Schönolt, Ohland, Erdmann Mitwirkende: Auger a. G., Perry — Calleo, Englert, Kroupa, Päckl	19.30—22.30 Uhr ● Jugend- abonnement der Stadt Linz	**Dienstag** **12.** Mai	Keine Vorstellung (in Wels: Haben)
Viktoria und ihr Husar Operette von Paul Abraham Leitung und Mitwirkende wie am 11. 5. Dirigent: Scherlich	20—22.30 Uhr Land- abonnement 2 Freier Verkauf	**Mittwoch** **13.** Mai	20—22.30 Uhr ● Mittwoch-Reihe Freier Verkauf **Haben** Schauspiel von Julius Hay Leitung: Buttler, Köttel, Erdmann Mitwirkende: Döberl, Falkenhagen, Fauland, Freiberg, Goetzloff, Gollmann, Hanke, Johannsen, Oesterheit, Rammer, Strambowski — Geiger, Gensichen, Goetz, Jager, Jirak, Meinecke, v. Pervulesko, Pfeiffer, Schossmann, Skumanz, Wildner, Zeller
Keine Vorstellung (in Steyr: Pique Dame)		**Donnerstag** **14.** Mai	20—22.15 Uhr Land- abonnement 4a Freier Verkauf Zum 25. Mal **Der Floh im Ohr** Schwank von Georges Feydeau Leitung: Degner, Fleisch, Erdmann Mitwirkende: Döberl, Falkenhagen, Fauland, Hanke, Strambowski — Beens, Englert, Goetz, Gorden, Jager, Mann, Meinecke, v. Pervulesko, Schossmann
Carmen Oper von Georges Bizet Leitung: Wöss, Schönolt, Ohland, Erdmann, Marik, Dimitrow Mitwirkende: Barizowa, Klippstedt, Perry, Wagner — Anderko, Berger-Tuna, Päckl, Varpio, Werner, Wolfrum u. a.	20—23 Uhr Geschl. Vorst. für den ÖGB	**Freitag** **15.** Mai	20—22 Uhr ● Freitag-Reihe Freier Verkauf **Heinrich IV.** Schauspiel von Luigi Pirandello Leitung: Degner, Ohland, Erdmann Mitwirkende: Fauland, Oesterheit — Englert, Gensichen, Höller, Jager, Köhn, Naumann, Pervulesko, Schossmann, Wildner
Boccaccio Operette von Franz v. Suppé Leitung: Rot, Steiner, Tellian, Marik, Vaughan Mitwirkende: Azarmi, Brehler, Hübl — Beens jun., Messany, Mohilicki, Päckl, Selenko, Siesz, Sofka, Werner, Wolfrum u. a.	19.30—22.30 Uhr ● Freier Verkauf	**Samstag** **16.** Mai	19.30—21.30 Uhr ┌─────────────────────┐ Erstaufführung **Baby Hamilton** Lustspiel von Anita Hart und Maurice Braddel Leitung: Steiner, Erdmann Mitwirkende: Brix, Döberl, Falkenhagen, Gollmann, Johannsen, Oesterheit, Strambowski — Beens, Brössner, Geiger, Kasten, Köhn, v. Pervulesko, Skumanz Premieren- abonnement └─────────────────────┘
Jenufa Oper von Leos Janacek Leitung: Wöss, Mirdita, Köttel, Erdmann, Marik, Figarowa Mitwirkende: Azarmi, Barizowa, Jungwirt, Novak, Perry, Popek, Tinsobin, Wagner, Zawrelowa — Calleo, Kroupa, Messany, Varpio	19.30—22 Uhr ● Freier Verkauf	**Sonntag** **17.** Mai	19.30—21.45 Uhr **Der Floh im Ohr** Freier Verkauf Schwank von Georges Feydeau Leitung und Mitwirkende wie am 14. 5.
My Fair Lady Musical von Alan Jay Lerner und Frederick Loewe Leitung: Marik, Steiner, Köttel, Vaughan Mitwirkende: Brehler, Fritz-Simader, Hagenbüchli, Halovanic, Hübl, Kostia, Milota, Tinsobin, Weber, Wunsch — Degner, Doblich, Friedrich, Grager, Hirt, Indra, Kathan, Klimesch, Kral, Messany, Mohilicki, Pavia, Päckl, Rothmaier, Selenko, Sofka, Werner, Wolfrum, Zeller	19.30—22.30 Uhr ● Freier Verkauf	**Montag** **18.** Mai	19.30—21.30 Uhr **Baby Hamilton** Freier Verkauf Lustspiel von Anita Hart und Maurice Braddel Leitung und Mitwirkende wie am 16. 5.
La Cenerentola (Aschenbrödel) Oper von Gioacchino Rossini Leitung: Lacovich, Schönolt, Tellian, Marik Mitwirkende: Azarmi, Barizowa, Wagner — Berger-Tuna, Calleo, Kroupa, Wolfrum	20—22.30 Uhr Dienstag-Reihe Freier Verkauf	**Dienstag** **19.** Mai	Keine Vorstellung (in Wels: Baby Hamilton)

● Diese Vorstellungen dürfen von Jugendlichen vom vollendeten 14. Lebensjahr an ohne Begleitung einer Aufsichtsperson besucht werden.

Kassezeiten: Dienstag bis Samstag 9—12.30 Uhr und 16 Uhr bis Beginn der Abendvorstellung. Sonn- und Feiertage 16 Uhr bis Beginn der Abendvorstellung. Montags ab 16 Uhr nur vor Abendvorstellungen. Außerdem eine Stunde vor Beginn von freien Nachmittagsvorstellungen. Eine halbe Stunde vor jeder Vorstellung findet kein Vorverkauf statt. Telephon: 24 2 42 (Großes Haus), 24 4 93 (Kammerspiele). Außerhalb der Kassezeiten bedienen Sie sich bitte des automatischen Auskunfidienstes des Landestheaters unter Telephon Nr. 24 2 42.

GENERALINTENDANT: KARL VIBACH

Bühnen der Hansestadt Lübeck

GROSSES HAUS

19 Gastspiel Martha Mödl / Bluthochzeit

20 Zum letzten Male / Der fliegende Holländer

22 Faust

23 Der Rosenkavalier

24 Zum vorletzten Male / Rita / Das Kind und der Zauberspuk

27 Gastspiel Martha Mödl / Bluthochzeit

28 Neuinszenierung / Gastspiel Benno Hoffmann / My Fair Lady

KAMMERSPIELE

19 Der Floh im Ohr

20 Arsen und Spitzenhäubchen

21 Mien Mann de fohrt to See

22 Cyprienne

23 Arsen und Spitzenhäubchen

24 Jagdszenen aus Niederbayern

25 Wiederaufnahme / Gastspiel Günther Lüders / Mein Freund Harvey

26 Gastspiel Günther Lüders / Mein Freund Harvey

27 Cyprienne

28 Der Floh im Ohr

STUDIO

21 Nur noch wenige Aufführungen / Ich versteh' kein Wort, wenn das Badewasser läuft

24 Seid nett zu Mr. Sloane

26 Ich versteh' kein Wort, wenn das Badewasser läuft

28 Seid nett zu Mr. Sloane

VORSCHAU

Großes Haus

Kammerspiele

Studio

städtische bühnen
mainz

Vorverkaufskasse: (Telefon 87 44 16) montags bis freitags von 10 bis 13 Uhr und von 16 bis 20 Uhr, samstags von 10 bis 13 Uhr und eine Stunde vor der Vorstellung, sonntags von 10.30 bis 12.30 Uhr und eine Stunde vor der Vorstellung.

Abonnementskasse: (Telefon 87 44 18) montags bis samstags 10 bis 13 Uhr und jeweils eine Stunde vor Beginn jeder Abonnementsvorstellung
Preise I   5,— bis 17,— DM   Preise II   4,— bis 14,— DM
Preise III 3,— bis 12,— DM   Preise IV   6,— bis 18,— DM
Preise V   7,50 bis 24,— DM   Preise VI 10,— bis 30,— DM
Kleine Bühne 4,50 bis 5,50 DM
Der Vorverkauf beginnt jeweils 7 Tage vor jeder Vorstellung

Vorverkaufsstellen: Mainz-Bretzenheim: Buchhandlung Christoph Eckert · Mainz-Gonsheim: Karl Rauch, Hauptstraße 58 · Wiesbaden: Zigarren-Witte, Theaterkolonnade 3, Telefon 30 09 66 · Ingelheim: Hapag-Lloyd-Reisebüro in Firma C. H. Boehringer Böhne

Nach Vorstellungsende besteht Verbindung in alle Stadtteile
(Beachten Sie bitte die Fahrpläne im Kassenraum)

4. Juni 1970 bis 10. Juni 1970

4. 6.	Donnerstag 16.45 Uhr Geschl. Vorstellung	**HEIRATEN IST IMMER EIN RISIKO** Komödie von Saul O'Hara · Deutsch von Hans-Joachim Pauli	Inszenierung: Küfle; Ausstattung: Domsdorf Bender, Lücke, Op gen Orth, Zifferer — Ackermann, Fieber, Franken, Schoenewolf
4. 6.	Donnerstag 19.30 — 21.45 Uhr Abonn. G (17. Vorstg.) und freier Verkauf Preise II	**LA TRAVIATA** Oper von Giuseppe Verdi · Deutsche Übersetzung von Walter Felsenstein	Musikalische Leitung: Wessel-Therhorn; Inszenierung: Meyer-Oertel Ausstattung: Göllner; Chöre: Wies Freitag, Landis, Schary — Bissmann, Krause, Krug, Kusch, Leyer, Lingel, Lübbert, Neubert, Zagovec, Caron
	20 — 22 Uhr Einheitspreis 2,50 DM	Theater in der Universität: Wie ein Ei dem anderen	
5. 6.	Freitag 19.30 — 21.45 Uhr Volksbühne 7 Geschl. Vorstellung	**HEIRATEN IST IMMER EIN RISIKO** Komödie von Saul O'Hara · Deutsch von Hans-Joachim Pauli	Mitwirkende wie am 4. 6. Fletcher: Mag
6. 6.	Samstag 20 — 22 Uhr Konzertabonn.	Städtische Konzerte **8. SINFONIEKONZERT**	
7. 6.	Sonntag 14.30 — 16.45 Uhr Volksbühne 8 Geschl. Vorstellung	**HEIRATEN IST IMMER EIN RISIKO** Komödie von Saul O'Hara · Deutsch von Hans-Joachim Pauli	Mitwirkende wie am 5. 6.
7. 6.	Sonntag 19.30 — 21.45 Uhr Jug.-Abonn. (11. Vorstg.) und freier Verkauf Preise II	Zum letzten Mal **FRA DIAVOLO** Komische Oper von Daniel F. E. Auber	Musikalische Leitung: Schenk; Inszenierung: Meyer-Oertel Ausstattung: Masson; Chöre: Wies Freitag, Schary — Krause, Krug, Kusch, Leyer, Neubert, Richter
8. 6.	Montag 19.30 — 21.45 Uhr Volksbühne 2 und beschr. Verkauf Preise III	Letztes Auftreten von Marta Zifferer **HEIRATEN IST IMMER EIN RISIKO** Komödie von Saul O'Hara · Deutsch von Hans-Joachim Pauli	Mitwirkende wie am 5. 6.
9. 6.	Dienstag 19.30 — 21.30 Uhr Abonn. A (17. Vorstg.) und freier Verkauf Preise II	**DIE KRÖNUNG DER POPPÄA** Oper von Claudio Monteverdi · Musikalische Bearbeitung von Erich Kraack Freie deutsche Nachdichtung von Günther Wilhelms	Musikalische Leitung: Wessel-Therhorn; Inszenierung: Meyer-Oertel Ausstattung: Masson; Chöre: Wies Drummond, Freitag, Herrmann, Landis, Schary — Krause, Krug, Leyer, Neubert, Richter
10. 6.	Mittwoch 19.30 — 21.15 Uhr Abonn. F (17. Vorstg.) und freier Verkauf Preise III	Zum ersten Mal **KABALE UND LIEBE** Bürgerliches Trauerspiel von Friedrich Schiller	Inszenierung: Aufenanger; Ausstattung: Domsdorf Bender, Frost, Johannsen, Op gen Orth — Dahlen, Fieber, Geissler, Sawizki, Seibt, Schoenewolf, Schwartz

kleine bühne

13. 6. und **14. 6.**	Samstag und Sonntag 20 — 22 Uhr freier Verkauf Preise 4,50 bis 5,50 DM	Voranzeige **BRAVE DIEBE** (Erstaufführung) Lustspiel von Jack Popplewell	Änderungen vorbehalten Druck: Dr. Hanns Krach

National theater

Großes Haus

Kleines Haus

MANNHEIM
191. Spielzeit 1969/70
vom 29. Mai bis 9. Juni 1970
Großes und Kleines Haus
am Goetheplatz
Kammerspiele in der Kunsthalle,
Moltkestraße
Intendant im Werkhaus
Mozartstraße 9

Vorankündigung
20. Juni, 23.00 Uhr
MEDEA
von Seneca
Gastspiel des
CENTRO TEATRO ESSE
NEAPEL

Vorverkauf in Ludwigshafen:
Mundenheimer Straße 220
(Theatergemeinde), Ruf 51 31 12)
In Speyer: Wormser Straße 17
(Theatergemeinde, Ruf 24 48)
Platzmietbüro: Mannheim
Collinistraße 26, Ruf 2 18 01,
Kassenstunden:
dienstags bis freitags von
10 bis 13 und 16 bis 18 Uhr,
montags, samstags, sonn- und
feiertags von 11 bis 13 Uhr
Kasseneröffnung 1 Stunde vor
Vorstellungen.
Samstag von 10 bis 12 Uhr

Sämtliche Vorbestellungen
für Platzmieten A bis E
jederzeit
Vorverkauf ab Dienstag
an der Theaterkasse
Goetheplatz
Ruf (0821) 2 48 44/45
Kassenstunden:
dienstags bis freitags von
10 bis 13 und 16 bis 18 Uhr,
montags, samstags, sonn- und
feiertags von 11 bis 13 Uhr
Kasseneröffnung 1 Stunde
vor Beginn

Vorstellungsänderungen und
Umbesetzungen vorbehalten.

Großes Haus

29.
Freitag
20.00 bis etwa 22.15 Uhr
Miete G
Freier Verkauf DM 3,50 bis 13,50

Tartuffe
Komödie von J. B. Molière
Deutsch von Hans Weigel
Leitung: v. Janko, Walter,
Weiher, Kleber a. G.
Mitwirkende: Achtermann,
de Graaf, Mollor, Nothhorn,
Wohlbauer — Abendroth,
Dietz, Krauel, Möller, Pawlik,
Radler, Witkowski

30.
Samstag
20.00 bis etwa 22.30 Uhr
Miete L
Freier Verkauf DM 4,— bis 16,70

Fidelio
Oper von
Ludwig van Beethoven
Leitung: Fuchs, Dietz, Walter,
Schulte, Momber
Mitwirkende: Bitzner
Schreiner, — Bernhöft, Cox,
Klepert, Mazura, Schneider,
Syri, Wendt

31.
Sonntag
19.45 bis etwa 22.45 Uhr
Miete L
Freier Verkauf DM 4,— bis 16,70

**Herzog
Blaubarts Burg**
Oper von Béla Bartók
Leitung: Eykman, Schubert,
Walter, Schulte
Mitwirkende: Schreiner —
Mazura

hierauf

Die Kluge
Oper von Carl Orff
Leitung: Eykman, Schubert,
Walter, Schulte, Momber
Mitwirkende: Bähr — Davidson,
Herr, Klepert, Reas, Rösaling,
Syri, Völker, Wendt —
Mikulski, Piep, Clos

Zum letzten Mal

1.
Montag
20.00 bis etwa 22.15 Uhr
Beschr. Verk. DM 4,— bis 16,70
Gutscheine anderer Stücke
von Umtausch ausgenommen

La Bohème
Oper von Giacomo Puccini
Leitung: Schubert,
Walter, Schulte, Momber
Mitwirkende: Bähr, Mohar
— Albrecht, Bernhöft, Davidson,
De Sica, Mazura, Reas,
Schneider, Wendt

2.
Dienstag
20.00 bis etwa 22.30 Uhr
Miete K
Freier Verkauf DM 4,— bis 16,70

Peer Gynt
Oper von Werner Egk
Leitung: Fuchs, Blum, Walter,
Stahl, Momber, Müller
Mitwirkende: Gasemann, Haas,
Jaeger, Köhler, Lehnert,
Schweninger — Albrecht,
Beyer, Blum, Teif — Falen, Piep
und Tanzgruppe

3.
Mittwoch
20.00 bis etwa 22.30 Uhr
Beschr. Verk. DM 4, — bis 16,70
Gutscheine anderer Stücke
von Umtausch ausgenommen

Gasparone
Operette von Carl Millöcker
Leitung: Gitschel, Blum, Walter,
Klein, Momber, Müller
Mitwirkende: Haas, Lehnert —
Albrecht, Beck, Bernhöft,
— Bernhöft, Cox, Davidson,
Ellerich, Herr, Rösaling, Wendt

4.
Donnerstag
20.00 bis etwa 22.30 Uhr
Miete A
Freier Verkauf DM 3,50 bis 13,50

Tosca
Oper von Giacomo Puccini
Leitung: Fuchs, Amberger, Krall,
Klein, Momber
Mitwirkende: Köhler, Schreiner,
— Bernhöft, Herr, Rösaling, Wendt

5.
Freitag
20.00 bis etwa 22.45 Uhr
Miete F grün
Freier Verkauf DM 3,50 bis 13,50

Maria Stuart
Trauerspiel
von Friedrich Schiller
Besetzung wie am 5. Juni

6.
Samstag
20.00 bis etwa 22.45 Uhr
Miete O
Freier Verkauf DM 3,50 bis 13,50

7.
Sonntag
20.00 bis etwa 22.45 Uhr
Miete A
Beschr. Verk. DM 4, — bis 16,70
Gutscheine anderer Stücke
von Umtausch ausgenommen

**Der
Freischütz**
Oper von Carl Maria von Weber
Leitung: Stein, Hager, Walter,
Amann a. G., Momber, Müller
Mitwirkende: Bitzner,
Gasemann — Badonik, Mazura,
Rösaling, Schneider, Syri,
Völker, Wendt

Neuinszenierung

8.
Montag
20.00 bis etwa 22.30 Uhr
Miete C
Freier Verkauf DM 4,20 bis 20,20

Norma
Oper von Vincenzo Bellini
Leitung: Latovski, Kortovav,
Kunstmacht, Petrakopic,
Milosavljeve, Pavcilic, Sopov
Mitwirkende: Bojadzic, Spov
Dobrokorova, Lipra — Bozikov,
Cancev, Surmajon, Todorovski
Gastspiel des Mazedonischen
Nationaltheaters Skopje

9.
Dienstag
20.00 bis etwa 22.45 Uhr
Miete C
Freier Verkauf DM 4,— bis 16,70

Kleines Haus

29.
Freitag
20.00 bis etwa 21.30 Uhr
Miete E gelb II
Freier Verkauf DM 3,50 bis 13,50

**Play
Strindberg**
August Strindbergs „Totentanz"
arrangiert von
Friedrich Dürrenmatt
Leitung v. Janko, Walter, Klein,
Mitwirkende: Mörger —
Kollhoff, Timmermann

30.
Samstag
20.00 bis etwa 21.45 Uhr
Miete H I
Freier Verkauf DM 3,50 bis 13,50

**Der
Belagerungs-
zustand**
Schauspiel von Albert Camus
Leitung: Gerstenberg, Stahl,
Tassa a. G.
Mitwirkende: de Graaf, Geiger,
Kocher, Meyer-Goslar,
Mollor, Nothhorn, Reymann,
Sosana, Walbröll, Weinreich,
Wohlbauer — Abendroth,
Anders, Berben, Brönel,
Dühren, Hönig, Köhler, Kollhoff,
Krauel, Krause, Pawlik, Pott,
Radler, Schmidtonz, Spahr,
Timmermann, Vito-Mühlen,
Weigang, Witkowski, Witta

31.
Sonntag
20.00 bis etwa 22.15 Uhr
Miete C I

König Johann
von Friedrich Dürrenmatt
nach Shakespeare
Besetzung wie am 4. Juni

Kunsthalle
20.00 bis etwa 22.00 Uhr
Schauspielmiete Gruppe III
Freier Verkauf DM 2,40 bis 5,70

Der Tiger
von Murray Schisgal
Deutsch von Rudolf Stoiber

hierauf

Oldenberg
von Barry Bermange
Deutsch von Jörg Wehmeier
Besetzung wie am 31. Mai

1.
Montag
20.00 bis etwa 22.30 Uhr
Theatergemeinde 1591 — 2120
Beschr. Verk. DM 3,50 bis 13,50

Der Snob
Komödie von Carl Sternheim
Leitung: Müller a. G., Walter,
Klein
Mitwirkende: Geiger, Sosana,
Weinreich, Wohlbauer —
Anders, Elisso, Pawlik,
Vito-Mühlen

Kunsthalle
20.00 bis etwa 22.00 Uhr
Schauspielmiete Gruppe IV
Freier Verkauf DM 2,40 bis 5,70

Der Tiger
von Murray Schisgal
Deutsch von Rudolf Stoiber

hierauf

Oldenberg
von Barry Bermange
Deutsch von Jörg Wehmeier
Besetzung wie am 31. Mai

2.
Dienstag
20.00 bis etwa 22.30 Uhr
Theatergemeinde 1061 — 1590
Beschr. Verk. DM 3,50 bis 13,50

Tartuffe
Komödie von J. B. Molière
Deutsch von Hans Weigel
Besetzung wie am 29. Mai

3.
Mittwoch
20.00 bis etwa 22.30 Uhr
Miete M c/t II
Freier Verkauf DM 3,50 bis 13,50

**Play
Strindberg**
August Strindbergs „Totentanz"
arrangiert von
Friedrich Dürrenmatt
Besetzung wie am 29. Mai

4.
Donnerstag
20.00 bis etwa 21.30 Uhr
Miete N I
Freier Verkauf DM 3,50 bis 13,50

König Johann
von Friedrich Dürrenmatt
nach Shakespeare
Leitung: Gerstenberg, Stahl,
Klein
Mitwirkende: Geiger, Sosana,
Weinreich, Wohlbauer —
Abendroth, Anders, Hönig,
Kollhoff, Krauel, Krause,
Küstelhardt, Pawlik, Pott, Radler,
Vito-Mühlen, Weigang
Schmidtonz, Timmermann,
Witkowski, Witta

5.
Freitag
20.00 bis etwa 22.15 Uhr
Miete N II
Freier Verkauf DM 3,50 bis 13,50

**Play
Strindberg**
August Strindbergs „Totentanz"
arrangiert von
Friedrich Dürrenmatt
Besetzung wie am 29. Mai

6.
Samstag
20.00 bis etwa 22.15 Uhr
Miete N II
Freier Verkauf DM 3,50 bis 13,50

**DiealteJungfer
und der Dieb**
Oper von Gian-Carlo Menotti

hierauf

Angélique
Oper von Jacques Ibert
Leitung: Eykman, Rasky a. G.
Stahl, Momber
Mitwirkende: Bähr, Fonseca,
Kapsmayer, Jaeger, Lehnert
Schweninger — De Sica, Gilvan
Herr, Reas, Syri, Völker, Wendt

7.
Sonntag
20.00 bis etwa 22.15 Uhr
Miete B II
Freier Verkauf DM 3,50 bis 13,50

**Die tollen
Zwanziger**
Eine Kabarett-Revue aus dem
Berlin zwischen 1918 und 1933
Zusammengestellt von
Herbert Hauck
Leitung: Hauck a. G., Gitschel,
Pillion, Klein, Guttmann a. G.
Geiger, Nothhorn, Wohlbauer —
Berben, Krauel, Pott,
Schmidtonz, Spahr
Bussmann, Schulz, Wagner,
Zeng

8.
Montag
geschlossen

9.
Dienstag
20.00 bis etwa 22.15 Uhr
Miete B II
Freier Verkauf DM 3,50 bis 13,50

König Johann
von Friedrich Dürrenmatt
nach Shakespeare
Besetzung wie am 4. Juni

MÜNCHNER FESTSPIELE

SCHWANENSEE
von Peter Iljitsch Tschaikowsky

in

RICHARD CRAGUN

und

MARGOT FONTEYN

Gastspiel

Montag, 8. Juni 1970

14. Juli bis 6. August 1970

Vorverkauf an der Eintrittskartenkasse der Bayerischen Staatsoper, Maximilianstraße 11
wochentags: Dienstag mit Freitag 10 Uhr bis 13 Uhr und 15 Uhr bis 18 Uhr, Samstag 10 Uhr bis 13 Uhr

---

29. Mai
Freitag 19.00 Uhr bis gegen 22.30 Uhr
Geschlossene Vorstellung
Don Carlos
In der Originalsprache
von Giuseppe Verdi
Patané, Hartha, Jürgens, Baumgart
Fahberg, Fassbaender, Schneider,
Björner, Fassbaender, Braun,
Hotter, Lenz, Tessaloni, Braun,
Freundörfer, Knapp, Sapell, Auer,
Wichartz

30. Mai
Samstag 18.00 Uhr bis gegen 22.00 Uhr
Tannhäuser
von Richard Wagner
von Dohnanyi, Lehmann, Heinrich,
Baumgart
Stilz, Bertold, Freedmann,
Schneider, Tentrop, Neubold,
Evangelatos, Böhme, Knzüb, Prey,
Hoffmann, Nöcker, Lenz, Auer

31. Mai
Samstag 18.00 Uhr bis gegen 22.30 Uhr
7. Sonntag-Platzmiete rot
Beschränkter Kartenverkauf
Don Carlos
In der Originalsprache
von Giuseppe Verdi
Patané, Hartha, Jürgens, Baumgart
Björner, Fassbaender, Schneider,
Fahberg, Fiorel, Lazaro, Braun,
Hotter, Lenz, Tessaloni, Sapell,
Freundörfer, Knapp, Sapell,
Auer, Wichartz

1. Juni
Montag 19.00 Uhr bis 22.30 Uhr
Die Hochzeit des Figaro
In der Originalsprache
von W. A. Mozart
Kuntzsch, Rennert, Heinrich, Baumgart
Kirschstein, Bertold, Schädle,
Evangelatos, Engen, Grumbach,
Kusche, Thaw, Proebstl, Falkenberger

2. Juni
Dienstag 19.00 Uhr bis 22.00 Uhr
Ein Maskenball
In der Originalsprache
von Giuseppe Verdi
Hager, Hasse, Jürgens/Dreher,
Baumgart
Stojanovic a. G., Töpper, Stefini,
Lazaro, Tentrop, Sapell, Peter,
Proebstl, Klarwein, Welter

3. Juni
Mittwoch 18.00 Uhr bis 22.00 Uhr
7. Mittwoch-Platzmiete weiß
Beschränkter Kartenverkauf
Tannhäuser
von Richard Wagner
von Dohnanyi, Lehmann, Heinrich,
Baumgart
Watson, Bertold, Freedmann,
Schneider, Tentrop, Neubold,
Evangelatos, Kohn, Esser,
Grumbach, Hoffmann, Nöcker,
Lenz, Auer

4. Juni
Donnerstag 19.00 Uhr bis 22.00 Uhr
Der Freischütz
von Carl Maria von Weber
Zanotelli, Hartmann, Gröbler, Eichhorn
Kirschstein, Schädle, Schneider,
Neubold, Tentrop, Evangelatos,
Grumbach, Peter, Böhme, Cox,
Klarwein, Kohn, Kehl, Haupt

5. Juni
Freitag 19.00 Uhr bis gegen 22.30 Uhr
Carmen
von Georges Bizet
Böhm, Rennolf, Bauer-Ecsy
Baumgart
Troyanos, Donath, Schädle,
Wewezow, Evangelatos, Roelialny,
Braun, Engen, Welter,
Grumbach, Klarwein, Lenz,
Sapell

---

6. Juni
Samstag 18.00 Uhr bis 22.00 Uhr
Tannhäuser
von Richard Wagner
von Dohnanyi, Lehmann, Heinrich,
Baumgart
Stilz, Martin, Freedmann,
Schneider, Tentrop, Neubold,
Evangelatos, Böhme, Koth,
Grumbach, Peukolla, Foerlit,
Brokmeier, Tessaloni

7. Juni
Samstag 18.00 Uhr bis nach 22.00 Uhr
Der Rosenkavalier
von Richard Strauss
Keilber, Hartmann, Jürgens, Baumgart
Hillebrecht, Bertold, Donath,
Wass, Wewezow, Böhme, Neubold,
Stolze, Peter, Klarwein,
Carruth, Knapp, Falkenberger,
Cox, Pawelita

8. Juni
Montag 19.00 Uhr bis gegen 22.30 Uhr
Schwanensee
Ballett von Peter Iljitsch Tschaikowsky
Kuntzsch, Cranko, Woollliams, Rose
Fonteyn a. G. Werner, Kraus-Nelschewa,
Algarotova, Cragun a. G., Peruni,
Madsen, Skrobila, Hradec, Nitsch,
Cragun a. G., Bertoy, de Luiry,
Erler, Hajek, Klaus, Rodzat,
Schöber, Leams

9. Juni
Dienstag 19.30 Uhr bis 22.15 Uhr
Geschlossene Vorstellung
Lucia di Lammermoor
von Gaetano Donizetti
Bender, Lisi, Hornsteiner, Baumgart
Michels, Benningsen, Murray,
Blankenship, Björnsson, Proebstl,
Klarwein

10. Juni
Mittwoch 19.00 Uhr bis 22.00 Uhr
Falstaff
von Giuseppe Verdi
Becker, Hartmann, Gröbler, Baumgart
Kirschstein, Stefini, Madeira,
Wewezow, Imdahl, Tipton,
Grabs, Peskolla, Lenz, Proebstl

11. Juni
Donnerstag 19.30 Uhr bis 22.15 Uhr
Fidelio
von Ludwig van Beethoven
Rieger, Hartmann, Jürgens, Baumgart
Björner, Stefini, Hotter,
Nöcker, Tschud Böhm,
Lenz, Falkenberger, Kell

12. Juni
Freitag 14.00 Uhr bis 18.15 Uhr
Geschlossene Nachmittags-Vorstellung
Don Pasquale
von Gaetano Donizetti
Zanotelli, Hartmann, Jürgens, Eichhorn
Schädle, Kohn, Wittrich,
Brokmeier, Knapp

12. Juni
Freitag 19.30 Uhr bis 21.45 Uhr
Geschlossene Abendvorstellung
Don Pasquale
von Gaetano Donizetti
Zanotelli, Hartmann, Jürgens, Eichhorn
Schädle, Böhme, Grumbach,
Grabs, Knapp

Druck J. Schweltzer, München

BAYERISCHE STAATSTHEATER

1970	Oper Nationaltheater	Schauspiel Residenztheater	Oper - Operette Theater am Gärtnerplatz
Mittwoch 3. Juni	Preise G 7. Mittwoch-Platzm. weiß u. beschr. Kartenverk. **Tannhäuser** von Dohnanyi - Lehmann - Heinrich Watson, Berthold, Kohn, Esser, Grumbach Beginn 18 Uhr — Ende 22 Uhr	Preise A 7. Vorstellung Mittwoch-Abonn. Serie gelb und freier Verkauf **Der Fächer** Beginn 19³⁰ Uhr — Ende 21⁴⁵ Uhr	Preise A **Die lustigen Weiber von Windsor** Beginn 19³⁰ Uhr — Ende 22 Uhr
Donnerstag 4. Juni	Preise A **Der Freischütz** Zanotelli - Hartmann - Grübler Kirschstein, Donath, Grumbach, Metternich, Böhme, Hoffmann, Kohn Beginn 19 Uhr — Ende 22 Uhr	Preise A 7. Vorstellung Donnerstag-Abonn. Serie gelb u. freier Verkauf **Der Fächer** Beginn 19³⁰ Uhr — Ende 21⁴⁵ Uhr	Preise A **Der Arzt wider Willen** Beginn 19³⁰ Uhr — Ende 21⁴⁵ Uhr
Freitag 5. Juni	Preise S **Carmen** Böhm - Rennert - Bauer-Ecsy Troyanos, Donath, Ilosfalvy, Braun, Engen, Grumbach Beginn 19 Uhr — Ende gegen 22³⁰ Uhr	Preise S 6. Vorstellung Freitag-Abonn. Serie grün und freier Verkauf **Maria Stuart** Beginn 19³⁰ Uhr — Ende 22⁴⁵ Uhr	Altes Residenztheater (Cuvilliés-Theater) Geschlossene Vorstellung — Kein Kartenverkauf **Der Barbier von Sevilla** Beginn 19³⁰ Uhr — Ende 22¹⁵ Uhr
Samstag 6. Juni	Preise G **Tannhäuser** von Dohnanyi - Lehmann - Heinrich Silja, Martin, Böhme, Kozub, Grumbach Beginn 18 Uhr — Ende 22 Uhr	Preise A 6. Vorstellung Samstag-Abonn. Serie grün und freier Verkauf **Der Fächer** Beginn 19³⁰ Uhr — Ende 21⁴⁵ Uhr	Preise S **Die lustige Witwe** Beginn 19³⁰ Uhr — Ende 22³⁰ Uhr
Sonntag 7. Juni	Preise A **Der Rosenkavalier** Kleiber - Hartmann - Jürgens Hillebrecht, Berthold, Donath, Wewezow, Böhme, Imdahl, Stolze, Peter, Fehenberger, Cox Beginn 18 Uhr — Ende nach 22 Uhr	Preise S 7. Vorstellung Sonntag-Abonn. Serie blau und freier Verkauf **Maria Stuart** Beginn 19³⁰ Uhr — Ende 22⁴⁵ Uhr	Preise S 6. Sonntag-Platzm. und freier Verkauf **Encores** **Yolimba** oder Die Grenzen der Magie Beginn 19³⁰ Uhr — Ende 21⁴⁵ Uhr
Montag 8. Juni	Preise G **Schwanensee** Kuntzsch - Cranko - Rose Fonteyn a. G., Werner, Cragun a. G., Barbay Beginn 19 Uhr — Ende gegen 22³⁰ Uhr	Preise S 7. Vorstellung Montag-Abonn. Serie gelb und freier Verkauf **Die Herren im Haus** Beginn 20 Uhr — Ende 22 Uhr	Preise A **Das Land des Lächelns** Beginn 19³⁰ Uhr — Ende 22 Uhr
Dienstag 9. Juni	Geschlossene Vorstellung **Lucia di Lammermoor** Bender - List - Hornsteiner Michels, Murray, Blankenship, Proebstl Beginn 19³⁰ Uhr — Ende 22¹⁵ Uhr	Preise A 7. Vorstellung Dienstag-Abonn. Serie grün und freier Verkauf **Der Fächer** Beginn 19³⁰ Uhr — Ende 21⁴⁵ Uhr	Preise A **Die lustigen Weiber von Windsor** Beginn 19³⁰ Uhr — Ende 22 Uhr
Mittwoch 10. Juni	Preise A **Falstaff** Bender - Hartleb - Grübler Kirschstein, Steffek, Madeira, Wewezow, Imdahl, Tipton, Grobe, Paskuda, Lenz, Proebstl Beginn 19³⁰ Uhr — Ende 22 Uhr	Preise S **Maria Stuart** Beginn 19³⁰ Uhr — Ende 22⁴⁵ Uhr	Preise S **Aufstieg und Fall der Stadt Mahagonny** Beginn 19³⁰ Uhr — Ende 22 Uhr

VORVERKAUF der Eintrittskarten für OPER (Nationaltheater an der Tageskasse, Maximilianstraße 11 (neben Nationaltheater), Tel. 221316, werktags von 10 bis 13 Uhr und von 15 bis 18 Uhr, an Sonn- und Feiertagen von 10 bis 13 Uhr, für SCHAUSPIEL an der Tageskasse, Max-Joseph-Platz 1 (Haupteingang Residenztheater), Telefon 225754 oder 2185413, Montag mit Freitag von 10 bis 13 Uhr und von 16 bis 18 Uhr, Samstag, Sonn- und Feiertag von 10 bis 13 Uhr, für GÄRTNERTHEATER, Telefon 261232, an der Tageskasse, Gärtnerplatz 3, Montag mit Freitag von 10 bis 13 Uhr und von 16 bis 18 Uhr, Samstag und Sonntag von 10 bis 13 Uhr und bei den bekannten Vorverkaufsstellen. Die Abendkasse in den jeweiligen Theatern ist eine Stunde vor Vorstellungsbeginn geöffnet.

Druck J Gotteswinter

39

one hundred fifty-nine

Städtische Bühnen Münster

Großes Haus

JUNI

MITTWOCH 3 20 – 22.30 Uhr	König Richard der Dritte	CTG-Besuchergruppe A und Freier Kartenverkauf Preise DM 2.50 bis 9.50	
DONNERSTAG 4 20 – 22 Uhr	*Zum letzten Mal* **Heiraten ist immer ein Risiko** Gastspiel in Viersen: Orpheus in der Unterwelt	Freier Kartenverkauf Preise DM 2.50 bis 9.50	
FREITAG 5 20 – 22.30 Uhr	The King and I mit Ilse Werner	CTG-Besuchergruppe B und Freier Kartenverkauf Preise DM 3.50 bis 12.50	
SAMSTAG 6 20 – 22.30 Uhr	The King and I mit Ilse Werner	Freier Kartenverkauf Preise DM 3.50 bis 12.50	
SONNTAG 7 20 – 22.30 Uhr	König Richard der Dritte	CTG-Besuchergruppe F und Freier Kartenverkauf Preise DM 2.50 bis 9.50	
MONTAG 8 20 – 22.30 Uhr	König Richard der Dritte	CTG-Besuchergruppe C und Freier Kartenverkauf Preise DM 2.50 bis 9.50	
DIENSTAG 9 20 – 22.30 Uhr	The King and I mit Ilse Werner	Großes Abonnement Dienstag A 13 und Freier Kartenverkauf Preise DM 3.50 bis 12.50	
MITTWOCH 10 19.30 – 22.45 Uhr	*Zum vorletzten Mal* Die Hochzeit des Figaro	Jugendring E und Beschr. Kartenverkauf Preise DM 3.50 bis 12.50	
DONNERSTAG 11 19.30 – 22 Uhr	König Richard der Dritte	Jugendring A und Beschr. Kartenverkauf Preise DM 2.50 bis 9.50	
FREITAG 12 20 – 22 Uhr	Die Perlenfischer	Großes Abonnement Freitag A 13 und Freier Kartenverkauf Preise DM 3.50 bis 12.50	
SAMSTAG 13 20 – 22.30 Uhr	The King and I mit Ilse Werner	Freier Kartenverkauf Preise DM 3.50 bis 12.50	
SONNTAG 14 20 – 22.15 Uhr	*Neuinszenierung* Die heimliche Ehe	Geschlossene Festvorstellung Kein Kartenverkauf	
MONTAG 15 19.30 – 22 Uhr	König Richard der Dritte	Jugendring B und Beschr. Kartenverkauf Preise DM 2.50 bis 9.50	

Kammerspiele
Annette von Droste-Hülshoff-Schule

JUNI

FREITAG 5 20 – 22.30 Uhr	Zicke-Zacke	Freier Kartenverkauf Preise DM 3.50 bis 7.—
SAMSTAG 6 20 – 22.30 Uhr	Zicke-Zacke	Freier Kartenverkauf Preise DM 3.50 bis 7.—
FREITAG 12 20 – 22 Uhr	*Erstaufführung* **Schönes Weekend, Mr. Bennett!**	Premieren-Abonnement und Freier Kartenverkauf Preise DM 3.50 bis 7.—
SONNTAG 14 20 – 22.30 Uhr	Zicke-Zacke	Freier Kartenverkauf Preise DM 3.50 bis 7.—

Im Spielplan

Großes Haus

König Richard der Dritte
von William Shakespeare
Deutsch von Hans Rothe
Leitung: Gnekow / Karafyllis / Schönbach
Mitwirkende: Böckstiegel, Claudius, Sagell, Ussat — Brambeer, Brüggemann, Buder, Erler, Friedrichsen, Gentsch, Gronau, Grüsser, Günther, Hönigschmid, Koch, Schlick, Scholkmann, Sudbrack a. G., Tecklenburg, Thiele u. a.

Ilse Werner in
The King and I   (Der König und ich)
Musical von Richard Rodgers und Oscar Hammerstein II
Leitung: Stulen / Vetter / Baer / Scherr a. G. / Böllert / van der Sloot
Mitwirkende: Liss, Pfirschinger, Werner a. G. — Buder, Walter, Jahreis, Klomser / Thiele, Schlick, Urich, Vehse — Hunt — Puech

Heiraten ist immer ein Risiko
Kriminalkomödie von Saul O'Hara
Leitung: Schmidt / Karafyllis / Flaskämper
Mitwirkende: Böckstiegel, Nippe, Koehler, Ussat — Erler, Gronau, Günther, Hönigschmid

Die heimliche Ehe
Komische Oper von Domenico Cimarosa
Neubearbeitung von Hans Stüwe
Leitung: Schwickert / Reinhold / Struck
Mitwirkende: Bähnke, Futran, Pröls — Bundschuh, Glawatsch, Jahreis, Nieders, Schütte

Die Hochzeit des Figaro
Oper von Wolfgang Amadeus Mozart
Leitung: Stulen / Reinhold / Karafyllis / Böllert / van der Sloot
Mitwirkende: Bähnke, Futran, Liss, Pfirschinger, Sapinski — Bundschuh, Lelgemann / Duesing, Glawatsch, Nieders / Jahreis, Schürmann / Nieders, Vehse

Die Perlenfischer
Oper von Georges Bizet
Leitung: Stulen / Werthenbach / Struck / van der Sloot / Böllert
Mitwirkende: Jones a. G. — Duesing, Kayrooz a. G., Schürmann — Hunt — Puech, van der Sloot

Kammerspiele

Schönes Weekend, Mr. Bennett!
Kriminalkomödie von Arthur Watkyn
Leitung: Schlick / Struck
Mitwirkende: Sagell — Brambeer, Erler, Gronau, Hönigschmid, Scholkmann, Tecklenburg, Thiele

Zicke-Zacke
Schauspiel von Peter Terson
Leitung: Koch / Janssens a. G. / Karafyllis / Weihe
Mitwirkende: Claudius, Didusch, Nippe, Ussat — Friedrichsen, Gentsch, Gronau, Grüsser, Günther, u. a.

Vorschau

GROSSES HAUS, Mittwoch, 24. und Donnerstag, 25. Juni, jeweils 20 Uhr

10. Symphoniekonzert

Das Symphonieorchester der Stadt Münster
Dirigent: André Vandernoot a. G.
Solist: Margot Schön, Klavier
Programm: HECTOR BERLIOZ: Liebesszene und Tod aus „Romeo und Julia"
LUDWIG VAN BEETHOVEN: Klavierkonzert Nr. 2 B-Dur
DIMITRI SCHOSTAKOWITSCH: 5. Symphonie

Vorverkauf ab 5. Juni für 9. Juni bis 15. Juni

Heben Sie bitte die UMTAUSCHGUTSCHEINE nicht bis zum Verfallstermin auf, da Sie Gefahr laufen, an den letzten Tagen keine Eintrittskarten mehr dafür zu bekommen.

Großes Haus

Vorverkauf	beginnt im Großen Haus (Telefon 4 01 01) und im Verkehrsverein Freitag für die jeweils kommende Woche von Dienstag bis einschließlich Montag der übernächsten Woche
Kassenstunden	Dienstag bis Freitag 10 bis 13.30 Uhr und 17 bis 18.30 Uhr Samstag 10 bis 13.30 Uhr Sonn- und Feiertag 11 bis 12.30 Uhr Montags keine Kassenstunden, dafür telefonische Kartenbestellung im Werbebüro (Tel. 5 64 02) während der üblichen Kassenstunden im Verkehrsverein, Berliner Platz, gegenüber dem Hauptbahnhof (Tel. 4 24 78) ständiger Kartenverkauf (auch montags) 8 bis 18 Uhr
Abendkasse	jeweils eine Stunde vor Beginn der Vorstellung

Abendkasse Telefon 4 01 01

Kammerspiele

Vorverkauf	siehe unter „Großes Haus"
Abendkasse	nur an Vorstellungstagen jeweils eine Stunde vor Beginn der Vorstellung. Annette-Schule, Grüne Gasse, zwischen Marienplatz und Aegidiistraße

Abendkasse Telefon 49 24 69

Spielzeit 1969/70   **Leitung: Dr. Horst Gnekow**

RHEINISCHES LANDESTHEATER NEUSS

SPIELZEIT 1969/70

2. SAMSTAG Mai
20 Uhr
Theater-Ring D und Freiverkauf
Preisgruppe III DM 6,50, 5,50 und 4,–
(einschließlich Sozialabgaben)
Erwerbsbeschäftigte, Jugendliche und Studierende: Ermäßigung

Zum letzten Male
Die Zofen
Tragödie von Jean Genet
Inszenierung: Rolf Heutz · Bühnenbild und Kostüme: Frank-Ulrich Schmidt
MITWIRKENDE: Damen: Dinkgräfe Meyer Piontek

---

18. MONTAG Mai
20 Uhr
Platzmiete B und Freiverkauf
Jugend-Abonnement Nr. 61–120

JOSEPH OFFENBACH in
Der Geizige

---

3. SONNTAG Mai
20 Uhr
Theater-Ring F und Freiverkauf
Preisgruppe III DM 6,50, 5,50 und 4,–
(einschließlich Sozialabgaben)
Erwerbsbeschäftigte, Jugendliche und Studierende: Ermäßigung

Zum letzten Male
Nekrassow
Schauspiel von Jean-Paul Sartre
Inszenierung: Hermann Wetzke · Bühnenbild: Paul Schneeloch
MITWIRKENDE: Damen: Berneker Büchner Stadler
Herren: Bauer Blatt Brox Conradt Dannell Eggert Grau
Handrick Held Jungermann Löbach Müller-Elmau
Oelrich Schnell Slindermann

---

29. FREITAG Mai
20 Uhr
Jugendring der Stadt Neuss und Freiverkauf
Jugend-Abonnement Nr. 1–60

JOSEPH OFFENBACH in
Der Geizige

---

10. SONNTAG Mai
Beginn: 20 Uhr
Ende: 22 Uhr
Platzmiete A und Freiverkauf
Preisgruppe I DM 12,–, 10,50 und 9,–
(einschließlich Sozialabgaben)

PREMIERE
JOSEPH OFFENBACH in
Der Geizige
Lustspiel von Molière
Inszenierung: Markwart Müller-Elmau · Bühnenbild und Kostüme: Frank-Ulrich Schmidt
MITWIRKENDE: Damen: Klamroth Meyer Piontek
Herren: Bauer Blatt Grau Held Jungermann Löbach
Oelrich Rauschenberger Schnell

IN VORBEREITUNG:

Baby Hamilton
Lustspiel von Anita Hart und Maurice Braddell

Vorverkauf: Theaterkasse Drususallee · Telefon 132 14 · Geöffnet: täglich von 11–13 Uhr und 17–19 Uhr · An Vorstellungstagen: vormittags 11–13 Uhr und ab 19 Uhr.

one hundred sixty-one

OPERNHAUS

Spielplan vom 30. Mai – 7. Juni 1970

Sa 30 20.00–22.45 Uhr
Preise von 3,40–15,60

Der Freischütz
Romantische Oper von Carl Maria von Weber

Musikalische Leitung: Hans Giersten
Inszenierung: Hans-Peter Lehmann
Bühnenbild: Annelies Corrodi
Kostüme: Margret Kaulbach · Chöre: Adam Rauh
Mitwirkende Damen: Kienzl, Kingdon
Herren: Gniffke, Licha, Mikorey, Supala, Thiemann, Vogler, Wolovsky

So 31 20.00–22.40 Uhr
Preise von 3,40–15,60

Der Vogelhändler
Operette von Carl Zeller

Musikalische Leitung: Edgar Schmidt-Bredow
Inszenierung: Kurt Leo Sourisseaux
Bühnenbild: Sepp Schick · Kostüme: Margret Kaulbach
Choreographie: Georges Lais · Chöre: Adam Rauh
Mitwirkende Damen: Hensel, Knittel, Krål
Herren: Besançon, Born, Graf, Lehrberger, Mikorey, Mirov, Sandbank
In Tänzen: Schönsteiner, Lang, Maslarevski, Braun und die Tanzgruppe des Opernhauses

Di 2 Juni 20.00–22.45 Uhr
Platzmiete A u G
und freier Verkauf
Preise von 3,40–15,60

Rendezvous bei Offenbach
Fortunios Lied
Operette von Jacques Offenbach
hierauf:
Die glückliche Insel
Operette nach Jacques Offenbach
von Leopold Schmidt

Musikalische Leitung: Otto Dinnebier
Inszenierung: Rolf Lansky
Bühnenbild und Kostüme: Waldemar Breidenbach

Mitwirkende Damen: Hensel, Sarata
Herren: Gentzen, Graf, Huemer, Loscher, Meier, Mikorey, Sandbank

Mitwirkende Damen: Coty, Kienzl, Krål
Herren: Gentzen, Graf, Loscher, Meier, Mikorey, Nowak, Sandbank

Neuinszenierung

Mi 3 20.00 Uhr
Platzmiete E u S
und freier Verkauf
Preise von 4,20–17,20

Die heimliche Ehe
Oper von Domenico Cimarosa

Musikalische Leitung: Konrad Peter Mannert
Inszenierung: Georg Goll
Bühnenbild und Kostüme: Walter Perdacher
Mitwirkende Damen: Astner, Hellmann, van Jüten
Herren: Hanner, Lange, Zimmermann

Do 4 20.00–21.20 Uhr
Platzmiete C u H
und freier Verkauf
Preise von 3,40–15,60

Intolleranza 70
Szenische Aktion von Luigi Nono

Musikalische Leitung: Wolfgang Gayler
Szenische Realisierung: Wolfgang Weber, Peter Heyduck, Günter Titt, Lajos Keresztes
Chöre: Karl Kaufhold / Adam Rauh
Mitwirkende Damen: de Francesca, Lammers
Herren: Curzi, Giongo, Hanner

Fr 5 20.00 Uhr
Preise von 3,40–15,60

Die heimliche Ehe
Oper von Domenico Cimarosa

Musikalische Leitung: Konrad Peter Mannert
Inszenierung: Georg Goll
Bühnenbild und Kostüme: Walter Perdacher
Mitwirkende Damen: Astner, Hellmann, van Jüten
Herren: Hanner, Lange, Zimmermann

Sa 6 19.00–23.30 Uhr
Fürther
Platzmieten A + B
und freier Verkauf
Preise von 4,20–17,20

Lohengrin
Romantische Oper von Richard Wagner

Musikalische Leitung: Max Loy
Inszenierung: Hans-Peter Lehmann
Bühnenbild: Walter Perdacher
Kostüme: Margret Kaulbach · Chöre: Adam Rauh
Mitwirkende Damen: Lammers, Rhein
Herren: Agrelli, Gniffke, Graf, Imdahl, Meier, Thiemann, Vogler, Wollitz

In neuer Besetzung

So 7 20.00 Uhr
Preise von 3,40–15,60

Die heimliche Ehe
Oper von Domenico Cimarosa

Musikalische Leitung: Konrad Peter Mannert
Inszenierung: Georg Goll
Bühnenbild und Kostüme: Walter Perdacher
Mitwirkende Damen: Kienzl, Krål, Schwenniger a. G.
Herren: Agrelli, Gniffke, Lehrberger

Voranzeige:
Mo 8 20.00 Uhr Rendezvous bei Offenbach
Di 9   20.00 Uhr Catulli Carmina hierauf: Carmina Burana
Mi 10 20.00 Uhr Die heimliche Ehe
Do 11 20.00 Uhr Lucrezia Borgia
Fr 12 20.00 Uhr Der Vogelhändler

Kassenöffnungszeiten:
Opernhaus
Schauspielhaus / Kammerspiele
wochentags 10–13 und 17–20 Uhr
sonntags 17–20 Uhr
bei Nachmittagsvorstellungen 1/2 Stunde vor Beginn

STÄDTISCHE BÜHNEN NÜRNBERG-FÜRTH

one hundred sixty-two

SCHAUSPIELHAUS

Spielplan vom 30. Mai – 8. Juni 1970

Sa 30 20.00–21.50 Uhr
Preise von 4,50–10,70

Das Glück zu dritt
Komödie von Eugène Labiche

Inszenierung: Konrad Höller
Bühnenbild: Ambrosius Humm
Kostüme: Margret Kaulbach · Musik: Otto Dinnebier
Mitwirkende Damen: Antonius, Pedersen, Schweizer,
Willick · Herren: Breitenfeld, Dardel, Thorwald, Ude

So 31 20.00–21.50 Uhr
Preise von 4,50–10,70

Das Glück zu dritt
Komödie von Eugène Labiche

Inszenierung: Konrad Höller
Bühnenbild: Ambrosius Humm
Kostüme: Margret Kaulbach · Musik: Otto Dinnebier
Mitwirkende Damen: Antonius, Pedersen, Schweizer,
Willick · Herren: Breitenfeld, Dardel, Thorwald, Ude

Mo 1
Juni
20.00–22.30 Uhr
☐ Beschränkter Verkauf
Preise von 4,50–10,70

Macbeth
von William Shakespeare

Inszenierung: Hesso Huber
Bühnenbild und Kostüme: Ambrosius Humm
Musik: Otto Dinnebier
Mitwirkende Damen: Gruß, Jacob, Kallei, Krost, Kuhl-
mann, Sanden, Stave, Thummet · Herren: Asner, Bieber,
Bösiger, Breinbauer, Busse, Cziesla, Eppe, Everth,
Hom, Honig, Hübbecker, Hüls, Kempken, Kreiser,
Mejstrik, Müller, Reindl, Riesenberger, Ulrich, Walter,
Walther

Di 2 20.00–22.00 Uhr
Platzmiete D u R
und freier Verkauf
Preise von 4,50–10,70

Toller
von Tankred Dorst

Inszenierung: Günther Büch
Ausstattung: Peter Heyduck
Mitwirkende Damen: Gruß, Sanden, Schweizer, Willick
Herren: Asner, Bieber, Bösiger, Breinbauer, Breitenfeld,
Brieger, Busse, Dardel, Everth, Holm, Hom, Huber, Hüls,
Kempken, Kohutek, Manger, Reindl, Riesenberger,
Thorwald, Ude, Ulrich, Wille, Wüpper

Mi 3 20.00–21.50 Uhr
Platzmiete B
und freier Verkauf
Preise von 4,50–10,70

Das Glück zu dritt
Komödie von Eugène Labiche

Inszenierung: Konrad Höller
Bühnenbild: Ambrosius Humm
Kostüme: Margret Kaulbach · Musik: Otto Dinnebier
Mitwirkende Damen: Antonius, Pedersen, Schweizer,
Willick · Herren: Breitenfeld, Dardel, Thorwald, Ude

Do 4 20.00–22.00 Uhr
Platzmiete F u L
und freier Verkauf
Preise von 4,50–10,70

Toller
von Tankred Dorst

Inszenierung: Günther Büch
Ausstattung: Peter Heyduck
Mitwirkende Damen: Gruß, Sanden, Schweizer, Willick
Herren: Asner, Bieber, Bösiger, Breinbauer, Breitenfeld,
Brieger, Busse, Dardel, Everth, Holm, Hom, Huber, Hüls,
Kempken, Kohutek, Manger, Reindl, Riesenberger,
Thorwald, Ude, Ulrich, Wille, Wüpper

Fr 5 20.00–22.30 Uhr
Preise von 4,50–10,70

Macbeth
von William Shakespeare

Inszenierung: Hesso Huber
Bühnenbild und Kostüme: Ambrosius Humm
Musik: Otto Dinnebier
Mitwirkende Damen: Gruß, Jacob, Kallei, Krost, Kuhl-
mann, Sanden, Stave, Thummet · Herren: Asner, Bieber,
Bösiger, Breinbauer, Busse, Cziesla, Eppe, Everth,
Hom, Honig, Hübbecker, Hüls, Kempken, Kreiser,
Mejstrik, Müller, Reindl, Riesenberger, Ulrich, Walter,
Walther

Sa 6 20.00–22.00 Uhr
Preise von 4,50–10,70

Der eingebildete Kranke
von Molière

Inszenierung: Panajotis Haritoglou
Bühnenbild und Kostüme: Walter Perdacher
Mitwirkende Damen: Jacob, Pedersen, Willick
Herren: Cziesla, Hausch, Honig, Hübbecker, Mejstrik,
Müller, Paulmann, Walter

So 7 20.00–21.50 Uhr
Preise von 4,50–10,70

Das Glück zu dritt
Komödie von Eugène Labiche

Inszenierung: Konrad Höller
Bühnenbild: Ambrosius Humm
Kostüme: Margret Kaulbach · Musik: Otto Dinnebier
Mitwirkende Damen: Antonius, Pedersen, Schweizer,
Willick · Herren: Breitenfeld, Dardel, Thorwald, Ude

Einmaliges Gastspiel
Westfälisches Landestheater Castrop-Rauxel

Mo 8 20.00 Uhr
Preise von 4,50–10,70

Arbeitgeber
von Gerhard Kelling

Voranzeige:
Di 9 20 Uhr Das Glück zu dritt
Mi 10 20 Uhr Macbeth
Fr 12 20 Uhr Zum letzten Male: Toller

Kassenöffnungszeiten:
Opernhaus
Schauspielhaus / Kammerspiele
wochentags 10–13 und 17–20 Uhr
sonntags 17–20 Uhr
bei Nachmittagsvorstellungen 1/2 Stunde vor Beginn

STÄDTISCHE BÜHNEN NÜRNBERG-FÜRTH

one hundred sixty-three

KAMMERSPIELE

Spielplan vom 23. Mai – 7. Juni 1970

Sa 23	20.00 Uhr Preise von 5,90–10,70	Erstaufführung **Magic Afternoon** von Wolfgang Bauer	Inszenierung: Nicolas Brieger Bühnenbild und Kostüme: Waldemar Breidenbach Mitwirkende Damen: Schweizer, Thimig Herren: Holm, Paulmann
So 24	20.00 Uhr Preise von 5,90–10,70	**Magic Afternoon** von Wolfgang Bauer	Inszenierung: Nicolas Brieger Bühnenbild und Kostüme: Waldemar Breidenbach Mitwirkende Damen: Schweizer, Thimig Herren: Holm, Paulmann
Mo 25	20.00–21.30 Uhr ☐ Beschränkter Verkauf Preise von 5,90–10,70	**Endspiel** von Samuel Beckett	Inszenierung: Stavros Doufexis Bühnenbild und Kostüme: Inge Keks Mitwirkende Damen: Keeser Herren: Bieber, Cziesla, Wille
Do 28	20.00 Uhr Preise von 5,90–10,70	**Magic Afternoon** von Wolfgang Bauer	Inszenierung: Nicolas Brieger Bühnenbild und Kostüme: Waldemar Breidenbach Mitwirkende Damen: Schweizer, Thimig Herren: Holm, Paulmann
Fr 29	20.00–21.30 Uhr Preise von 5,90–10,70	**Endspiel** von Samuel Beckett	Inszenierung: Stavros Doufexis Bühnenbild und Kostüme: Inge Keks Mitwirkende Damen: Keeser Herren: Bieber, Cziesla, Wille
Sa 30	20.00–21.40 Uhr Preise von 5,90–10,70	**Play Strindberg** August Strindbergs »Totentanz« arrangiert von Friedrich Dürrenmatt	Inszenierung: Stavros Doufexis Bühnenbild und Kostüme: Inge Keks Mitwirkende Damen: Kroat Herren: Richards, Riesenberger
So 31	20.00–21.30 Uhr Preise von 5,90–10,70	**Endspiel** von Samuel Beckett	Inszenierung: Stavros Doufexis Bühnenbild und Kostüme: Inge Keks Mitwirkende Damen: Keeser Herren: Bieber, Cziesla, Wille
Mi 3 Juni	20.00–21.30 Uhr Preise von 5,90–10,70	**Endspiel** von Samuel Beckett	Inszenierung: Stavros Doufexis Bühnenbild und Kostüme: Inge Keks Mitwirkende Damen: Keeser Herren: Bieber, Cziesla, Wille
Do 4	20.00 Uhr Preise von 5,90–10,70	Gastspiel Quichotte · Herr Meck **José Gomez** Idyllen · Pantomimen · Szenen ohne Wort	
Fr 5	20.00 Uhr Preise von 5,90–10,70	**Magic Afternoon** von Wolfgang Bauer	Inszenierung: Nicolas Brieger Bühnenbild und Kostüme: Waldemar Breidenbach Mitwirkende Damen: Schweizer, Thimig Herren: Holm, Paulmann
Sa 6	20.00 Uhr Preise von 5,90–10,70	Gastspiel Quichotte · Herr Meck **José Gomez** Idyllen · Pantomimen · Szenen ohne Wort	
So 7	11.00–12.30 Uhr Geschlossene Vorstellung 20.00–21.30 Uhr Preise von 5,90–10,70	**Endspiel** von Samuel Beckett	Inszenierung: Stavros Doufexis Bühnenbild und Kostüme: Inge Keks Mitwirkende Damen: Keeser Herren: Bieber, Cziesla, Wille

Voranzeige:
Di 9 20 Uhr Play Strindberg
Mi 10 20 Uhr Magic Afternoon
Do 11 20 Uhr Endspiel

Kassenöffnungszeiten:
Kammerspiele
wochentags 10–13 u. 17–20 Uhr
sonntags 17–20 Uhr

STÄDTISCHE BÜHNEN NÜRNBERG-FÜRTH

one hundred sixty-four

SONDERPROGRAMME

Spielplan vom 16. Mai – 6. Juni 1970

Sa 16 — Schauspielhaus 20.00 Uhr, Preise von 5,40–11,60

Neuinszenierung

Macbeth

von William Shakespeare
Deutsch von Alf Leegaard

Mi 20 — Kammerspiele 20.00 Uhr, Eintritt frei

Einführungsvortrag zum VII. Philharmonischen Konzert

Mit musikalischen Beispielen von Dr. Alfred Kosel

Fr 22 — Meistersingerhalle Abonnementkonzert, Preise von 4,20–12,50

VII. Philharmonisches Konzert

Maros	Eufonia Nr. 1 Erstaufführung
Brahms	Konzert für Violine, Violoncello und Orchester a-Moll op. 102
Beethoven	8. Symphonie F-Dur op. 93
Dirigent	György Lehel
Solisten	Michael Sigler, Violine
	Claus Reichardt, Violoncello

Das Philharmonische Orchester der Stadt Nürnberg

Sa 23 — Kammerspiele 20.00 Uhr, Preise von 5,90–10,70

Erstaufführung

Magic Afternoon

von Wolfgang Bauer

Do 28 — Stadttheater Fürth 20.00 Uhr, Freier Verkauf, Preise von 3,70–12,20

und

Fr 29 — Schauspielhaus 20.00 Uhr, Preise von 7,20–12,20

Gastspiel »Berliner Tournee«

Aus Mangel an Beweisen

Schauspiel von G. del Torre

Mit **Hilde Krahl** und **Hannes Messemer**

Di 2 Juni — Kammerspiele 20.00 Uhr, Eintrittskarten DM 1,50 am Eingang der Kammerspiele

Bildungszentrum der Stadt Nürnberg in Verbindung mit den Städtischen Bühnen Nürnberg-Fürth

Das Theatergespräch

Magic Afternoon
von Wolfgang Bauer

Leitung Dr. Paul Dreykorn in Verbindung mit Chefdramaturg Alf Leegaard

Mi 3 — Opernhaus 20.00 Uhr, Platzmiete **E u S** und freier Verkauf, Preise von 4,20–17,20

Neuinszenierung

Die heimliche Ehe

Oper von Domenico Cimarosa

Do 4 — Kammerspiele jeweils 20.00 Uhr, Preise von 5,90–10,70

und

Sa 6

Gastspiel
Quichotte · Herr Meck

José Gomez

Idyllen · Pantomimen · Szenen ohne Wort

STÄDTISCHE BÜHNEN NÜRNBERG-FÜRTH

THEATER OBERHAUSEN

SPIELZEIT 1969-70

INTENDANT DR. CHRISTIAN METTIN

Dienstag, 26. Mai
20.00 bis 22.30 Uhr

DIE KEUSCHE SUSANNE
Operette von Jean Gilbert

DGB-Freizeitwerk 9
und Freiverkauf
3,00 bis 9,00 DM

Reinhardt/Schödel/Schreiber/Igudin/May/Schenk
Andrée, Kempe, Köhler, Thissen — von Iwen, Koszhutzke, Pokorny, Schödel,
Schulte, Stießel-Preuß
Vicsk — Maurer, Pergler, von't Stot

Mittwoch, 27. Mai
20.00 bis 22.30 Uhr

DIE LANDSTREICHER
Operette von Carl Michael Ziehrer

Blau 18, O 11
und Freiverkauf
3,00 bis 9,00 DM

Pflüger/Walter u. G./Ahlers u. G./Bode u. G./Iguchi/May
Andrée, Friedrichs, Kempe, Köhler, Kühnemann, Thissen — Boding, von Iwen,
Jahst, Jüngl, Koszhutzke, May, Pokorny, Reinhardt, Schulte, Stießel-Preuß —
Angus, Ritter, Rüter, Vicsk, Walder — Emslie, Maurer, Pergler, von't Stot

Donnerst. 28. Mai
20.00 bis 22.30 Uhr

● Einmaliges Gastspiel Landestheater Halle
DIE AULA
Schauspiel von Hermann Kant
(s. Sonderplakat)

Freiverkauf
2,00 bis 7,00 DM

Gastspiel in Moers „Die Blume von Hawaii"

Freitag, 29. Mai
20.00 bis 22.30 Uhr

DIE LANDSTREICHER
Besetzung siehe 27. Mai

Grün 18
und Freiverkauf
3,00 bis 9,00 DM

20.00 bis 22.15 Uhr

Kammerspiele Stadthalle
HEIRATEN IST IMMER EIN RISIKO
von Saul O'Hara

J 9b
und Freiverkauf
3,00 bis 7,00 DM

Richter/Schröter/Schenk
Klüwvein, Schreiber, Wohry, Wronitz — Burkn, Burdan, Fuchs, Matthes

---

Samstag, 30. Mai
20.00 bis 22.30 Uhr

DIE KEUSCHE SUSANNE
Besetzung siehe 26. Mai

Freiverkauf
3,00 bis 9,00 DM

20.00 bis 22.15 Uhr

Kammerspiele Stadthalle
HEIRATEN IST IMMER EIN RISIKO
Besetzung siehe 29. Mai

Freiverkauf
3,00 bis 7,00 DM

Sonntag, 31. Mai
20.00 bis 21.30 Uhr

Studio 99 auf der Probebühne
MAGIC AFTERNOON
von Wolfgang Bauer

Freiverkauf
Studiopreis 3,00 DM

Zum letzten Mal

Haser u. G. / Fleischer
Daniel, Klüwvein — Hollmund, Rupprecht
Die Intendanz ist der Ansicht, daß dieses Stück für Jugendliche unter 16 Jahren
nicht geeignet ist.

Gastspiel in Remscheid „Die Landstreicher"

Montag, 1. Juni

Gastspiel in Kevelaer „Der Bettelstudent"

Dienstag, 2. Juni
20.00 bis 22.15 Uhr

Kammerspiele Stadthalle
HEIRATEN IST IMMER EIN RISIKO
Besetzung siehe 29. Mai

Weiß 19
und Freiverkauf
3,00 bis 7,00 DM

Mittwoch, 3. Juni

Gastspiel in Den Haag „Die Blume von Hawaii"

Donnerst., 4. Juni

Gastspiel in Den Haag „Die Blume von Hawaii"

Freitag, 5. Juni
20.00 bis 22.30 Uhr

DIE LANDSTREICHER
Besetzung siehe 27. Mai

Rosa 19, G 10
und Freiverkauf
3,00 bis 9,30 DM

Vorschau

6. 6.	DIE LANDSTREICHER	Birken 6
	HEIRATEN IST IMMER EIN RISIKO	
7. 6.	DIE LANDSTREICHER (14.30)	
	DIE LANDSTREICHER	
	IRRGARTEN/STRIPTEASE	
9. 6.	ARABELLA (19.30)	Blau 17, O 12
12. 6.	DIE GEISEL	Grün 17, J 10
13. 6.	HEIRATEN IST IMMER EIN RISIKO	
14. 6.	DIE KEUSCHE SUSANNE	

Vorverkauf: THEATERKASSE. — Kassenstunden:
Dienstag bis Samstag 10 Uhr bis 13 Uhr und ab 17 Uhr
bis zu Beginn der Vorstellung. Sonntag von 11 bis 13 Uhr
und eine Stunde vor Beginn der Vorstellung. — Fernruf 2 18 73.

HIESIGE VORVERKAUFSSTELLEN
Verkehrsverein, Oberhausen, Berliner Platz 4
Reisebüro Kauffof, Oberhausen, Marktstraße
Buchhandlung von Huet, Ob.-Beuthausen, Friesenstr. 100
Tabak-Pavillon Lehnhausen, Ob. Marktstr. 34a
Büroofen Zimenski, Ob.-Lirich, Wilmstr. 66
Verkehrsverein, Ob.-Sterkrade, Kantstr. 4
Verkehrsverein, Ob.-Osterfeld, Gildenstr. 17
Fa. Karl Frintrop, Ob.-Sterkrade, Schmachtend. Str. 150
Fa. Osterkamp, Ob.-Sterkrade, Steinbrinkstr. 231
Bücherstube Utten, Ob.-Sterkrade, Steinbrinkstr. 249

Für auswärtige Theaterbesucher: Kartenbestellungen schriftlich oder telefonisch bei der Werbeabteilung, 42 Oberhausen, Ebertstraße 82, Fernruf 85 22 44 (Direktwahl).

STÄDT. BÜHNEN

LICHTSCHEID-DRUCK, OBERHAUSEN · TELEFON 2 18 69

THEATER AM DOMHOF

OSNABRÜCK
STUDIO 99

EINMALIGES GASTSPIEL
Samstag, 9. Mai, 20 Uhr

GESPENSTER

Schauspiel von Henrik Ibsen

mit

Marianne Hoppe, Karin Baal, Helmut Lohner

STUDIO 99
Freitag, 15. Mai, Premiere

WAS IST AN TOLEN SO SEXY?

Lustspiel von Ann Jellicoe

Inszenierung:	Volker Jeck
Bühnenbild:	John Dew
Mitwirkende:	Angelika Thomas
	Michael Derda, Paul Doetsch
und als Tolen	Klaus Spürkel

Theaterkasse geöffnet: montags von 11 bis 13 Uhr; dienstags bis sonnabends von 11 bis 13 Uhr und von 17.30 bis 19.30 Uhr, sonntags eine Stunde vor Beginn jeder Vorstellung.
Fernruf: 2 75 44 - 46, Kasse I App. 14, Kasse II App. 24. Vorbestellte Karten müssen spätestens bis 12.30 Uhr des Vorstellungstages abgeholt sein, da sonst anderweitig darüber verfügt wird. Vorverkauf 3 Tage vor jeder Vorstellung.

Mai

4. Montag — 20 Uhr
5. Dienstag — 20 bis 22.15 Uhr — **9. Hauptkonzert des Musikvereins**
Leitung: Alfred Walter — Werke von Dvořák, Dvořák, Kodály
Abschlussvorstellung Regine Treffer - Claus Walther — **Sinfonie in C-Dur** — Ballett von Georges Bizet — Zum letzten Male
Die Geschichte von Babar, dem kleinen Elefanten
Ballett von Francis Poulenc
Die spanische Stunde — Einmalführung

6. Mittwoch — 20 bis 22 Uhr — **Die Schule der Frauen** — Komödie von Molière
7. Donnerstag — 20 bis 22.45 Uhr — **Ein Maskenball** — Oper von Giuseppe Verdi
8. Freitag — 20 bis 22.30 Uhr — **Die Schule der Frauen** — Komödie von Molière
9. Samstag — 20 Uhr — Einmaliges Gastspiel — **Gespenster** von H. Ibsen
10. Samstag — 11 Uhr — **5. Konzert für junge Hörer** — Werke von Hermann Schroeder, Antonín Dvořák
Die Schule der Frauen — Komödie von Molière

11. Montag — 20 bis 22 Uhr — **Kiss me, Kate** — Musikalische Komödie von Cole Porter
Die Schule der Frauen — Komödie von Molière
12. Dienstag — 20 bis 22 Uhr — **Die Schule der Frauen** — Komödie von Molière
13. Mittwoch — 20 bis 22.45 Uhr — **Ein Maskenball** — Oper von Giuseppe Verdi
14. Donnerstag — 20 bis 22 Uhr — **Die Schule der Frauen** — Komödie von Molière
15. Freitag — 20 bis 22.45 Uhr — **Kiss me, Kate** — Musikalische Komödie von Cole Porter
16. Samstag — 20 bis 22.45 Uhr — **Ein Maskenball** — Oper von Giuseppe Verdi
17. Pfingst-samstag — 20 bis 22 Uhr — Abschlussvorstellung Andreas Becker — **Die Zauberflöte** — Oper von Wolfgang Amadeus Mozart — Zum letzten Male
18. Pfingst-montag — 20 bis 22.45 Uhr — **Kiss me, Kate** — Musikalische Komödie von Cole Porter

STUDIO 99
Freitag, 15. Mai — 20 Uhr — **Was ist an Tolen so sexy?** — Lustspiel von Ann Jellicoe
Weitere Vorstellungen: Fr., 15. 5., 20 Uhr — So., 16. 5., 20 Uhr — Di., 19. 5., 20 Uhr — Mi., 20. 5., 20 Uhr
Sombrero
Weitere Vorstellungen: Di., 12. 5., 15 Uhr — Zum letzten Male: Do., 14. 5., 15 Uhr

SPIELZEIT 1969/70

April 1970

Donnerstag 9. 20.00 gegen 21.30
Freier Verkauf Foyer des Stadttheaters
Kunstverein Remscheid e. V.
Elisabeth Jacobi
Fontane
ein Meister des Gespräches und des Briefes

Freitag 10. 20.00– gegen 23.15
Freier Verkauf und Abonnement B.15 Erhöhte Preise
Städtische Bühne Hagen
Boris Godunow
Oper von Modest Mussorgsky

Sonntag 12. 20.00– gegen 21.30
Freier Verkauf und Konzertreihe 5. Preis: DM 5.50
5. Kammerkonzert - Foyer des Stadttheaters
Klavierabend Barbara Fry
Ludwig van Beethoven: Sonate f-moll op. 2/1
Ludwig van Beethoven: Sonate e-moll op. 90
Giovanni Paisiello: Sechs Variationen über "Nel cor più non mi sento"
Ludwig van Beethoven: Sonate f-moll op. 57 (Appassionata)

Mittwoch 15. 20.00– gegen 22.00
Freier Verkauf und Konzertreihe A Preise: DM 3.40–8.40
Sinfoniekonzert
(9. Abonnementskonzert)
Arnold Schönberg: Fünf Orchesterstücke op. 16
Robert Schumann: Konzert für Violoncello und Orchester a-moll op. 129
Peter I. Tschaikowsky: Symphonie Nr. 5 e-moll op. 64
Solist: Antonio Janigro, Violoncello
Das Städtische Orchester – Leitung: Alexander Rumpf

Donnerstag 16. 20.00– gegen 22.30
Freier Verkauf und Abonnement D.12 Erhöhte Preise
Städtische Bühne Hagen
Die verkaufte Braut
Oper von Friedrich Smetana
Musikalische Leitung: Alexander Rumpf

Samstag 18. 17.00– 19.00
Freier Verkauf und Jugendkonzertreihe.3 Preis: DM 3.40
3. Jugendkonzert
Ludwig van Beethoven: Ouvertüre "Leonore" Nr. 1 op. 138
Ludwig van Beethoven: Konzert für Klavier und Orchester Nr. 3 c-moll op. 37
Ludwig van Beethoven: Symphonie Nr. 3 Es-dur op. 55 (Eroica)
Solist: Fritz Emonts, Klavier
Das Städtische Orchester – Leitung: Alexander Rumpf
Begin 19.30

Sonntag 19. 19.30 gegen 22.00
Freier Verkauf und Volksbühne.9 Erhöhte Preise
Städtische Bühne Hagen
Die verkaufte Braut
Oper von Friedrich Smetana

April 1970

Mittwoch 22. 20.00 gegen 22.15
Freier Verkauf und Abonnement C/10 Erhöhte Preise
Düsseldorfer Schauspielhaus
Coriolan
Trauerspiel von William Shakespeare

Donnerstag 23. 20.00– gegen 22.30
Freier Verkauf und Abonnement D/13 Preisgruppe I
Wuppertaler Bühnen
Der Barbier von Sevilla
Komische Oper von Gioacchino Rossini

Dienstag 28. 20.00– gegen 22.00
Freier Verkauf Preisgruppe 6
Das Kom(m)ödchen
Von der Freiheit eines Christenmenschen

Mittwoch 29. 20.00– gegen 22.00
Freier Verkauf und Abonnement C.11 Erhöhte Preise
Einmaliges Gastspiel
Jugoslawisches Nationalballett "IVO LOLA RIBAR" Belgrad

Mai 1970

Freitag 1. 20.00– gegen 22.30
Freier Verkauf und Abonnement B.16 Erhöhte Preise
Städtische Bühne Hagen
Die verkaufte Braut
Oper von Friedrich Smetana

Sonntag 3. 19.30– gegen 21.30
Freier Verkauf und Volksbühne.10 Preisgruppe I
Direktion Landgraf
Donna Diana
Lustspiel von Agustín Moreto
Begin 19.30

Freitag 8. 20.00– gegen 22.15
Freier Verkauf und Abonnement B.17 Erhöhte Preise
Düsseldorfer Schauspielhaus
Der Biberpelz
von Gerhart Hauptmann mit Heidemarie Hatheyer

Abstecher des Orchesters: 26. April - Wermelskirchen

Der Vorverkauf für alle Veranstaltungen beginnt jeweils 1 Woche vor der Vorstellung

Volkstheater Rostock

Leitung: Gerd Puls

Mai 1970

	13. Mittwoch	14. Donnerstag	15. Freitag	16. Sonnabend	17. Sonntag	18. Montag	19. Dienstag	20. Mittwoch	21. Donnerstag	22. Freitag
GROSSES HAUS	19.30–21.45 1. EOS und freier Verkauf **Zwischen den Gewittern** Schauspiel von Alexander Stein	19.30–22.15 B 4 und freier Verkauf **Don Carlos** Oper in fünf Akten von Giuseppe Verdi	19.30–21.45 C 5 und freier Verkauf In der Inszenierung der Kammerspiele des Deutschen Theaters Berlin **Tagebuch eines Wahnsinnigen** von Nikolai Gogol	19.30–22.15 B 6 und freier Verkauf **Mein Freund Bunbury** von Gerd Natschinski	19.30–21.30 B 7 Premiere **Der Türke in Italien** Oper von Gioacchino Rossini	19.30–22.15 B 24 + EA und freier Verkauf **Ein Sommernachtstraum** Komödie von William Shakespeare	19.30–21.30 B 2 und freier Verkauf **Zwischen den Gewittern** Schauspiel von Alexander Stein	19.30–21.45 B 3 / 2. EOS und freier Verkauf **Madame Butterfly** Oper in drei Akten von Giacomo Puccini	19.30–21.30 A 4 / 3. EOS und freier Verkauf **Der Türke in Italien** Oper von Gioacchino Rossini	19.30–21.45 B 5 und freier Verkauf In der Inszenierung der Kammerspiele des Deutschen Theaters Berlin **Tagebuch eines Wahnsinnigen** von Nikolai Gogol
KLEINES HAUS	19.30 Im freien Verkauf Premiere **Becher-Matinee**	19.30–21.30 D 44 und freier Verkauf Premiere **In Sachen Adam und Eva** Komödie von Rudi Strahl	19.30–21.30 A 55 und freier Verkauf **Cyprienne** Musikalische Komödie nach dem Lustspiel von Sardou und Najac	19.30–21.15 D 43 und freier Verkauf **Affäre Palomares** von José Maria Camps	19.30–21.30 D 73, 74 und freier Verkauf **Das Fräulein wird Minister** Komödie von Margit Gáspár	19.30–21.30 A 1 / D 1 + EA und freier Verkauf **Das Fräulein wird Minister** Komödie von Margit Gáspár	19.30–21.30 C 21, D 2 und freier Verkauf **Das Fräulein wird Minister** Komödie von Margit Gáspár	19.30–21.30 C 3 und freier Verkauf **Das Uhrenständchen**	19.30–21.30 C 42, 44 und freier Verkauf **Das Fräulein wird Minister** Komödie von Margit Gáspár	19.30–21.30 D 51 + EA und freier Verkauf **Das Fräulein wird Minister** Komödie von Margit Gáspár
INTIMES THEATER	19.30–22.00 Im freien Verkauf **Laurette** Komödie von Marc-Gilbert Sauvajon	19.30–22.00 Im freien Verkauf **Laurette** Komödie von Marc-Gilbert Sauvajon	19.30–22.00 Im freien Verkauf **Laurette** Komödie von Marc-Gilbert Sauvajon	19.30–22.00 Im freien Verkauf **Laurette** Komödie von Marc-Gilbert Sauvajon	19.30–22.00 Im freien Verkauf **Laurette** Komödie von Marc-Gilbert Sauvajon	19.30–22.00 Im freien Verkauf **Laurette** Komödie von Marc-Gilbert Sauvajon	19.30–22.00 Im freien Verkauf **Laurette** Komödie von Marc-Gilbert Sauvajon			19.30–22.00 Im freien Verkauf **Laurette** Komödie von Marc-Gilbert Sauvajon

Ausgabe der Anrechtskarten:

Beschwerdeabteilung Rostock
für Betriebe u. a.
20. und 25. Mai 1970
für Schüler und Studenten
26. bis 28. Mai 1970

Kleine Komödie Warnemünde
Am 22. und 25. Mai 1970
von 15.00 bis 17.00 Uhr

Kulturzentrum Lütten Klein
Am 20. und 21. Mai 1970
von 17.00 bis 18.00 Uhr

In Vorbereitung!

Premiere am 29. Mai 1970
im Intimen Theater
Fisch zu Vier

Premiere am 7. Juni 1970
im Kleinen Haus
Der lange Weg zu Lenin
Abenteuerliche Reise nach Sowjetrußland 1919
von Helmut Baierl

KLEINE KOMÖDIE WARNEMÜNDE

20.00–22.15 Im freien Verkauf
Kleinekortes Große Zeiten

VORANZEIGE

	Großes Haus	Kleines Haus	Kleine Komödie Warnemünde
Sonnabend, 23. Mai 1970	Madame Butterfly	Kleinekortes Große Zeiten	Kleinekortes Große Zeiten
Sonntag, 24. Mai 1970	La Traviata	Das Fräulein wird Minister	Kleinekortes Große Zeiten
Montag, 25. Mai 1970	Im Montag-Klub Reiner Süß, Kammersänger	Das Fräulein wird Minister	

Rufen Sie VTR-Kartendienst 36251, Apparat 4

Vorverkauf
für alle Häuser in Rostock:
Vorverkaufskasse Doberaner Straße 134/135, Ruf 23 33
Montag bis Freitag 10.00 – 13.00 und 16.00 – 18.00 Uhr
Sonnabend 18.00 – 19.30 Uhr an der Abendkasse
des Großen Hauses
Telefonische Kartenbestellungen für alle Häuser Montag bis Freitag 10.00 – 13.00 und 16.00 – 18.00 Uhr
Die Theaterkassen in allen Häusern öffnen eine Stunde vor Beginn der Vorstellung.

Besucherabteilung:
Doberaner Straße 134/135, Ruf 36251, App. 3,
und 2 35 34
Montag bis Freitag 10.00 – 13.00 und 16.00 – 18.00 Uhr
Kartenausgabe für Anrechtsgruppen von 20. bis 25. jeden Monats.
Außenstelle: Montag bis Freitag 8.00 – 12.00 Uhr
und Montag 13.00 – 18.00 Uhr
Dienstag 13.00 – 18.00 Uhr
Außenstelle Warnemünde an den bekanntgegebenen Tagen.
In der Kleinen Komödie an den bekanntgegebenen Tagen.

one hundred sixty-nine

Stadt—THEATER Saarbrücken

1.6. — 11.6. 1970

INTENDANT HERMANN WEDEKIND

Großes Haus	JUNI	Kammerspiele		Großes Haus		Kammerspiele	

Großes Haus

19.30 bis etwa 22.00
Othello
Oper in 4 Akten von Arrigo Boito
Neue deutsche Übertragung
von Walter Felsenstein
unter Mitarbeit von Carl Stueber
Musik von Giuseppe Verdi
Leitung: Köhler, Wedekind, Wilke, Kulke, Hoschke
Mitwirkende: Kathe, Matthieu, Roberts — Andrulonis, Fuger, Krogh, Ludwig, Nathge, Pampuch, Stricker
8. Vorstellung MIETE H und freier Verkauf

1. MONTAG

Kammerspiele

20 bis etwa 22.30
Die verkaufte Braut
EINMALIGES GASTSPIEL DER NATIONALOPER SKOPJE
Nur freier Verkauf
Gastspielpreise DM 3,50 bis 17,10
Oper von Friedrich Smetana
Soli, Chor, Ballett und Orchester des Mazedonischen Nationaltheaters
20

7. SONNTAG

Play Strindberg
von Friedrich Dürrenmatt
nach August Strindbergs „Totentanz"
Besetzung siehe 2.6. 1970
20.15 bis etwa 21.45
Nur freier Verkauf

19.30 bis etwa 22.00
Don Carlos
Oper in 4 Akten nach Schillers Drama
von Joseph Méry und Camille du Locle
Musik von Giuseppe Verdi
Leitung: Köhler, Wedekind, Wilke, Dahm, Hoschke
Mitwirkende: Matthieu, Purtonen, Roberts — Andrulonis, Baciu, Fuger, Morris, Nimagern — Hofmann, Steinebach, Weller
8. Vorstellung MIETE G und freier Verkauf

2. DIENSTAG

Play Strindberg
von Friedrich Dürrenmatt
nach August Strindbergs „Totentanz"
Leitung: Dryander, Meyer, Hoschke
Mitwirkende: Roosch — Alisch, Rainer
20 bis etwa 21.30
8. Vorstellung KAMMERSPIEL-MIETE Dienstag und freier Verkauf

19.30 bis etwa 22.00
Aida
Oper in 4 Akten von Antonio Ghislanzoni
Musik von Giuseppe Verdi
Leitung: Süss, Fischer a. G., Wilke, Jezic, Munz a. G., Hoschke
Mitwirkende: Eisele, Fraenkel, Purtonen — Baciu, Daniel, Krogh, Morris, Pampuch — Chlubek, Sala
9. Vorstellung Volksbühne Saar eV MIETE 2

8. MONTAG

Play Strindberg
von Friedrich Dürrenmatt
nach August Strindbergs „Totentanz"
Besetzung siehe 2.6. 1970
20.30 bis etwa 22.00
Geschlossene Vorstellung

---

15 bis etwa 17.30
Die lustige Witwe
Operette in 3 Akten von Franz Lehár
Leitung: Ott, Könemann a. G., Wilke, Graseck a. G., Jezic, Sala, Hardt a. G., Hoschke
Mitwirkende: Eisele, Flemming — Brüning, Ludwig, Pampuch, Pauli, Trefny, von Wachtmeister — Finzel, Hippler, Schelthase, Borré, Hofmann, Peter — Andonowa, Billik, Chlubek, Reck, Radonjic, Sala, Schober
Geschl. Vorstellung Kein Verkauf

3. MITTWOCH

19 bis etwa 21.45
Madame Pompadour
Operette in 3 Akten
von Rudolph Schanzer und Ernst Welisch
Musik von Leo Fall
Leitung: Ott, Eichner a. G., Wilke, Alkov a. G., Kulke, Hoschke
Mitwirkende: Alsen, Flemming, Matthieu — Bächle, Brüning, Horstmann, Trefny, von Wachtmeister — Borré, Disner, Maurer, Peter, Weller — Andonowa, Chlubek — Sala, Schober
8. Vorstellung Kulturring d. Jugend (Landesjugendring) Gruppe 1 Kein Verkauf

9. DIENSTAG

Play Strindberg
von Friedrich Dürrenmatt
nach August Strindbergs „Totentanz"
Besetzung siehe 2.6. 1970
20 bis etwa 21.30
Nur freier Verkauf

19.30 bis etwa 22.00
Die lustige Witwe
Operette in 3 Akten von Franz Lehár
Camille de Rosillon: Stricker
Njegus: Horstmann
sonst siehe Besetzung vom Nachmittag
18. Vorstellung MIETE C und freier Verkauf

Magic Afternoon
Stück von Wolfgang Bauer
Leitung: Neu, Kulka, Hoschke
Mitwirkende: Alsen, Jelinek — Lichtenstein, Rainer
20 bis etwa 21.15
Nur freier Verkauf

4. DONNERSTAG

19.45 bis etwa 22.15
Lulu
Oper von Alban Berg
Leitung: Köhler, Rothacker a.G., Munz a.G., Hoschke
Mitwirkende: Ghadiali a. G., Kathe, Matthieu, Reinhardt-Kiss — Andrulonis, Bächle, Brüning, Fuger, Ludwig, Nimagern, Pampuch, Stricker, Trefny, v. Wachtmeister
18. Vorstellung MIETE A und freier Verkauf

Zur schönen Aussicht
Komödie in 4 Akten von Ödön von Horváth
Leitung: Stok a. G., Meyer, Hoschke
Mitwirkende: Dryander, Jelinek — Dilg, Johow, Kraus, Menzel, Saager
20.15 bis etwa 22.15
Nur freier Verkauf

Der Preispokal
(The Silver Tassie)
Eine Tragikomödie in 4 Akten
von Sean O'Casey
Deutsch von Kunred Dorst
Liedertexte von Karl Wesseler
Leitung: Johow, Imig, Kulka, Hoschke
Mitwirkende: Alsen, Ammann, Schaun, Wilhelmus a. G. — Brüneke, Dilg, Flöth, Greuel, Kraus, Lakenmacher, Lichtenstein, May, Nordmann, Petersen, Rollauer, Saager, Schindler, Weverinck
8. Vorstellung MIETE D D 10 Volksbühne Saar eV und freier Verkauf

10. MITTWOCH

19.45 bis etwa 22.15
Die lustige Witwe
Operette in 3 Akten von Franz Lehár
Besetzung siehe 3.6. 1970 nachmittags
18. Vorstellung MIETE B und freier Verkauf

5. FREITAG

Play Strindberg
von Friedrich Dürrenmatt
nach August Strindbergs „Totentanz"
Besetzung siehe 2.6. 1970
20.15 bis etwa 21.45
8. Vorstellung KAMMERSPIEL-MIETE Freitag und freier Verkauf

19.30 bis etwa 22.00
Die lustige Witwe
Operette in 3 Akten von Franz Lehár
Njegus: Horstmann
sonst siehe Besetzung 3.6.1970 nachmittags
18. Vorstellung MIETE E

6. SAMSTAG

Zur schönen Aussicht
Komödie von Ödön von Horváth
Besetzung siehe 4.6. 1970
20 bis etwa 22.00
Nur freier Verkauf

19.45 bis etwa 22.15
La Traviata
Oper in 4 Akten
nach A. Dumas von F.M. Piave
Musik von Giuseppe Verdi
Leitung: Köhler, Johow, Wilke, Heyduk, Hoschke
Mitwirkende: Eisele, Kathe, Roberts — Daniel, Fuger, Krogh, Ludwig, Pampuch, Pauli
Neuinszenierung
18. Vorstellung MIETE A1 und freier Verkauf

11. DONNERSTAG

Zur schönen Aussicht
Komödie von Ödön von Horváth
Besetzung siehe 4.6. 1970
20.15 bis etwa 22.15
Nur freier Verkauf

VORSCHAU
Grosses Haus

Freitag, 12.6.1970	Dornröschen	(freier Verk.)	
	(Gastspiel Studio Dryander)		
Samstag, 13.6.1970	Aida	(Miete F)	
Sonntag, 14.6.1970	Lumpazivagabundus	(Fremden-Miete, Volksbühne Miete 1)	
	My Fair Lady	(freier Verk.)	
Montag, 15.6.1970	Der Troubadour	(Jugendring 2)	
Dienstag, 16.6.1970	Die lustige Witwe	(Saarl. Theatergem. Dienstag-Miete)	
Mittwoch, 17.6.1970	Lulu	(Miete C)	
Donnerstag, 18.6.1970	Die lustige Witwe	(Miete A)	

VORSCHAU
Kammerspiele

Freitag, 12.6.1970	Kinder fallen nach oben	(Première)	(freier Verk.)
Samstag, 13.6.1970	Zur schönen Aussicht		(freier Verk.)
Sonntag, 14.6.1970	Play Strindberg		(freier Verk.)
Dienstag, 16.6.1970	Zur schönen Aussicht		(freier Verk.)
Mittwoch, 17.6.1970	Play Strindberg		(freier Verk.)
Donnerstag, 18.6.1970	Kinder fallen nach oben		(freier Verk.)

Gastspiele

Freitag, 12. Juni 1970, 19.30 Uhr
Großes Haus

BALLETT-STUDIO KATJA DRYANDER

„Dornröschen"

Ballett von Peter Tschaikowsky

Eintrittspreise: DM 3,50 / 4,— / 4,50 / 5,—

Vorverkauf

ab Sonntag: für Montag — Donnerstag
ab Mittwoch: für Freitag — Sonntag
Theaterkasse: werktags von 10—13 Uhr und 17—18 Uhr,
sonn- und feiertags von 11—13 Uhr – Abendkasse ab 18 Uhr.
Reisebüro „Saarbrücker Zeitung", Dudweilerstraße 5

Eintrittspreise

Großes Haus:
Gastspiel 3,60 bis 17,10 DM Oper u. Operette 3,10 bis 13,20 DM
Schauspiel 2,10 bis 9,00 DM - Konzert 4,30 bis 14,80 DM

Kammerspiele:
Schauspiel: 1. Pl. 4,20, 2. Pl. 3,60, 3. Pl. 2,90
Musikalische Aufführung: 1. Pl. 5,10, 2. Pl. 4,50, 3. Pl. 3,70
Gastspiel: 7,60 und 5,90 DM
(Preise einschl. Altersversorgungs-Abgabe)

Öffnungszeit der Mietenkasse: 8.00 bis 13.00 Uhr
Sonntags geschlossen!

Fernruf 2 96 96 - 97 - 98 und 2 47 44

...auch das druckt buchdruckerei gebr. adam, saarbrücken 1, tel. 5 29 44

one hundred seventy

Volkstheater Rostock

Leitung: Gerd Puls

Mai 1970

	13. Mittwoch	14. Donnerstag	15. Freitag	16. Sonnabend	17. Sonntag	18. Montag	19. Dienstag	20. Mittwoch	21. Donnerstag	22. Freitag
GROSSES HAUS	Zwischen den Gewittern	Don Carlos	Tagebuch eines Wahnsinnigen	Mein Freund Bunbury	Premiere — Der Türke in Italien	Ein Sommernachtstraum	Zwischen den Gewittern	Madame Butterfly	Der Türke in Italien	Tagebuch eines Wahnsinnigen
KLEINES HAUS	Premiere — Becher-Matinee	In Sachen Adam und Eva	Cyprienne	Affäre Palomares	Das Fräulein wird Minister	Das Fräulein wird Minister	Das Fräulein wird Minister	Das Uhrenständchen	Das Fräulein wird Minister	Das Fräulein wird Minister
INTIMES THEATER		Laurette	Laurette	Laurette	Laurette	Laurette		Laurette		Laurette

In Vorbereitung!

Premiere am 29. Mai 1970 im Intimen Theater
Fisch zu Viert
Komödie von Marc-Gilbert Sauvajon

Premiere am 7. Juni 1970 im Kleinen Haus
Der lange Weg zu Lenin
Abenteuerliche Reise nach Sowjetrußland 1919
von Helmut Baierl

Ausgabe der Anrechtskarten:

Besucherabteilung Rostock
für Betriebe u. a.
20. bis 25. Mai 1970
für Schüler und Studenten
26. bis 28. Mai 1970

Kleine Komödie Warnemünde
Am 22. und 23. Mai 1970
von 15.00 bis 17.00 Uhr

Kulturzentrum Lütten Klein
Am 20. und 21. Mai 1970
von 17.00 bis 18.00 Uhr

KLEINE KOMÖDIE WARNEMÜNDE

Kleinekortes Große Zeiten
Komödie von Claus Ulrich Wiesner

VORANZEIGE

	Großes Haus	Kleines Haus	Kleine Komödie Warnemünde
Sonnabend, 23. Mai 1970	Madame Butterfly	Kleinekortes Große Zeiten	
Sonntag, 24. Mai 1970	La Traviata	Das Fräulein wird Minister	Kleinekortes Große Zeiten
Montag, 25. Mai 1970	Im Montag-Klub Reiner Süß, Kammersänger	Das Fräulein wird Minister	

Rufen Sie VTR-Kartendienst 3 6251, Apparat 4

Vorverkauf für alle Häuser in Rostock:
Vorverkaufskasse Doberaner Straße 134/135, Ruf 2333
Montag bis Freitag 10.00 – 13.00 und 15.00 – 18.00 Uhr
Sonnabend 18.00 – 19.30 Uhr an der Abendkasse
Telefonische Kartenbestellungen für alle Häuser Montag bis Freitag 10.00 – 13.00 und 16.00 – 18.00 Uhr
Die Theaterkassen in allen Häusern öffnen eine Stunde vor Beginn der Vorstellung

Besucherabteilung:
Doberaner Straße 134/135, Ruf 36251, App. 3, und 25534
Montag bis Freitag 10.00 – 13.00 und 14.00 – 18.00 Uhr
Kartenausgabe für Anrechtsgruppen von 8.00 bis 25. jeden Monats.
Außenstelle Lütten Klein: Montag bis Freitag 8.00 – 18.00 Uhr.
Termine: Werktäglich an den bekanntgegebenen Tagen.
Außenstelle Warnemünde: Von 13.00 – 17.00 Uhr in der Kleinen Komödie an den bekanntgegebenen Tagen.

one hundred sixty-nine

INTENDANT HERMANN WEDEKIND

Großes Haus

JUNI

1. MONTAG

19.30 bis etwa 22.00
8. Vorstellung
MIETE
H
und freier Verkauf

Othello
Oper in 4 Akten von Arrigo Boito
Neue deutsche Übertragung
von Walter Felsenstein
unter Mitarbeit von Carl Stueber
Musik von Giuseppe Verdi
Leitung: Köhler, Wedekind, Wilke,
Kulke, Hoschke
Mitwirkende: Katha, Matthieu, Roberts —
Andrulonis, Fuger, Krogh, Ludwig, Nathge,
Pampuch, Stricker

2. DIENSTAG

19.30 bis etwa 22.30
8. Vorstellung
MIETE
G
und freier Verkauf

Don Carlos
Oper in 4 Akten nach Schillers Drama
von Joseph Méry und Camille du Locle
Musik von Giuseppe Verdi
Leitung: Köhler, Wedekind, Dahm,
Hoschke
Mitwirkende: Matthieu, Purtonen,
Roberts — Andrulonis, Baciu, Fuger,
Morris, Nimsgern — Hofmann, Steinebach,
Weller

3. MITTWOCH

15 bis 17.30
Geschl. Vorstellung
Kein Verkauf

Die lustige Witwe
Operette in 3 Akten von Franz Lehár
Leitung: Ott, Könemann a. G., Wilke,
Graeck a. G., Jezic, Sala, Herdt a. G.,
Hoschke
Mitwirkende: Eisele, Flemming —
Brüning, Ludwig, Pampuch, Pauli, Trefny,
von Wachtmeister — Finzel, Hippler,
Schellhass, Borré, Hofmann, Peter —
Andonowa, Billik, Chlubek, Reck, Radonjie,
Sala, Schober

19.30 bis etwa 22.00
18. Vorstellung
MIETE
C
und freier Verkauf

Die lustige Witwe
Operette in 3 Akten von Franz Lehár
Camilla de Rosillon: Stricker
Njegus: Horstmann
sonst siehe Besetzung vom Nachmittag

4. DONNERSTAG

19.45 bis etwa 22.15
18. Vorstellung
MIETE
A
und freier Verkauf

Lulu
Oper von Alban Berg
Leitung: Köhler, Rothacker a. G., Munz a.G.,
Hoschke
Mitwirkende: Ghadiali a. G., Kathe,
Matthieu, Reinhardt-Kiss — Andrulonis,
Bächle, Brüning, Fuger, Ludwig, Nimsgern,
Pampuch, Stricker, Trefny, v. Wachtmeister

5. FREITAG

19.45 bis etwa 22.15
18. Vorstellung
MIETE
B
und freier Verkauf

Die lustige Witwe
Operette in 3 Akten von Franz Lehár
Besetzung siehe 3.6.1970 nachmittags

6. SAMSTAG

19.30 bis etwa 22.00
18. Vorstellung
MIETE
E
und freier Verkauf

Die lustige Witwe
Operette in 3 Akten von Franz Lehár
Njegus: Horstmann
sonst siehe Besetzung 3.6.1970 nachmittags

Kammerspiele

2. DIENSTAG

Play Strindberg
von Friedrich Dürrenmatt
nach August Strindbergs „Totentanz"
Leitung: Dryander, Meyer, Hoschke
Mitwirkende: Roosch — Aliach, Rainer

20 bis etwa 21.30
8. Vorstellung
KAMMERSPIEL-
MIETE
Dienstag
und freier Verkauf

3. (Magic Afternoon listed)

Magic Afternoon
Stück von Wolfgang Bauer
Leitung: Neu, Kulka, Hoschke
Mitwirkende: Alzen, Jelinek —
Lichtenstein, Rainer

20 bis etwa 21.15
Nur freier Verkauf

4. DONNERSTAG

Zur schönen Aussicht
Komödie von Ödön von Horváth
Leitung: Stok a. G., Meyer, Hoschke
Mitwirkende: Dryander, Jelinek — Dilg,
Johow, Kraus, Menzel, Saager

20.15 bis etwa 22.15
Nur freier Verkauf

5. FREITAG

Play Strindberg
von Friedrich Dürrenmatt
nach August Strindbergs „Totentanz"
Besetzung siehe 2.6.1970

20.15 bis etwa 21.45
8. Vorstellung
KAMMERSPIEL-
MIETE
Freitag
und freier Verkauf

6. SAMSTAG

Zur schönen Aussicht
Komödie von Ödön von Horváth
Besetzung siehe 4.6.1970

20 bis etwa 22.00
Nur freier Verkauf

Großes Haus

20 / 7. SONNTAG

20 bis etwa 22.30
Nur freier Verkauf
Gastspielpreise
DM 3,80 bis 17,10

EINMALIGES GASTSPIEL
DER NATIONALOPER SKOPJE
Die verkaufte Braut
Oper von Friedrich Smetana
Soli, Chor, Ballett und Orchester
des Mazedonischen Nationaltheaters

8. MONTAG

19.30 bis etwa 22.30
8. Vorstellung
Volksbühne Saar eV
MIETE 3

Aida
Oper in 4 Akten von Antonio Ghislanzoni
Musik von Giuseppe Verdi
Leitung: Süss, Fischer a. G., Wilke, Jezic,
Munz a. G., Hoschke
Mitwirkende: Eisele, Fraenkel, Purtonen —
Baciu, Daniel, Krogh, Morris, Pampuch —
Chlubek, Sala

9. DIENSTAG

19 bis etwa 21.45
8. Vorstellung
Kulturring d. Jugend
(Landesjugendring)
Gruppe 1
Kein Verkauf

Madame Pompadour
Operette in 3 Akten
von Rudolph Schanzer und Ernst Welisch
Musik von Leo Fall
Leitung: Ott, Eichner a. G., Wilke,
Alkov a. G., Kulke, Hoschke
Mitwirkende: Alzen, Flemming, Matthieu —
Bächle, Brüning, Horstmann, Trefny,
von Wachtmeister — Borré, Diener,
Maurer, Peter, Weller — Andonowa,
Chlubek — Sala, Schober

10. MITTWOCH

19.30 bis etwa 21.30
19. Vorstellung
MIETE
D
8. Vorstellung
MIETE
D 10
Volksbühne Saar eV
und freier Verkauf

Der Preispokal
(The Silver Tassie)
Eine Tragikomödie in 4 Akten
von Sean O'Casey
Deutsch von Tankred Dorst
Liedertexte von Karl Wesseler
Leitung: Johow, Imig, Kulka, Hoschke
Mitwirkende: Alzen, Ammann, Schaun,
Wilhelmus a. G. — Brünska, Dilg, Flöth,
Greull, Kraus, Lakenmacher, Lichtenstein,
May, Nordmann, Petersen, Rollauer,
Saager, Schindler, Weverinck

11. DONNERSTAG

19.45 bis etwa 22.15
19. Vorstellung
MIETE
A 1
und freier Verkauf

La Traviata
Oper in 4 Akten
nach A. Dumas von F.M. Piave
Musik von Giuseppe Verdi
Leitung: Köhler, Johow, Wilke, Heyduk,
Hoschke
Mitwirkende: Eisele, Kathe, Roberts —
Daniel, Fuger, Krogh, Ludwig, Pampuch,
Pauli

Neuinszenierung

Kammerspiele

7. SONNTAG

Play Strindberg
von Friedrich Dürrenmatt
nach August Strindbergs „Totentanz"
Besetzung siehe 2.6.1970

20.15 bis etwa 21.45
Nur freier Verkauf

8. MONTAG

Play Strindberg
von Friedrich Dürrenmatt
nach August Strindbergs „Totentanz"
Besetzung siehe 2.6.1970

20.30 Geschlossene Vorstellung

9. DIENSTAG

Play Strindberg
von Friedrich Dürrenmatt
nach August Strindbergs „Totentanz"
Besetzung siehe 2.6.1970

20 bis etwa 21.30
Nur freier Verkauf

11. DONNERSTAG

Zur schönen Aussicht
Komödie von Ödön von Horváth
Besetzung siehe 4.6.1970

20.15 bis etwa 22.15
Nur freier Verkauf

...auch das druckt buchdruckerei g:br adam, saarbrücken 1, tel. 5 29 44

Gastspiele

Freitag, 12. Juni 1970, 19.30 Uhr
Großes Haus

BALLETT-STUDIO KATJA DRYANDER

„Dornröschen"
Ballett von Peter Tschaikowsky

Eintrittspreise: DM 3,50 / 4,— / 4,50 / 5,—

Vorverkauf

ab Sonntag: für Montag — Donnerstag
ab Mittwoch: für Freitag — Sonntag
Theaterkasse: werktags von 10—13 Uhr und 17—18 Uhr,
sonn- und feiertags von 11—13 Uhr - Abendkasse ab 18 Uhr.
Reisebüro „Saarbrücker Zeitung", Dudweilerstraße 5

Eintrittspreise

Großes Haus:
Gastspiel 3,80 bis 17,10 DM - Oper u. Operette 3,10 bis 13,20 DM
Schauspiel 2,10 bis 9,60 DM - Konzert 4,30 bis 14,50 DM

Kammerspiele:
Schauspiel: 1. Pl. 4,20, 2. Pl. 3,60, 3. Pl. 2,90
Musikalische Aufführung: 1. Pl. 5,10, 2. Pl. 4,50, 3. Pl. 3,70
Gastspiel: 7,60 und 5,90 DM
(Preise einschl. Altersversorgungs-Abgabe)

Öffnungszeit der Mietenkasse: 8.00 bis 13.00 Uhr
Samstags geschlossen!

Fernruf 2 90 96 · 97 · 98 und 2 47 44

---

one hundred seventy

20. April bis 13. Mai 1970

20 Montag 20-22.30 Ring C

Gastspiel Städtebundtheater Hof
Intendant Hannes Keppler

Hallo, Dolly!
Nach »The Matchmaker« von Thornton Wilder
Buch von Michael Stewart - Musik und Gesangstexte von Jerry Herman
Deutsch von Robert Gilbert

21 Dienstag 20-22.30 Ring D

Inszenierung: Hannes Keppler
Musikalische Leitung und Chöre: Ludwig de Ridder
Bühnenbild: Gernot D. Zahel - Kostüme: Alheid Lupp

22 Mittwoch 20-22.30 Ring E

Irene Gebart - Brunhild Rüttinger
Charlotte Sender - Gerda Stagnier - Eva-Maria Teubel
Wolfgang Babl - Helmut Dicke - Arno Frost
Wilhelm Gartner - Leo Hermann - Hermann Nocker
Harry Walther

23 Donnerstag 20-22.30 Ring A

Chor und Tanzgruppe

10. Gemischtes Abonnement
Karten im freien Verkauf:
DM 12.- ,10.- ,8.- ,6.60

24 Freitag 20-22 Freier Verkauf

Albert-Mangelsdorff-Quartett
Albert Mangelsdorff - Heinz Sauer
Günter Lenz - Ralf Hübner

Sonderkonzert
Jazz im Theater
Karten im freien Verkauf:
DM 4.- auf allen Plätzen

26 Sonntag 19.30-22.15 GRÜN

Gastspiel Düsseldorfer Schauspielhaus
Generalintendant Prof. Karl Heinz Stroux

Der Biberpelz
Diebskomödie von Gerhart Hauptmann

27 Montag 20-22.15 BLAU

Inszenierung: Karl Heinz Stroux
Ausstattung: Pit Fischer

28 Dienstag 20-22.45 ROT

Christiane Hammacher - Heidemarie Hatheyer
Johanna Liebeneiner - Annemarie Schmid
Dom de Beern - Helmut Everke - Marius Flachsmann
Wolfgang Grönebaum - Gunther Malzacher
Otto Rouvel - Frank Robert Schneider - Waldemar Schütz

11. Schauspielmiete
Karten im freien Verkauf:
DM 15.- ,12.- ,10.- ,8.- ,6.50

30 Donnerstag 19.30-22.45 Ring C

Gastspiel Landestheater Coburg
Intendant Hannsjoachim Worringen

Don Carlos
Oper von Giuseppe Verdi

2 Samstag 19.30-22.45 Ring A

Musikalische Leitung: Hellmut Pape
Inszenierung: Hannsjoachim Worringen
Bühnenbild: Dr. Fritz Mahnke - Chöre: Helmut Henze
Kostüme: Nina Kemper

4 Montag 19.30-22.45 Ring E

Gudrun Ebel - Gertraute Keil - Renate Lüke
Anneli Rauhala
Hartmut Bauer - Gustav Brunn - Urs Guldimann
Werner Kessler - Gregor Schildknecht - Erhard Weis

6 Mittwoch 19.30-22.45 Ring D

11. Gemischtes Abonnement
Karten im freien Verkauf:
DM 15.- ,12.- ,10.- ,8.-

11 Montag 20-22.15 GRÜN

Gastspiel Ulmer Theater
Intendant Detlof Krüger

Unbeständigkeit auf beiden Seiten
Komödie von Pierre Chamblain de Marivaux
Deutsch von Peter Gilbert

12 Dienstag 20-22.15 ROT

Inszenierung: Joachim Engel-Denis/Detlof Krüger
Bühnenbild und Kostüme: Gisela Spahlinger

13 Mittwoch 20-22.15 BLAU

Antje Holtz - Doris Steinmüller - Renate Völkner
Peter Dolder - Volker K. Bauer
Robert J. Bosshardt - Henning Köhler

12. (letzte) Schauspielmiete
Karten im freien Verkauf:
DM 12.- ,10.- ,8.- ,6.50

Änderungen vorbehalten!
Vorverkauf ab 21.4.1970 für alle Vorstellungen und Konzerte. Tageskasse (Tel. 51475). Eingang Rüßmannstr. 2, montags-samstags 9.30/12.30 Uhr, an der Abendkasse 1 Stunde vor Beginn. In den Preisen sind Garderobe und Altersversorgungsabgabe enthalten - mieten in Konzerten DM 1.- für Schauspielmieten im Gemischten Abonnement (bzw. umgekehrt): Theater- mieten in Konzerten (bzw. umgekehrt)
Jugendliche und Studierende (gegen Ausweis) DM 3.- im Hochparkett und Rang
Zuspätkommende können erst nach der Ouvertüre bzw. dem 1. Akt eingelassen werden

7

one hundred seventy-one

THEATER

SOLINGEN

11. Mai
Montag
19.45 bis 22.00 Uhr
Kulturgemeinde
Volksbühne, Kreis J I
6. Vorstellung
Kein Kartenverkauf

Monsieur chasse oder
Wie man Hasen jagt
Komödie von Georges Feydeau

Inszenierung:	Marianne Kehlau	Wilhelm Beck	Bernt Hahn	Theater
Pierre Léon	Helmka Segebiel	Carl-Johannes	Ernst von Klipstein	der Stadt Bonn
Bühnenbild	Gudrun Velisek	Eberhardt	Jochen Kroeber	
und Kostüme:		Hans Faber	Reinhard Papula	
Ottowerner Meyer				

19. Mai
Dienstag
19.00 bis 22.30 Uhr
Miete gelb
10. Vorstellung
und freier Verkauf
Preise von
4,60 bis 10,60 DM
Vorverkauf ab 11. 5.

Der Teufel und der liebe Gott
Schauspiel von Jean Paul Sartre

21. Mai
Donnerstag
19.45 bis 22.30 Uhr
Schauspielmiete
9. Vorstellung
und freier Verkauf
Preise von
4,60 bis 10,60 DM
Vorverkauf ab 19. 5.

Vor der Nacht
Schauspiel von David Rudkin

23. Mai
Samstag
19.45 bis 21.45 Uhr
Freier Verkauf
Preise von
4,60 bis 11,60 DM
Vorverkauf ab 19. 5.

Aus Mangel an Beweisen
Komödie von Giulio del Torre

25. Mai
Montag
19.45 bis 22.30 Uhr
Kulturgemeinde
Volksbühne, Kreis E 1
8. Vorstellung
und freier Verkauf
Preise von
4,60 bis 11,00 DM
Vorverkauf ab 19. 5.

Die Zauberflöte
Oper von Wolfgang Amadeus Mozart

27. Mai
Mittwoch
19.45 bis 22.00 Uhr
Miete grün
11. Vorstellung
und freier Verkauf
Preise von
4,60 bis 11,00 DM
Vorverkauf ab 19. 5.

Ballett-Abend
Der Weg
Elektronische Musik und das Brötzmann Free-Jazz-Quartett
Der wunderbare Mandarin von Béla Bartók
Scherzo italiano von Gioacchino Rossini

28. Mai
Donnerstag
20.00 bis 21.15 Uhr
Freier Verkauf
Preis 2,50 DM
Vorverkauf ab 19. 5.
Karten vom 27. März
haben Gültigkeit

Orgelkonzert Herbert Rafflenbeul

29. Mai
Freitag
20.00 Uhr
Eintrittspreis
1,50 DM

Unser Theater und Konzerthaus
Ein Blick hinter die Kulissen
Hans Demmer

30. Mai
Samstag
19.45 bis 22.15 Uhr
Miete grau
11. Vorstellung
und freier Verkauf
Preise von
4,60 bis 11,60 DM
Vorverkauf ab 25. 5.

Undine
Oper von Ernst Theodor Amadeus Hoffmann

31. Mai
Sonntag
19.00 bis 22.00 Uhr
Freier Verkauf
Preise von
5,50 bis 12,60 DM
Vorverkauf ab 25. 5.

My Fair Lady
Musical von Alan Jay Lerner / Frederick Loewe
Zum letzten Male

1. Juni
Montag
19.45 bis 22.45 Uhr
Kulturgemeinde
Volksbühne, Kreis J I
7. Vorstellung
Kein Kartenverkauf

My Fair Lady
Musical von Alan Jay Lerner / Frederick Loewe

2. Juni
Dienstag
20.00 bis 22.00 Uhr
Konzertreihe A
10. Konzert
und freier Verkauf
Preise von
2,50 bis 7,— DM
Vorverkauf ab 25. 5.

10. Hauptkonzert

one hundred seventy-two

WÜRTTEMBERGISCHE STAATSTHEATER STUTTGART

GROSSES HAUS		JUNI		KLEINES HAUS
Der fliegende Holländer Romantische Oper von RICHARD WAGNER Leitung: Dünnwald / Wieland Wagner / Mende Watson, Mödl — Neidlinger, Callio, Linke, Kraus	20 - 23 Uhr Miete J 8 und Plätze zu DM 5.— bis 23.—	Freitag **5**	19 - 22¼ Uhr Miete W 9 und Plätze zu DM 4.— bis 16.50	Zum 25. Mal **Heinrich IV.** von WILLIAM SHAKESPEARE Leitung: Palitzsch / Minks / Löffler Fassung Peter Palitzsch und Jörg Wehmeier Burde, Diekhoff, Schiemmer, Schwarz, Wiecke — Baender, Becker, Bock, Buhre, Elste, Enz, Haars, Haenel, Hennig, Höper, Just, Korff, Kuhlmann, Lang, Matschoß, Roggisch, Solinger, Schwartzkopff, Schwuchow, Steck, Steinmüller, Tächl, Toetzke, Walther, Wennemann, Wiedmann, Wildgruber
Ballettabend **Brouillards** Ballett von John Cranko / Musik von CLAUDE DEBUSSY Leitung: Cranko / Lautner Keil, Reyn, Hanke, Landon, Ishimatsu, Griffiths — Madsen, Cragun, Clauss, Berg, Stripling, Sutherland, Anderson, Ammann, Delmar, Klos, Kylian Erstaufführung **Orpheus** Musik von IGOR STRAWINSKY Leitung: Cranko / Kontarsky Keil, Landon, Griffiths — Clauss, Anderson, Kylian, Klos Erstaufführung **Agon** Musik von IGOR STRAWINSKY Leitung: Balanchine / Neary / Kontarsky Reyn, Hanke, Landon, Griffiths — Cragun, Stripling, Kylian, Klos	19½ - 22 Uhr Außer Miete DM 5.— bis 23.—	Samstag **6**	19 - 22½ Uhr Auswärtige Miete III 9 und Plätze zu DM 4.— bis 16.50	**Die Tage der Commune** von BERTOLT BRECHT / Musik von HANNS EISLER Leitung: Hollmann / Richter-Forgach / Löffler Engelmann, Gandre, Goetzen, Höger, Ohngemach, Rohweder, Schiemmer, Schroeder, Strien, Thomann — Anschütz, Baender, Becker, Bernhardt, Bock, Buhre, Eckart, Elste, Enz, Gerth, Haars, Haenel, Hanus, Höper, Kemmer, König, Korff, Lang, Matschoß, Michaeli, Moland, Roggisch, Schramm, Schwalm, Schwuchow, Solinger, Steck, Steinmüller, Tächl, Thurau, Toetzke, Treichler, Walther, Wennemann, Wöhrmann, Wöbben
Die Teufel von Loudun Oper in drei Akten von KRZYSZTOF PENDERECKI Text vom Komponisten nach Aldous Huxley / John Whiting Leitung: Kulka / Rennert / Bauer-Ecsy / Mende Lorand, Becker-Egner, Gutmann, Schulz-Pickard, Krüger a. G., Karen — Alexander, Fourie, Kraus, Linke, Pfeifle, Holm, Bertram, Cramer, Grefe, Eichler, Kosso, Hirte, Baender	19½ - 22 Uhr Miete So IV 9 und Plätze zu DM 5.— bis 23.—	Sonntag **7**	20 - 22¼ Uhr Miete KI 9 und Plätze zu DM 4.— bis 16.50	**Koralle Meier** Ein Stück mit Musik von MARTIN SPERR Leitung: Palitzsch / Heitmüller Diesel, Engelmann, Kuschnitzky, Schiemmer — Elste, Höper, Jeker, Kemmer, Korff, Matschoß, Schramm, Schwuchow, Steinmüller, Toetzke, Wildgruber
Aida In italienischer Sprache Oper von GIUSEPPE VERDI Leitung: Dünnwald / Puhlmann / Richter / Mende / Berlozoff Löw-Szöky, Hoffman, Sutter — Callio, Wolansky, Wildermann, Kosso, Krämer	19½ - 22⅓ Uhr Geschl. Vorst. Volksbühne DGB Gruppen A u. F	Montag **8**	19½ - 22½ Uhr Geschl. Vorst. Volksbühne DGB Gruppen N u. Q 21	**Guerillas** Tragödie in fünf Akten von ROLF HOCHHUTH Leitung: Palitzsch / Schubert / Löffler Burde, Kopp, Wodetzky — Andersson, Anschütz, Baender, Blech, Buhre, Diemer, Elste, Haars, Haenel, Just, Knuth, Roggisch, Schwalm, Schwuchow, Steck, Walther, Wildgruber
Tosca In italienischer Sprache Musikdrama von GIACOMO PUCCINI Leitung: Nagora / Puhlmann / Fritzsche / Mende Hillebrecht, Bence — Alemanno a. G., Nurmela, Hirte, Bertram, Pfeifle, Eichler	20 - 22½ Uhr Miete A 10 und Plätze zu DM 4.— bis 22.—	Dienstag **9**	19½ - 22½ Uhr Miete X 9 und Plätze zu DM 4.— bis 16.50	**Guerillas** Tragödie in fünf Akten von ROLF HOCHHUTH Leitung: Palitzsch / Schubert / Löffler Besetzung wie 8. Juni
BALLETTWOCHE 1970 **Apollo** Musik von IGOR STRAWINSKY Leitung: Balanchine / Stolze · Einstudierung: Clauss Keil, Reyn, Hanke — Clauss **Orpheus** Musik von IGOR STRAWINSKY Leitung: Cranko / Kontarsky Keil, Landon, Griffiths — Clauss, Anderson, Kylian, Klos **Agon** Musik von IGOR STRAWINSKY Leitung: Balanchine / Neary / Kontarsky Reyn, Hanke, Landon, Griffiths — Cragun, Stripling, Kylian, Klos	19½ - 22 Uhr Miete Mi II 8 und Plätze zu DM 5.— bis 23.—	Mittwoch **10**	20 - 22¼ Uhr Miete Mi III 9 und Plätze zu DM 4.— bis 16.50	**Koralle Meier** Ein Stück mit Musik von MARTIN SPERR Leitung: Palitzsch / Heitmüller Besetzung wie 7. Juni
Brouillards Ballett von John Cranko / Musik von CLAUDE DEBUSSY Leitung: Cranko / Lautner Keil, Reyn, Hanke, Landon, Ishimatsu, Griffiths — Madsen, Cragun, Clauss, Berg, Stripling, Sutherland, Anderson, Ammann, Delmar, Klos, Kylian **Poème de l'extase** Ballett von John Cranko / Musik von ALEXANDER SKRJABIN Leitung: Cranko / Stolze / Rose Haydée — Madsen, Cragun, Clauss, Berg, Stripling und das Corps de ballet **Katalyse** Nach dem Konzert für Klavier, Trompete und Streichorchester von DIMITRI SCHOSTAKOWITSCH Leitung: Cranko / Stolze Cragun — Keil, Krause — Madsen, Stripling und das Corps de ballet	19½ - 22 Uhr Miete E 10 und Plätze zu DM 5.— bis 23.—	Donnerstag **11**	20 - 21½ Uhr Miete O 10 und Plätze zu DM 4.— bis 16.50	**Was der Butler sah** Komödie von JOE ORTON / Deutsch von Georg Klausen Leitung: von Wiese / Heyduck Engelmann, Rohweder — Bock, Höper, Kuhlmann, Matschoß
Romeo und Julia Ballett nach Shakespeare / Musik von SERGE PROKOFIEFF Leitung: Stolze / Cranko / Rose Haydée, Heim, Papendick — Madsen, Barbay a. G., Stripling, Sutherland, Beale, Anderson und das Corps de ballet	19½ - 22¼ Uhr Miete M 9 und Plätze zu DM 5.— bis 30.—	Freitag **12**	19 - 22¼ Uhr Miete Z 9 und Plätze zu DM 4.— bis 16.50	**Heinrich IV.** von WILLIAM SHAKESPEARE Leitung: Palitzsch / Minks / Löffler Fassung: Peter Palitzsch und Jörg Wehmeier Besetzung wie 5. Juni
Der Widerspenstigen Zähmung (nach Shakespeare) Ballett in zwei Akten. Musik nach D. SCARLATTI von KURT-HEINZ STOLZE Leitung: Stolze / Cranko / Dalton Haydée, Keil, Griffiths, Papendick — Cragun, Madsen, Berg, Kylian und das Corps de ballet	19½ - 21½ Uhr Außer Miete DM 5.— bis 30.—	Samstag **13**	19 - 22½ Uhr Miete IX 9 und Plätze zu DM 4.— bis 16.50	**Die Tage der Commune** von BERTOLT BRECHT / Musik von HANNS EISLER Leitung: Hollmann / Richter-Forgach / Löffler Besetzung wie 6. Juni
Apollo Musik von IGOR STRAWINSKY Leitung: Balanchine / Stolze · Einstudierung: Clauss Neary a. G., Landon, Griffiths — Clauss **Orpheus** Musik von IGOR STRAWINSKY Leitung: Cranko / Kontarsky Keil, Landon, Griffiths — Clauss, Anderson, Kylian, Klos **Agon** Musik von IGOR STRAWINSKY Leitung: Balanchine / Neary / Kontarsky Neary a. G., Reyn, Hanke, Landon — Cragun, Stripling, Kylian, Klos	19½ - 22 Uhr Miete So 10 und Plätze zu DM 5.— bis 23.—	Sonntag **14**	19 - 22 Uhr Auswärtige Miete IV 9 und Plätze zu DM 4.— bis 16.50	**Guerillas** Tragödie in fünf Akten von ROLF HOCHHUTH Leitung: Palitzsch / Schubert / Löffler Besetzung wie 8. Juni
Ballett-Gastspiel **Paul Taylor Dance Compagny** New York	19½ - 22 Uhr Miete L 9 und Plätze zu DM 5.— bis 30.—	Montag **15**	19½ - 21½ Uhr Geschl. Vorst. Volksbühne DGB Gruppen R u. Q 22	**Leonce und Lena** Lustspiel von GEORG BÜCHNER Leitung: Fischer / Richter-Forgach / Löffler Diekhoff, Schwarz, Wiecke — Anschütz, Baender, Enz, Hanus, Kuhlmann, Mahnke, Steck, Toetzke, Wildgruber
Onegin Ballett in drei Akten nach Puschkin Musik von PETER I. TSCHAIKOWSKY eingerichtet und instrumentiert von Kurt-Heinz Stolze Leitung: Stolze / Cranko / Rose Haydée, Hanke, Papendick — Clauss, Berg, Stripling und das Corps de ballet	19½ - 21½ Uhr Miete C 9 und Plätze zu DM 5.— bis 30.—	Dienstag **16**	20 - 22½ Uhr Miete XV 9 und Plätze zu DM 4.— bis 22.—	**Der Tod des Empedokles** Concerto scenico in 2 Akten Musik von HERMANN REUTTER Leitung: Paulmüller / Poettgen / Bauer-Ecsy / Mende Orchester: Die Stuttgarter Philharmoniker Bence, Sailer — Wolansky, Reich, Harper, Hirte, Krämer Wiederaufnahme **Die Witwe von Ephesus** von HERMANN REUTTER Leitung: Paulmüller / Poettgen / Bauer-Ecsy Orchester: Die Stuttgarter Philharmoniker Rebmann, Sauter, Becker-Egner, Brivkalne, Gutmann, Schulz-Pickard — Callio, Bertram, Grefe, Kraus, Schwer
Gala-Abend Siehe rechte Randspalte	19½ - 22½ Uhr Außer Miete DM 5.— bis 40.—	Mittwoch **17**	19 - 22½ Uhr Miete VIII 10 und Plätze zu DM 4.— bis 16.50	**Die Tage der Commune** von BERTOLT BRECHT / Musik von HANNS EISLER Leitung: Hollmann / Richter-Forgach / Löffler Besetzung wie 6. Juni
Die Entführung aus dem Serail Singspiel von WOLFGANG AMADEUS MOZART Leitung: Nagora / Puhlmann / Bauer-Ecsy Pütz, Freedmann a. G. — Herndon, Unger, Linke, Cramer	20 - 22½ Uhr Geschl. Vorst. Volksbühne DGB Gruppen G u. K	Donnerstag **18**	19 - 21½ Uhr Miete V 9 und Plätze zu DM 4.— bis 22.—	Zum 70. Geburtstag von Hermann Reutter **Der Tod des Empedokles** Concerto scenico in 2 Akten Musik von HERMANN REUTTER Leitung: Paulmüller / Poettgen / Bauer-Ecsy / Mende Orchester: Die Stuttgarter Philharmoniker Bence, Sailer — Wolansky, Reich, Harper, Hirte, Krämer **Die Witwe von Ephesus** von HERMANN REUTTER Leitung: Paulmüller / Poettgen / Bauer-Ecsy Orchester: Die Stuttgarter Philharmoniker Rebmann, Sauter, Becker-Egner, Brivkalne, Gutmann, Schulz-Pickard — Callio, Bertram, Grefe, Kraus, Schwer

41

LIEDERHALLE

14. Juni, 11 Uhr: Voraufführung
15. Juni, 20 Uhr: Hauptaufführung

7. Symphoniekonzert

Dirigent: VACLAV NEUMANN
Solist: CHRISTOPH ESCHENBACH, Klavier

WOLFGANG FORTNER
Marginalien für Orchester (Erstaufführung)

LUDWIG VAN BEETHOVEN
Konzert für Klavier und Orchester Nr. 5, Es-Dur, op. 73

JOHANNES BRAHMS
2. Sinfonie D-Dur, op. 73

Preise von DM 3.— bis DM 10.—

VORSCHAU

GROSSES HAUS

Mittwoch, 17. Juni, 19.30—22.30 Uhr

Gala-Abend der Stuttgarter Ballettwoche

Brouillards
Ballett von John Cranko / Musik von CLAUDE DEBUSSY
Leitung: Cranko / Lautner

Divertissements
Gastspiel Margot Fonteyn

Poème de l'extase
Ballett von John Cranko / Musik von ALEXANDER SKRJABIN
Leitung: Cranko / Stolze / Rose

Der Ring des Nibelungen

von RICHARD WAGNER / Inszenierung: Wieland Wagner
Musikalische Leitung: Heinrich Hollreiser
Einzige Gesamt-Aufführung des Spieljahres

Samstag, 20. Juni 1970, 19.30—22.00 Uhr
Das Rheingold
Hoffman, Stadler, Bence, Rebmann, Wachmann, Sutter — Wildermann, Windgassen, Harper, Hirte, Neidlinger, von Rohr, Linke, Kraus

Sonntag, 21. Juni 1970, 17.30—22.00 Uhr
Die Walküre
Ligendza, Hillebrecht, Hoffman, Stadler, Löw-Szöky, Plümacher, Bence, Rebmann, Gutmann, Sutter — Ward, Windgassen, von Rohr

Mittwoch, 24. Juni 1970, 18.00—22.45 Uhr
Siegfried
Ligendza, Bence, Pütz — Windgassen, Ward, Neidlinger, Linke, Kraus

Samstag, 27. Juni 1970, 17.00—22.30 Uhr
Götterdämmerung
Ligendza, Stadler, Hoffman, Rebmann, Wachmann, Hellmann, Bence — Windgassen, Alexander, von Rohr, Neidlinger

Preise für den gesamten Zyklus — gegenüber Einzelkartenverkauf um 10% ermäßigt: DM 23.40 bis DM 82.80, für Mieter mit besonderem Gutschein 20% ermäßigt: DM 20.80 bis DM 73.60.

Vorverkauf für den gesamten Zyklus ab Samstag, 30. Mai, 10.30 Uhr,

Einzelkarten ab 13. Juni, 10.30 Uhr

In Vorbereitung
Ende Juni, Kleines Haus
Neuinszenierung

Onkel Wanja

Schauspiel von ANTON TSCHECHOW
Deutsch von Peter Urban
Inszenierung: Niels-Peter Rudolph
Bühne: Karl Kneidl

Neueinzeichnung für die Spielzeit 1970/71

Die Opern-, Schauspiel- und Orchestermieten bieten einen Preisnachlaß von 20-40% gegenüber den Kassenpreisen. Neueinzeichnungen im Verwaltungsgebäude der Württ. Staatstheater Stuttgart, Oberer Schloßgarten 6 ab 15. Juni

Geschäftsstunden: 10.30 - 13.00 und 17.00 - 18.30 Uhr
samstags: 10.30 - 13. Uhr

Vorverkauf für 12. Juni bis 18. Juni ab 6. Juni

für alle Aufführungen: Kassenhalle des Großen Hauses: dienstags bis samstags 10.30—13.00 und 17.00—18.30 Uhr, sonntags 10.30 bis 13.00 Uhr, montags geschlossen · ABENDKASSE jeweils ½ Stunde vor Beginn
TELEFONISCHE KARTENBESTELLUNG — Telefon 2 49 51 — werktags von 10.30—18.30 Uhr, sonntags von 10.30—13.00 Uhr
PROGRAMMDURCHSAGEN — auch plötzliche Änderungen — über Telefon 1 15 16
WEITERE VORVERKAUFSSTELLEN: Buchhandlung Wildt, Königstraße 44 und Königsbau, Verkehrsverein im Hauptbahnhof, unter den Arkaden und Zweigstelle des Verkehrsvereins im [illegible] Kaufhaus Breuninger; Kartenhäusle, Kleiner Schloßplatz; Musikhaus Mayer, Bad Cannstatt, Marktstraße 14; in Ludwigsburg: Buchhandlung Aigner, Arsenalstraße 8

Theater Trier
Spielplan

Kasse: Mo–Fr 11.00–13.00 Uhr
Sa–So 11.00–12.30 Uhr
Telefon: 7 5777
Vorverkauf: ab Freitag für nachfolgende Woche
Spielplandurchsage: Telefon 11 56
Die Kasse ist Dienstag bis Freitag 2 Stunden,
Samstag und Sonntag 1 Stunde vor der Vorstellung
geöffnet. Montag geschlossen.

Mittwoch 13 Mai

20.00–ca. 22.00 Uhr
Konzertanrecht
und freier Verkauf
Preise 4,50—10,50 DM

9. Orchesterkonzert
Werke von Ravel, Chopin, Mozart

Leitung: Francis Travis
Solist: André Tschaikowsky
Siehe auch Sonderplakat

Freitag 15 Mai

20.00–ca. 22.00 Uhr
Premierenanrecht
und freier Verkauf
Preise 3,50—9,50 DM

Erstaufführung
Die Troerinnen
Schauspiel von Matthias Braun nach Euripides

Leitung: Pohl, Rechtern, Frehner
Besetzung: Adam-Quot, Benesch, Franzmann a. G., Gmeinböck,
Haller, Kabus, Kolf, Lais, Minkwitz, Opitz a. G., Remy, Riedel a. G.
Sanne — Filges, Hassenstein, Saxen, Saxen jun.

Samstag 16 Mai

20.00–22.30 Uhr
Lkr. Trier, Ring IV
und freier Verkauf
Preise 4,50—10,50 DM

Das Land des Lächelns
Operette von Franz Lehar

Leitung: Kubica, Krämer, Saxen, Giersch, Frehner
Besetzung: Haller, Kammerl, Remy, Schmid — Buder, Fiorente,
Habernicht, Henning, Helfer, Stelten, Wiersich — Menzel, Saxen

---

Sonntag 17 Mai

19.00–21.00 Uhr
Nur freier Verkauf
Preise 4,50—10,50 DM

Frühlingsluft
Operette von Joseph Strauß

Leitung: Bihlmaier, Krämer, Giersch, Nunnemann, Gmeinböck
Besetzung: Berson, Gmeinböck, Kreitmair, Remy, Snortland —
Buder, Dittebrand, Habernicht, Krämer, Reim, Stelten, Wiersich
Kabus

Montag 18 Mai

20.00–21.45 Uhr
Nur freier Verkauf
Preise 4,50—10,50 DM

Der Mann von La Mancha
Musical von Dale Wassermann, Joe Darion und Mitch Leigh

Leitung: Bihlmaier, Schnitzler a. G., Hruby, Hutter, Saxen
Besetzung: Gubkova, Horn, Lara-Paredes, Menzel, Remy,
Snortland — Borchert, Dittebrand, Evans, Fell, Fiorente, Gubka,
Habernicht, Kaschenz, King, Pikl, Rabben, Rathke, Reim,
Saxen, Schreer

Mittwoch 20 Mai

20.00–22.15 Uhr
Theatergemeinde
und freier Verkauf
Preise 3,50—9,50 DM

Biografie: Ein Spiel
Schauspiel von Max Frisch

Leitung: Spörri a. G., Frehner
Besetzung: Adam-Quodt, Gmeinböck, Horn, Lais, Menzel,
Minkwitz, Remy, Schmid, Snortland, Tröber-Fink, Ullrich —
Borchert, Fell, Filges, Habernicht, Hassenstein, Henning,
Kaschenz, Kovacs, Pikl, Rabben, Rathke, Reim, Sallowsky,
Saxen, Saxen jun., Schönfeld, Wagner, Wiersich

Freitag 22 Mai

20.00–21.45 Uhr
Anrecht rot
und freier Verkauf
Preise 4,50—10,50 DM

Der Mann von La Mancha
Musical von Dale Wassermann, Joe Darion und Mitch Leigh

Wie am 18. Mai

---

studio

Neuer Studio-Raum:
Jugendzentrum Mergener Hof, Rindertanzstraße 4

Von Mäusen und Menschen
Schauspiel von John Steinbeck

Leitung: Pohl, Körner, Frehner
Besetzung: Gmeinböck — Borchert, Evans, Fell, Hassenstein,
Henning, Kaschenz, Pikl, Saxen, Tibes

Montag, 11. Mai, 20.00 Uhr (Jugendanrecht, Ring IV und freier Verkauf)
Donnerstag, 21. Mai, 20.00 Uhr (Nur freier Verkauf)
Preise 3,50 und 4,50 DM

Raymund Richter · Köln

Volksfreund-Druckerei Nik. Koch, Trier

Theater Trier
Spielplan

Kasse: Mo–Fr 11.00–13.00 Uhr
Sa–So 11.00–12.30 Uhr
Telefon: 7 57 77
Vorverkauf: ab Freitag für nachfolgende Woche
Spielplandurchsage: Telefon 11 56
Die Kasse ist Dienstag bis Freitag 2 Stunden,
Samstag und Sonntag 1 Stunde vor der Vorstellung
geöffnet. Montag geschlossen.

Freitag 22 Mai — 20.00–22.00 Uhr — Anrecht rot und freier Verkauf — Preise 4.50–10.50 DM

Der Mann von La Mancha
Musical von Dale Wassermann, Joe Darion und Mitch Leigh

Leitung: Bihlmaier, Schnitzler a. G., Hruby, Hutter, Saxen
Besetzung: Gubkova, Horn, Lara-Paredes, Menzel, Remy, Snortland — Borchert, Dittebrand, Evans, Fell, Fiorente, Gubka, Habernicht, Kaschenz, King, Pikl, Rabben, Rathke, Reim, Saxen, Schreer

Samstag 23 Mai — 19.30–21.30 Uhr — Anrecht beige und freier Verkauf — Preise 3.50–9.50 DM

Die Troerinnen
Schauspiel von Mattias Braun nach Euripides

Leitung: Pohl, Rechtern, Frehner
Besetzung: Adam-Quot, Benesch, Franzmann a. G., Gmeinböck, Haller, Kabus, Kolf, Lais, Minkwitz, Opitz a. G., Remy, Riedel a. G. Sanne — Filges, Hassenstein, Saxen, Saxen jun.

Sonntag 24 Mai — 19.30–21.30 Uhr — Lkr. Trier Ring V ausverkauft

Das Land des Lächelns
Operette von Franz Lehar

Leitung: Kubica, Krämer, Saxen, Giersch, Frehner
Besetzung: Haller, Kammerl, Remy, Schmid — Dittebrand, Fiorente, Habernicht, Hassenstein, Helfer, Steffen, Wiersich — Menzel, Saxen

Dienstag 26 Mai — 20.00–22.00 Uhr — Anrecht grün und freier Verkauf — Preise 3.50–9.50 DM

Die Troerinnen
Schauspiel von Mattias Braun nach Euripides

Wie am 23. Mai

Mittwoch 27 Mai — 20.00–22.00 Uhr — Nur freier Verkauf — Preise 4.50–10.50 DM

Zum letzten Male:
Frühlingsluft
Operette von Joseph Strauß

Leitung: Bihlmaier, Krämer, Giersch, Nunnemann, Gmeinböck
Besetzung: Berson, Gmeinböck, Kreitmair, Remy, Snortland — Buder, Dittebrand, Habernicht, Krämer, Reim, Steffen, Wiersich Kabus

Donnerstag 28 Mai — 19.00–21.30 Uhr — Nur freier Verkauf — Preise 4.50–10.50 DM

Das Land des Lächelns
Operette von Franz Lehar

Wie am 24. Mai

Freitag 29 Mai — 20.00–22.00 Uhr — Volksbühne und freier Verkauf — Preise 4.50–10.50 DM

Der Mann von La Mancha
Musical von Dale Wassermann, Joe Darion und Mitch Leigh

Leitung: Bibl, Schnitzler a. G., Hruby, Hutter, Saxen
Besetzung: Wie am 22. Mai

Samstag 30 Mai — 19.30–22.00 Uhr — Nur freier Verkauf — Preise 4.50–10.50 DM

Das Land des Lächelns
Operette von Franz Lehar

Wie am 24. Mai

Sonntag 31 Mai — 20.00–22.00 Uhr — Volkshochschule und freier Verkauf — Preise 3.50–9.50 DM

Die Troerinnen
Schauspiel von Mattias Braun nach Euripides

Wie am 23. Mai

Dienstag 2 Juni — 20.00–22.00 Uhr — Nur freier Verkauf — Preise 4.50–10.50 DM

Der Mann von La Mancha
Musical von Dale Wassermann, Joe Darion und Mitch Leigh

Wie am 22. Mai

studio

Neuer Studio-Raum:
Jugendzentrum Mergener Hof, Rindertanzstraße 4

Von Mäusen und Menschen
Schauspiel von John Steinbeck

Leitung: Pohl, Körner, Frehner
Besetzung: Gmeinböck — Borchert, Evans, Fell, Hassenstein, Henning, Kaschenz, Pikl, Saxen, Tibes

Montag, 25. Mai, 20.00 Uhr (Jugendanrecht Ring I und freier Verkauf)
Montag, 1. Juni, 20.00 Uhr (freier Verkauf)
Preise 3,50 und 4,50 DM

Raymund Richter · Köln

Volksfreund-Druckerei Nik. Koch, Trier

STAATSOPER

Wien I, Opernring

Spielplan für die Zeit vom 31. Mai bis 7. Juni 1970

Tag	Vorstellungen		Proben

Sonntag, 31. Mai

Preise I — **19** Uhr **Aschenbrödel** (Cinderella)
Schwarz
Kirnbauer, Klemisch, Zimmerl, Maar, Karl, Cech, Scheuermann, Barth, Zlocha, Wolf, Wilhelm, P. Vondrak, Reischütz
Dill – Nowotny – Ursuliak   E. Vondrak

Theater an der Wien
Vorstellung der Wiener Staatsoper
19.30 Uhr **Fidelio**
Bernstein
Jones, Popp
King, Ridderbusch, Adam, Crass, Dallapozza, Terkal, Lackner
Zehetgruber   Koller

Montag, 1. Juni

Preise II — **17.30** Uhr **Tristan und Isolde**
Böhm
Nilsson, Hesse
Thomas, Kreppel, Wiener, Bunger, Klein, Dermota, Pröglhöf
Dostal   Cserjan

Redoutensaal:
18 Die Entführung aus dem Serail, mit Klavier

Proben:
Bühne: 16.15 Tristan und Isolde, mit Klavier (Statisten)
Probebühne: 11 Iphigenie auf Tauris, mit Klavier
Ensembleprobesaal: 18.30 Iphigenie auf Tauris, Ensembleprobe

Dienstag, 2. Juni

Preise I — **20** Uhr **Iphigenie auf Tauris**
Stein
Jurinac, De Groote, Yachmi, Dutoit, Kmentt, Paskalis, Kreppel, Frese, Pernerstorfer
Dostal   Koller

Im Redoutensaal
Preise I — **19** Uhr **Die Entführung aus dem Serail**
Swarowsky
Rothenberger, Grist, Christian, Schreier, Unger, Jungwirth
Meinert   Cserjan

Proben:
Bühne: Fidelio, technische Einrichtung
Direktion: 9 Regiesitzung
Probebühne: 17.30 Tosca, mit Klavier

Mittwoch, 3. Juni

Preise II — In italienischer Sprache
19.30 Uhr **Tosca**
Klobučar
Rysanek-Gausmann, Yachmi, King, Wächter, Dönch, Braun, Equiluz, Pröglhöf, Pantscheff
Usunow   Cserjan

Proben:
Bühne: Fidelio, Dekorations- u. Beleuchtungsprobe (1. u. 2. Bild)
Probebühne: 10.30 Der fliegende Holländer, mit Klavier

Donnerstag, 4. Juni

Preise I — **19.30** Uhr **Der fliegende Holländer**
Märzendorfer
Jones, Rössel-Majdan, Kreppel, Beirer, Unger, Vermeersch a. G.
Wopmann   Homola

Proben:
Bühne: Fidelio, Dekorations- u. Beleuchtungsprobe (3. u. 4. Bild)
Ensembleprobesaal: 18 Ariadne auf Naxos, Ensembleprobe

Freitag, 5. Juni

Preise I — **19.30** Uhr **Ariadne auf Naxos**
Hollreiser
Ludwig, Grist, Della Casa, Popp, Lilowa, Mechera, Christian, Berry, Thomas, Pröglhöf, Dickie (2 Partien), Frese, Pantscheff, Kerns, Equiluz, Lackner
Meinert   Koller

Proben:
Bühne: Fidelio, mit Klavier (Soli und Chor)
Probebühne: 10 Der Prozeß, mit Klavier, ca. 11.30 Der Prozeß, Ensembleprobe

Samstag, 6. Juni

Preise I — **19.30** Uhr **Der Prozeß**
Hollreiser
Pilou, Hermann, Stolze, Equiluz, Jungwirth, Zednik, Bunger, Dermota, Gutstein, Czerwenka, Lackner, Pernerstorfer
Dostal   Homola

Proben:
Bühne: Fidelio, mit Klavier (Soli)
Probebühne: 10 Capriccio, mit Klavier
Ensembleprobesaal: 10 Don Giovanni, Ensembleprobe

Sonntag, 7. Juni

Preise II — In italienischer Sprache
19 Uhr **Don Giovanni**
Krips
Janowitz, Jurinac, Holm, Crass, Wächter, Berry, Schreier, Holecek
Zehetgruber   Koller

In Vorbereitung: **Einakterabend** (Redoutensaal), **Don Carlos**

---

1. Wenn ein Mitglied krankheitshalber verhindert ist, an den angesetzten Proben oder Vorstellungen teilzunehmen, hat es dies der Direktion sofort anzuzeigen und gleichzeitig ein ärztliches Zeugnis einzusenden.
Theaterarzt ist Medizinalrat Dr. Götz Kende (Ordination im Dienstzimmer Montag, Mittwoch, Donnerstag, Freitag 10.30 bis 11.30 Uhr). Ihm obliegt lediglich die amtsärztliche Bestätigung bzw die Ausfertigung eines Krankheitszeugnisses.
2. Die Mitglieder sind verpflichtet, eine halbe Stunde vor Beginn des Aktes, in dem sie aufzutreten haben, im Theater anwesend zu sein. Der

Abendspielleiter ist verpflichtet, Verspätungen der Direktion sofort zu melden.
3. Auch die in den angesetzten Vorstellungen nicht beschäftigten Mitglieder haben eine Stunde vor Theaterbeginn in ihrer Wohnung die eventuelle Erreichbarkeit sicherzustellen.
4. Es wird neuerlich in Erinnerung gebracht, daß das Anprobieren von Kleidern nur in den Werkstätten des Operntheaters selbst, und zwar innerhalb der Arbeitsstunden (8 bis 12 Uhr und 13 bis 16 Uhr) erfolgen kann.

Die Mitglieder sind ausnahmslos verpflichtet, jeden Urlaub sowie Mitwirkungen jeder Art vor Abschluß der Direktion anzuzeigen

Die Mitglieder sind verpflichtet, sich selbst über die Proben des nächsten Tages entweder telephonisch (Regiekanzlei) oder persönlich zu informieren

Eine Verständigung durch die Regiekanzlei erfolgt nicht!

Telephon der Regiekanzlei: 52 76 41/2315/2316

Das jeweilige Wochenrepertoire ist jeden Samstag abend in der Regiekanzlei erhältlich

Druck: AGENS-WERK – Geyer + Co. – Wien 5, Schloßgasse 18 a

VOLKSOPER

Währinger Straße 78
1090 Wien

Spielplan für die Zeit vom 31. Mai bis 7. Juni 1970

Tag	Vorstellungen	Proben	
Sonntag, 31. Mai	Im Abonnement XXI. Gruppe und allgemeiner Kartenverkauf Preise I **19** Uhr **Puccini-Einakter** (Triptychon) Schaenen **DER MANTEL** Zschau, Malaniuk, Szep Buzea, Konya, Witte, Schöfer, Drahosch Kaiser Pecinovsky **SCHWESTER ANGELICA** Sorell, Hermann, Draksler, Herze, Wald, Kaiser, Plaschka, Fez, Sobota, Papouschek, Kindler, Kowa, Wittich, Stadtler, Mozart-Sängerknaben Kaiser Pecinovsky **GIANNI SCHICCHI** Steffek, Hermann, Felbermayer, Sobota Dönch, Baillie, Drahosch, Ruzicka, Schöfer, Strohbauer, Nidetzky, Laurer, Stajnc, Temple, Mozart-Sängerknabe Laurer Pecinovsky		
Montag, 1. Juni	Bei aufgehobenem Abonnement – Preise III PREMIERE 19.30 Uhr **Die Italienerin in Algier** Weller Samar, Higueras-Aragon, Draksler Czerwenka, Papulkas, Peters, Nicolai Laurer Lehner	**Bühne:** Die Italienerin in Algier, Dekorations- und Beleuchtungsprobe	
Dienstag, 2. Juni	Im Abonnement II. Gruppe und allgemeiner Kartenverkauf Preise II **19** Uhr **Fra Diavolo** Bernet Sobota, Henery Buzea, Serafin, Witte, Nidetzky, Kuchar, Dönch, Haider, Laurer Laurer Lehner	**Bühne:** 11 Die Kluge, mit Klavier	
Mittwoch, 3. Juni	Im Abonnement X. Gruppe und allgemeiner Kartenverkauf Preise II 19.30 Uhr **Die Italienerin in Algier** Weller Samar, Higueras-Aragon, Draksler Czerwenka, Papulkas, Peters, Nicolai Laurer Lehner	**Bühne:** 10 Der Mond, mit Klavier	
Donnerstag, 4. Juni	Bei aufgehobenem Abonnement – Preise III 19.30 Uhr **Eine Nacht in Venedig** Bauer-Theussl Leigh, Löwinger, Kowa, Längauer, Kindler Dallapozza, Drahosch, Pilz, Nidetzky, Zimmer, Strohbauer, Ruzicka, Drexler, Jenewein, Randers Fritz Pecinovsky	**Bühne:** 10 Der Mond, mit Klavier	
Freitag, 5. Juni	Preise III **19** Uhr **Die Fledermaus** Paulik Lorenz, de Groote, Sobota, Kindler Serafin, Gutstein, Dönch, Kuchar, Terkal, Carl, Strohbauer Fritz Pecinovsky	**Bühne:** 10 Die Kluge, mit Klavier	
Samstag, 6. Juni	Preise III Zum 50. Male **19** Uhr **Die Csardasfürstin** Paulik Leigh, Löwinger, Längauer Minich, Kuchar, Prikopa, Diehl a. G., Zimmer, Unterkircher, Laurer, Randers, Fritsch, Pirringer Laurer Pecinovsky	**Bühne:** 10 Die Kluge, mit Klavier	
Sonntag, 7. Juni	Im Abonnement XXII. Gruppe und allgemeiner Kartenverkauf Preise II 19.30 Uhr **Werther** Bernet Lorenz, Sophie ? Dallapozza, Hagegaard, Korn, Drahosch, Strohbauer, Mozart-Sängerknaben Kaiser Pecinovsky	**Weiterer Spielplanentwurf:** 8. VI.: Die Italienerin in Algier 9. VI.: Der Bettelstudent 10. VI.: Die Zauberflöte 11. VI.: Die Italienerin in Algier 12. VI.: Der Graf von Luxemburg 13. VI.: Ein Walzertraum 14. VI.: Die Italienerin in Algier	

In Vorbereitung: **Der Mond – Die Kluge, Die heimliche Ehe**

Hessisches Staatstheater Wiesbaden

Großes Haus | | Kleines Haus

Montag 25 Mai

Titelpartie Dagmar Koller
Das Taxigirl Sweet Charity
Tanzmusical von Neil Simon – Musik von Cy Coleman
20.00–22.45 Uhr · Bes.-Ring · Freiverkauf · Preise 3,50–17,00 DM

Die Schule der Frauen
Komödie von Molière
20.00–22.00 Uhr · Th.-Gem. Gr. MA 1 · Freiverkauf · Preise 4,00–12,50 DM

Dienstag 26 Mai

Theaterkasse abends geschlossen
Wegen Vorbereitung der Wiederaufnahme von „Aida" geschlossen

Theaterkasse abends geschlossen
Wegen Vorbereitung des „Multimedia"-Abends geschlossen

Mittwoch 27 Mai

IMF Gala-Abend
Titelpartie: Tamara Milaschkina – Radames: Bruno Prevedi
Aida (in italienischer Sprache)
Oper in vier Akten von Giuseppe Verdi
19.30–22.45 Uhr · Freiverkauf · Preise 10,00–60,00 DM

IMF Multimedia-Abend
Canzona für Sopran und ein Environment von Dieter Schönbach
La Fabbrica Illuminata von Luigi Nono
Der Sturm von Dieter Schönbach und Edmund Kieselbach nach William Shakespeare
20.00–22.15 Uhr · Freiverkauf · Preise 4,00 u. 8,00 DM

Donnerstag 28 Mai

Zum letzten Male in dieser Spielzeit!
Aida
Oper in vier Akten von Giuseppe Verdi
19.30–22.45 Uhr · Bes.-Ring · Freiverkauf · Preise 3,50–17,00 DM

Die Schule der Frauen
Komödie von Molière
20.00–22.00 Uhr · Th.-Gem. Gr. GK 22 · Beschränkter Verkauf · Preise 4,00–12,50 DM
Studio-Souterrain 19.00 Der amerikanische Traum/Der Sandkasten

Freitag 29 Mai

Royal Ballet Covent Garden London
Der Schwanensee
Ballett von Peter I. Tschaikowski
19.30–22.45 Uhr · Freiverkauf · Preise 8,00–35,00 DM

Theaterkasse abends geschlossen
Wegen Vorbereitung der Premiere „Landshuter Erzählungen" geschlossen

Sonntag 30 Mai

Royal Ballet Covent Garden London
Ernest Bloch
Lazarus Choreographie Caley
Igor Strawinsky
Danses concertantes Choreographie Mac Millan
Schubert-Martino
La Symphonie Pastorale Choreographie Cauley
20.00–22.30 Uhr · Freiverkauf · Preise 8,00–35,00 DM

Pepsie
Französische Komödie von Pierrette Bruno
19.50–21.30 Uhr · Freiverkauf · Preise 4,00–12,50 DM

IMF Multimedia-Abend
La Fabbrica Illuminata von Luigi Nono
Der Sturm
22.30–0.45 Uhr · Freiverkauf · Einheitspreis DM 4,50
Studio-Souterrain 20.00 Der amerikanische Traum/Der Sandkasten

Sonntag 31 Mai

Royal Ballet Covent Garden London
Der Schwanensee
Ballett von Peter I. Tschaikowski
20.00–22.45 Uhr · Freiverkauf · Preise 8,00–35,00 DM

Premiere
Landshuter Erzählungen
Schauspiel von Martin Sperr
19.30–22.15 Uhr · Premieren-Miete/1 · Freiverkauf
Studio-Souterrain 20.00 Ars longa, vita brevis/Deutsches Rondo/Selbstbezichtigung

Montag 1 Juni

Das Rheingold
Oper von Richard Wagner
20.00–22.30 Uhr · Th.-Gem. Gr. G · Freiverkauf · Preise 3,50–17,00 DM

Zum letzten Male!
Rund um den Kongreß
Posse von Ödön von Horvath
20.00–22.15 Uhr · Th.-Gem. Gr. MB · Freiverkauf · Preise 4,00–12,50 DM

Dienstag 2 Juni

Don Giovanni
Oper in zwei Akten von Wolfgang Amadeus Mozart
19.30–22.30 Uhr · Ju-Ring I (7. Vorstellung) · Freiverkauf · Preise 3,50–17,00 DM

Zicke Zacke
Schauspiel von Peter Terson mit der bekannten Wiesbadener Band „The Ducks"
20.00–22.00 Uhr · St.-Reihe 8/12 · Freiverkauf · Preise 4,00–12,50 DM

Mittwoch 3 Juni

Zum vorletzten Male!
Wozzeck
Oper in drei Akten von Alban Berg
20.00–21.45 Uhr · St.-Reihe F/13 · Freiverkauf · Preise 3,50–17,00 DM

Landshuter Erzählungen
Schauspiel von Martin Sperr
20.00–22.15 Uhr · St.-Reihe B/12 · Freiverkauf · Preise 4,00–12,50 DM

Donnerstag 4 Juni

Zum letzten Male in dieser Spielzeit!
Eugen Onegin
Oper in drei Akten von Peter I. Tschaikowski
20.00–22.45 Uhr · Bes.-Ring · Freiverkauf · Preise 3,50–17,00 DM

Pepsie
Französische Komödie von Pierrette Bruno
19.50–22.00 Uhr · Freiverkauf · Preise 4,00–12,50 DM

Freitag 5 Juni

Zum vorletzten Male!
Titelrolle Werner Rundshagen
Napoleon oder Die hundert Tage
Schauspiel von Christian Dietrich Grabbe
20.00–22.45 Uhr · Th.-Gem. Gr. GK 21, 22 · Freiverkauf · Preise 3,50–15,00 DM

Kurhaus
5. Jugendkonzert
Dirigent Ludwig Kaufmann
Solisten Helmut Lang (Violine), Elmer Baumann (Flöte)
Ludwig Kaufmann (Klavier)
Das Wiesbadener Symphonie-Orchester
20.00 Uhr

Was ist an Toten so sexy?
Komödie von Arn Jellicoe
20.00–21.45 Uhr · Freiverkauf · Preise 4,00–12,50 DM

Spielplanvorschau | | | Studio-Souterrain

Premiere: „Landshuter Erzählungen" von Martin Sperr am 31. 5.

Schauspielhaus

Do 28. Mai Fronleichnam 19.00–22.00	Volksbühne A 7 und Kartenverkauf 4,00–13,00 DM	**Ein Freudenfeuer für den Bischof** von Sean O'Casey		Inszenierung Günter Ballhausen Bühnenbild und Kostüme Jürgen Dreier / Wilfried Reckewitz	Donata Höffer Rosel Zech	Helmuth Ebba Claus Eberth Hans W. Hamacher Roland Kenda	Heinz G. Kilian Hermann Schlögl Adalbert Stamborski Heinz Voss	Kurt Weinzierl Helmut Wiedermann
Fr 29. Mai		Austausch-Gastspiel in Köln **Vor der Nacht**						
Sa 30. Mai 19.00–22.00	Theatergemeinde Gr. 4 Volksbühne A 9 und Kartenverkauf 4,00–13,00 DM	**Margarete in Aix** Komödie von Peter Hacks	Zum letzten Mal	Inszenierung Günter Ballhausen Bühnenbild und Kostüme Jürgen Dreier Musik Hans Gerbes	Musikalische Leitung Udo Gefe Akrobatik und choreographische Mitarbeit Bozo Krog	Ute Cremer Maria Krasna Ursula von Reibnitz	Edgar M. Böhlke Joachim Boldt Helmuth Ebba Hans Günther Werner Grossmann Roland Kenda	Heinz G. Kilian Hans-Jürgen Mayer Walter Orth Christian Quadflieg Hermann Schlögl Robert Zimmerling Corps de ballet
Sa 30. Mai 22.00–0.30	Freier Kartenverkauf Der Vorverkauf hat bereits begonnen 3,00–8,00 DM	**Magic Afternoon** Ein Stück von Wolfgang Bauer	Nachtvorstellung Zum letzten Mal	Inszenierung Peter Löscher	Bühnenbild und Kostüme Wilfried Sakowitz	Ute Cremer Geneta Fischer	Edgar M. Böhlke Lutz Hochstraate	Ermäßigungsscheine haben Gültigkeit für Sperrsitz und I. Parkett
So 31. Mai 15.30–18.00	Freier Kartenverkauf 4,00–13,00 DM	**Das Haus in Montevideo** Komödie von Curt Goetz	Nachmittagsvorstellung auf vielfachen Wunsch	Inszenierung Hannes Tannert Bühnenbild Gerhard Völker Kostüme Ortrud Himmelreich	Ute Cremer Geneta Fischer Donata Höffer	Maria Krasna Martha Kusztrich Dorothea Walda	Werner Grossmann Hans Günther Friederich Kutschera	Otto Payer Christian Quadflieg Kurt Weinzierl Ermäßigungsscheine und Gutscheinen haben Gültigkeit
So 31. Mai 19.00–21.30	Freier Kartenverkauf 4,00–13,00 DM	**Das Haus in Montevideo** Komödie von Curt Goetz	Zum letzten Mal	Inszenierung Hannes Tannert Bühnenbild Gerhard Völker Kostüme Ortrud Himmelreich	Ute Cremer Geneta Fischer Donata Höffer	Maria Krasna Martha Kusztrich Dorothea Walda	Werner Grossmann Hans Günther Friederich Kutschera	Otto Payer Christian Quadflieg Kurt Weinzierl
Di 2. Juni 20.00–22.30	Abo K rot und Kartenverkauf 4,00–13,00 DM	**Einer muß die Zeche zahlen** Komödie von Georges Feydeau		Inszenierung Karl Guttmann Bühnenbild Jürgen Dreier Kostüme Edith Biskup	Musikalische Leitung Udo Gefe	Doris Gallart Maria Krasna Martha Kusztrich	Renate Reger Helena Rosenkranz Inge Wilhelm	Wolfgang Arnold Gerd Mayen Walter Orth Karl-Heinz Vosgerau Helmut Wiedermann	Otto Payer Herbert Temme Franz Trager Robert Zimmerling
Mi 3. Juni 20.00–23.00	Volksbühne J 2 und beschr. Kartenverkauf	**Ein Freudenfeuer für den Bischof** von Sean O'Casey		Inszenierung Günter Ballhausen Bühnenbild und Kostüme Jürgen Dreier / Wilfried Reckewitz	Donata Höffer Rosel Zech	Helmuth Ebba Claus Eberth Hans W. Hamacher Roland Kenda	Heinz G. Kilian Hermann Schlögl Adalbert Stamborski Heinz Voss	Kurt Weinzierl Helmut Wiedermann
Do 4. Juni 20.00–22.30	Abo B blau und Kartenverkauf 4,00–13,00 DM	**Einer muß die Zeche zahlen** Komödie von Georges Feydeau		Inszenierung Karl Guttmann Bühnenbild Jürgen Dreier Kostüme Edith Biskup	Musikalische Leitung Udo Gefe	Doris Gallart Donata Höffer Maria Krasna Martha Kusztrich	Renate Reger Helena Rosenkranz Inge Wilhelm	Wolfgang Arnold Werner Grossmann Gerd Mayen Karl-Heinz Vosgerau Helmut Wiedermann	Otto Payer Herbert Temme Franz Trager Robert Zimmerling
Sa 6. Juni 19.00–21.30	Volksbühne A 12 und A 13 und beschr. Kartenverkauf 4,00–13,00 DM	**Einer muß die Zeche zahlen** Komödie von Georges Feydeau		Inszenierung Karl Guttmann Bühnenbild Jürgen Dreier Kostüme Edith Biskup	Musikalische Leitung Udo Gefe	Doris Gallart Donata Höffer Maria Krasna Martha Kusztrich	Renate Reger Helena Rosenkranz Inge Wilhelm	Wolfgang Arnold Werner Grossmann Gerd Mayen Walter Orth Karl-Heinz Vosgerau Helmut Wiedermann	Otto Payer Herbert Temme Franz Trager Robert Zimmerling
So 7. Juni 19.00–21.30	Volksbühne B und Kartenverkauf 4,00–13,00 DM	**Ein Freudenfeuer für den Bischof** von Sean O'Casey		Inszenierung Günter Ballhausen Bühnenbild und Kostüme Jürgen Dreier / Wilfried Reckewitz	Donata Höffer Rosel Zech	Helmuth Ebba Claus Eberth Hans W. Hamacher Roland Kenda	Heinz G. Kilian Hermann Schlögl Adalbert Stamborski Heinz Voss	Kurt Weinzierl Helmut Wiedermann
So 14. Juni 19.00–22.30	Freier Kartenverkauf Vorverkauf ab Mo., 1. Juni, 17.30 Uhr 4,00–13,00 DM	**Wallenstein** von Friedrich Schiller Bearbeitung von Hansgünther Heyme	Austausch-Gastspiel der Städtischen Bühnen Köln	Inszenierung Hansgünther Heyme Bühnenbild Klaus Weiffenbach Kostüme Jan Skalicky	Bühnenmusik Werner Haentjes	Berkewicz / Hennings Bendgens / Faber Geiger / Hildebrandt / Hilken	Hinze / Landeck Lerche / Liecke Meinertzhagen / Mitterer Müller / Niggemann Ostermann / Palser	Quadflieg / Reichmann Samariter / Schnitzer Schulze / Stickan Volling / Walter u. a. Ermäßigungsscheine und Gutschriften haben Gültigkeit

WUPPERTALER BÜHNEN

Generalintendant Arno Wüstenhöfer

Vorverkauf:

Für die Vorstellungen im Opernhaus: Nur Kasse Opernhaus   Ruf 55 00 50 / 55 00 07

Für die Vorstellungen im Schauspielhaus: Nur Kasse Schauspielhaus   Ruf 44 44 62 / 44 23 62

montags 17.30 bis 20.00 Uhr, dienstags bis samstags 9.00 bis 13.00 Uhr.

Beginn der Vorverkaufs für die angekündigten Vorstellungen jeweils montags 17.30 Uhr.

Telefonische Bestellungen können erst ab dienstags berücksichtigt werden.

Abendkasse: 1 Stunde vor Beginn der Vorstellung. Vorbestellte Karten bitte eine halbe Stunde vor Beginn abholen.

Bitte beachten Sie die Anfangszeiten.

Einlaß für Zuspätkommende nur bei Bildwechsel möglich.

Opernhaus

Do 28. Mai Fronleichnam 19.00–22.00	Volksbühne J 3 und beschr. Kartenverkauf 6,00–14,00 DM	**My Fair Lady** Musical von Alan Jay Lerner / Frederick Loewe nach Bernard Shaw „Pygmalion"	ausverkauft	Zu Gunsten der Genossenschaft deutscher Bühnenangehörigen	Musikalische Leitung Georg W. Schmöhe Inszenierung Karl Wesseler Bühnenbild Jürgen Dreier	Kostüme Edith Biskup Chöre Willi Fues Choreographie Ivan Sertic	Albrecht / Bäumler Becker / Gallart Holstein / Pfrengle Lang / Maass Overhoff / Walther	Banse / Dimitriadia Fünkel / Hartkopf Havenstein / Hohmann Hügen / Kern Laborcz / Lohrum Meiser / Orth	Remscheid / H. P. Schmidt Vosgerau / Weckbrodt Wyzner / Ziegler	Brunner / Kretzschmar Hartley / Volkers Wenninger / Krog Kryszka / Mittelbach Corps de ballet
Sa 30. Mai		Gastspiel in Solingen **Undine**							
So 31. Mai		Gastspiel in Solingen **My Fair Lady**							
Mo 1. Juni		Gastspiel in Solingen **My Fair Lady**							
Di 2. Juni 20.00–22.15	Abo D grün und Kartenverkauf 5,00–13,00 DM	**Die Teufel von Loudun** Oper von Krzysztof Penderecki	Zum letzten Mal		Musikalische Leitung Wolfgang Schmid Inszenierung Kurt Horres Hanns Jordan	Kostüme Edith Biskup Marianne Dorka Willi Fues Pantomimische Mitarbeit Jean Soubeyran	Shari Boruvka Jutta Heller Ingeborg Krüger Käthe Maass Hildegund Walther	Fred Banse Wolfgang Fünkel Herbert Grabe Zsolt Ketszery Kurt Moll	Hans-Georg Moser Willi Nett Siegfried Schmidt Tom Swift Denis Trussas	Erich Weckbrodt Heinz Wildhagen Franz Wyzner
Mi 3. Juni 20.00–22.30	Abo Z violett und Kartenverkauf	**Der Barbier von Sevilla** Komische Oper von Gioacchino Rossini			Musikalische Leitung Wolfgang Schmid Inszenierung Kurt Horres Bühnenbild Wilfried Sakowitz	Kostüme Edith Biskup Chöre Willi Fues	Marianne Dorka Annika Melén	Fred Banse Wolfgang Fünkel Zsolt Ketszery Ernst Remscheid	Helmut Schorr Denis Trussas Franz Wyzner	
Fr 5. Juni 20.00–22.30	Abo A rot Volksbühne O 1 und Kartenverkauf 5,00–13,00 DM	**Undine** Oper von E. T. A. Hoffmann			Musikalische Leitung Wolfgang Schmid Inszenierung Harro Dicks	Bühnenbild und Kostüme Fabius von Gugel Chöre Willi Fues	Marianne Dorka Käthe Maass Barbara Rondelli	Zsolt Ketszery Hans-Georg Moser Willi Nett Franz Wyzner		
Sa 6. Juni 19.00–21.15	Abo S gelb und Kartenverkauf 5,00–13,00 DM	**Der Troubadour** Oper von Giuseppe Verdi			Musikalische Leitung Friedrich-Wilhelm Hidding Inszenierung Gerrit ter Horst Bühnenbild und Kostüme Wilfried Sakowitz	Chöre Willi Fues Pantomimische Mitarbeit Jean Soubeyran	Shari Boruvka Tatjana Kralj Hildegund Stieger	Paris Dimitriadia Gernot Kern Hans-Georg Moser	Raffaele Polani Tom Swift	
So 7. Juni 19.00–21.00	Freier Kartenverkauf Der Vorverkauf hat bereits begonnen 5,00–13,00 DM	**Aus Mangel an Beweisen** Schauspiel von Giulio del Torre	Einmaliges Gastspiel		Regie Wolfgang Liebeneiner Bühne Timm Zorn	Hilde Krahl	Hannes Messemer			

In Vorbereitung

Orpheus in der Unterwelt

Klassische Operette von Jacques Offenbach   Premiere: 28. Juni 1970

Breker

Landes theater

Mai	Schülervorstellung	Beginn 15 Uhr
21. Donnerstag Schillersaal 15–17.00 Uhr	**Der zerbrochene Krug** Lustspiel von Heinrich v. Kleist Inszenierung: Wolfgang Müller Bühnenbild und Kostüme: Monika Bauert	Bäumker - Brugger - Burkhardt Holt - vom Scheidt Allendorf - Herff - Leiser Rühring - Stoll - v. Stolzmann

---

	Zum letzten Mal	
21. Donnerstag Schillersaal 20–22.30 Uhr Fremdenmiete II. 9. Vorstellung	**Arsen und Spitzenhäubchen** Kriminalkomödie von Joseph Kesselring Deutsch von Annemarie Artinger Leitung: Ganz - Korntner	Bäumker - Holt - vom Scheidt Allendorf - Am Acher - Bödiger Butschke - Hans - Herff - Idler Liebsch - Rühring - Stoll

---

	Schülervorstellung	Beginn 15 Uhr
22. Freitag Schillersaal 15–17.30 Uhr	**Was ihr wollt** Komödie von William Shakespeare Übersetzt von Axel Plogstedt Inszenierung: Ernst Seiltgen Bühnenbild und Kostüme: Monika Bauert Musik: Laszlo Farago	Brugger - Hees - Walter Am Acher - Butschke Hans - Herff - Hospowsky - Idler Krebs - Leiser - Liebsch - Pfisterer Rühring - Stoll

---

22. Freitag Schillersaal 20–22.30 Uhr Miete B, 13. Vorst. Miete M. 9. Vorst. Freiverkauf	**Amphitryon** Komödie von Peter Hacks Inszenierung: Wolfgang Müller Bühnenbild und Kostüme: Peter Korntner	Burkhardt Balzer - Hans - Pfisterer v. Stolzmann

---

	Afrikanisches Nationalballett Guinea	Beginn 19.30 Uhr
26. Dienstag 19.30–22.00 Uhr Schillersaal Miete P, 14. Vorst. Freiverkauf DM 6.- bis 14.-	**Black Afrika** 50 Tänzerinnen und Tänzer, Sänger und Musiker **Wegen des starken Erfolges zweites Gastspiel**	(siehe Sonderplakat)

Juni	Zum letzten Mal	
3. Mittwoch Schillersaal 20–22.30 Uhr Fremdenmiete II, 10. Vorstellung Freiverkauf	**König Johann** nach Shakespeare von Friedrich Dürrenmatt Inszenierung: Gerhard Jelen Bühnenbild: Hansheinrich Palitzsch Kostüme: Marlene Bode / Peter Korntner	Barth - Bäumker - Hees - vom Scheidt Walter - Am Acher - Bödiger Butschke - Ganz - Hans - Herff Hospowsky - Idler - Krebs - Leiser Liebsch - Mey - Pfisterer - Rühring Stoll - v. Stolzmann

---

4. Donnerstag Schillersaal 20–22.30 Uhr Miete A, 14. Vorst. Jugendm. 9. Vorst. Freiverkauf	**Amphitryon** Komödie von Peter Hacks Inszenierung: Wolfgang Müller Bühnenbild und Kostüme: Peter Korntner	Burkhardt Balzer - Hans - Pfisterer v. Stolzmann

---

	Operettengastspiel des Stadttheaters Pforzheim	
5. Freitag Schillersaal 20–22.15 Uhr Fremdenmiete I, 9. Vorstellung Freiverkauf	**Ein Walzertraum** Operette von Oscar Straus Musikalische Leitung: Hans Werner Kalcher Inszenierung: Peter Sonnberger Bühnenbild: Alexander Blanke Chöre: Werner Eckhardt Choreographie: Emy Knautz	(siehe Sonderplakat)

	Premiere	
11. Donnerstag Schillersaal 20–22.30 Uhr Miete P, 15. Vorst. AStA Freiverkauf	**Minna von Barnhelm** Lustspiel von Gotthold Ephraim Lessing Inszenierung: Ernst Seiltgen Bühnenbild und Kostüme: Peter Korntner	Brugger - Burkhardt - Walter Hans - Herff - Hospowsky - Idler Krebs - Liebsch - Pfisterer v. Stolzmann

---

Auswärtige Gastspiele des Landestheaters

Sa. 23. 5.	Saulgau	König Johann	Di. 2. 6. Reutlingen	Amphitryon
Mo. 25. 5.	Dettingen	König Johann	Mo. 8. 6. Freudenstadt	Endspiel
Di. 26. 5.	Tuttlingen	Amphitryon	Mi 10. 6. Tuttlingen	Minna von Barnhelm
Do. 28. 5.	Hagen	Hamlet	Do. 11. 6. Reutlingen	König für einen Tag (Opern-Gast)

Vorverkauf werktags von 10 bis 13 Uhr an der Theaterkasse. Schillersaal. Grabenstr. (Tel. 22801). Werktags von 8 –16 Uhr im Verkehrsverein an der Neckarbrücke. Montags ist die Theaterkasse nur an Spieltagen geöffnet. Soweit verfügbar ermäßigte Karten für Studenten und Schüler an allen Spieltagen ab 18 Uhr an der Abendkasse. Studentenkarten für AStA - Vorstellungen täglich von 10 - 12 Uhr in der Neuen Aula.

Opernhaus Zürich

Leitung:
Hermann Juch

Im Rahmen der Juni-Festwochen
Neuinszenierung
In italienischer Sprache

30. Don Giovanni

Preise: Fr. 8.— / 60.—

Mai
Samstag
20—nach 23.15 Uhr

Oper von Wolfgang
Amadeus Mozart

Leitung:
Ferdinand Leitner
Leopold Lindtberg
Max Röthlisberger
Hans Erismann

Antigone Sgourda
Gerry de Groot
Renate Lenhart

Cesare Siepi
Horst R. Laubenthal
Aurelian Neagu
Jozsef Dene
Rupert Oliver Forbes

Im Rahmen der Juni-Festwochen
In Anwesenheit des Komponisten

31. Karl V.

Preise: Fr. 4.— / 22.—

Mai
Sonntag
20—ca. 22 Uhr

Bühnenwerk mit Musik
von Ernst Křenek

Leitung:
Ferdinand Leitner
Imo Moszkowicz
Max Röthlisberger
Hans Erismann

Susan Wold
Erika Wien
Ruth Rohner
Renate Lenhart
Anneliese Fackler
Marga Schiml
Costanza Cuccaro

Roland Hermann
Wolfgang Warncke
Glade Peterson
Nigel Douglas
Howard Nelson
Andor Kaposy
Fritz Peter
Paul Späni
Ralph Telasko
Gottlieb Zeithammer
Ernst-August Steinhoff
Werner Ernst
Renato Premoli

Im Rahmen der Juni-Festwochen

1. Gastspiel Kaiserliche Hofkapelle GAGAKU Japan

Preise: Fr. 5.50 / 35.—

Montag
Juni
20 Uhr

Japanische Musik und Tänze

I. Kangen: «Netori»
«Ringa»
«Etenraku»

II. Ninjomai: «Sonokoma»

III. Bugaku: «Shundeika»
«Ryo-O»
«Bairo»

---

2. Die Zauberflöte

Vorstellung für den
Lebensmittelverein
Zürich

Juni
Dienstag
20—23 Uhr

Oper von Wolfgang
Amadeus Mozart

Leitung:
Ferdinand Leitner
Leopold Lindtberg
Max Röthlisberger
Hans Erismann

Renate Lenhart
Costanza Cuccaro
Ina Dressel
Klara Barlow
Alexandra Kunosiková
Marga Schiml
Paula Smeikal
Hildegard Eilmann
Annelies Böttcher

Frans van Daalen
Manfred Schenk
Heinz Holecek
Fritz Peter
Howard Nelson
Ernst-August Steinhoff
Ralph Telasko
Renato Premoli
Gejza Zelenay

Im Rahmen der Juni-Festwochen
In italienischer Sprache

3. Don Giovanni

Preise: Fr. 8.— / 60.—

Juni
Mittwoch
20—nach 23.15 Uhr

Oper von Wolfgang
Amadeus Mozart

Leitung:
Ferdinand Leitner
Leopold Lindtberg
Max Röthlisberger
Hans Erismann

Antigone Sgourda
Gerry de Groot
Renate Lenhart

Cesare Siepi
Horst R. Laubenthal
Aurelian Neagu
Jozsef Dene
Rupert Oliver Forbes

Im Rahmen der Juni-Festwochen

4. Der Nussknacker

Donnerstag-Ab. 12
und freier Verkauf

Preise: Fr. 4.— / 22.—

Juni
Donnerstag
20—ca. 22.30 Uhr

Ballett von Peter
Iljitsch Tschaikowsky

Leitung:
Frank Egermann
Nicolas Beriozoff
Toni Businger

Gaye Fulton
Irena Milovan
Angela Bishopp
Phoni Samaropoulo
Colette Cerf

Matti Tikkanen
Stefan Schuller
Rudolf Budavary
Max Natiez
und das Corps de Ballet

---

5. Das Land des Lächelns

Preise: Fr. 4.— / 22.—

Juni
Freitag
20—ca. 22.30 Uhr

Operette
von Franz Lehár

Leitung:
Matthias Aeschbacher
Martin Markun
Toni Businger
Hans Erismann
Nicolas Beriozoff

Wilma Lipp
Ina Dressel
Ellen Schwanneke
Alexandra Kunosiková
Hannelore Maile
Inez Graf
Hildegard Eilmann

Frans van Daalen
Paul Späni
Gottlieb Zeithammer
Ralph Telasko
Werner Ernst
Franz Drosg
Erwin Froese
Giacomo Tavoli

Im Rahmen der Juni-Festwochen
Gesamtgastspiel des National-Theaters Prag

6. Dalibor

Preise: Fr. 5.50 / 35.—

Juni
Samstag
20—ca. 23 Uhr

Oper von
Friedrich Smetana

Leitung:
Jaroslav Krombholc
Vaclav Kaslik
Josef Svoboda
Milan Maly

In den Hauptpartien:

Hans Janků

Vilém Přibyl

7.

Juni
Sonntag
20—ca. 23 Uhr

Vorverkauf

Theaterkasse, Telefon 32 69 22/23, werktags von 10—19 Uhr, sonntags 10—12 und 15—17 Uhr. Reisebüro Kuoni, Bahnhofplatz, Telefon 27 55 15/17/18, 8.30—17.30 Uhr, samstags 8.30—12 Uhr, sonntags geschlossen. Reisebüro Hafner AG, Schaffhauserstr. 339 (beim «Sternen» Oerlikon), Telefon 48 48 00, von 8—12 und 14—18 Uhr, samstags von 8—12 Uhr, sonntags geschlossen. Vorbestellte Billette bleiben, ohne besonderen Auftrag, nur bis einen Tag vor der Vorstellung reserviert. Vorbestellte Billette für Juni-Festwochen-Vorstellungen bleiben nur bis 5 Tage vor der betreffenden Vorstellung reserviert. Über bis dahin nicht abgeholte Karten muss verfügt werden.

Schauspielhaus
Zürich

29.
Mai
Freitag
20–22 h

Die nächtliche Huldigung

Schauspiel in drei Akten von Lars Gustafsson
Deutsch von H. C. Artmann

Regie: Carl M. Weber
Bühnenbild: Karl Kneidl
Musik: Peter Fischer

mit Danegger Giskes G. Knuth G. Lampe Siegi Stix Wildenauer

Zum voraus-
sichtlich
letzten Male

30.
Mai
Samstag
20–22 h

Die nächtliche Huldigung

Besetzung wie oben

31.
Mai
Sonntag
20 h

1.
Juni
Montag
20 h

Preise:
Fr. 6.–/30.–

Im Rahmen der Juni-Festwochen
Teatro Stabile di Genova

I Rusteghi

di Carlo Goldoni

Regia di Luigi Squarzina
Scene e costumi di Gianfranco Padovani
Musiche di Fernando C. Mainardi

con Morlacchi Ruspoli Spina Volonghi Antonutti Battain
Galavotti Milli Pagni Zanetti

2.
Juni
Dienstag
20 h

3.
Juni
Mittwoch
20 h

4.
Juni
Donnerstag
20 h

Preise:
Fr. 6.–/30.–

Im Rahmen der Juni-Festwochen
The Abbey Theatre, Dublin

The Hostage

by Brendan Behan

Directed by Hugh Hunt
Designed by Christopher Baugh
Costumes by Anne McCabe

with Hayes ni Ghrainne Johannes Lalor Newman O'Kelly
Alcock Buggy Dowling Foley Lamb McCann McSwiney Newham
O'Brian O'Callaghan O'Flynn

5.
Juni
Freitag
20–22 h

Die nächtliche Huldigung

Besetzung wie oben

6.
Juni
Samstag
20–22 h

Die nächtliche Huldigung

Besetzung wie oben

7.
Juni
Sonntag
15–17 h

Die nächtliche Huldigung

Besetzung wie oben

20–22 h

Die nächtliche Huldigung

Besetzung wie oben

Sonntagabend-
abonnement 11
und freier Verkauf

Vorverkauf

Rämistrasse 34, 1. Stock (Eingang Schauspielhaus), 10–19 Uhr (Sonntag 10–12 Uhr), Telefon 32 11 11 und 32 33 60
Kuoni, Bahnhofplatz, geöffnet 8.30–17.30 Uhr (Samstag bis 12 Uhr), Telefon 27 55 16
Theaterkasse Schauspielhaus, eine Stunde vor Beginn jeder Vorstellung, Telefon 32 11 11 und 32 33 60

Index

Index

one hundred eighty-four

one hundred eighty-six